BACK TO ASCETICISM II: THE TRAPPIST OPTION

A Translation with Introduction and Notes of Armand-Jean de Rancé's *De la sainteté et des devoirs de la vie monastique*

Vincent Ryan, Translator

Lee Gilbert, Editor

"Haec est voluntas Dei, sanctificatio vestra" I Thess 4:3
"This is the will of God, your sanctification."

ARTHUR M. GILBERT & SON, PUBLISHERS
2019

De la sainteté et des devoirs de la vie monastique by the Abbé Armand-Jean de Rancé was originally published in Paris by Francois Muguet in 1683. In 1830 it was translated and titled *On the Sanctity and the Duties of the Monastic State* by Abbot Vincent Ryan, founding abbot of Mount Melleray in Cappoquin, Ireland and published in Dublin by Richard Grace. This derivative edition in two volumes has been re-typeset, re-titled, edited, updated, annotated, and its many citations corrected and amplified. In addition, it has been supplied with 44 illustrations from the public domain together with an Image Index and an Index of Scriptural Citations. For the public domain provenance of all images in this volume see page 343.

© Arthur M. Gilbert & Son, Publishers, 2019.

All rights reserved. No part of this book may be reproduced in any form or by any electronic or mechanical means, including information storage and retrieval systems, without permission in writing from the publisher, except by reviewers, who may quote brief passages in a review.

www.auldsnu.com

12051 SE 31st Place, Ste 15
Milwaukie, Oregon 97222

ISBN 978-0-578-55796-0
Library of Congress Control Number:2019911469

PRINTED IN THE UNITED STATES OF AMERICA

Cover image: The Virgin Appearing at Mass, Agostino Masucci 1692–1758.

Praise for *On the Sanctity and Duties of the Monastic State:*

"His *De la Saintete* is unquestionably one of the most important works of post-medieval Cistercian writing and occupies a major place in the history of spirituality."

>David N. Bell, medievalist, theologian, professor at the Memorial University of Newfoundland, author of *Everyday Life at La Trappe Under Armand-Jean Rancé, Understanding Rancé*, etc.

"No book within the memory of man has won for itself greater esteem at court, amongst the people, in the upper circles of society. But that would be little, if it had not at the same time produced inestimable fruits of virtue whereof I am myself a witness."

>Olivier Lefèvre d'Ormesson: (b.1616-d.1686) French magistrate, friend of Bossuet, Madame de Sévigné, Racine, Boileau, La Fontaine.

"This work, treating of the sanctity and the duties of the monastic life, contains a doctrine accurately derived from Holy Scripture and the tradition of saints. The reading of it will discover to monks the obligations and the perfection of the angelic state to which they have been called. It will prove not less profitable to people in the world by making them understand, from the austerities and the humiliations practiced in the cloister, how great is the corruption in which we live, how deeply the poison has penetrated our hearts, and how violent and incessant must be our efforts against ourselves if we hope not merely to prevent the growth of vicious habits but to pluck them up by the roots."

>Jacques-Bénigne Lignel Bossuet: (1681-1704) disciple of Saint Vincent de Paul, theologian, Bishop of Meaux, thought to be one of the greatest orators of all time, "the Eagle of Meaux."

As to the results of its publication Bossuet wrote to de Rancé, "The book has produced all the good effects I had anticipated. It has done great good everywhere. You ought to give thanks to God for giving you so happy an inspiration."

"What is this new work which the Eagle of Meaux has covered under his wings? Its language has all the harmonies of the organ, rich and majestic. One moves through its pages as through a basilica whose rose-windows are ablaze with the shimmering light of the sun. Oh, what a wealth of imagination in a work wherein, from its character, one would least expect to find it! . . . . Its first appearance was followed by an interval of profound silence, the silence of astonishment and admiration."

Chateaubriand, preeminent French literary figure in the early 19th c.

"It used to be said formerly that one should have lived like Saint John Climacus so as to be able to compose his divine *Ladder of Perfection*. The same can be said of the author of this book. Five years ago I had the consolation both to hear from his lips and to see put in practice the grand and holy maxims which are contained in his volume, so that what is written in these pages is but the expression of his thoughts and actions. I have read the work attentively. Everything in it, as far as I can judge, is calculated to edify, and full of the Spirit of God. The sentiments are noble and elevated, and on the whole, gives one a sublime conception of the religious life."

ETIENNE LE CAMUS: The Bishop of Grenoble (1681-1707) and Cardinal.

Contents

Foreword   vii

16 | On Retirement   6

17 | On Silence   104

18 | On Abstinence and Austere Food   121

19 | On Manual Labor   167

20 | On Night Watchings   213

21 | On Poverty   221

22 | On Patience under Sickness and Infirmities   272

23 | On Mitigations   310

Foreword

"Angels are a light for monks, and the monastic way of life is a light for all men"—Saint John Climachus

Re-titling Rancé's *On the Sanctity and Duties of Monastic life* as *Back to Asceticism: The Trappist Option* was intended both as homage to Rod Dreher's *The Benedict Option* and as an alternative to it, just as Trappist life is an intensification and an alternative interpretation of the Rule of Saint Benedict. Dreher foresees a time when it will not be possible for Christians to be part of mainstream society without betraying their consciences. In the face of ongoing civilizational collapse—which he characterizes as a flood—manifest in narcissistic consumerism and the normalization of sexual deviancy, Dreher recommends strategic withdrawal from the world. He hopes to see nodes of Christian intentional communities established throughout the West to seed a new civilization on the wreckage of the old, in rough approximation of the spread of Benedictine monasticism on the ruins of the Roman Empire. While not prescribing the exact form of such communities, he recommends that they take what wisdom they can from the Rule of Saint Benedict. He writes with fondness of a particular community in Italy, the Tipi Loschi of San Benedetto del Tronto; and it was notable that a recent panel discussing the Benedict Option included a leader of an Australian Bruderhof community. Yet, of all such communities one can surely say that they are difficult to inaugurate and still harder to preserve.

The Benedict Option does provoke serious thinking on how we might, like Noah, ride out the deluge and rebuild. Rancé's book, on the other hand, presents such a radically more intense way of Catholic living that it raises the real possibility that we have the resources to roll back the flood altogether if we exploited them to the full.

Rolling back the flood is not out of the question, for our resources are truly infinite: the Father, Son and Holy Ghost. With divine initiative they have already incorporated us into an intentional community, a community intended by the Father (John 6:44; John 6:65) and animated by the Spirit of His Son, Jesus Christ: the Catholic Church. With Him we have a communion in flesh and blood, for we are part of the Body of Christ, of which He is the head. With Him we form a living, intimately connected communion, universally distributed and nourished with supernatural life at the sacramental founts of grace: the Church Militant, the Body of Christ on earth.

At one time we understood this very well. When Pius XII issued *Mystici Corporis Christi* (On the Mystical Body of Christ) on June 29th, 1943, the Lord greatly renewed us in mind. A thrill of life surged through the Body of Christ. "You then are the body of Christ. Every one of you is a member of it" (1 Cor 12:27). What we did, or did not do, profoundly affected the Church. We mattered. Our lives made a difference. The Church flourished as we bore one another's burdens in mystical union with one another. This was shortly to be overwhelmed by post war prosperity and the import of rival pulpits into our own homes, but in the meantime we had a vitality practically unparalleled in the life of the Church. Our monasteries, convents, rectories and schools were full.

One could say, too, that this flourishing was due in great part to the asceticism imposed by the great Depression and World War II. "See if you can do without" was a motto of the times, and "The Greatest Generation" rose to the occasion, but evidently with the firm resolve that their children would *not* do without. That generation and their parents had been driven to their knees. Whatever Catholics may have been in the Roaring Twenties, it was not so long ago, eighty years, during the Depression and World War II, that the Basilica of Our Lady of Sorrows in Chicago had an ongoing novena to the Mother of Sorrows that filled and re-filled that huge space hour after hour. This in turn inspired 2200 other parishes across the country to erect their own stations to the Mother of Sorrows and to have their own novenas to her. In the immediate post war years, then, we were a prayerful, disciplined people, ascetics in all but name. The body of Christ was vigorous and full of grace.

To take just one small corner of the flourishing Catholic world at that time, Our Lady of New Melleray Abbey (Cistercian) near Dubuque, Iowa had 65 novices; Gethsemane Cistercian Abbey near Bardstown, Kentucky had 270 men total. Had Cistercians the wisdom and grace to sustain that trajectory and had the Church as a whole supported these men with prayer and sacrifice—for even saintly Trappist monks cannot say to the rest of the Church, "We have no need of you" (1 Cor 12:21)—we might well have entered upon a new age of faith as in the time of Saint Bernard.

It would take amazingly little, though, to take up where we left off in the mid-fifties, so little to re-group, to slake our thirst in the living streams of grace and to continue our triumphal march. Our Lord's saying to Simon, "Thou art Peter and upon this rock I will build my church and the gates of Hell will not prevail against it," is usually taken to mean, "Don't worry, no matter how bad things get, the Church will perdure, we will not be over-run and defeated by Satan." However, our Lord rather promises that the defensive gates of the strongholds of Satan will not hold. They will not prevail against the onslaught of the Church.

> For though we live in the flesh, we do not wage war according to the flesh. The weapons of our warfare are not the weapons of the world. Instead, they have divine power to demolish strongholds (2 Cor 10:3,4).

In other words, we are not primarily in a defensive, holding position, but we are on the move and we are irresistible. We are a stronghold demolishing force. In principle.

Yet, though we are irresistible in principle, this does not mean that we are not presently so wounded, so under-nourished, so dis-spirited that the idea of being "more than conquerors in Jesus Christ"(Rom 8:37) seems almost laughable. Moreover, there are not lacking any number of pundits who note the data points, plot the trajectory, forecast the ongoing decline of the Church and predict her persecution in the not too distant future. From a Biblical standpoint, though, how is this not superstitious? Judas, too, could see the way things were going and acted accordingly, but he was wrong. From a Catholic point of view, plotting the trajectory is roughly equivalent to reading tea leaves. Saul waiting for Samuel saw that his army was melting away, plotted the trajectory, offered sacrifice and lost the kingdom because of his disobedience (1 Sam 13).

Rather than playing the prophet and forecasting doom, better we should ask why are we so wounded, so undernourished and so dis-spirited that the enemy is over-running us. There is a principle in medicine, enshrined in the Hippocratic oath, "First, do no harm" and perhaps it applies in its own way to the Body of Christ as well. In medicine the idea is that the body will tend to heal itself if physicians do not injure it further by their interventions. Yet, in practically every Catholic family, we, the Church militant, as a matter of settled routine have been putting ourselves in the way of being spiritually wounded years on end, since the early 1950's at least.

From the *Austin Daily Herald,* Austin, Minnesota, December 10, 1951, page 16:

Archbishop Warns on TV Programs

ST. PAUL (/T) — In a letter read in Catholic churches of the St. Paul archdiocese Archbishop John Gregory Murray warned that television is having "disastrous results, especially on children."

It is the "serious responsibility of parents," he wrote, "to supervise and limit the presence of children at programs presented so as to safeguard their health and morals." The letter was read as Catholics were asked to renew the pledge of the Legion of Decency.

A few years later, in 1954, Pope Pius XII addressed the bishops of Italy:

"The painful picture of the evil and disturbing power of the cinema is ever present before Our mind. But it is impossible not to be horrified at the thought that through the medium of Television it may be possible for that atmosphere poisoned by materialism, fatuity and hedonism, which is too often breathed in so many cinemas, to penetrate within the very walls of the home. One could not, indeed, imagine anything more fatal for the spiritual forces of the nation, if these impressive revelations of pleasure, passion and evil, which are capable of shaking and ruining for ever a whole construction of purity, goodness and healthy individual and social education, were performed in front of so many innocent souls, in the very midst of the family.[1]

What if we stopped placing our souls and those of our children in harm's way and shielded them from the evil influence of the mass media? Surely we would heal quickly with the aid of the Sacrament of Reconciliation and the Eucharist. From what do we need to be healed? Sloth, certainly; wasting time; sinful curiosity; gluttony; lust; covetousness; to say nothing of distracted minds. There are so many things we need to see happen, and which would happen practically of themselves once we cast off our

---

[1] quoted in the *Tablet* 16th January 1954, page 10.

lethargic receptivity to whatever harmful meme the media wants to lodge in our minds, our open-armed acceptance of whatever artist they use to play upon our passions: "If only my people would hear me and Israel walk in my ways. Quickly I would humble their enemies: against their foes I would turn my hand" (Ps 80:14). The battle is the Lord's, a fact that we have been neglecting at our peril.

"Therefore, since we are surrounded by so great a cloud of witnesses, let us also lay aside every weight, and sin which clings so closely, and let us run with endurance the race that is set before us" (Heb 12:1). Such is the ascetic exhortation the Lord addresses to every age. In ours throwing off the yoke of the mass media would free us to live lives pleasing to God, to run our race victoriously, and to see the blessing of God.

For more than seventy years we have been spiritually malnourished by false teaching of many kinds together with abundant bad example, most of it coming through the mass media. By this point our minds and imaginations—to an extraordinary extent—are creations of the mass media. Besides all this, the nightly TV habit has displaced many encounters with the good, the true, and the beautiful that would have come with our spending more of our evenings together *sans* screen. We could have been happy, prayerful, peaceful families, enjoying one another's company, perhaps reading together, playing board games, singing together, being human beings together instead of passive receptors of commercial propaganda and putty in the hands of hostile opinion makers.

Also, television extinguished the saints that never were, for when one reads the lives of saints who came to the altar by way of innocence, one frequently encounters a mother of whom it is said, "When Johnny was a little boy, his mother used to read to him from the Gospels and the lives of the saints." Essentially that is the way the biography of St. John Vianney, the patron saint of priests, begins, and the way our lives did not. There was a time when sending our children to Catholic school would have remedied that to some extent, but that was before the advent of content-less catechisms and sister free classrooms.

We too little realize how much we depend on one another and sustain one another in our life of grace, especially within the family, for many of us belong to another intentional community nested within that larger Mystical Body of Christ, a community formed by our own marital vows and those of our parents: our families. Dreher happily refers to our Christian homes as domestic monasteries, and so they are. Like religious, are not children bound to live lives of poverty, chastity and obedience until their majority, and are not their father-abbots and his prioress obligated to shelter them, instruct them and discipline them in this holy endeavor? In chapter 16, which is roughly one third of Volume II, De Rancé in making the case for retirement from the world—that is, for leaving the world and entering religious life—gives domestic father-abbots inspiration should they wish to appropriate his wisdom in a way suitable for families. The domestic analogue would operate much differently, of course, and, so to speak, in the opposite direction, with expulsions and excommunications. For whether a man leaves the world and enters the monastery, or whether the father of a family casts the world out of the domestic monastery, the result is analogous, for both the monk and the child begin to breathe a holy atmosphere.

Yet domestically the very opposite happened in the early fifties, for then the world entered the Catholic home, and to our eternal loss we welcomed it with great enthusiasm. Though we are heartened now by the rapid expansion of the Church in the Southern Hemisphere, and though the Church is flourishing there today as it did in the United States in the fifties, the world is following close on. Within the past forty years a pastor in Andrah Pradesh could walk through his village and hear family after family reciting the rosary, but now all he hears is the television. As happened here, the family Rosary has been extinguished there. Too, as the laity gave way to the lure of prosperity what was in reality a familial culture of vocation went by the way, and individual members fell away for lack of prayer and good habits. Less life was flowing through the vine to nourish the branches. In Cardinal Newman's phrase, we were out of grace, for in our senseless complacency and self-indulgence we had cut ourselves off from it.

It is around this time that the abuse crisis began to really take off. Shortly, the vocations crisis was underway. In religious life the traditional Trappist wisdom was being undermined within the order itself, and an identity crisis not only permitted but fomented. Confusion was rife, wisdom in short supply. The population of both New Melleray and Gethsemane collapsed, and this was emblematic of what was happening through the West in virtually every religious order and in the diocesan priesthood as well. Worst of all was a spirituality of resentment that was fomented in many motherhouses, resentment against authority, against the demands of religious life, and eventually against God the Father. The Body of Christ was bleeding out grace. Given our interconnectedness, it is not fanciful to wonder if clergy and cloister were failing because the light of Christ was going out in family after family, because father after father offered no resistance to what was already a tsunami of darkness.

It is, after all, in the power of a father to throw the world out of his domestic monastery. Moreover, it is his obligation. He is the gatekeeper, and should never have let it in. In an allocution on Radio and Television to the Italian bishops in 1954 Pope Pius XII quotes the pagan poet, Juvenal: "Nothing impure in the home." In the meantime oceans of filth have swept through the Catholic home, carrying children out of the grace of God, and out of the Church. Television is a blind guide, an open pit, dark light, an accessory to gluttony, entertainment unto death, a window for voyeurs, an ambo for comedians, the enemy of fathers, and their shame, the child of cupidity, and its father, a fount of impurity, the preaching of demons, instant solace, inanimate companion, displacer of prayer, the idler's agenda, the student's failure, the seducer of children. The fact that we can hardly live without it ought to make us numb with apprehension. Where is such a habit taking us?

Within the Church of our day there is a very strong current of opinion that lays our present anemic ecclesial situation at the feet of the Second Vatican Council, but others say, no, it was rather those who hijacked the council, did and taught many things in the name of the "Spirit of Vatican II." However, is there not a great danger of falling into the "post hoc, propter hoc" (after this, because of this) logical fallacy in attributing the entirety of our collapse to Vatican II and its mis-appropriation? How can we hold blameless the entertainment industry and its vectors, given the persuasive power of audio-visual media?

From the early fifties on we were being secularized in our own homes night after night, our morals being constantly walked down, our prayer lives and our family lives practically annihilated. And then in a kind of self-indulgent obtuseness we attribute the vocations crisis to Vatican II!? As far as that goes, in the Catholic Italian daily newspaper, *Avvenire*, there was an article heading years ago, a flash of revelation in the night: "The Culture of Distraction vs the Culture of Vocation." Does this require comment? Is it not overwhelmingly obvious? And yet vocation directors throughout the Church imagine they are promoting a culture of vocation by encouraging the presentation—with ceremony—of the "vocation cross" to a different family every week at Sunday Mass, or they promote "Come and See" weekends and the like. Fine. Yet, if one wanted to evoke a culture of vocation that actually produces vocations, he would take on the culture of distraction and brave the wrath of those domestic father-abbots addicted to televised sports, of whom there are not a few.

If only bishops, priests and vocation directors would urge upon the Church the parental philosophy and domestic routine, quasi-monastic, found in the home of Louis and Zellie Martin, the parents of Saint Therese of Lisieux. Certainly the Church has made much of her and her spirituality, even to the extent of making her a doctor of the Church, but given our situation today, do not her parents deserve even more attention? Given the fact that they gave four daughters to the Carmelites and one to the Visitation nuns, one would think that *The Story of a Family: The Home of St. Therese of Lisieux* by Fr. Stephane-Joseph Piat, O.F.M would warrant far more attention than *The Story of a Soul*. Saint Therese herself says, "God gave me a father and a mother more worthy of Heaven than of earth." When you read Fr. Piat's book, take a look at their evenings, at their family time together.

To take another example, the upbringing of Blessed Solanus Casey:

> "At a time when television and movies were not even imagined, stories and songs provided the Casey family with sufficient entertainment. Especially when snows landlocked the family, this kind of entertainment kept spirits from becoming morose. Often the children played games. Other times Barney Sr. and Ellen gathered everyone around the dining room for an evening of literature. Barney Sr. would read the poems of Tom Moore besides those of Longfellow and Whittier. Stories like Cooper's *The Deerslayer* held the children fascinated for long periods of time."
>
> "Bernard and Ellen Casey were creating a caring environment which enabled young Casey to become well-integrated and balanced. For their role in his spiritual formation, the future Solanus would be forever grateful... In many ways Solanus was able to be who he was precisely because of the way his parents norurished him in his youth"[2]

That is the culture of vocation, even if there is no mention of reading

---

[2] Fr. Michael Crosby OFM, Cap, *Thank God Ahead of Time*, (Chicago: Franciscan Herald Press, 1985)11.

the lives of the saints or the catechism. We know that such an evening manifests the culture of vocation because in fact it produced a priest and a saint. Such was the way of life lived by many Catholic and Christian families before the invasion of the Catholic home by the media.

Again, in a life of St Angela Merici (1474-1540), Sigrid Undset relates St. Angela's memories of her father:

> In the evening the fire blazes on the hearth in the great kitchen. Giovanni reads aloud to his household from the holy scriptures, from the lives of the saints and from the great book about the life of the desert Fathers which made a particular impression on Angela and her sister.[3]

Accounts such as this encourage us to think that *all will be well with the Church when we recover our evenings.* Yes, it may be just that simple, This will happen practically of itself when Catholic families rid their homes of mainstream mass media, not excluding secular newspapers and magazines. How often does it not happen that a Catholic family will go to Sunday Mass, return home, have breakfast, repair to the family room and sit down with the Sunday paper, sanctified, only to rise up secularized an hour later. Will not this cleansing of secular media from the monasteriolum (little monastry) be a kind of domestic asceticism? Will it not be felt as a death to self? For many it will be such a wrench that they will feel at first as if they are staring into the abyss.

Suddenly, alarming aeons of empty time will open up before the domestic father-abbot and his prioress, time that must be filled with something. According to their talents, interests and needs they will hit upon one thing and then another to fill up their evenings with the good, the true and the beautiful. There are many possibilities, of course. One family of our acquaintance gave half an hour to good secular literature (*The Chronicles of Narnia*, The Tom Playfair Series, *Robinson Crusoe* and the like); half an hour to the lives of the saints (long, book length versions lest sanctity seem to be a thing merely of visions and miracles); and twenty minutes of catechism (for the catechism explains the lives of the saints and the lives of the saints bring the catechism alive) followed by brief night prayer of one sort or another, and off to bed you go. Thirty years later the adult children still practice the faith, and one is a contemplative nun.

---

[3] *Stages on the Road* (Notre Dame, Indiana: Christian Classics, 2012), 69.

Another family that has already given a priest and a nun to the Church—with three more sons in the seminary pipeline—is a kind of modern day version of the Trapp Family Singers, but solely for their mutual enjoyment. Their evenings are musical, their lives a hymn to God.

There are many ways to recover our evenings and to make them family evenings together. This is key to making the Catholic family a "school of the Lord's service." Parenthetically, this is the perfect solution for those families who can neither afford parochial school nor agree on homeschooling the children. It is, among other things, semi-homeschooling, where the children routinely have their minds and hearts lifted to God, though a wise parent will call such evenings recreation and not school. Here instruction takes place line upon line, syllable upon syllable, year after year. This done now by even one percent of Catholic families will give us in fifteen to twenty years rectories full of holy priests, convents full of teaching sisters and flourishing monasteries.

With all retiring to sleep at a decent hour with holy thoughts and happy memories of an evening well spent, since they need less sleep than their children the parents now have the option of incorporating another Trappist option into their daily lives: early rising. The early morning really is a privileged, hallowed part of the day. No one else is up, either in the house or the town. What a perfect time to pray, to set the tone for the day, to bring our concerns before God, to intercede for the children. One could say the Rosary while walking to daily Mass, or while strolling through town. One could read Scripture, sing hymns to God, or say the Divine Office. There are many ways to be a Catholic, and many ways to pray.

Another benefit of such wonderful evenings together—if another Trappist motif were to be adopted—would be reading some portion of the life of a saint. In the monastery this is done at the noon meal, or in private reading known among monastics as *Lectio Divina*, but for a family the evening gathering is the optimal setting. Reading such lives to the children is a wonderful way to give their imaginations—the practical intellect—a Catholic formation. This will affect the choices they make throughout their lives. Such reading may kindle friendship with a saint, lead to a noble and holy life, and possibly to a vocation to the priesthood or religious life besides. Cultivating their minds and imaginations with such stories now will give them an orientation toward Heaven and resources sufficient to nourish them spiritually throughout their formative years. Here it would be well to recall the remark of an apostolic nuncio about the wonderful state of the Church in the United States before the Baltimore Catechism was put on the index of forbidden books. He was speaking ironically, of course, but its disappearance has been a great loss.

A parent could not read very deeply in the lives of the saints with his children without coming to the realization sooner or later that in addition to being prayerful, holy people, the saints also had a penitential aspect to their lives, an aspect that greatly amplified their impact, or rather the impact of Our Lord through them. For example, in his biography we read that Saint Anthony Mary Claret accomplished wonders in Cuba during his eleven years there as archbishop of Santiago.[4] Among other things, he confirmed some 300,000 persons and rectified many marriages. Then we discover in another book—the autobiography he wrote under obedience—that he wore a hairshirt three days a week and took the discipline the other three, Sundays being exempt.[5] Again, in a life of Saint Louis of France we read, "The king kept his body in subjection by fasting and discipline and secretly wore haircloth under his royal robes."[6] Examples could be multiplied ad infinitum, but sooner or later it will occur to the parent, "Wait, these people were made of flesh and blood and had much greater responsibilities. What if I took a leaf from their book and for my family fasted on Wednesdays and Fridays, or took my coffee black, or finished off my hot shower with a long, cold shower . . . or *something* self sacrificial on some regular basis to make my prayers heard on high?"

For those who might say or think, "I make sacrifices enough for my family, thank you very much," there is a difference between simply making such laudable sacrifices and offering them up to the Father in union with Jesus Christ, especially at the Eucharistic Sacrifice.

To do any such thing is to fall in with Our Lord's life of redemptive suffering. It is penitential, and a Trappist sort of thing to do. Essentially it is the effective strategy Saint Monica employed year after year in the hope of rescuing her wayward son from a life of unbelief and sin. How much

---

[4] Fanchón Royer, *The Life of St. Anthony Mary Claret* (Rockford, Tan, 1957).

[5] *The Autobiography of St. Anthony Mary Claret,* tr. Louis Joseph Moore, C.M.F. (Rockford, Tan, 1945) 114.

[6] *Il Libro D'Oro*, tr. Mrs. Francis Alexander (Boston: Little Brown, 1905), 374.

more effective it would be in the lives of the parents of young children, for it is much easier by our prayers to keep our children Catholic than to recover them if they fall away. Such asceticism would be effective not only in keeping them in the right way, but in bringing down blessing upon blessing on the family, not excluding vocations to the priesthood and religious life, but also vocations to happy and holy marriages and a plethora of grandchildren.

That suffering is redemptive is a premise of all Catholic and Christian life. Acsesis, then, is not merely a method of keeping the flesh under, nor a rung on the ladder to contemplation, nor spiritual athleticism, but a union with the sufferings of Christ crucified, whose sufferings are redemptive. Uniting our sufferings to those of Jesus Christ brings down graces and blessings from Heaven both on ourselves and others. Put differently, it changes things, or rather Divine Providence changes things in response to such lives, and we Catholics of 2019 have a very great many things that need changing. If the Church of 2019 in any massive fashion were to wake up to the fact that suffering is redemptive, that it changes things, we could with the help and blessing of God roll back the flood that threatens to overwhelm us.

There are many things that Catholics and many Christians want to see happen that would unfold *almost of themselves* if a few of these fairly simple and perfectly obvious Catholic and Trappist principles were applied to our personal and familial lives on a fairly wide basis, particularly in our prayer lives, but not only there. A few of the things we would like to see happen, and that are very much in reach are: tuition credits for the education of our children; the roll-back to zero of the homosexual juggernaut; the suppression of pornography; the end of abortion; full rectories; convents full of teaching sisters; the purification of our clergy; the restoration of monasticism; a vigorous episcopacy; the reunion of Christendom; the conversion to the faith of our country; the return to the faith of our siblings, children, grandchildren, nieces and nephews.

Since we are so used to being pushed back on all these fronts, saying that triumph is within reach will surely come across as unrealistic. Yet, since we Catholics and Christians all believe firmly in the resurrection of the dead, what Scriptural grounds do we have for saying that any of these things are unrealistic? Does not Our Lord say, "*Whatsoever* you ask for in faith . . . .?" God does not work miracles for saints who weigh the evidence, plot the trends, and surrender to reality as they find it. We absolutely need to become the saints we have needed for so long, men and women who by their prayers, words and works, faith, hope and charity will roll back the tide that threatens to extinguish us.

For a layman to read de Rance' is to be jolted by new possibilities, things that never occurred to him in all his Catholic life. He will find himself thinking, "Wait, they did that? Were they not also flesh and blood? They prayed for compunction? They prayed for humility and humiliations? I see that in their time they lit up Europe with the light of Christ that shone though them. And I, cannot I do my part in this our time? Can I not rise to the occasion, at least for the salvation of my children?"

Now in days gone by whenever anyone (any well-formed Catholic, that is) had a serious concern, he would call the nearest contemplative monastery to ask for prayers, for the prayers of monks or nuns obtained answers. Yet, why would this be? Surely, fidelity to their vows of poverty, chastity and obedience humbled them and plunged them into many fiery trials. Having passed through these, they would have been purified and their prayer rendered more acceptable to God. They became individually and corporately living sacrifices of praise. Also, they were living in community, and their unity drew God into their midst (Mt. 18:20). Too, fasting and other penances undergirded their prayer (Is 58: 2,3). They were friends with Our Lady and the saints. *Of course,* the Lord would answer their prayers.

Yet all these factors are available to laymen as well, albeit in much mitigated form. Moreover, as monks disappear and we increasingly lack anywhere to outsource our lives of prayer and penance, responsibility for sustaining other members of the Body of Christ increasingly falls on laymen. We too are capable of having prayer lives, of saying a Rosary on the way to daily Mass. A long commute makes the Breviary possible for us. We also are under vows that make heavy demands on us from time to time, our baptismal vows especially, and these lead us into truly purifying trials. Although we do not have a vow of obedience, are we not often pressed to yield to the will of our spouses, our co-workers or our boss on this or that matter, both large and small, thus growing in patience, generosity and self-sacrifice? The exigencies of daily life make many demands on our fidelity and purify us secretly. We have no abbot to humble us, yet daily life supplies that need. For many of us, the Sacrament of Matrimony situates us in that unity which is so pleasing to God and in addition to a spouse gives us children to join us. God granting us wisdom to keep it so, the Catholic family hearth always finds two or three gathered in His name. Moreover, we have a significant advantage over monastics, an advantage that fosters close intimacy with God, for we have no abbot to provide for us, but must learn to trust in God to guide us and to provide for us. "Those who are proven are proven everywhere," says St. John Climachus.

In the mid-fifties just as we then triumphal Catholics were entering into one of the most insidious temptations the world or the Church has ever known, Friedrich Jurgensmeier, diocesan priest and seminary professor offered the rationale for this test, a test it is safe to say we failed on a grand scale:

> "The vital energy of the Mystical Body... should be manifested in progressive, ascetical growth in Christ....The depth and sincerity of the member's fellowship with Christ must be put to the test through the trials and afflictions to which temptation daily exposes him. Christ's member can attain perfect fellowship only by means of battle and victory; he can grow into the likeness of the head and share in His transfiguration only when he becomes victor with Christ in the battle of life"[7]

All this was implicit in the long abandoned honorific for the confirmed Catholic: "Soldier of Christ." Could it be that for lack of soldiers—that is, Catholics spiritually militant—we are losing the war?

As for physical penance, this is available to us in many different forms: in taking smaller portions at table, in avoiding something particularly delectable, by not using salt, by skipping dessert, in avoiding sweeteners, in taking cold showers, by fasting twice a week, by taking the discipline or wearing a hairshirt. Take your pick. It is a very large buffet of possibilities. A search for some of these items on the internet will show that a) they are commercially available and b) there is therefore a market, and so it must be that c) many persons in the Church are doing penance.

---

[7] Friedrich Jurgensmeier, *The Mystical Body of Christ as the Basic Principle of Spiritual Life* (trans. Harriet G. Strauss; New York: Sheed and Ward, 1954) 188.

Then there are the interior sufferings that can come from many directions, from memory, from a rebuke, from misunderstandings, from financial or marital stress, from unrelenting temptation: "A troubled mind and a contrite heart are a sacrifice to thee, O Lord." There are a very great many things which we can offer up to the Father through Jesus Christ, the Son of God who lives in us, all of it pleasing to God and evocative of blessings. At one time this was well understood throughout the Church, and the mantra, "Offer it up" often heard, well understood and acted upon. We knew that trials would come and we knew what to do with them, to the glory of God and for the salvation of His people.

In his wonderful book, *The Mystical Body of Christ,* in a section entitled, "Ascetical Theology as Derived from the Doctrine of Christ's Mystical Body" Friedrich Jurgensmeier dwells on consciousness of membership in the body of Christ as a tremendous help in dealing with temptation:

> "Viewed from this standpoint, temptation has a particular ascetical significance. The member who is conscious of being afflicted with temptations through the very fact of his membership in Christ, finds greater strength to bear his burden with willingness and joy. He battles directly for Christ; he defends his personal union with Him and his own personal salvation while he also establishes a solidarity with Christ by continuing and completing the victory which he has won. It is a battle with Him and a participation in His victory. This realization is particularly a help to the member grievously tried by temptation, guarding him from the discouragement and weariness which are the result of this daily battle." [8]

Such writing makes one think that the generation that was so enchanted by reading of silence and contemplation in Thomas Merton (*Seeds of Contemplation*, etc.) would have done better reading of battle and victory in Friedrich Jurgensmeier.

As attractive as the Trappist Option is—and a more ardent imitation of Christ will always be attractive to the children of God—there is a danger of falling into a kind of spiritual athleticism that would not only be unhealthy, it would be suicidal. Growth in Christ is a matter of co-operating with

---

[8] Jurgensmeier, Mystical, 188.

grace, not of raw will power or resolutions. If, for instance, one takes cold showers every day for one hundred days, all the while avoiding sweets and screens of every sort, prays thirty minutes a day and has a vigorous workout program besides, at the end of this long battle he will surely be very disciplined person. Yet, unless he takes it a step further and prays for humiliations and compunction, as Rancé would urge him to do, he runs a great risk of being swollen with pride. And if he speaks vaingloriously of his accomplishment, he has not only lost any spiritual benefit of this exercise, but runs the risk of being humbled to the dust by his Lord.

Any program undertaken on the strength of mere resolutions and holy ambition will fail, but it will be a salutary failure because a wonderful discovery: namely, that no one is allowed to be his own savior, not a parent, not an abbot nor a penitential order. Jesus Christ is the Savior, He alone. The sooner this dawns on us the better. Undertaking a programmatic shift in the life of a family on the basis of resolutions and will power is one thing; praying ardently for guidance and wisdom and good success quite another. The holiest among us will always have good reason to pray, "Lord Jesus Christ, Son of the Living God, have mercy on me a sinner." It will ever be thus, for Jesus Christ is not going to deny Himself the joy of rescuing us from our difficulties and so winning our love. In our battle with the world, the flesh and the devil, which will not end till we take our last breath, Trappist Option or no, He is our savior. He is our Savior as breadwinners, as parents, as spouses and children, in our health both physical and mental, in our relationships, in every aspect of our lives.

For that reason, it would be presumptive to jump into any approximation of the Trappist Option all at once. We are weak creatures whose reach typically exceeds our grasp. It is fatal to sketch out a new, comprehensive rule of life, implement it all immediately and hope to follow it for any length of time. Better to take one thing at a time and build new habits of life gradually, now the Rosary, now daily Mass, one habit building on another. The exception, of course, is that everything sinful, scandalous and *distractive from the main business of life,* namely getting to Heaven, must go, and now. The mass media generally and television especially fit this description perfectly. It is, besides, war on the Gospel, hostility to Jesus Christ, cheap grace, pseudo peace, the hollowing out of one's life and soul, inurement to evil, bad example, interminable distraction, delightful illusion, self-set snare, the destruction of the family, amusement until the darkness comes and no one can work, pleasant path to eternal misery.

Some version of a much more ascetic way of life–undertaken by many– will cause a surge of new life throughout the Church. As in Ezechiel 37, it will be like the amazing sound of bones joining bones, the sight of flesh covering the bones, till finally we are the Body of Christ standing on our feet, cleansed, re-newed, vigorous and implacable in our assault on the strongholds of Satan. Then we shall roll back the poisonous tide in the name of the Lord. "Under God we shall do valiantly. It is He who will tread down our foes" (Ps 60:14). Such is the glorious future offered the Church and the world by an ascetical life, "The Trappist Option."

Lee M. Gilbert

BACK TO ASCETICISM:
THE TRAPPIST OPTION

16 | ON RETIREMENT—CONTENTS:

QUESTION 1.—*Having now treated of interior penance, tell us something as to that of the body: in what does it consist.* 6

Q. 2.—*A religious, therefore, cannot leave the monastery in which he has made profession?* 14

Q. 3.—*May not a religious go out of his monastery to unbend his mind, and to seek a little agreeable diversion and innocent recreation?* 16

Q. 4.—*Must a religious, therefore, live in discouragement, and sadness, without any consolation?* 16

Q. 5.—*Ought not a religious be allowed to go out when he is afflicted with disquiet or sadness, for the purpose of seeking some ease and consolation?* 19

Q. 6.—*Is not sickness a sufficient reason to go out of the enclosure of the monastery?* 22

Q. 7.—*If a religious cannot leave his monastery for the purpose of recovering his health, can he do it for that of engaging in necessary affairs and lawsuits?* 27

Q. 8.—*Does it not seem that you do not think it proper for religious to have lawsuits, since you say, if they may sometimes have important reasons and necessities?* 29

Q. 9.—*What are the occasions in which it is allowed for religious persons to go to law?* 40

Q. 10.—*Is it not to be feared, that the property of monasteries shall soon be destroyed, if all possible precautions are not taken to preserve them by law?* 42

Q. 11.—*Are not real poverty and pressing necessities of fathers and mothers, sufficient motives to oblige religious persons to leave their solitude, and to remain out of their monastery?* 44

Q. 12.—*Does it not seem that the similarity between those alliances is quite distant, and that is very difficult to deduce just consequences from them?* 48

Q. 13.—*You have now removed all our difficulties, by furnishing us with proper means to assist our relations; but we request that you will explain more in detail the precept of honoring our parents.* 50

Q. 14.—*What were the sentiments of the holy fathers on this subject?* 54

Q. 15.—*From what sources did the saints derive those maxims?* 65

Q. 16. —*What answer can be made to several passages of the holy scripture, which appear contrary to your reasons?* 71

Q. 17. —*May it not be objected that a religious cannot contract a new obligation with God, contrary to that which already binds him to honor and assist his parents?* 73

Q. 18.—*Does it not seem reasonable, that the obligation of religious vows ought to yield to that of assisting our parents, since a vow is a free act, whereas the other is a necessary duty, and necessary things are to be preferred to such as are not so?* 76

Q. 19.—As the religious state, according to the opinion of some, essentially consists only in the vows of poverty, chastity, and obedience, which may be equally observed in all places, does it not seem that nothing can oblige the members of that state to remain so constantly in their monasteries, since they can preserve the principle and essence of what they have promised in any place out of them?   77

Q. 20.—Is it not a divine precept to love and honor our parents, and is not the obligation it imposes consequently indispensable?   79

Q. 21.—Ought we not submit to the great number of doctors and casuists who maintain the contrary opinion?   80

Q. 22.—Are not, therefore, the advantages of retirement very great, since they preponderate over those important considerations?   87

Q. 23. —Are we to consider that retirement is as necessary for superiors as for their subjects?   90

Q. 24. —May a superior go out of his monastery for the purpose of making visits?   93

Q. 25.—Is not the motive of instructing the faithful sufficient to authorize a superior, when he leaves his regiment for that purpose?   94

Q. 26.—Before you conclude this instruction concerning retirement, tell us whether it is proper to invite the relations and friends of the religious to the monastery on the day of profession.   97

16

ON RETIREMENT

Question 1.—Having now treated of interior penance, tell us something as to that of the body: in what does it consist?

Answer.—The ancient monks and solitaries were always persuaded that exterior penance consists in some principal virtues and particular exercises, namely, in retirement, silence, fasting, austere food, watching, poverty, and in patiently enduring sickness and infirmities.

To begin with the first, which is retirement, I will tell you, my brethren, that the desert has been, at all times, the paradise of true solitaries. In it the plenitude of the divine favors met, as in their center, and replenished souls with heavenly joy; in it they received all those extraordinary graces, the effects of which we so justly admire in their lives. And what is much more, it was in the desert that Jesus Christ, the divine author of all grace, took particular delight in communicating Himself to them.

In solitude, they who have preserved their baptismal innocence, receive the fruit and reward of their fidelity. As the world never lived in their hearts, so are they free from having any remembrance of what they never loved; and as they are entirely separated from it, so are they never molested by the least idea of it. They are inaccessible to all its attacks; they have eyes, only to close them to everything mortal; hands, only to raise them continually to Heaven; tongues, only to sing the praises of God day and night; minds and reason only to meditate on His infinite perfections; and hearts, only to consume them, like so many victims, in the flames of his love.

Those faithful souls live as if they were alone, and as if there were none but themselves and God in the universe; they enjoy Him in peace, without interruption; they repose in His arms with profound tranquility; purified by the infusions of the Holy Spirit, which are always new, they enjoy an uninterrupted communication with their heavenly spouse, by which they become worthy to enjoy forever, the object of their love.

The condition of those who had unfortunately provoked His anger by their sins is not less happy. Conducted into solitude by His merciful hand, and separated from the places and the persons which were the cause of their fall, they recover the justice they had lost, they preserve it when found, and being healed of the wounds they had received from their sins, they become as vigorous as those whose health had never been impaired. Animated with the most fervent desires of being united to God, as well as with the most sincere regret for having ever separated from Him, they employ everything that may assist them in their holy enterprise. The remembrance of their sins is the only object they retain of the world; they accuse themselves of them, day and night, in the presence of God; they punish themselves by severe penance, and the only thought of having ever offended and lost their God, makes them sigh and mourn continually. Like the dove, when beholding herself deprived of her companion, she makes the utmost recesses of the forest resound with her plaintive notes.

Our Lord, who excites these dispositions in their souls, and delights to behold them penetrated with sorrow and love, never fails to unite secret joys, and ineffable consolations, to their interior grief. He produces in these re-animated souls the same happiness, and makes them enjoy the same pleasures in their retreats as those whom He preserved from the death of sin. Thus the same happiness unites both the one and the other, and they enjoy a felicity as complete as is compatible with the condition of this mortal life.

There is nothing that you should have more carefully remarked, my brethren, in all I have said, than the strict obligation by which a religious is bound to live retired in the repose of his cloister. Yet, though this duty is as important as it is unattended to, you ought to be persuaded that you cannot sufficiently fortify your minds against the example of the great number of monks, who, instead of sanctifying themselves in retirement, dissipate themselves in the intrigues and affairs of the world, as if they were not obliged to have nothing to do with them.

Is it not astonishing, my brethren, that religious men can be found, unacquainted with a truth so evident, and living as if they did not know, that by their profession they had closed to themselves for ever every avenue leading to the world; that they renounced all its cares and business, as well as its riches and pleasures; and that the service of Jesus Christ, in which they are engaged, will not allow them to engage, lawfully, in anything belonging to men; that they are dead to all visible things; that their monasteries are their tombs, and that they ought to remain buried in them, until their Redeemer calls them forth, as He formerly did Lazarus, when He raised him from the dead; that they are like vessels consecrated to God, and to the sacred ministry of His altars, and that without profanation, they cannot be employed in any profane use; that their rules abound with precepts and instructions which they can accomplish only in entire retirement; that the saints recommend nothing more strenuously than to live and die in a constant fidelity to this observance; that every one who meets them when they are so unhappy as to leave their solitudes, reproaches them in the following words of Saint Bernard, at least does so in his heart: "What have you to do with the world, who have already renounced it?"[1] In fine, that the perfection which our Lord requires of them, and concerning which He will undoubtedly judge them, can neither be acquired nor preserved in the noise and occupations of the world.

But, notwithstanding all this, nothing can be imagined equal to the blindness of men, nor to the astonishing insensibility in which they live, with regard to their real miseries. If, for example, that religious who lives without scruple in the commerce of the world, if I say, he saw a magistrate acting on the theater, a soldier pleading at the bar, an ignorant artisan striving to deliver lectures in one of our academies of science, he would be extremely surprised; yet, though his own situation, every time he leaves his retreat for the sole purpose of entertaining himself with men, is much more extravagant. Still he can discover nothing in his conduct that can give him anxiety, and though the sacred livery with which he is clothed makes him appear so different from others, and will not allow him to forget what he is, nevertheless, he is quite satisfied with his life, and finds nothing in it that can deserve the least reprehension.

In effect, can anything be more strange than to behold a religious, whose whole life ought to be a constant penance, in the midst of those who think only of their pleasures? To behold a solitary, whose state obliges to unlimited poverty and humiliation, in the company of men whose only occupation is the acquisition of the riches and glory of the world; to see a man, who

---

[1] Epistola II, Ad Fulconem. PL182:81a (1854) / "But you, who had already rejected the world, what had you to do with following a man of the world?" Bernard, *Works*, 1:121.

by his silence is bound to stem that torrent of words which produce such frightful evils in the different classes of society, insinuating himself into companies, diffusing himself in superfluous words, and wasting his time in idle conversation; to see him who, like a luminous planet, ought to dart his rays from the deep recesses of his solitude, and enlighten the world, appear in the midst of the same world, like an extinguished lamp, that emits nothing but smoke, says Saint Bernard.[2] To behold that man, whom the Lord had appointed to be a mediator between His justice and the sinner, committing the same sins, to deprecate which he ought to employ his continual mediation, prayers, and tears. In fine, to behold him who, by his thoughts, words, and actions, ought to dwell in Heaven, degrading his noble state by obtruding himself into the actions and affairs of those whose hearts and affections are sensible only to earthly things.

Behold, my brethren, the conduct and occupation of monks who leave their retirement, and appear in the company and affairs of the world. This is a faithful portrait of those who pretend to unite things so contrary and incompatible. Would to God they would discover all its deformity, and persuade themselves that they have at last succeeded—by means of those unlawful communications—in expelling the spirit of Jesus Christ from their cloisters, and in introducing the spirit of Satan in His place; that, by the same, they have dishonored both their state and their own persons, and so have justly drawn down on themselves the hatred of God and the contempt of men.

The saints employed every possible means to prevent those disorders. To inspire us with a horror of them, they foretold them long before they existed. They endeavored to nip them when in the bud, sometimes by describing all their deformity and exposing all their scandalous consequences; at other times by representing the beauty and advantages of the opposite virtues. But, alas! their counsels and exhortations have been ignored; for when a religious unhappily succeeds in making himself deaf to the voice of Jesus Christ, who speaks to him interiorly by His grace, he no longer has the docility to hear the advice and instructions of men.

Saint Anthony commanded his religious not to have anything to do with the affairs of worldly people. He maintained, as a constant maxim,

---

[2] "Non quidem lucens sed fumigans." De moribus et officio episcoporum seu Epistola XLII, ad Henricum, PL 182:809c (1854)..

that as a fish cannot live out of water, so a religious loses the life of piety and recollection if he forsake his all to converse with men.[3]

Saint Basil says,

> In order to lead an exact life, exempt from useless thoughts, it is necessary to separate from worldly persons, who live in ease and pleasure; and to converse with those who do not apply themselves to the study of the law of God is to expose ourselves to evident danger.

He tells us that retirement is necessary, and that no one can occupy his soul in devout prayer and meditation unless he expels from his mind the various thoughts and affairs which divide the soul, and link it to worldly occupations. He demonstrates the necessity of breaking off all commerce with people of the world by those words of our Lord: "If any man will come after me, let him renounce himself" (Matt 16:24); and concludes, "If we desire to fulfill that duty, we must separate ourselves from the society of men."

"If you desire to be a true religious," says Saint Jerome, "What business have you in cities, which are common and ordinary habitations, and not solitudes." [4]

Saint John Climacus says:

> He who is once retired into solitude, ought to have nothing more to do with the things of the world; for nothing is more pleasing to the passions which we have expelled from the dwelling of our hearts than to recover their former habitation. He tells us, To have our affections engaged by our relations, or by strangers, is extremely dangerous, because they may allure us to the world again, and extinguish in our hearts the fire of our fervor and compunction.[5]

"He is a true solitary, " says the saint in another place,

Who, being unwilling to lose the divine sweetnesses with which his heav-

---

[3] Saeculari nullo modo commiscearis—In sua Reg art. 6./ S. Antonius, *Regulae ac Praecepta*, SS. Patrum Aegyptiorum . PG 40:1068B (1863).

[4] S. Hieronymus, Epistola XVI, ad Heliodorum Monachum, PL 22:347 (1845).

[5] *Scala*, PG 88:663 (1864) / *Ladder*, 64.11.

enly spouse consoles him, is as solicitous to fly from the company of men, (although he has no aversion for them) as others are to seek it.[6]

It is to be remarked, my brethren, that the primitive monks did not keep a retirement so rigorous and exact. They made frequent visits to each other for the purpose of mutual consolation and instruction. Animated with the desire of greater perfection, some earnestly sought the company of those whom they considered as persons better qualified to assist them in that noble pursuit. Others, being attacked by their invisible enemies who pressed them with violent temptations, went to seek comfort from those whom they hoped could apply proper remedies to their evils.

But, as God alone is immutable (Mal 3:6), and as the most holy practices are liable to be corrupted in time, that custom which in itself was so charitable and useful was not exempt from this misfortune. In a short time monks, who before could not be induced to go out of their monasteries but by the most holy considerations, were seen in after time straying through the deserts, passing from one monastery to another, and even going to cities, for no other purpose but to satisfy their restless curiosity, and to hear something new. This contagion was quickly communicated; intercourse carried it from place to place; it penetrated the most distant parts; it changed the beauty of the desert, and plunged the monastic state into an almost universal desolation. "The earth mourned and languished: Libanus is confounded, and is in a state of misery" (Isa 33:9).

Saint Benedict, who was raised up by God to be the reformer of monastic discipline in the West, and to repair the ruins which time and circumstances had introduced into that part of the Church of Christ, considering that this liberty of mutually visiting and communicating together, was the cause of all the disorder he beheld, resolved to put a stop to the inconstancy of monks by obliging them to remain steadfast in the house in which they had made their profession. So that their engagement in that point might be the more solid, he required that it should be distinctly expressed in the form of the vows: "I promise stability, "[7] that is, I promise to live constantly in this house, and to serve God all my life in this place, unless obedience obliges

---

[6] *Scala*, PG 88:1095 (1864) / *Ladder*, 224.27.

[7] Promitto stabilitatem meam.—-Reg. c. 58 / The form of the promise is not found in Chapter 58 of the Rule of St. Benedict, but several instances of it as used in several monasteries are noted at PL 66:820 (1847)

me to change my situation. And to explain his sentiments more clearly, he adds, that the religious must remember that their profession prohibits all future egressions from the enclosure of the monastery without particular orders. In fine, to remove every occasion of pretext, he commands that every care be taken to furnish each establishment with all things necessary; so that they may not be obliged to leave their solitude for any reason, because, says he, there is nothing more dangerous for their eternal welfare.[8]

The founders of the order of Citeaux, who were entirely animated with the spirit of Saint Benedict, and who proposed to observe his rule to the letter, resolving to separate themselves for ever from all communication with the world made choice of the most inaccessible deserts for their abode, according as they were directed by the spirit of God. They made a statute by which they prohibited any monastery of the order to be built in any place, but such as might be found entirely sequestered from the commune and intercourse of men.[9]

Pope Eugenius III, writing to the abbots of this order, speaks in just the same manner:

> Consider that our fathers, who founded our holy order, forsook the world and despised all things in it; that they left the dead to bury their dead, and fled into solitude, there to place themselves like Mary at our Lord's feet, and that they gathered the heavenly manna so much the more abundantly as they were more separated and removed from Egypt. Take care therefore, that you do not degenerate from your fathers' virtue, so that you may be in the branches, what they were in the stock.[10]

Saint Bernard recommended nothing more earnestly to his brethren than retirement and solitude. He says, "The marks by which a true religious is known are retirement, manual labor, voluntary poverty," and "Nothing is more shameful, than to see monks in cities and towns, except when charity obliges them to appear in such places." He speaks of nothing so much as of the dangers to which religious persons are exposed in the world. He represents it as a place full of rocks, precipices, and destruction. He teaches

---

[8] *RB* 66

[9] In ex. Cister. Cap. 15. P. 246.

[10] Ad capitulum Cister. congreg, in lib. Epist. S. Bernardi.

that the religious life consists in obedience to the superior, and in stability in the monastery. He exclaims in one of his sermons:

> It is lamentable to behold religious persons, after having embraced the service of Jesus Christ, embarrassing themselves in worldly affairs, and engaging themselves in the passions and interests of men. It is pitiful to behold them flattering the rich, and even paying compliments to ladies. Is it thus that they imagine the world is dead to them, and they to the world? Before they entered religion they were scarcely known in a town or village, and now they are seen exhibiting themselves to public notice in whole provinces, and insinuating themselves eagerly to the knowledge of courts and kings.[11]

It was the love of retirement that made the first Carthusians form a statute by which they prohibited themselves the possession of anything beyond the limits of their enclosure, so that they might prevent every occasion of leaving their retirement:

> Being resolved to prevent every desire and occasion of inconstancy in ourselves and successors, we decree by the authority of the present statute, that none of the inhabitants of this place shall possess anything without the bounds of their solitude. That is to say, that they shall not possess lands, nor vineyards, nor churches, nor offerings, nor tithes, nor burying places, nor any other thing of the like nature.[12]

The same motive animated and inspired those holy men to reduce the number of the members to a few,[13] lest the increase of earthly possessions might also increase evil among them and withdraw them from their beloved solitude. By this wise ordinance they prevented the unhappy consequences of worldly dissipation, and the dangerous intercourse of men. Nothing is more just and remarkable than the instructions delivered by Saint Guigo to those who were to succeed him: "We have reduced ourselves to this small number," says that great man,

---

[11] Homilia IV, in *Super Missus Est Homiliae*. PL 183:85 (1854).

[12] Guigonis I Carthusiae Majoris Prioris V, *Consuetudines, Capitulum XLI,* PL 153:719 (1854).

[13] They would never allow more than thirteen in their communities cf. *Consuetudines,* Capitulum LXXVIII, PL 153:751.

That being exempt from all necessities, we may live more secure. We have determined to possess no means of accommodation for the retinue of those who might visit us, nor even places to lodge the poor, lest engaging ourselves in expenses beyond our abilities, we might be forced to seek assistance beyond the bounds of our solitude, which is a thing we much abhor. If it should happen by circumstances and reasons which we cannot at present foresee, that our successors cannot keep even that small number, without yielding to the odious and detestable necessity of going forth and seeking assistance; they will even yet diminish this number, if they follow the advice we here give them, and reduce it still in such proportion, as the means of the house may suffice, without exposing itself to such great danger. For although at present we are but few, we would choose to be still less in number, rather than to fall into such inconveniences for the purpose of either preserving or increasing our members.[14]

We read in Gratian, quoting Eugene III, that a religious ought to remain contented in his cloister, "Because," says he, "a monk can preserve his life no more assuredly out of his retirement, than a fish can live out of water. Let the solitary," he adds, "remain in silence and repose, since he is dead to the world, and lives now only for God."[15]

Pope Alexander, conformably to a decree of the Council of Chalcedon, orders all persons who profess the rule of Saint Benedict, to remain in their cloister, and prohibits them all visits to cities, villages, or private seats.[16]

Q. 2.—A religious, therefore, cannot leave the monastery in which he has made profession?

A.—Although there is no precept more positive in Saint Benedict's rule than that of stability, nor, I may add, more important, yet it must be allowed that it admits of some exceptions. Saint Benedict sent Saint Maurice into France, and Saint Placid into Sicily, to make new foundations

---

[14] Guigonis I, *Consuetudines,* Capitulum LXXIX, Quare tam parvus sit numerus, PL 153:753 (1854).

[15] Sedeat itaque solitarius et taceat, quia mundo mortuus est, Deo autem vivit.—Grat. decret. 2. part. caus. 6, cap. 8. Plac. 9.1./ Aemilius Ludwig Richter, *Corpus juris canonici: Decretum Gratiani.* Pars I, Volume 1 (Lipsia: Bernh. Tauchnitz, 1839) 654.

[16] Monachis quamvis religionis ad norma Sancti Benedicti, intra claustra morari praecipimus: vicos, urbes, castella peragrare prohibemus: et a populorum praedicatione omnino cessare censuimus: nisi forte quia de sua animae salute sollicitus, ut eorum habitum assumat eos intra claustram consulere voluerit.–Ibid.11, c. juxta. / Richter, *Corpus,* 654.

of his order. Saint Bernard, though he made profession in the Abbey of Citeaux, went to Clairvaux, formed that house, and was its first abbot. We find by Saint Benedict's rule, and by other monastic rules, that the religious were frequently employed out of the enclosure in cultivation of land and in other employments relative to agricultural economy; besides which, we find that they were sent out on the affairs and wants of the house. One of the councils of Mayence prohibits all egressions to religious persons, unless when obliged by necessity, or the command of the superior; and it may be said with truth, that a religious does no injury to the promise he made to Jesus Christ of living and dying in his monastery, when he goes from it by the direction of the divine will, which is the Lord of all things, and the rule of all rules.

But this divine will ought to be declared by a just and lawful command of his superiors, who cannot oblige him to go forth from his enclosure but on motives of just necessity, and by considerations which are in conformity with his rule and profession. For the vow of stability is not subject to their authority; it depends not on the manner in which they are pleased to explain it.

This is what Saint Bernard teaches when he says, that the vow of stability ought not to injure that of obedience, nor should obedience militate against the promise of stability; that is to say, that the vow of stability does not exempt a religious from the duty of obeying, when the command is just, and contains nothing contrary to the rules or duties of the state. But when it is divested of all these conditions, stability must not yield to it, but must stand immoveable and in full force, as to the possession of its own rights.

It should be remembered here, as well as in all cases of the same kind, that in all matters of doubt, the superior is to be exactly obeyed, because it is reasonable to conclude that he has the best reason to understand the nature of the affair; and besides that of being invested with authority, he is possessed of the privilege which, in the conflict of opinions, entitles him to a preference.

The saint explains himself more clearly on the subject in another place, where he tells us, that the vow of stability ought to exert all its influence, when there is question of leaving the monastery for the purpose of leading a more easy life; or when the motion arises from anxiety, humor, curiosity, levity, inconstancy, or any other spring of the like nature, for it then has every right to exert all its strength, but not when a religious is obliged to a change, by a lawful authority, that places him in such employments or occupations as are in harmony with his duties, and the rules of his state.[17]

We find the same thing exactly, inculcated in a statute of one of the general chapters of the Cistercian order. These are its expressions: "Let no person be translated to another house at his own request; but let each religious remain in his own house, let him live and die in the house of his profession."[18]

This has been so much the doctrine of antiquity, that we learn from Saint Basil, that it was not lawful for anyone to go out of the monastery, without being obliged by a particular order, or by a very pressing necessity.[19] He tells us in another place, that if anyone feels inclined to separate himself from his brethren, he ought to endeavor to heal this malady of his soul; and that if he does not effect it, he should be expelled from his religious community.

To this we must add that a religious may change his monastery, when by the evil example of its members it forms a real danger and opposition to his eternal salvation; or when he feels inspired by God to embrace a life more austere and perfect than that followed in the place in which he made his first engagement. This is a part of the holy liberty of the children of God (Rom 8:21), which, as we have already said, the Church never takes from them.

Q. 3.—*May not a religious go out of his monastery to unbend his mind, and to seek a little agreeable diversion and innocent recreation?*

A. Every religious should remember that he ought not to seek the satisfaction of the world; that being dead to it, he has renounced all its joys and pleasures as well as its riches; that all such enjoyments are equally unlawful to him; that the only consolations which are proper and lawful for him are those which are to be found in his state; that is to say, in the peace and testimony of a good conscience, which is the effect of interior purity, submission to the will of God, and fidelity in the accomplishment of all that the holy law of God prescribes.

---

[17] *De praecepto*, PL 182:885 (1854). / *Treatise* I, 139.

[18] Nemo ad propriam instantiam ad aliam domum emittatur; sed in domo sua aut moriatur aut vivat. Cap. Gen. an. 1224.

[19] S. Basilius, *Fusius*, PG 31:1007 (1857).

Now, how incompatible must not the enjoyment of worldly amusements be with this purity of heart, and with the obligation of living in the practice of holy sighs and tears, in which all religious persons ought to spend their lives, as we have already demonstrated in so many parts of this work.

Q. 4.—Must a religious, therefore, live in discouragement and sadness without any consolation?

A.—You ought to remember, my brethren, that there are two sorts of sadnesses; the one, which is merely human, is wicked, unprofitable, and produces death; like that of which the wise man speaks when he says, "Drive sadness far from thee, for sadness hath killed many, and there is no good in it" (Ecclesiastic. 30:24). It is wicked, for sadness is a disorder of the heart, a passion irritated by the privation of some desired good or by the presence of some unavoidable evil. There is no good in it. It is unprofitable, because by its violent motions it can neither deliver us from the evil that afflicts us, nor procure us the enjoyment of the good we desire. It produces death, for all the passions are sure to wound us mortally, when they are neither moderated nor regulated by grace.

There is another sadness according to God; this is holy, profitable, and fortifies the soul instead of discouraging it. This is what the prophet pointed out, when he said, "According to the multitude of my sorrows, with which my heart was oppressed, thy consolations have rejoiced my soul" (Ps. 93:19).

This sadness is holy, because our Lord produces it in our souls by the operation of His Holy Spirit. It is profitable, because it stimulates our compunction, produces tears, and purifies our souls from the stains of sin, which they had contracted. It is a source of consolation and joy for the sighs proceeding from a penitent heart, while they console it, are both an assurance of the already received influence of the Divine Mercy, and are so many pledges of the favors prepared to be in future its more delightful reward. Thus the religious who passes his whole life without any worldly enjoyments, is so far from being overwhelmed under the weight of that grief, with which it is supposed he must be daily contending, that on the contrary he feels, that the sorrow of penance, according to Saint John Climacus, produces spiritual joy and exultation, and contains a delight much sweeter than anything the world can afford. It affects the soul, but it is accompanied with pleasures, which spring from the great source of true comfort above, the God of peace, who never fails to pour down the invisible dews of His holy love, on a heart broken and afflicted with holy compunction.[20]

He tells us that the lively and profound sorrow of penance attracts and obtains the divine consolations, in the same manner as purity of heart receives the splendor of celestial gifts and lights.... That these consolations are the refreshment of the soul afflicted with the view of its infidelities, and who like a child weeps and laments interiorly, by the impulses of love and tenderness. That being revived by these refreshments, and delivered from the weight of its grief, it changes its bitter tears into others which are sweet and agreeable.

Q. 5.— Ought not a religious be allowed to go out when he is afflicted with disquiet or sadness, for the purpose of seeking some ease and consolation?

A.—I admit, my brethren, that there are some religious, who, deprived of the consolations of their state, find all things hard and difficult and live in continual grief and anxiety; but the affliction is not the same in all those who are thus affected. There are some who are afflicted by the loss of the sensible presence of God, who is sometimes pleased to conceal Himself from them, and to withdraw the sweet delights He usually communicates to those who serve Him; but this is only to try their fidelity, and to give them an occasion to maintain themselves by the vigor of their faith, and by the strength of their confidence in Him, that thus their merits may be hereafter crowned more abundantly. But it frequently happens, that seeing themselves in a state of aridity, and deprived of all sensible graces, instead of submitting to the will of an all-wise Providence, and of being satisfied with the position wherein He would have them, they afflict and torment themselves, without considering that the violent agitations to which they are the willing victims only increase their pains and make their burden more insupportable.

There are others, whose natural melancholy makes them feel a disgust for retirement, and plunges them into a state of interior darkness, makes them sink under the loneliness of solitude, and pass their days in affliction and obscurity.

Some may be found, and would to God the number were not so great, who by the corruption of their minds, and by their disaffection for all holy

---

[20] *Scala,* PG 88:811 (1860). / *Ladder,* 116.45.

things, consider the monastery as a prison, and subjection to regularity as a cruel slavery. Indifferent both to the exactitude and fidelity which God expects to find in all who are consecrated to Him, they deprive themselves of all the happiness of their state and of the fruit of their labors, and in the land of peace and tranquility reap nothing but trouble and confusion.

Now as to those of the first class, they ought to reflect, that their state being a disposition of the divine will, they ought to conform themselves to it without reserve, and bless the Lord, who is to be adored in all His ways, considering that He only tries their patience and fidelity by those momentary privations. In effect, the cloud that obscures the beauty of the heavenly light will be soon dispelled, and the sun, emerging from the transitory veil, will appear more resplendent than ever. Their afflictions will be to them a salutary means, if they support them with patience, and excite in themselves the dispositions which animated the prophet, when addressing himself to God, he said, "My soul, O Lord! had refused every consolation; thou alone were the object of my thoughts, and I have been abundantly consoled" (Ps 76:3).

The infirmities of the second are to be considered as deserving of compassion. They ought to be comforted in their weaknesses, and assisted in their conflicts. Their superiors and spiritual guides ought to console them by endeavoring to raise their souls to God, and by giving them the advice that Saint James the Apostle addressed to all Christians who are in a state of sadness: "Is anyone sad, let him pray" (James 5:13). Let all superiors remember, too, that it is never allowed to aspire to any good, however necessary it may be, unless by lawful means.

As to those of the last class, they ought to be convinced that they are unhappy only because they are unfaithful; that affliction and anxiety are the effects of their disorders; that they ought not to be astonished if their consciences are disturbed, since they are not pure; for if they were faithful to the law of God, they would enjoy a peace as profound as those depths of the ocean, over which the raging billows flow, according to the prophet (Isa 48:18).

Let them be moved to say from the bottom of their hearts: "Woe to us, because we have sinned; for this reason our hearts are become sad, and therefore our eyes are obscured, and deprived of the enjoyment of lights" (Lam 5:16). Thus acknowledging that they themselves are the authors of the evils they suffer, that the sadness and anxiety, which like a dark cloud covers their interior man, is an effect of their own sin, may they return to the Lord by a sincere conversion, implore His divine assistance, so that having dispersed the clouds and shades of darkness which surround them, He may preserve them from sinking into the obscurities of an eternal sleep. "Enlighten my eyes that I may never sleep in death "(Ps 12:4).

Such are the remedies to be employed when a religious is attacked with sadness. These are the means which are to be used in healing his disorders, instead of presenting to him the cup of worldly pleasures and amusements, which at best only deceive those who drink its contents; because they cannot produce any real or solid comfort, and more particularly because they are adverse to the sanctity of his state. Jesus alone is the true principle of peace for all those who belong to Him. In Him alone their true glory is contained. This peace is of Him, it is His own peace; He has merited it for us by the blood He shed for the redemption and reconciliation of all men. And it would be miserably deceiving ourselves to expect to find it in the world, since He himself assures us that the world does not know it, and consequently is incapable either to give it or procure it for us. "My peace I give you; not as the world gives do I give you" (John 14:27).

Hold it for a constant maxim, my brethren, that the pleasures and amusements of the world are never more dangerous for a religious person than when he foolishly imagines he has most reason to desire and allow himself their enjoyment—that is to say, in the time of temptations and sickness. For as our natural impenitence and immortification make us seek to be delivered from the evils we suffer, whether they are corporal or spiritual, so they excite us to seek ardently everything that may produce the effect we desire and when found to attach ourselves no less firmly to them. This is so much the case that if we allow ourselves the liberty of tasting the pleasures and enjoyments of the world, it is not to be doubted but that — being agreeable to self-love—they will solicit our irregular desires, allure our affections to themselves, destroy in us all the virtues of our state, and thus separating us from the principal duties of our profession, will, by the same, separate us from God.

In fine, whether we entirely lose the remembrance of our duties, or the desire of fulfilling them as we ought, in either case we make a new covenant with death. We renew our bonds, we recall into existence our engagements with the world, and by a sacrilegious infidelity we restore to the enemy the place in our hearts which had been in the possession of Jesus Christ since we first consecrated ourselves to His service. Hence, my brethren, to allow religious persons the enjoyment of worldly diversions and amusements, in the circumstances and cases of which we have spoken, is so far from being allowable in conscience, that superiors ought to become more exact, and oppose all the force of their authority against the injustice of such unreasonable attempts, laboring without intermission to deter their subjects from either executing, or even desiring such pernicious liberties.

Present meat and wine to a man who is neither hungry nor thirsty, place before him the most delicious food; all these things cannot be to him the matter of any serious temptation; it is sufficient in such circumstances to possess the most ordinary virtue, in order to practice temperance. But if you surprise this man with the same things at a time when he is extremely hungry and parched with a violent thirst, he will certainly find it very difficult to resist and preserve his virtue unstained. In like manner, when the pleasures of the world present themselves alone, at a time when we feel no way inclined to enjoy them, the danger is not so imminently great. But if on the contrary, they join themselves with our infirmities, our wants, our necessities, and present themselves under the influence of the passions, Ah! then everything speaks in their favor. The poison becomes more quick and subtle, the malignity more pernicious, and it is almost a thing impossible that they can be prevented from making the most dreadful impressions.

Q. 6.—*Is not sickness a sufficient reason to go out of the enclosure of the monastery?*

A.—The motive of illness, and that of preserving health, can never be considered sufficient for such egressions by any but by those who have no knowledge of the monastic state.

First, if in the order of God, all Christians live only to die, if all their lives should be a constant preparation for death, and if, according to Saint Augustine, he is not worthy of a good death who has not a sincere will to die, what ought to be the dispositions of a religious on this subject? With what fervor ought he not to desire and expect the moment in which he is to enter on that happy journey, since he is bound to fulfill in a perfect manner the duties which are common to him and to all Christians, and being no longer of the world, has neither affairs, nor pleasures, nor affections which might bind him to it. His life is a continual desire of and meditation on death, and his chief employment consists in preparing for its arrival. Yet, notwithstanding all this, could it be thought that a man bound by these sacred ties were in the dispositions of accomplishing his duties, or rather could it be doubted that he were influenced with dispositions entirely contrary, if he abandoned his retirement for the purpose of seeking health in the world?

Is it not a lamentable extravagance to see a man who had shut himself up in a cloister in order to prepare himself for a happy death—and to avoid everything that might become the cause of an evil one—forsaking his retirement when he is about to terminate his mortal existence, and exposing himself to the same, and even to greater dangers, than those he had avoided by his first retreat from the world? He flies from the society of men, according to his own expressions, in order to die well; but he returns to the company of men when he is near the important term! Not unlike a man, who having spent his life at a distance from the enemies of faith for fear he might unfortunately die amongst them, no sooner beholding himself at the end of his course, and having only a few moments to live, than he returns amongst them and thus renders all his precautions unprofitable.

Secondly, a religious forsakes the world and shuts himself up in a monastery in order to satisfy the justice of God for his sins. He delivers up his body to a voluntary death that he may redeem the life of his soul. All his exercises of religion, his watchings, fastings, labors, solitude and all the corporal mortifications he endures are the instruments of his punishment. He renounces a life of a few moments, so that he may deserve to obtain of the Divine Goodness one that is eternal, according to the words of Jesus Christ: "He that hates his life in this world, keeps it to life eternal"(John 12:25). He desires nothing more than that Almighty God would destroy everything mortal and perishable that may be found in him, that He may employ His avenging justice to punish him in time in order to treat him with mercy and clemency in eternity. "Here cut, here burn, but spare me in eternity."[21]

Now after all this, what opinion can be formed of a religious, who in the state of illness (which is nothing more than the real effects, and the natural consequences of his engagement) leaves his monastery in order to seek amongst men the means to avoid death? No other, certainly, than that he retracts the resolution that he had made, or at least, that he has quite lost all thought of it, since being thus influenced by the fear of death, and by the desire of prolonging life, he plainly demonstrates that he values his health more than his salvation; that he prefers the welfare of his body to that of his soul; and that he makes no difficulty in exchanging an immortal life, for a

---

[21] Hic ure, hic seca, modo in aeternum parcas.- S. August.

life whose frailty, incertitude, and short duration, are such as make it to be esteemed only as a fleeting vapor and an empty shadow.

Thirdly, if you saw a martyr, who being near the moment in which he were to offer his life as a sacrifice to the honor of his God by a death which ought to be the sole object of his desires, as it certainly is the principle of his real glory, instead of awaiting the final stroke with constancy, would burst his bonds and chains and shamefully fly to conceal himself from the torments prepared for him, you would undoubtedly say that he would not have less dishonored the name of Jesus Christ by his scandalous flight, than if he had renounced his faith.

Now the religious state, according to the saints, being a martyrdom, we may consequently form the same idea of the monk, who, instead of showing the world what account men ought to make of a future life by his contempt of the present, and of bearing testimony to the truths taught us by our divine Lord, by faithfully persevering in the penitential labors annexed to his state, and by finally completing his sacrifice in a voluntary acquiescence to the stroke of a sweet and peaceful death, evinces by public evidence that he is unwilling to accept it. For he leaves his monastery and goes to seek the assistance and remedies of men, thus making all his resolutions and engagements yield to the immoderate desire of a longer life.

Fourthly, sicknesses are harbingers of death, since they are, as it were, the passages or natural ways by which we arrive at the end of life. By infirmities, says Saint Gregory, God knocks at the door of our souls.[22] By them He admonishes us to hold ourselves in readiness, and to prepare, when called upon, to appear in His presence, to the end that He may not surprise us in any improper condition that might oblige Him to judge us in His anger.

Now, this being supposed, is it not an insupportable conduct in a religious, who, beholding himself in the state of sickness, instead of profiting by the warning of his fast-approaching dissolution given him by God, and of employing for that end all the means he has received from His goodness, forsakes his monastery, that sacred asylum in which Divine Providence had placed him as in a strong fortress; withdraws from the society of his brethren; deprives himself of all the assistance he might derive from the

---

[22] Pulsat vero cum iam per aegritudinis molestias, mortem vicinam designat.– S. Greg. Hom. 13 in *Evangelica*./ Gregorius Magnus, *Homilia XIII*, PL 76:1124 (1878).

good example and regularity of the cloister, from his submission to his superior, from silent solitude, and from all the other advantages which are found in the exact observance of his rule.

Is it thus he prepares himself for the coming of Jesus Christ, his judge, by withdrawing himself from the state in which He was pleased to station him? Does he imagine that this unerring Judge will consider such conduct as an effect of his zeal and solicitude? Or rather, can he entertain any doubt, that such liberty being so opposite to the dispositions the Lord requires in him, that He will not punish it severely? Ah! there is just reason to fear that the great King will treat him as a deserter, who cowardly forsook his post through fear of death, and will deliver him up to all the passions and all the evils of which an unfortunate religious is capable, when he prefers the ease and satisfaction of his body, to the discharge of his duty, to the voice of his God, and to the salvation of his immortal soul.

Do you desire to know, my brethren, what those religious become, when they leave their monasteries, for the purpose of seeking the recovery of their health? Some run over distant countries and provinces in search of waters and baths to cure their distempers. There you might see them in public places and assemblies, in the midst of persons of all conditions, sexes, ages, and manners. There they pass whole days in conversations, in enquiring after news and worldly affairs, or in discourses concerning their particular infirmities; the operations, the remedies to be employed, or those they have already applied; by which those ideas are recalled to their minds, which ought to be eternally forgotten. They live in public effeminacy and impenitence, as empty of, and as inattentive to the things of God as they are full of themselves. Their blindness is so great that they do not perceive that though they may avoid the more enormous sins to which they expose themselves, yet their conduct dishonors the sanctity of their habit, and the sanctity of their habit condemns the impropriety of their conduct.

You might behold others going from one monastery to another on pretext that the change of air will reestablish their health. They are there received and treated as strangers and sick persons. And as they live without rule or subjection, they never fail to diffuse the poison of their libertinism and immortification, leaving in all places the marks of their pernicious disorders as the reward of the charity with which they were entertained.

There are others who return to their relations, and to their fathers' house, in order, as they say, to breathe their native air; but, in reality, to retake the spoils of the old man which they had previously forsaken, for they find their former customs, and their ancient affections. The tenderness of a father, the caresses of a mother, the pleasures and satisfactions they enjoy in the company of their friends soon effect the entire extinction of their enfeebled piety. Their hearts being softened like wax, receive, indifferently, every impression.

In brief, they become again what they were before they left the world, and return to their monasteries as to insupportable evils. They import the world with them, and instead of living there by the spirit of Christ, they know no other rules or maxims but such as had been revealed to them by flesh and blood.

Here you see the inevitable consequences of leaving the monastery on the motive of health. Let all such religious remember that as often as they sue for such permissions, they open to themselves so many pits, and that the superiors who consent to their requests, do nothing less than plunge them into the gulf

Q. 7.—If a religious cannot leave his monastery for the purpose of recovering his health, can he do it for that of engaging in necessary affairs and lawsuits?

A.—If in some cases, and for important necessities, it may be lawful for monks to pursue their rights by the way of lawsuits, it is scarcely even lawful to leave their monasteries for the purpose of supporting them personally. Such employments are so opposite to all the duties of their state, that there can be no doubt but they are to be numbered amongst those things which are prohibited to them.

There would be no diversity of opinion on this subject, if sufficient care were taken to examine what the life of a religious ought to be, and what are the employments of a man who support lawsuits. Let it be remembered that a religious is called by God to a life of interior piety; that he is obliged to live in innocence, in simplicity, in repose, in continual recollection, in a separation from the company of men, and in the presence of God, as uninterruptedly as human weakness can allow; and it will appear evident that he can never, in conscience, expose himself to the dreadful dissipation inseparable from the pursuit of secular affairs, nor that he can entangle himself in these refinements and artifices without which, as it frequently happens, the best founded pretensions are frustrated.

In effect, nothing will appear more sensible than that the necessity of appearing in secular courts of justice, before tribunals where nothing is

heard but noise and clamor, is incompatible with the presence of God, which a religious ought to preserve at all times. This, together with the affairs and other distracting concomitants, would not only dissipate his mind, but also so absorb all his time, that he would not have a single moment to give to Him who ought to be the only object of all his thoughts during the whole course of his life. Hence all lawsuits that cannot be maintained without the immediate concurrence of religious persons in this manner are to be relinquished; nor is it lawful for them to leave their retreat on such motives.

Now, let us reflect on the extremities to which a religious is exposed, when employed in such negotiations. He is deprived of the advantages of his retirement; he no longer tastes the sweets of silence, nor enjoys the assistance of a regular life. The affairs with which he is charged engage his whole attention, and he sacrifices to them all his time, attention, and industry. They are like a rapid torrent that hurries him away in its current, with so much the more violence as he has no time to make the least useful reflection.

He lives amongst men who frequently follow the impulse of covetousness or hatred. He is soon infected with the same evils, and learns both their morals and maxims. He is without unction in his discourses, dissipated in his conduct, attached to his own opinion, ardent in his interests, prompt in engaging in business, an enemy to reconciliation. In a word, he is a religious without religion, who evinces in all his words and actions the disorder and confusion of his soul. He is the vineyard mentioned in the holy scriptures, which being formerly beautiful and fertile, is now become wild and barren, whose fruit is sour and disagreeable to the taste.

Hence we may without difficulty judge whether a superior, who is invested with authority only for the purpose of saving others, can, without betraying his ministry, engage a religious in employments which are merely temporal, which oblige him to leave his cloister, prevent him from the discharge of his duties, and by inevitable consequences destroy in him the holy qualities and principal virtues of his state. How can such conduct be reconciled with the instruction which our Lord gives to all monastic pastors, by the mouth of Saint Benedict. "Above all things," "says that saint,

> Let the superior be careful not to neglect the souls committed to his care, or to prefer the care of temporal and perishable things to the duties he owes to them; but let him never forget that he is the pastor and guide of souls, and that he shall be obliged one day to give an account of them. Let him

not seek to excuse himself by alleging the poverty of his monastery, but let him remember that it is written: seek first the kingdom of God and his justice, and all other things shall be given you over and above (Matt 6:33).[23]

One of the councils of Mayence forbids religious persons to appear before secular tribunals, and declares that in case the abbot is necessarily obliged to appear, he shall not consent to do so without the approbation and command of his bishop; but even then he must take care not to be the cause of any disputes or suits, and that any requests or solutions he may want, must be done by the ministry of advocates.[24]

If there are some canons which allow a religious to plead, with the permission of his superior, in cases relating to the affairs of the community, that such is to be understood of lawful and pressing occasions, just merely to inform the judge of his right, the justice of his cause, for his interest; but not to engage himself the pursuit of law, to solicit and support his suits, or pass any considerable time out of his cloister for that purpose.

Everything, my brethren, ought to yield to the salvation of souls, since Jesus Christ did not hesitate to lay down His life for them, to the end that He might deliver them from the slavery of sin. They are worth an infinite price. Nothing created, nothing of all perishable things can be put in the balance with them; and it is even denying the faith not to be persuaded that whole worlds ought not to be sacrificed to save one only soul.

Q. 8.—Does it not seem that you do not think it proper for religious to have lawsuits, since you say, if they may sometimes have important reasons and necessities?

A.—Every person well knows the instruction given us by Jesus Christ, in these words: "If anyone take away what belongs to you, do not seek to have it again" (Luke 6:30). And if He has been careful to recommend the same thing in many places of the scripture, and in so many different ways, it was only that it might be more forcibly impressed on our minds, and to teach us more correctly what account we ought to make of such things. All agree, that not to plead, to forsake our property, rather than preserve it by lawsuits and contentious ways, is an evangelical counsel; that all Christians

---

[23] *RB* 2.33.

[24] M.L. Bail, *Summa Concilium Omnium* (Paris, Fredericum Leonard, 1622), 309.

are obliged, in the interior dispositions of their souls, to observe it as a precept.

However, it is really strange that nobody takes any notice of the cases and circumstances which ought to have an exterior effect, and hold the place of a command; and that even those persons who live according to the more severe maxims, and who make profession of a more exact piety, are the first to find reasons to dispense themselves in its observance. In truth, if we were to judge of our Lord's intention by what we see every day amongst men, we could believe nothing more than that He merely proposed a truth, and a speculative perfection, without ever requiring that we should exemplify it in our actions, or in the conduct of our lives.

But we find that Saint Paul, after having reprimanded the Corinthians for having differences and disputes amongst them, and for contending before the tribunals of pagan judges, tells them, "There is now indeed, sin amongst you, since you have suits with one another: Why do you not rather suffer to be injured? Why do you not rather suffer the wrong that is offered to you? " (I Co. 6:7)

If we cannot say that the apostle considered all lawsuits and disputes as so many sins and violations of the divine law, we may at least confidently say that he believed them to be faults and imperfections; and that it is so difficult to observe the rules of a just defense in the disputes which arise among men; to remain within the bounds of that mildness and reserve prescribed by our great Master; and to command the motions of our hearts in such a manner as may secure charity from the dangers which surround and attack it; that he did not hesitate to tell them, you offend God every time you contend in law (1 Cor 6:7).

Not that to plead, positively speaking, offends God, but because it is almost impossible to plead without offending Him. Our divine Redeemer, who always applied Himself to the sanctification of His disciples, and took such particular care to smooth all their ways, and to remove everything that might be an occasion of error or scandal, and thus, to raise them to a state of perfection that might be pleasing to His heavenly Father: "Be ye perfect, as your heavenly Father is perfect" (Matt 5:48); for this end lays down as the rule and maxim for our conduct to avoid all disputes; to offer our cloak to him who would take away our coat; not to resist evil when we are injured; and not to endeavor to regain possession of what had been taken from us (Matt 5:39).

The instructions, my brethren, are general. Jesus Christ delivered them to all Christians, and there is no individual but ought to consider himself as having a part in them. And so that you may clearly understand this matter, I will tell you that every Christian being a disciple of Jesus Christ is obliged to attend to these words: Not to endeavor, by contending ways, to regain the possession of what had been taken from him (Luke 6:30), and to consider them in the dispositions of his heart as a commandment. He ought not only to be sincerely disposed to forsake his goods, his honor and everything that the injustice of men may take from him as soon as he perceives and understands that God requires such a sacrifice from him, or finds that the service and glory of his Creator calls on him to make it, but also, whenever he is forced to resist evil, and oppose the designs of those who would deprive him of what belongs to him, he must be as disengaged from them interiorly, as if he had really given up all care and solicitude concerning them. For, though God allows Christians to use the things of this world, He forbids them to have their affections engaged in them, so that as to the interior dispositions of the heart, there ought to be no difference between a Christian who repels an injury or an injustice, and a Christian who suffers it without any resistance at all.

As to the exterior effect and accomplishment of those words of our Lord, it is not the will of God that all persons should equally observe it. He holds out perfection to all men, as we have already said, but He does not call all men to perfection. Thus these words; "He that takes away what belongs to you," etc. (Luke 6:30) are a counsel for some, and a command for others. They are a counsel for the generality of Christians, though there are some occasions in which all are obliged to understand them literally and to execute them as a precept. But those who are called by God to a perfect state, who are raised by His grace to the practice of superior virtue and eminent piety, such Christians as these ought to consider them as an obligation. The will of God requires that they should exemplify this duty in their lives, and there are but very few cases in which they can consider the above words as containing no more than a counsel for them.

Hence it is easy to conclude, my brethren, what the duty of religious persons is in this matter, and in what manner they ought to conduct themselves in it. We shall advance nothing beyond the truth when we shall say that being called by God to the practice of all that is great and holy in the Christian religion, and being obliged by their state to labor without interruption to become perfect men, they are obliged, on every occasion, to follow the advice of Jesus Christ, and to practice the evangelical counsels;

and that, consequently, all judicial contests are prohibited them. From this we may infer that religious persons cannot lawfully begin or entertain any law affairs, whether they are attacked in their persons, injured in their reputation, or despoiled of their property; that the only defensive arms they can wield to resist the wickedness of men are patience, faith, and prayer; unless on some extraordinary and important occasions, when they may be forced by the motives of the interest of our great master, the edification of the Church, and for the defense of truth, to depart from those general rules, and to oppose the designs of malicious persons; for there their resistance will be sanctified, and will be no more than an exception to the precept, and a dispensation from the evangelical counsel.

It must be allowed, my brethren, that unless religious persons behold the loss of transitory goods with a disinterested and indifferent eye, and unless they are always ready to sacrifice their rights and pretensions rather than to lose the sacred repose of their solitude, it is impossible they should be able to answer the designs of God, or correspond with the graces He has given them; nor, consequently, to attain the perfection to which they are obliged to aspire. God requires two principal things; the one is their own particular sanctification in a perfect measure and degree; the other is the edification of the Church.

Now, in what manner could they accomplish His will, and acquire a perfection so eminent and pure, amidst all the agitations, disorderly motions, and different passions, either of anger, covetousness, envy, and revenge, which excite and inflame such persons as engage in litigation? By what means could they give public edification, if they held out the example of that ardent attachment to temporal things, than which, nothing produces a more evil effect in the minds of worldly people, nor furnishes them with more unfavorable sentiments against persons consecrated to God. Such dispositions remove them as far distant from the purity of their state, from the example of the saints, and from the end for which they were formed by God in His Church, as the heavens are from the earth.

Do not imagine, my brethren, that this is my particular opinion. Saint Basil declares, "Monks ought not to contend about temporal things before secular tribunals."[25] He tells us in another place, and Saint Gregory Nazianzen with him:

---

[25] S. Basilius, *Fusius,* PG 31:942.

The worldly man may contend and employ all his abilities to preserve his goods and maintain his rights; but a religious, on the contrary, ought to renounce both willingly rather than go to law with those who unjustly deprive him of them; and thus obey without difficulty the precept. Let the man of the world defend himself when struck, and repel one injury by another, persuading himself that in so doing he observes the rules of exact justice; but a religious ought to extend his patience so far as to allow him who treats him ill to weary and satisfy himself with the outrages he lays upon him.[26]

Saint John Chrysostom, explaining these words of the apostle: "There is really a sin"(1 Cor 6:7), says:

It is a double fault to plead before unbelievers; it is one to have any difference, and another to decide them before the judgment-seat of pagans: when two persons go to law, they give scandal, and they are both equally criminal; nor does he allow us to examine which of the two is right or wrong.[27]

Saint Augustine says:

It might be thought that it is no sin to have disputes with one another, but only to decide them before pagans; but the apostle, by employing the phrase, and there is really a sin, shows the contrary; and in order to remove every motive of excuse by which men might exculpate themselves, saying: the cause I maintain is just, I am injured, and I require nothing more of the judges, than that they put an end to the cause of my vexation, the apostle adds, Why do you not rather suffer the injustice, and allow them to take away your goods (I Cor 6:7), rather than to contend in lawsuits; and thus exemplify the instruction given us by Jesus Christ in these words: Let him who desires to go to law with you for your robe, have your cloak also (Matt 5:40); and in another place: Do not seek to recover the possession of what had been taken from you unjustly (Luke 6:30).[28]

Saint Gregory the Great speaks nearly in the same terms, when he asks:

---

[26] S. Basilius, *Constitutione Monasticae,* PG 31:1359 (1857).

[27] S. Joannes Chrysostomus, *Homiliae XVI in Mathaeum,* PG 57:248 / *Saint Chrysostom: Homilies on the Gospel of Saint Matthew* (New York: Christian, 1889, NPNF1/10:110).

[28] S. Augustinus, *Enchiridion, sive de Fide, Spe et Caritate,* PL 40:231 (1845).

How can a perfect Christian defend by contentions those temporal things which God commands him to despise? He says, When we love the perishable goods of this life, if we follow Jesus Christ in a perfect manner, so far from being afflicted at such accidents, we shall consider ourselves as travelers delivered from the weight of a heavy burden and though necessity may sometimes oblige us to take care of our property, yet there are persons whose injustice we must suffer when they injure us in that respect.

Saint Bernard, writing to the religious of Marmoutiers, tells them:

I am really astonished that some amongst you (God forbid I should suspect you all to be in the same case) either by simplicity or cupidity, are so indifferent as to the celebrated reputation you have acquired that they prefer an inconsiderable revenue to the esteem of an entire people. You ought not, my brethren, appreciate more seriously any temporal advantage, whatever it may be, when placed in competition with the reputation you have always possessed, even in the minds of those who are strangers to you. You have acquired it by the merit of your lives. Be careful therefore to preserve it.

You will tell me perhaps, that you do no harm to any person, that you only preserve what is your own, and that you are quite disposed to acquiesce to the decision of the judge, if anyone should dispute your pretensions. Right well, but if anyone should tell you that to have any suits at law is in itself a sin, why do you not rather suffer injustice? (1 Cor 6:7) If again it were told you, that it is written: If anyone take away your goods, do not seek them again; if anyone strike you on one cheek, turn to him the other also; let him that takes away your coat, have your cloak also (Luke 6:30; Matt 5:39); what would you reply? To all this we might add many other things of the same nature; but we choose rather to excite you to a proper amendment of life than to confound you; therefore, we tell you plainly, that to possess less goods and to preserve peace is a more certain mode of conduct for every Christian, and chiefly for a monk, than to enjoy more by means of lawsuits; for you sing every day: A little is better to the just man, than the abundant riches of sinners (Ps 36:16)[29].

The same holy abbot, reprimanding a bishop of Angus for going to law, tells him that his conduct would be more glorious and more holy, and that he would do much more for the glory of God by patiently suffering the

---

[29] Epistola CCCXCVII, Ad Odonem, PL 182:606 (1854) / St. Bernard, *The Letters of St. Bernard of Clairvaux* (trans. Bruno Scott James; Athens, Ohio: Cistercian, 1998), 498.

injury than by seeking indemnification by law; that he (the saint) could not conceive how he could have an easy conscience, after having given such great scandal; and he cites this passage from Saint Paul: "Certainly this is sinful "(1 Cor 6:7).

We read that Saint John the almoner was earnestly solicited by the stewards of the church of Alexandria to enter a lawsuit against a person who unjustly detained the money the saint had lent him to the end, said they, that it may be given to the poor. He answered them that it was true that by giving alms he would fulfill one precept of Jesus Christ, but that by going to law he would violate two: the first, by the scandal he would give, inasmuch as he would thereby give occasion to people to believe that he acted through the motive of self-interest; and the other, by neglecting this commandment of the gospel: "Do not seek to have that again that has been taken from you." [30]

"Be assured, my children," continues that great saint and bishop, "that it is a much more holy way of conduct to prove our patience than to contend for our property, according to the remonstrance of the apostle: 'Why do you not rather suffer the injustice?'" (1 Cor 6:7).

Saint Stephen of Grandmont forbids his brethren ever to employ lawsuits for the conservation of their property or for increasing it, because the apostle teaches that he who is engaged in the service of God should not embarrass himself in earthly things in order that he may please Him in whose service he is engaged. He would never allow them to appear in any affair of this nature (2 Tim 2:4). "You are dead," says he to them, "and your life is hidden with Jesus Christ in God" (Col 3:3).[31]

Here you see the truth that I have advanced evidently proved. You see, my brethren, that these are not our own imaginary productions that we inculcate, but the sentiments of the saints. You behold in what manner they maintained in the same sense as we do, that these words of our Lord, "Do not contend for what has been taken from you" (Luke 6:30), contain a precept for all who are called to a life of perfection. Namely, that lawsuits and contestations are forbidden them either because such disputes fill the mind with solicitude and anxiety and impede them in the practice of that meekness which they are bound to observe; or, because they are the cause of public scandal. Besides people in the world, as Saint Basil remarks,

---

[30] Leontius, *Vita Sancti Joannis, Eleemosynarii,* PG 93:1644D (1865).

[31] S. Stephanus Grandmontensis, *Regula,* PL 204:1131(1855).

when they see those who make profession of exact piety straying ever so little from the paths and rules of that state, load them with injuries and calumnies;[32] or, in fine, because it is a conduct more holy, more perfect, and more worthy of a true follower of Christ to suffer the violences and injustices of men in peace and without resistance than it would be to repel them, and to defend our property by any litigious means.

But to the end that you may not say that those severe maxims were good in former times, but that they are not so for those in which we live, I will here insert the testimony of a great saint of our times, which certainly ought to be of so much the more weight with us as it is universally allowed that he never gave excessive counsels, and that his conduct was no less conspicuous for wisdom and mildness than for spiritual light. I speak of the amiable Saint Francis of Sales, who writing to a lady to deter her from entering on a lawsuit speaks to her in such edifying terms, that I think it necessary to insert the saint's words here in detail. "How long my dear daughter," says he,

> Will you pretend to gain any other victory over the world, and over the affection you may have for it, than that which our Lord Himself won, and to the example of which He exhorts you in so many ways? In what manner did this Lord of all things conduct Himself? It is true, my daughter, that He was the lawful master of the whole world; and yet do we find that He ever went to law to obtain the least place whereon to repose His head? He suffered a thousand injuries: what suits did He ever undertake at law to obtain satisfaction? before what tribunal did He ever cite any person?
>
> Never before any indeed: He would not cite the traitors who crucified Him before the tribunal of God; on the contrary, He invoked the Divine Mercy in their favor, and this is what He so much recommended to us: "Let him who contends with you for your coat, have your cloak also." I am no way superstitious, and I do not blame those who go to law, provided that they do it in truth, judgment, and justice; but I say, I exclaim, and I write, and were it necessary, I would write it with my blood, that whoever desires to become perfect, and to become a true child of Jesus Christ, ought to exemplify this doctrine of our Lord.
>
> Though the world should fret and fume; let the prudence of the flesh tear its hair with spite, if it so pleases; let the wise ones of the world invent as many different pretexts and excuses as they will, this sentence ought to be preferred to all prudence; "Let him who contends with you for your

---

[32] S. Basilius, *Constitutiones,* PG 31:1359D (1857).

coat, take your cloak also." But you will tell me, that we ought to understand it in that sense in certain cases only: it is true, my dear daughter, and thanks be to God, we are in those cases; for we aspire to perfection, and we desire to imitate Him as near as possible, who with a truly apostolical affection said: "Having food and raiment let us be content"; and who cried out to the Corinthians; "Now there is plainly a fault amongst you, since you have lawsuits one with another."

But give ear my daughter, give ear to this man, who no longer lived to himself, but in whom Jesus Christ lived; hear his sentiments and his solicitude: "Why," says he, "do you not rather take wrong? Why do you not suffer yourselves to be defrauded?" And remark, my daughter, that he speaks not to a young woman, who after making so many efforts, and in such a particular manner aspires to perfection, but to all the people of Corinth in general; take notice that he requires that they should suffer wrong; take notice that he says there is a fault among you because you have lawsuits with one another, though he knew that some had defrauded and were guilty of injustice: but what sin? Sin, because by that means they scandalized the unbelieving worldlings, who said, behold how these Christians observe the law of Christians: their Master says, "If a man goes to law with thee for thy coat, let him have thy cloak also"; behold how for the sake of temporal goods they expose themselves to lose those which are eternal, and hesitate not to destroy that tender and fraternal love they ought to have for one another. Take notice again (says Saint Augustine) how our Lord in His divine lesson does not say, if anyone take away your ring, let him have your necklace, though they are both superfluous; but He speaks of the coat and the cloak, which are necessary garments.

O my dear daughter, behold the wisdom of God, behold His prudence, which consists in that most holy and most adorable simplicity which makes us become like little children; and to speak in a more apostolic style, in the sacred folly of the cross. But I hear human prudence asking me, to what a state do you intend to reduce us? What! do you require that we suffer ourselves to be ill-treated, trodden under foot; that we allow every one who thinks fit, to wring us by the nose, and to sport with us as children do with a puppet, and hold our peace, letting them clothe and unclothe us as they think proper? Yes, it is true, I do require all that; but it is not I who commands it, but Jesus Christ who required it in me: and the apostle of the cross and of Him who was crucified cries out: "Even unto this hour we both hunger and thirst, and are naked, and are buffeted; and, in fine, we are ill spoken of; we are made as the refuse of the world, the off-scouring of all even till now." The inhabitants of Babylon do not understand this language; but the inhabitants of mount Calvary reduce it to practice.

Oh! daughter, will you tell me, Father, you are really very severe all of a sudden? It is not really all of a sudden, for as soon as I tasted a little of the fruit of the cross, this sentiment entered into my soul, and remained there ever since. If I have not lived conformably to this principle, it was rather the effect of weakness of heart than that of sentiment. The tumult of the world made me do the evil which I detested interiorly; and I will now presume to speak this word to my confusion, to the ear of my daughter's heart: I have never sought any indemnity, nor done any ill, but against my will. I am not making any examination of conscience, but I speak as I see things in general, according to which, I think that 1 say the truth, and so much the more inexcusable do I acknowledge myself to be: but now, daughter, I consent; be as prudent as the serpent, who strips himself entirely, not of his clothes but of his skin, in order to grow young again; who hides his head, says Saint Gregory, by which we are to understand fidelity to the truths of the gospel; and exposes all the rest to the mercy of his enemies, in order to save his head.

But what am I saying? You have so many people of honor, wisdom, cordiality and capacity, would it not be easy for them to reduce M . . . .? Are people become like tigers: will they not give ear to reason? What duplicity and artifices, what profane words, and perhaps what untruths, how many little concealed and perhaps unveiled injustices, how many calumnies, or at least half-calumnies, are there not employed in those lawsuits and procedures? Will you say that you will marry, and thus scandalize the world by an evident lie? Such might be the case, if you had not a faithful and a continual preceptor, who would keep the love of sincerity alive in your soul. Will you tell me, that you will live in the world and be entertained according to your birth? that you have no need of this and of that? To what purpose all this multitude of thoughts and imaginations which those pursuits shall produce in your mind?

Leave! Leave to worldlings their world. What need have you of those things which are requisite for making a figure in it? Two thousand crowns, and even less, will more than abundantly sufficient for a young woman who loves her crucified Lord; one hundred and fifty, or two hundred crowns of board money, are riches for a young woman who believes in the counsel of evangelical poverty. But if I were not a cloistered nun, but merely associated to some convent, I would not then have sufficient to entitle me to be called madam, except by one or two servants. But what do you say? Have you ever learned that our Blessed Lady had so many? What great matter is it, whether it be, or be not known, that you belong to a good house, according to the world, provided that you belong to the house of God?

O yes, but I desire to establish a house of piety, or at least to give some great and important assistance to some religious house; because, being subject to many corporal infirmities, that consideration would encourage me to support them with greater cheerfulness. Admirable! indeed, my daughter; I well knew, that your piety served as a plank to your self-love, because your devotion is so wretchedly human; and really to say all in a word, we are not fond of crosses, unless they are all of gold, studded with pearls and precious stones. To be considered as the foundress, or at least as a great benefactress to a community, is a rich though a very devout and admirable spiritual abjection. Lucifer would have been satisfied to remain in Heaven on the same condition.

But to live by alms, like our Lord; to receive charity from others in our illnesses and maladies; we, who by our extraction and fine qualities are this and that; really that is very disagreeable and very difficult: I allow it is too difficult to man, but not to the Son of God who will effect it in us. But is it not a good thing to possess what is our own, and to employ it. as we please in the service of God? The phrase, as we please, explains all our difference. Yes, but I say, as you please, father; for 1 am still your daughter, God having disposed things so.

Well then, be satisfied that my pleasure is, that you will be advised in all the affair by M. M. N.; and that you sacrifice the rest to the love of God, to the edification of your neighbour, and to the glory of the Christian spirit. Oh! what blessings, what graces and spiritual riches will you not merit for your soul, my most dear daughter. Ah, yes, by doing this you shall abound and overflow. God will diffuse his blessings on your little stock, and will fully satisfy you: no, no, it is no way difficult for our Lord to do as much with five barley loaves, as Solomon did with so many cooks and agents. Rest in peace, I am . . .

This instruction is of itself so explicit, that I find no necessity to make the application; and really, religious persons must have lost all remembrance and feeling of what they are, if they do not perceive that it is entirely addressed to them, that it particularly points out their spirit and duty, and regards them more than any other persons.

Q. 9.— *What are the occasions in which it is allowed for religious persons to go to law?*

A.—The cases in which religious persons may, or ought to appear before judges in order to defend themselves and maintain their interests ought to be determined by Christian prudence and charity. We do not presume to say that the duty of not going to law, particularly regards the perfect, and consequently the religious and the solitary, admits no exceptions, nor that there are no extraordinary circumstances in which those exceptions are to be attended to; on the contrary, the will of God sometimes decides in favor of them.

Saint Basil says that there are some cases in which, when cited before secular tribunals by unjust persons, we ought to answer, for the better finding out the truth, and submit our innocence to such a trial: that we ought not to be the first, but only follow those who assault us first. He adds that such a line of conduct will evince that animosity is not the motive by which we are impelled, but the love of truth; that when we defend the interests of truth within the limits of just moderation we not only do not violate the commandments of God but we preserve him who stirs up the affair from a great many sins, and that we thus act as ministers of God.[33]

Saint Gregory the Great after having testified his astonishment how a Christian can presume to defend temporal things by lawsuits and disputes, and having said that when we love the goods of this life by imitating Jesus Christ in a perfect manner, we ought to consider ourselves as travelers delivered from a heavy burden, adds, that we may sometimes resist those who endeavor to take our goods from us unjustly, provided that we do it without injuring charity; and that our motive be not merely to deter them from taking our goods, but lest in taking them they should lose themselves.

It is in this manner that it may be sometimes lawful for religious persons to go to law for important reasons; such as to prevent considerable losses, to deliver themselves from some violent oppression, to hinder the effect of an enterprise that might ruin a whole community, or disturb its tranquility, or to stem the course of some injustice; and, as the same Saint Gregory says, to compel the aggressor to enter into himself; so that preserving meekness and charity, we ought to be more attentive to the salvation of our neighbor than to our own temporal advantage.

But before making the least advances in the way of rigor, religious persons ought to employ all possible efforts to reconcile their differences by peaceable means. They ought to represent to the unjust aggressor, either by themselves personally, or by the intermedium of friends common to

---

[33] S. Basilius, *Fusius,* Interrogatio IX, PG 31:942 (1857).

both, the injustice of his proceedings. Let them endeavor to convince him how great a crime it is to usurp the goods of the Church, or to persecute the servants of Jesus Christ; let them offer to submit the affair to the judgment of arbiters, and to consent to their decisions; let them suffer some little loss, in order to make the accommodation more easy. To this let them unite their fervent prayers and implore the assistance of Almighty God, that being forced to dispense themselves in the literal observance of His law, He may preserve them from being so unfortunate as to lose its spirit, or to do anything contrary to His holy will and commandments. Above all let them remember never to engage in doubtful lawsuits, as there is nothing that more exposes their reputation to the piercing darts of human malice, than the bad success of ill-founded enterprises.

Now if religious persons are careful to observe these rules, if they conduct themselves by these maxims, it will scarcely ever happen that their names shall be heard spoken of before the tribunals of secular judges. They will avoid a great number of embarrassments, dissipations, and condescensions; they will enjoy much repose within and without the enclosure of their monastery; their patience will edify the Church; they will have peace with all; and they may indeed say with the prophet: "I was peaceable with those who hated peace" (Ps. 119:7).

If it should happen that some extraordinary occasions compel religious persons to engage in acts of litigation, the care they shall have taken to avoid them will secure them from being suspected of either covetousness or cupidity. Tranquil and moderate in their conduct, they will be respected even by their enemies, and perhaps become the instruments of their conversion to better sentiments. In fine, they shall have the advantage of preserving the merit of patience, charity, and meekness in the midst of involuntary disgusts, as well in the judgment of God as in the opinion of men.

Q. 10.—Is it not to be feared, that the property of monasteries shall soon be destroyed, if all possible precautions are not taken to preserve them by law?

A.—Can you believe, my brethren, that having received gratuitously from the hand and liberality of God whatever you possess, He will allow any person to deprive you of them if they are necessary for you? And that He who prompted His servants to give them to you will not deter the wicked from taking them from you? Be assured, that as it was not by your industry you have acquired them, so neither can you preserve them by your vigilance.

Besides, what reason can there be adduced to make religious persons prefer their temporal interest which so many holy solitaries entirely despised to the good example which they are commanded by God to hold out to all his Church? How can they think of losing their good name, by which they edify the world, for the purpose of gaining a piece of land, a portion of an inheritance, a claim to a title, a measure of corn; and by this tenancy to keep everything which they believe is their property, they are willing to relax their attachment to their exercises; they disgrace their persons and state, and become in the sight of God, servants stained with vice, and deserving to be called men of little faith, while they are considered by men, as persons self-interested, covetous, and unjust.

In fine, my brethren, can anyone disapprove their conduct, who viewing things in the light of the divine appointments, prefer those which are best and most estimable to those which are less valuable, and who, influenced by a most holy and religious discernment and commerce, relinquish goods of little consequence so that they may obtain the possession of others which are of incomparable worth? This is just what those religious perform, who, to avoid lawsuits, give up a part of their property, and thus secure their precious time, which when employed in a just and rational manner, is worth a whole eternity of happiness.

They behold with pleasure the hand of injustice despoiling them of some temporal advantages, but they are unwilling to sacrifice for its conservation the repose they enjoy, and which is to them the source of much greater profit; for they make no comparison between the gain that might be the result of succeeding in any lawsuit, whatever might be its importance, and the blessings which accompany the tranquility of those souls, whose only affair is that of the service of God, and of seeking the means to accomplish His holy will.

This is what Saint Augustine teaches when explaining those words of Saint Paul, "Redeeming the time for the days are evil" (Eph 5:16). He says that when we are solicited to enter suits at law, and that rather than engage therein and so lose our time, we thereby choose to lose something of our goods, that such a mode of conduct is redeeming the time. Every day, says that great saint, beholds you exchanging your money for necessary things, such as wine, bread, oil, wood . . . . you give something to have some other thing, and that is properly buying. Do the same, and give something of your property to purchase repose to your souls, and thus you will redeem the time.[34]

Ah! are you not convinced that the acquisition of peace, the liberty of employing all your time in the service of God, and the being delivered from a thousand perplexities, a thousand solicitudes and occasions of sin, are much more preferable than the money you may gain by contending at law? If the obligation of preserving the property of the monastery should be alleged as a chief reason, you may answer, my brethren, with Saint John the almoner, that God does not oblige you to preserve it by all sorts of means; that lawsuits are not those He requires you to employ; and that though it may be lawful to have recourse to litigation on some unavoidable occasions, such occasions are still to be considered as extraordinary and as contrary to the instructions, maxims, and precepts of Jesus Christ as they are to the repose, disengagement, and sanctity in which you ought to live without interruption.

Some may, perhaps, tell you that you perform an act of charity, when you oblige your neighbor to restore what he unjustly possesses. To this it is easy to reply, that such a plea has the appearance of rectitude, provided that in forcing the property out of his possession, you could eradicate covetousness from his heart. But this is so far from being the case, that the heart becomes irritated by the resistance it meets; its cupidity is inflamed by opposition, whether it succeeds or not in its designs; and as nothing is more effectual to calm the mind, and to stem the passion of a violent character, than to bear his injurious treatment with patience, so nothing is better calculated to convert a covetous man than to show him by our disinterested behavior, the contempt he ought to have for everything that can serve as an incentive to a passion so shameful and unjust.

To say all in a word, my brethren, let religious persons never entertain the least doubt concerning the goods they relinquish for the purpose of avoiding lawsuits and shunning all litigious affairs. God will preserve their property by more innocent ways, if it be necessary for their salvation. On the whole, to become poor for the sake of Christ Jesus is really the way to become rich; and to purchase eternal happiness with the perishable goods of this life is undoubtedly to act according to His spirit and commandment.[35]

---

[34] De Verbis Apostoli, Sermo CXI, PL 39:1966 (1844)

[35] S. Paulinus Nolanus, *Poemata,* PL 61:655 (1847).

Q.11.—Are not real poverty and pressing necessities of fathers and mothers sufficient motives to oblige religious persons to leave their solitude, and to remain out of their monasteries?

A.—If the holy fathers were persuaded that the first and most essential disposition necessary for those who embrace the monastic state was to forsake their country, or at least the place of their birth, and to separate themselves from their parents forever, there can be of course nothing more opposite to their sentiments than to maintain that a religious may leave his cloister and forsake the service of Jesus Christ—to which alone he ought to consider himself bound—for the purpose of going to assist his parents in their wants and necessities.

But we ought not to be astonished to find this opinion so generally established, or to behold so many persons of every state and condition defending it, since there is nothing so deeply rooted in nature, nothing that it inspires and teaches more constantly and universally. Children for the most part do not desire to afford these assistances to their parents with less ardor than the parents wish to receive them. In a word, this sentiment being in all appearance so conformable to all laws, divine and human, there seems to be nothing found sufficient to excite the least doubt in the minds of any persons concerned therein, about its veracity.

Nevertheless, they who measure things, not according to the generally received opinion and customs of men, but by the rules of truth, shall without difficulty discover, that though this opinion is common, yet it is not on that account true and equitable; that it militates against reason enlightened by faith; that it attacks the maxims of the saints, the conduct of all holy monks, the example and words of Jesus Christ, who on all occasions, and everywhere teaches us, that He came with the sword, in order to make divisions amongst relations, and to separate those who were united by the bonds of nature and blood.

The reason why people in general persuade themselves that religious persons cannot in conscience remain in their monasteries, when the extreme necessities of their parents seem to require their presence with them, is, that they consider persons consecrated to God as being equally obliged with other men to assist them; and that the precept of honoring father or mother is the same at all times, for all persons, of whatever state or condition they may be; and that it is not lawful to engage in any state which imposes any obligations contrary to its accomplishment.

This principle seems just, but is not so in effect; for this obligation is not so extensive, but it admits exceptions on many occasions.

Amongst many that we might adduce, there is one which all must allow, because it is evident from the words of Christ Himself: "A man shall leave father and mother, and cleave to his wife"(Matt 19:5) Now every one allows that it is a lawful right and consequence of marriage, to separate children from the subjection and dependence of their parents, not merely for any limited time, but for all their lives; nor will anyone contend that those who are engaged in the indissoluble bonds of the conjugal state, are not bound to live continually therein; consequently are dispensed from giving their parents those exterior marks of charity, of duty, and service, which are incompatible with that state and holy society in which the law of God obliges them to remain. From hence, it may be inferred, that either children who are engaged in the state of matrimony, are dispensed from the observance of the precept of honoring their fathers and mothers; or that the precept still subsisting, they are unable to observe it; or, in fine, that there are other means besides that of being personally present with their parents, by which they may satisfy that duty.

The first cannot be admitted, because the commandment is general and indispensable for all men. The second is equally inadmissible, for God never commands impossible things. It must therefore necessarily follow that there are means to accomplish it, proportioned to the different states and conditions of children; and that these means are not merely personal, nor such as the children can be obliged to communicate to their parents in that sense, when the extreme necessities of the latter may make such assistance necessary.

It is in this point of view, we may with all reason, consider those persons who are engaged in the bonds of religious vows. This holy connection unites them to Jesus Christ in a manner much more strict and elevated than that of which we have just spoken. As more strict, it binds more closely. As more elevated, it separates more widely. Every other difference which distinguishes the two conditions demonstrates evidently that if the obligations of marriage are a lawful impediment which excuse children from going to their parents in the time of extreme necessity, there is much less reason to expect that those who are once consecrated to Jesus Christ, and who have shut themselves up alive in cloisters, as it were in tombs, in order to live only for Him and in Him, should separate themselves from

their retreat and duty, and plunge themselves again into the cares of the world, in order to relieve the necessities of their parents.

For however great and extreme their wants may be, the alliance formed by the religious engagement is much more important and intimate, because the union contracted by men with their creator obliges them incomparably more than those which they make with creatures. It is more sublime, because it excludes all that is not God, He alone being its principle, its object, and its end. Moreover, it tends to unite us intimately and exclusively to Him by perfect charity, and, to speak according to the language of the saints, to make us become partakers—even in this mortal life—of the immortality of angels.

All this proves, my brethren, that our consecration can admit nothing impure; that it is incompatible with the occupations of the world; that those who have forsaken it by the vows of religion have, by the same, deprived themselves of all future possibility of returning to it; that it is an error to refuse to religious vows what must be granted to those of marriage; that it is doing an injury to Jesus Christ to tear His spouses from His arms, and to expose those holy souls who are consecrated to Him to the defilements of the world after they had been secured from them in the enclosure of monasteries, as in the secrets of the divine countenance.

Q. 12.—Does it not seem that the similarity between those alliances is quite distant, and that it is very difficult to deduce just consequences from them?

A.—I allow that the disparity between them is very great; that the advantages of the one are almost infinitely superior to those of the other; but then it must be allowed, that the more the former surpasses the latter in dignity and excellence, the more it ought to be preferred; nor is it less unreasonable and irreligious to place the spouses of Christ in a state of subjection, from which the spouses of men are exempt; and to maintain that notwithstanding the religious profession the world has a right to receive services of them, from which the bonds of matrimony emancipate the others.

Neither will it be anything to the purpose to suppose, that civil marriage, consisting in a reciprocal donation, and mutual giving up of the persons of the parties to one another, necessarily supposes a separation from parents; for although the consecration of ourselves to God by vow is entirely spiritual and holy, yet it is an oblation as well as that of our soul, and by which, as by an evident consequence, a new order of dependence is established with respect to God and us, which is incompatible with that wherein we formerly lived, with regard to our parents and relatives.

Religious persons have means proper to themselves, and conformable to their state, by the application of which they may, without any egression from the pale of their solitude, accomplish the precept which obliges them to honor their parents. If anyone is anxious to know what those innocent means are by which a religious may assist an indigent parent, it is easy to answer, according to the opinion of the saints, and particularly that of Saint Basil, that those means do not consist in giving him a part of the goods of the monastery, since no private religious can attribute to himself any individual right to them. Neither can a religious assist his father or mother by his labor, because he can no longer dispose either of his time or actions as he pleases; even his own person is not in his power. Nor can he console them by letters or discourses, since he has no more communication with the world, all exterior intercourse being prohibited by his state.

But the means he can employ are his exercises of mortification, penitential works, and fervent and assiduous prayers. These he ought to offer to the Lord continually, not so much to beseech Him to deliver his parents from the poverty they may endure, as to give them the grace to make good use of it; that He may make them patient after having made them poor, and convince their hearts of that truth which the world can never understand, that happiness consists in being poor; that abundance is found in poverty, (according to the words of incarnate truth) when it is united to the grace of God, and an entire resignation to the orders of His Divine Providence.

This is the manner in which a true religious ought to fulfill the precept that binds him to honor his parents, and not by adopting a mode of conduct more according to the sentiments of flesh and blood, which is proper only for persons in the world; and which, in violating the integrity of his engagement, would hurt his conscience, withdraw him from the ordinance of God, and from the purity of his state.

Nevertheless, if religious persons are dispensed from giving to their parents that assistance which, if free, they could not refuse them without the greatest ingratitude, Divine Providence, which extends its munificent influence over all its works, has not neglected to furnish a supply for those indigent parents, as well as a refuge for their children: and thus is afforded a proper solution of the present difficulty. For if the children have lost their parents according to the flesh, by retiring from and renouncing the world, religion repairs the loss, by uniting them to others according to the spirit, by a new and holy affinity.

Here they find relations, friends, and parents, not only in those who bear the same sweet yoke of Christ, but moreover, in all those whom our Lord acknowledges for His true members, who, being destitute of all the advantages of the fortune and goods of this world, have no other inheritance but that which the eternal Father gave to His Son, when He introduced Him amongst men, clothed with our flesh; which the Son himself declared by these words: "Foxes have holes, and the birds of the air have nests, but the son of man hath no where to lay his head"(Matt 8:20).

And as the goods which monasteries receive from the goodness and liberality of God are common both to the religious and to the poor, as they are equally the patrimony of both, it is certain that parents, as poor persons, have a right to partake of them; and that they ought to find a subsistence therein, preferably to all other poor, as well as every necessity for the preservation of their lives. And as a religious ought to have no other employment but that of meditating on the law of God day and night, to hear His sacred word so as to sanctify himself in his retirement by the exercises of his state, so it is evident that the application of this charity does not concern him.

That care, according to Saint Basil, belongs to the superior, so that the obligation which ceased in the person of this religious at the moment he consecrated himself to the service of Jesus Christ, began to exist in, or was transferred under another title to the person of his superior. The superior then is obliged to communicate the assistance, in the name of the religious, and may do so without his participation or intermediacy, and even without his knowledge.

Saint Basil adds to this an essential condition; namely that the parents and relations must be of the number of those of whom our Lord spoke when being told that His family, according to the flesh, waited for Him. He answered that His mother, His brother and His sister, were those who did the will of His heavenly Father (Matt 12:50). That is to say, according to Saint Basil, that the assistance given to parents by religious houses should be only given to those who lead holy and Christian lives. It would be very improper to employ holy things in evil pursuits, or to become benefactors of unworthy persons, who would thereby make the inheritance of Christ, which was destined to relieve the wants and necessities of those who belong to Him as brethren, serve as means of sin in the hands of those who, by their irregular and scandalous lives, can only be considered His enemies.

Q. 13.— You have now removed all our difficulties, by furnishing us with proper means to assist our relations; but we request that you will explain more in detail the precept of honoring our parents.

A.—It is certain, my brethren, that the precept of honoring our parents is indispensable, not only because it is a positive commandment given by Almighty God, but because it is conformable to eternal truth, which is always the same, and never admits either of change or vicissitude. A man as father establishes in his son a necessary grateful respect, the principle of which he communicates to him by communicating life to him. And the gratitude that a son owes to his father is no less essential than the necessary dependence of the one on the other, as an effect and its natural cause. Hence this duty is common to every age and condition; nor can anyone pretend to be exempt from it.

But though in this respect such obligations are common to all men, yet the manner of complying with their injunctions is different. Indeed, it may be said that the acts and obligations of these duties are regulated by the various states and employments of individuals, or rather by the appointed destinations of God; for here I suppose no other states of life than those which are appointed by Him. A son who is free is obliged to employ his time, application, and study in relieving the necessary wants of his parents. He is bound to console them in their afflictions, assist them in their affairs, and support their decrepit state. He owes them as many proofs of love and tenderness as he finds means and occasions of displaying them. But if he be engaged either in religion or in the nuptial state, or as a pastor devoted to the care of souls, he is then bound to regulate his conduct according to the duties of the vocation in which the divine will has placed him. Though he still preserves in his heart the same respect and gratitude for his parents, yet he cannot lawfully give them the same exterior demonstrations thereof, as he would do, were he not deterred by those lawful impediments.

Our Divine Lord has inculcated this truth by so many circumstances of His life, and in a manner so evident and precise, that it is impossible to mistake His real intentions. He declares that when there is question of the service of God, He knows neither mother nor brethren. Nothing is more remarkable than what passed between Him and His holy mother when she found Him in the temple and declared how much she had suffered by

His absence. He answered her: "Why have you thus sought me; did you not know that I need to be about those things that belong to my Father?" (Luke 2:49) as if he would say, you ought to know that my obligations cease with regard to you, when they are contrary to those which I owe to my Father.

Now it is according to this principle that we are to elucidate the present question. The precept of honoring parents obliges religious persons as well as other men, but the means of accomplishing that duty are peculiar to the religious state. Those which are contrary to this state, and incompatible with its rules, are unlawful to them, nor can they employ them. Now as religious persons are consecrated to God, and obliged to remain in their solitude during their whole lives; and as they have, by their profession, equally renounced all communication with the world and its affairs, as well as everything that might engage them in it, they not only cannot be obliged to leave their monasteries for the purpose of going to assist their parents in distress, though extreme, but they cannot even willingly entertain the thought of such a thing without infringing on the promises they have made to God, and standing in opposition to what their state requires of them.

Every person must allow, my brethren, that God has established a constant and immutable order in the exercise of charity. Though He is the only object of our love, as He ought to be its end as well as He is its principle, yet it is no less true that there are more immediate, more intimate objects on which we may lawfully place our affections. By these, as by certain intermediaries, our love and desires may ascend to Him as to our ultimate end. For if we love anything other than Him, that we do not love for Him, our love would then be irregular, according to Saint Augustine. Thus it is with regard to these different objects; there is a certain invariable order established, by which they occupy different places in our hearts, and obtain a distinctive preference with respect to one another, from which the order of our duties is formed.

Hence, God holds the first place in the order of charity. The duties we owe to ourselves, of which it is unnecessary to say anything, present themselves in the second rank. After these appear our parents, brothers, sisters, relations, etc. These obligations are universal, and never suffer any mutation or destruction; neither are they inimical to one another. But though it can never happen that our love of God should destroy the love of our parents, nor should the love of our parents annul that of our brethren; nevertheless it frequently happens that the exercises of those duties are contrary and incompatible; so much so, that the assistance we desire to give to our parents is impeded by that which our brethren require; and the service binding us close to God discharges us from all exterior duties of every other nature.

It would certainly be wrong to infer from this that the natural law would be thus destroyed; and that those obligations which ought to stand invariable would be enervated. For in reality, they remain always the same; their exercise alone is suspended. The ordinary means which may be employed to accomplish them are obstructed, but the obligation remains entire. Therefore, the law of nature is not violated. And while impeded from assisting our parents by attending to the necessities of our brothers, and from giving them exterior proofs of our love, our hearts do not fail to perform, by ardent desires, what our hands are unable to effect. Now the same thing may, with every reason, be said with regard to God; so that when His appointment, interest, and service require our attendance, by which we are unable to assist our parents or friends, in that case we must, according to Saint Ambrose, prefer the duty we owe to our great parent, before the duty and tenderness we owe to our natural parents. [36]

And it is in such cases that we accomplish the precept of hating them, that is only to say, of treating them with apparent rigor, and as we would behave to such persons as we separate from, lest we should incur the dreadful sentence already pronounced by the Son of God, against all those who prefer the love and attachment to their parents, to the love and obedience they owe to Him. "He that loves father or mother more than me, is not worthy of me" (Matt 10:37).

From this malediction they preserve themselves, who, without consulting the wants or resistance of their parents, follow the voice of their Redeemer, whether He withdraws them from the embraces of their parents to place them within the pale of a religious state, as in a secure haven; or whether, being already engaged therein, they remain constant to the duties imposed on them by the will of God, without yielding to the influence of the requests or necessities of their parents, however urgent they may be; or allowing themselves to be moved by motives of a false compassion, which would induce them to leave their retreat, and administer such assistance as is no longer compatible with the state of a religious.

---

[36] "Magnum pietatis officium, sed religionis uberius." S. Ambrosius, *Opera Omnia*, PL 16:236 (1845).

This disposition, so far from doing any injury to the natural obligation of children to their parents, on the contrary, proves that they have the most lively sentiments of love and tenderness for them, by which they frequently serve them in a manner much more profitable, because they thus become more agreeable to God, and by their fidelity in immolating all the dearest inclinations of nature to His love, become more worthy to obtain for their parents goods which are real and solid, which certainly are infinitely superior to anything they could procure for them by their personal endeavors.

In fine, there is nothing more unreasonable, nor more unworthy of Christians, who ought to live by faith and in the expectation of eternal things, than to require that a soul, who after being shipwrecked on the tempestuous sea of this world, finds security in the port of religion, and having contracted an unlimited engagement by making lawful vows, which like so many anchors keep her from being again tossed about at the mercy of storms and tempests, should break through all these secure barriers, and expose herself again in the same world in which she had been so often lost. Convinced by experience that her vessel is too weak to resist a new storm, she trembles at the idea of being exposed, for she well knows that the least wind is sufficient to overcome her resistance and to plunge her into her former excesses.

This man, for example, who had the misfortune to offend his God, and who knows by his experience that nothing less than the assistance which he finds in the cloister is sufficient to preserve him pure in the divine presence, returns to the world. This man, I say, according to Saint Bernard's words, is like a bird when leaving its nest, without feathers, without strength, without defense, exposing itself naked to the air, the rigors and violence of which it is unable to resist.

Now let me ask, what proportion is there between what he is about to lose and what he intends to preserve? He exposes himself to losses eternal and unchangeable for the fleeting vanities of time. He exchanges the life of his own immortal soul for the bodily life of one of his relations, which at best he can only prolong for a few uncertain moments. This is really a strange misreckoning. The house is all on fire, the flames are gaining every part, but he who would fly from the danger is prevented by some persons who stand before him and will not allow him to come out, and they will even force him back into the fire after he had the good fortune to escape.[37]

Q. 14.— What were the sentiments of the holy fathers on this subject?

A.—Although the holy fathers have not treated of this question in a particular manner, nevertheless the maxims and instructions they have left us evidently demonstrate what they thought of the matter.

Saint Basil is the first whom we behold introduced by antiquity. That saint teaches in many places of his writings that a true monk ought to have renounced all affections to flesh and blood from the time he first entered the religious state; and that no consanguinity can oblige him to return to the world, who has once separated himself from it and consecrated himself to the service of Jesus Christ, raised up by God to be our guide in a special manner, and to give us clear and certain rules for the accomplishment of our duties.

That great doctor teaches us, with Saint Gregory of Nazianzen in his monastic institutions, that a religious cannot in any manner attend to the management of his parents affairs without doing an injury to his own conscience, and failing in what he owes to the duties of his state. Nor could he declare his sentiments on the subject in terms more clear than by telling us that truly religious persons ought to be more separated from their relations, from their friends, and from their parents, than the dead are from the living; that every one who has taken off his clothes to wrestle in the combats of virtue, who has renounced the world and all its affairs, and to speak more forcibly, who is crucified to the world, and dead to all who are in it, ought to consider himself as entirely dead to the world, and even to his father, to his mother, and to his nearest kindred and relations.

These two great doctors go yet farther; and to remove every occasion that might be taken to explain their sentiments in any manner opposite to the real sense in which they understood them, they say:

> Either the parents have renounced the world like their children, or they remain in the same state of life. If they have forsaken it, they are then in a true sense the relatives of their children, not as fathers and mothers, but only as brethren; and if they remain engaged in the world, they form a part of what we have renounced, and from which we are separated.

---

[37] Epistola CXI, Ex persona Eliae, PL 182:254c (1854). / Bernard, *Works*, 373.

"Yes," continue the same saints, "Since we have forsaken the carnal man, they are entirely foreign to us, nor should we have any more alliance with them." They add, "A monk has only two fathers, one in Heaven, who is the common father of all men, the other in the monastery, who is the spiritual father of the community."

They ground this sentiment on the words of Jesus Christ, by which he prohibited those whom he calls from the society of men to have anything more to do with the affairs of their families, or to exercise the duty of charity towards their relations, to which those who are free, are indispensably obliged; nor would He allow his disciples to withdraw from Him for a single moment, lest they should be guilty of anything that might be unworthy of the sublime and divine elevation, which ought to be the possessive quality of souls destined to fill the brilliant thrones of His glorious kingdom. "Thus it is," continue these great saints,

> That our Lord demonstrates that it is no longer lawful for those who are called to an uninterrupted study of heavenly things to have any concern for what passes here below, because they ought to have already departed from, and be far elevated above the region of this lower orb.

Finally, they object against themselves those passages of holy writ, which seem to militate against their opinion; as that of Isaiah: "Do not despise thy own flesh" (Isa 58:7) and that of Saint Paul to Timothy: "But if any man take no care of his own and chiefly of his household, he has denied the faith, and is worse than an infidel"(1 Tim 5:8); the solution of which they give by saying:

> Those words are addressed to men who live in the world, and not to such as have forsaken it; to the living, but not to the dead, for the dead are no longer obliged to anything of that nature. A man who is consecrated to the service of God, being in the same state as one dead, is discharged thereby from every obligation of contributing to the subsistence of his parents. As one poor he has nothing to give them, not even his own body, over which he no longer can claim dominion, because he has given it to God. Therefore, he cannot employ himself in the service of men, except for the advantage of those who are united to him by the same bonds.

To affirm that Saint Basil speaks not here of extreme necessity, would be certainly a mistake. We allow that he does not speak of such a case precisely, but then if he intended to except it, he would have pointed out the exception. Therefore, as he writes in general terms, it is evident that his discourse admits of no reserve. What other sense can be given to these words, "A religious ought to be more separated from his relations, from his friends, and even from his father and mother, than the dead are from the living"? No other undoubtedly but this, that as the dead no longer meddle with the affairs of the living, so ought children, when consecrated to God, be considered as deprived of all power and capacity of attending to the wants or affairs of their parents, this mystical and spiritual death having produced in them, with regard to their parents, the same effect as the natural death does in those whom it lays in the grave, with regard to the living.

Hence, unless we willingly close our eyes, it is easy to see that this saint declares positively that religious persons cannot assist their parents, or have any commerce with them even in their wants. For he tells us that they have only two fathers, God and their superior, making no account of the third, but placing him in the number of those things they have forsaken, and from which they are separated for ever. The case in which he allows us to have a father, being founded, not on the old affinity of flesh and blood, but on the new alliance of the spirit.

This is so entirely Saint Basil's opinion, that in the answer to the question, "What ought to be our disposition with regard to our relations and parents according to the flesh?" he says positively:

> The superior ought to exert all his authority to prevent those who are once engaged in the society of his brethren, from ever leaving the monastery for the purpose of assisting their parents, whatever the motives may be that might induce them to solicit such improper permissions. If the indigent parents live in piety, it is just that the community should consider them as their common parents, and as such open to them their unanimous charity; and it is the duty of the superior to undertake the execution of it. But if, on the contrary, they lead a criminal, worldly life, it ought to be remembered, that in such a case they have nothing common with such persons, and that they ought to attend to the service of God, without giving themselves any anxiety concerning their wants or distress.

Saint Jerome, influenced by the same thought, forcibly exhorts his friend Heliodonis to raise himself above all human considerations, to walk over his father and mother if they lay on the ground before him in order to obstruct his passage, and to fly to solitude, without being deterred either by the resistance of the one, or by the tears and importunities of the other; adding, that it is real piety to be cruel on such occasions.[38] Now if he spoke in this manner to a person free, what would he not have said, if he had been engaged by vow in the religious state?

Saint Arsenius, animated with the same spirit, answered a person who brought him the will of one of his relations, in the following manner, "I am really astonished how my relation could think of making me his heir, seeing that I am dead much longer than he." And one of the solitaries having asked him one day, why he so much avoided the company of men, he returned this so much admired answer:

> God knows, brother, how much I love men, but I cannot converse with God and men at the same time. All the heavenly spirits have only one and the same will, but men have many wills opposite to one another, and therefore cannot resolve to forsake God in order to entertain men. [39]

By which he gave us a twofold instruction; the one, that the charity which we are commanded by God to have for our neighbor, may exist, though we decline giving any exterior proofs thereof; the other, that it is more difficult than is frequently believed to live as faithful to God, and as conformable to the sanctity of our state, as we ought and at the same time to entertain intercourse and engagements with men.

Guided by this principle, Saint Simeon Stylites saw his mother standing at the foot of his pillar during three days, without being moved either by her tears or menaces, though she told him in a reproachful manner that this obduracy would put an end to her life, as his retreat had already terminated his father's existence. Yet notwithstanding, he would not comply with her request, and he thus let her die, overwhelmed with grief and affliction. But he offered the incense of most fervent prayers for her and while that incarnate angel refused her a momentary satisfaction, his inviolable attachment to God obtained for her eternal consolations. Eventually she died, and her body being brought to him, he then saw her dead, whom he would not see when alive. But the tears and prayers full of tenderness which he poured forth publicly for the repose of her soul, as well as every other circumstance of his conduct on that occasion, evidently show that

---

[38] S. Hieronymis, Epistola XVIII, De Laude Religionis, PL 30:374C (1865).

[39] Rufinus. *De Vitis Patrum*, Libellus Quintus, PL 73:888D (1849).

persons consecrated to God have other means of fulfilling the precept of honoring their parents, besides those which appear exteriorly.

Saint Fulgentius performed an action nothing inferior to that of this great saint. Knowing that his mother came to see him, he became insensible to the piercing cries which she sent forth at the gate of the monastery in which he lived. And though she loudly complained that being the only support of her family, his retreat exposed it to inevitable ruin, to which she added all that grief and tenderness could inspire and place in the mouth of a desolate mother, yet, resisting all her efforts, he remained constant in his resolution, and, as the author of his life says, he overcame natural affection by a holy cruelty.

Saint Theonas was inspired by God to do something still more extraordinary, which certainly ought not to be imitated as a rule of conduct. That saint left his wife against her will, and embraced the solitary state. To justify an action so very singular, Almighty God made the sequel of his life famous by many miracles.[40]

That great solitary, Theodorus, was of the same opinion, when he refused to see his mother when she came to see him in the monastery of Tabenna. When Saint Pachomius, his superior, solicited his acquiescence at the request of some bishops, Theodorus replied, "Will you assure me that I shall have nothing to answer for this visit, at the judgment seat of Christ?" adding that having—according to the precept of Jesus Christ—forsaken his mother and the whole world, he could not resolve to see her again, lest he should thereby scandalize all those with whom he had the happiness to live; that if before the new covenant the sons of Levi were obliged to renounce their parents in order to accomplish the commandments of the law, with how much more reason ought he not to prefer the love of God to that of his relations, seeing that he is now made partaker of the graces of the new covenant, according to these words of our Lord: "He who loves father or mother more than me, is not worthy of me" (Matt 10:37).

These words induced Saint Pachomius to acquiesce to his sentiments, telling him that such a refusal was the peculiar character of those who had perfectly renounced the world and themselves; and that if anyone is induced by natural affection to think that he ought to love his parents because they are his own flesh, though he has forsaken them, he should remember these words of Saint Peter: "He who is overcome, becomes the

---

[40] *Collationes*, PL 49:1180 (1846) /Cassian, *Conferences* 3.21.9-10 (NPNF2/11:506-7).

slave of him by whom he is overcome" (2 Pet 2:19); and thus, he who is overcome by the flesh, is made a slave to the flesh.

Cassian relates in his conferences, that a brother of the holy abbot Saint Apollo, once came to him at midnight, requesting him to come out of his cell for a moment, and assist him in withdrawing one of his oxen from a pit into which he had fallen. The holy abbot told him to address himself to another of their brothers who was not far from the place in which the accident had happened; but he having replied, "You send me to a man who is dead now fifteen years," the abbot answered,

> And how can you require such a thing of me, who am dead to the world these twenty years past; and being buried in my cell as in a tomb, I can no longer have any intercourse with the things which belong to this world? Can you imagine that Jesus Christ would be satisfied, if I should relax the least part of this mortification to which I have once consecrated myself, by going to assist you in drawing your oxen out of the pit; since He would not allow one moment to the man who only requested to have the permission to go and bury his father, though such a request seemed much more just and pious than yours ?[41]

From those examples it is easy for all persons to conclude what those men who were so animated with the spirit of God would have said or thought if anyone endeavored to make them forsake their monasteries for any considerable time; seeing that they were inflexible when there was question of granting a few moments, a few words, or even a few looks, for the comfort of their relations.

The same venerable abbot, as Cassian teaches in his *Institutions*, said that in his time an entire forgetfulness of parents was requisite as a principal disposition in all those who were admitted in the monasteries of Palestine. The holy abbot Paphnutius, speaking to his religious said,

> Do not suffer the remembrance of your parents, nor your former affections to occupy your thoughts lest engaging yourselves again in the cares and embarrassments of the world, you only put your hand to the plough, and looking back, may thereby become unfit for the kingdom of Christ (Luke 9:62).[42]

---

[41] Cassianus, *Collationes*, PL 49:1297 (1846) / *Conferences* 3.24.9 (NPNF2/11:535).

[42] Institutiones, PL 49:196 (1846) / *Institutes* 4.36 (NPNF2/11:231).

Saint John Climacus who had penetrated the depth of the duties of the monastic state more profoundly than any other person, thought this separation so necessary, that he inculcates nothing so forcibly. He says,

> We ought to imitate Lot, but not his wife;[43] it is better to displease our parents than to offend God.[44] The same God is also our Savior, whereas parents frequently destroy those whom they love, and consign them to eternal torments. We are not influenced to retire into solitude by any aversion for our parents or country, but to avoid the loss to which their presence and company might expose us.[45]

Our conduct in doing so is vindicated by the example of our Lord Jesus Christ, who frequently withdrew from His parent according to the flesh,[46] and who being told that His mother and brethren were seeking Him, immediately returned such an answer as evinced the innocent aversion that we ought to have for our relations (Matt 12:50). The love of God extinguishes the carnal love of parents. If anyone pretends to possess those two loves, he deceives himself, for, according to our Redeemer's words, "No man can serve two masters" (Matt 6:24). Jesus Christ came not on earth to bring peace, that is to say, the love of fathers and mothers for their children or brethren who desire to consecrate themselves to His service, but war and the sword (Matt 10:34), in order that He might separate those who love God from those who love the world, the spiritual from the carnal, the humble from the proud; for the Lord takes pleasure in this division of spirit, and in this separation of body which is effected by His love.

"Be not affected," continues the saint,

> With the tears of your parents and friends, if you desire to secure yourself from eternal weeping,[47] for as it is impossible for a man to turn one eye towards Heaven and the other towards the earth at the same time, so is it equally impossible to secure our souls from the danger of losing our eternal

---

[43] *Scala*, PG 88:666c (1864). / *Ladder*, 64.11.

[44] *Scala*, PG 88:666d(1864). / *Ladder*, 65.12.

[45] *Scala*, PG 88:667a (1864). / *Ladder*, 65.14.

[46] *Scala*, PG 88:667b(1864). / *Ladder*, 65.14.

[47] *Scala*, PG 88:667d (1864). / *Ladder*, 65.17.

salvation, if we do not separate our souls and bodies from all commerce with men.[48]

When in our solitude the devil endeavors to inflame our minds with the tender remembrance of our dear parents, brothers, and sisters, let us fly to the arms of prayer, to defend ourselves against the attack. Let us in spirit approach the eternal fire below so that the thoughts of those never-ending flames may extinguish the indiscreet ardor of that fire which he blows up in our hearts. [49]

All this clearly proves how far that great director of souls was, from being persuaded that the necessities of parents were sufficient reasons to induce a religious to forsake his monastery, since he thought that he was obliged to combat even the thought of such an affair, and to consider the very remembrance of them as one of the most dangerous temptations by which he might be attacked.

Saint Bernard everywhere teaches the same truth. He requires that those souls who have given themselves entirely to Jesus Christ by the vows of religion should constantly remain in solitude, so that they may preserve themselves in a state worthy the purity of him to whom they are consecrated. He says with Saint Jerome that those whom God calls to the cloister ought to obey His voice without being deterred by any consideration for their parents, and that to treat them severely for the love of Christ is a proof of their perfect piety.[50]

He everywhere exhorts children to leave their parents, for the purpose of embracing the monastic state, without giving the least attention to their resistance. He declares that a vocation to religion is a lawful and just reason to resist and disobey them, that the service of Christ is to be preferred to them, and that it is in such cases that we are to consider them not as our parents but as our enemies (Matt 10:36), that in the order of charity, the salvation of children ought to antecede the consolation of parents, and that if it be impious to despise a mother, yet when done for the love of Christ, it is the mark of singular piety;[51] and that He who said, "Honor thy father

---

[48] *Scala*, PG 88:670a (1860). / *Ladder*, 66.23.

[49] *Scala*, PG 88:658c (1860). / *Ladder*, 62.10.

[50] Epistola CCCXXII, Ad Hugonem, PL 182:527d (1854). / Bernard, *Works,* 2:846.

[51] Epistola CIV, Ad Gualterum, PL 182:240b (1854). / Bernard, *Works,* 1:350.

and thy mother " (Matt 15:4) said also: "He that loves father or mother more than me, is not worthy of me" (Matt 10:37).

Now if any should think that Saint Bernard speaks here only of the rich, of such as find abundance and pleasures in their parents' house, it can be answered that having spoken in opposition to the dangers of the world, he addressed his discourse to all sorts of persons in general; that abundance is not the only cause of the loss of souls; that there is danger in poverty as well as in riches, in huts as well as in palaces, on the dunghill as well as in gilded chambers; that the poor may be even more licentious than the rich; that even amongst them crimes are sometimes more frequent and more enormous, for when the rich are not withheld by piety, probity deters them; but as this latter virtue is not so much known in general amongst the poor, and as piety is less prevalent than licentiousness, vice frequently prevails amongst them in all its malignity.

Saint Thomas speaks decisively on this subject. Treating the question, whether the indigence of parents ought to be considered as a sufficient impediment to prevent young persons from embracing the religious state, he maintains the affirmative; and having objected to himself, that as the wants of parents cannot oblige a religious to leave his cloister after his profession, so they ought not be considered as a lawful impediment to his engaging in it. He answers that the case in both is not the same; for the one being free, are consequently obliged to assist their parents; and the other being dead to the world, and as it were buried with Christ in the cloister, it cannot be reasonably expected that they should re-engage in the cares and solicitudes of life.[52] In fine, he could not speak more positively than by affirming that religious persons are not less dispensed from every duty to their parent by the spiritual death than by the natural. [53]

Behold what the saints thought concerning the obligation by which religious persons are bound to renounce their relations. Few opinions can be found in the Church, I mean opinions of the saints, so well supported and so universally approved. Indeed examples on the subject might be adduced almost without number. But we ought not to be astonished, for they were the true disciples of a master who taught nothing more generally than the science of renunciation. As they constantly applied themselves

---

[52] S. Thomas Aquinas, Summa Theologiae 2a2ae, 101,4.

[53] S. Thomas Aquinas, Quodlibet III, Art. XVI in *Sancti Thomae Aquinatus Questionae Disputatae, Opera Omnia,* Stanislaus Frette, ed., Vol 15 (Paris, Vives, 1885), 414.

to the study of perfectly understanding His maxims, so they made all their glory consist in embracing and following them without consulting either the inclinations of nature or the lights of reason. Their unlimited disengagement from all created things gave them an unimpeded facility in that divine study. Dead to themselves and to all creatures, nature formed no affections in them opposite to those truths, dispositions which cannot exist in those who do not imitate their mortification nor virtues.

Almighty God delivers His sacred oracles and speaks equally to all men; but His voice is not equally heard by all, because the hearts of all are not equally prepared. Divine truths may be compared to scented liquors which always lose something of their strength and sweetness when they are put into unclean vessels. So the truths of life always lose something of their invigorating purity, when they are received in hearts which are not perfectly pure.

Q. 15.—From what sources did the saints derive those maxims?

A. The saints taught us those truths, not as having been derived from their own ideas, but as having come to them from truth itself. Indeed it can be safely asserted that they are deposited in so many parts of the sacred writings, that nothing can be more easily discovered, if a long habit of attending to contrary opinions did not form a prejudice in favor of the latter. As the end which our Lord proposed to Himself in becoming man was the sanctification of the world, so did He take particular care to inculcate those sanctifying truths, by which alone the world was raised to a perfection known only by very few persons, before the great master of perfection taught it by the efficacious means of renunciation and separation. According to this principle He tells us in Saint Matthew, that He came not to bring peace on earth, but the sword (Matt 10:34); that He came to separate the daughter from the mother, the son from his father; that he who loves his father or mother more than Him is not worthy of Him(Matt10:37); and again, 'Who is my mother and my brethren?" He asked, and extending His hand towards His disciples, "Behold my mother and my brethren for whoever doth the will of my Father who is in Heaven, he is my brother, my sister, and my mother"(Matt 12:48-50). And in the same gospel He expressly says, "Whosoever shall leave his house or brethren, or sisters, or father, or mother, or wife, or children, or lands, for my sake, shall receive an hundredfold, and he shall hereafter possess eternal life" (Matt 19:29).

Again, when a certain young man presented himself to become his disciple, but first requested leave to bury his father, our Lord said to him: "Follow me, and let the dead bury their dead" (Matt 8:22). To another who said: "Lord I will follow thee, but allow me first to take leave of those who are at home"; He replied, "He who puts his hand to the plough, and looks back, is not fit for the kingdom of God"(Luke 9:62). And in another place He declares, "If anyone comes to me, and hates not his father, mother, wife, children, brothers, sisters, and even his own life, he cannot be my disciple" (Luke 14:25).

That Christians ought to be always ready to leave all things, and to divest themselves of every obligation for the love of Christ is at once both the most natural and the most holy sense that can be given to those words. Yes, my brethren, we ought to conclude from them that the interest of our great master ought to occupy the first place in our hearts; that the most indispensable duties are to be considered as ceasing to bind when there is question of going where His voice calls and of persevering where His divine will determines; that even the duty and exercises of piety which bind us to those by whom we have received existence are to be forsaken when they oppose those we owe to God.

Moreover, this is to be understood not only of those things by which our relatives would induce us to violate His holy law, or engage us in the execution of anything injurious to our eternal welfare; but also when they would deter us from entering or persevering in that state of perfection to which we are raised by His sacred providence and commands. That is to say we are not only obliged to prefer the love of Jesus to everything evil and prohibited, but also to such as are lawful, and even to such as are good, and commanded at another time, when He requires something more perfect at our hands, and which consequently is to be preferred.

This being supposed, it must be allowed that these instructions are directed in a very particular manner to those persons who renounced the world, and have consecrated themselves to God by the solemn vows of religion; and who, by a special disposition of His grace have so chosen Him for their inheritance that their only employment on earth consists in making a continual progress in perfection, meditating on His holy law day and night, and in seeking the accomplishment of His adorable will.

Since this is the case, should the world endeavor to recover the right it formerly had to their services; should parents claim that their children are obliged to help and assist them after their profession in the same manner as before it, and require any services incompatible with the purity and sanctity of their state, whatever motives might seem to sanction such demands, or oblige such children to leave their solitude and engage them in the cares of the world, I maintain that they ought to remember the danger of incurring an eternal exclusion from the kingdom of Christ to which they expose themselves, if they prefer the love of their parents in any case to His love. For the first condition He requires on the part of all who desire to follow Him is an entire separation from all those persons to whom they are most strictly united by the ties of nature and blood.

Here it would be to no purpose if anyone would reply, that the religious engagement cannot be lawfully formed at the expense of that in which young persons are placed by nature, which obliges them to assist their parents, because, as we have already shown, there is a primary and superior obligation by which all others are formed and regulated. This link is no other than that which binds us to God, who is the chief and efficient cause of our existence. As our Creator He possesses a sovereign and unlimited dominion over His creatures. It places them in His hand, and gives Him an indisputable right to dispose of them as He pleases—in the order of grace as well as in that of nature—according to the views of His wisdom and providence.

This is an inalienable right, inseparable from His omnipotence, subsisting in Him from all eternity, and from which He himself cannot derogate. And as He could if He pleased, unhinge the frame of the universe, if I may use the expression, stop the sun in the midst of his course for whole ages with the same facility as He did at a former period for a few moments; and, that I may say something more analogous to our subject, as by His command the Levites innocently stained their hands with their parents' blood, so might He call the whole race of mankind before His throne to pay Him their homages and services, if the glory of His name required it; making all services cease, and suspending or abrogating all the obligations and customs they may have with one another. The parents would be obliged to give up their children, husbands their wives, masters their servants, princes their subjects, without having any lawful cause to complain of His justice.

All this evidently proves, that those persons who will not allow Him a sacrifice much less important, and who refuse Him the power of suspending the rules and changing the exercise of piety on the part of children to their

parents, in the manner we have already explained, are entire strangers to the just ideas that the knowledge of the supreme dominion of God inspires.

Moreover, it is certain that a religious engages in inevitable ruin when he undertakes a life opposite to that in which God requires he should sanctify himself. Now it is beyond a doubt that the design of God was to remove him from the dangers of the world so that He might sanctify him in retirement, when He had prepared all necessary assistance, by the good use of which he might labor more successfully in that great affair.

These dangers which form so great an impediment in a worldly life are commerce with the world, attachment to parents, application to family affairs, solicitude for the necessaries of life, dissipation of mind, which is their inseparable consequence; in fine, so many occasions of losing God by sin, which are found almost at every step and at every movement in the society and conversation of men. The means, on the contrary, laid up and prepared in the cloister by the divine goodness are regular discipline, vigilance of superiors, good example, the prayers of pious associates, subjection of the will, variety of exercises, the austerities of fasting, humiliating practices, and inviolable silence.

Now when a religious forsakes his cloister for the purpose of assisting his parents, by the same act he not only leaves his house, but his state also, and suddenly finds himself in the midst of all those obstacles and impediments, both destitute of all those important advantages and surrounded by all the enemies from whom the power of God had before delivered him. In such a position am I not justified in forming this conclusion, that as his state is more dangerous than that in which he finds his parents, so it will produce in his soul more dangerous effects. Ah! yes, he becomes a prey to wearisomeness and anxiety, a stranger to the sacred repose of the religious life, which contains the unexhausted treasure of its members.

His soul, weighed down by continual solicitude and application for the present wants of his parents, and with future apprehensions, is no longer free to soar to the contemplation of heavenly things. He loses the enjoyment of that holy peace in which his subdued passions were buried, and but which now unrestrained arise with more furious impetuosity than ever. In fine, he lives, or rather miserably languishes, in a strange land, exposed to all the various temptations which are inseparable from extreme want, and from the indiscriminate and unavoidable conversation of every sex.

Such a state being entirely opposite to that in which the hand of God had placed this religious soul, as it destroys all the means and advantages he enjoyed in His service, so it must terminate in producing an equally contrary end; the one being the way of life, the other, must of course be that of death. Hence it is, that there is no case in which the word of God more earnestly recommends the forsaking our parents than this, because the services we do them produce such great disorders, and evidently show that it is impossible to assist them, and to be attached to their persons, without losing ourselves and being eternally separated from Jesus Christ.

Hence we ought to conclude, my brethren, that a religious being emancipated by God from those exterior duties of charity and justice with regard to the world; delivered from the engagements which bind men to one another; filling the place which the martyrs formerly held in the Church, as I have said before, as well with respect to their courage as to their sanctity; and being obliged by his state to retrace in himself the perfect renunciation of the ancient monks and solitaries; we must, I say, conclude that such a man cannot leave his cloister, nor return to the world to re-engage himself in its employments and cares for the purpose of assisting his parents, however extreme their wants may be.

Moreover, if he ultimately decides and leaves it on that pretext, he leaves at the same time the way appointed for him by God, and destroys the designs He had on his person. He opposes his own will to the unerring appointment of Heaven, and withdraws himself from the society of those who are appointed to adore the Lord in spirit and in truth. He wounds his profession in its most tender part; exposes the purity of his body as well as that of his soul; prefers a common life to one both heavenly and divine; he descends from the mysterious house-top of the gospel to dwell amidst the filth and vermin of the earth; he looks behind, after having put his hand to the plough. He prefers the alliance of the flesh to that of grace, instead of saying with Saint Bernard: "Why do you disturb me in the state, wherein being engaged, I endeavor to please the great Father of all things? Why do you endeavor to withdraw me from the service of him whose true servants are so many kings?"[54]

From hence it follows that religious persons are precisely in the case in which they are commanded to renounce their fathers, mothers, and in general all other things, for the love of Christ; and that in leaving their monasteries, they not only contemn all the advantages we have adduced,

---

[54] Epistola CXI, PL 182:254a. / Bernard, *Works*, 372.

but moreover perform an action condemned by the sacred words of Jesus Christ Himself.

Finally, all the proofs I have cited, clearly demonstrate, that we have advanced nothing but truth and justice, when we have said, that the opinion of those who maintain and justify such religious persons as leave their monasteries, for the purpose of assisting their parents in their temporal wants, is quite unfounded; that it has no degree of truth; that it is condemned by reason, enlightened and regulated by faith, as well as by the maxims of the saints; and that it is derogatory to the majesty of God, and contrary to the sacred words of Jesus Christ.

Q. 16.— What answer can be made to several passages of the holy scripture which appear contrary to your reasons?

A.—It is true, my brethren, that we read in the prophet Isaiah: "Do not despise thine own relations" (Isa 58:7); in Saint Paul to Timothy: "If any man have not care of his own, and chiefly those of his household, he has denied the faith, and is worse than an infidel" (1 Tim 5:8); our Lord also, speaking to the Pharisees, says: "Why do you transgress the law of God for your traditions?" (Matt 15:3) But Saint Basil answers the two first passages by saying, that those words are addressed to persons who live in the world, and not to those who have renounced it; and to answer more explicitly, says the saint; those words the apostle addresses to the living, but not to the dead, because the dead are certainly not obliged to anything of that nature. You are crucified and dead to the world; in renouncing it and its perishable riches, you have embraced a life of entire poverty. Consecrated to God, you are become His riches and treasure. As persons dead, you are emancipated from the law which obliged you to contribute to the subsistence of your relatives.

To this we may add, according to the opinion of the same saint, as we have already remarked, that though a religious be no longer able to assist his parents, either personally or with his goods, yet he can do it by the care of his superior, and by the property of the house; and hence he is secured from being of the number of those whom the scripture reprehends.

As to the third passage, "Why do you transgress the law of God for your traditions?" we can affirm, without fear of being rash, that to infer from this that a religious is obliged to leave his cloister for the purpose of assisting his parents, would be doing violence to our Lord's intention. The discrepancy that exists between the facts against which our Lord declaims, and those of which we are treating here, is so great that whoever attentively considers them will easily perceive that no parallel can be formed between things so distinctly dissimilar. For if the dispositions of the persons, the quality of the things offered, or the consecration in itself, be well considered, as well as the effects and inconveniences which might result from them, were they employed in any other manner than that to which they were destined, it will evidently appear that there is no comparison to be found, from which any consequence can be deduced against our position.

First, Jesus Christ condemns the inhumanity of the Pharisees towards their parents; their avarice, hypocrisy, and dissimulation. For, as Saint John Chrysostom says, it was not true that they would have consecrated their property to God as they pretended. Now nothing of all this can be found in truly religious persons. On the contrary, their piety is sincere, their disengagement is complete, their sacrifice is real, their love for their parents is tender, though tempered by the duties of their state; and if they refuse to assist them in their wants, the motives by which they are deterred are no other than deference to the orders of God, and a fear of displeasing Him.

Secondly, the gifts which the Pharisees refused to their parents were only a few animals, which were said to have been previously destined to the service of God; but here they are souls redeemed by the blood of Jesus Christ, who are to be made one day partakers of the divinity.

Thirdly, the pretended offering of the Pharisees was only an external sanctification, whereas that which is done by a religious profession is interior and divine, by which souls are made the spouses of Jesus Christ. His Holy Spirit is, as it were, the link and sacred bond of the spiritual union then effected; and though by virtue of this consecration He is not precisely given, because the sacraments alone have that peculiar efficacy, nevertheless He is inseparable from the piety which ought to accompany it. This the holy fathers affirm when they speak of a religious profession, so we find that they all agree in declaring that those who perform it with the necessary dispositions receive the divine spirit with such plenitude, that the religious profession is in some sort equal to a new baptism, and it is also a true martyrdom.

Fourthly, the effect of one of the oblations here spoken of, is only to separate the thing offered from the common and ordinary use, and destine it to be consumed by fire or by the priests. That of the other is to separate the creature from all transitory things, to extinguish in his heart all love of what is not eternal, and to unite him in a perfect manner to Jesus Christ, that by thus filling the great void He there finds, by His ineffable and reciprocal communication, He constantly dwells in the soul, and the soul in Him; and by anticipation becomes the object of its beatified fruition here in time, and the beginning of that immortal state signified by those words of the prophet: "They shall exult for all eternity, and thou shalt dwell in them"(Ps 5:12). This shall only be finally accomplished when our Lord having subjected all creatures to Himself, and being all in all, as the apostle says, "He shall repose in them for ever, replenishing them by His presence with glory and consolation"(1 Cor 15:28).

As to inconveniences, it cannot be said that any such would arise, except that ox or lamb might have been applied to some other use besides that to which they were destined. But the same notion cannot be entertained of a religious, who being engaged in the service of God by vow, should return to the world, and become once more a slave to its cares and dissipations. For, as I have already endeavored to demonstrate, besides the infidelity of which he would thereby become guilty, he would expose himself to a thousand accidents, the least of which would be sufficient to deprive him forever of the fruit of his retirement.

Every person who reflects in a proper and judicious manner on all we have said will understand without difficulty that the above passage of the sacred writings does not really apply to our subject; neither is it reasonable nor just to conclude from the reproach made by our Lord to the Pharisees, who according to the hardness of their hearts and their attachment to the things of the world—contrary to the divine precept, and under the appearance of false piety and an imaginary offering—refused their parents that assistance which they had a right to claim. It is, I say, unreasonable and unjust to conclude from such a fact that a religious who has renounced the world, and is now consecrated to God by an engagement so real, so holy, and so lawful as is that which is effected by solemn vows, is still obliged to return to the world for the purpose of assisting his parents in their extreme want.

Q. 17.—May it not be objected that a religious can not contract a new obligation with God, contrary to that which already binds him to honor and assist his parents?

A. This objection, my brethren, contains nothing solid; and though it has been already sufficiently refuted, nevertheless, I think it yet necessary to remark that we belong to God by a dependence incomparably more intimate and binding than that by which we are united to our parents.

We are His property on so many titles both of nature and of grace, that it may be said with truth, that man is a composition of relations and connections with His mercy and omnipotence. He alone deserves the title of true Father, because He gives life both to our bodies and souls. He preserves them by the continual influence of His power and uninterrupted vigilance; and is, as Saint Paul teaches, the source of all paternity in Heaven and on earth (Eph 3:15).

For this reason we owe Him the tribute of our goods, time, labor, industry, liberty, health, life; in a word, of our whole persons, and of everything belonging to our bodies and souls, senses and reason; so that, to speak in a proper manner, when we consecrate ourselves to Him by religious vows, we contract no new obligation with Him; we do no more than offer Him what already belongs to Him, the use of which He only allowed us, but by our vocation recalls the loan; that is to say, by the motion of His spirit manifesting that His sacred will requires on our part a renunciation of all cares and solicitudes for creatures, so that we may give ourselves entirely to Him. Thus He retakes only the time, assiduity, and all the assistance that we should have employed in favor of our parents, which we undoubtedly owe to Him preferably to them.

But let it be remarked, that he does not annul the obligation of honoring them, He only regulates the manner of fulfilling that duty, forbidding us to give them some certain testimonies thereof, because they are incompatible with the services to which He requires our constant application. Thus, instead of abrogating that divine and natural law, He only changes its use and functions.

In a word, this duty subsists in the hearts of children, after profession as well as before. They love and honor their parents now as well as they did at any other time, since they love them according to the order and disposition of God; and if they refuse them more sensible proofs of their affection, the reason of such conduct is that the will of God prohibits it, according to this expression of Saint Augustine. [55]

We ought to love our parents, but we are obliged to prefer the love we owe to God to that which may be due to them. A pastor who is charged with the care of souls, cannot leave those who are under his direction for the purpose of assisting his parents, though indigent, because the duty which binds him to the care of his flock is the first in the order of charity.

---

[55] Amandus genitor, sed praeponendus Creator.

Yet by his attendance to this duty he does not injure that of filial affection. Likewise a religious may remain in his cloister without giving any just reason to censure his conduct, or doing the least thing thereby that can deserve the title of a violation of any law or obligation natural or divine.

In fine, He who dispensed Abraham from the care he ought to have taken for the preservation of his son; who even commanded him to deprive his only child of life by immolating him in sacrifice; and who of a heinous crime could make an act of heroic virtue; may also call children to a state in which they shall be dispensed from the duty of assisting their parents. And as the father, by the same divine command, might raise the sword over his son's head without offending against natural tenderness; so the son may, without offending against the same law, oppose his father, when the divine will requires it.

God will never destroy the sentiments of nature, either in the parents or in the children, of which He is Himself the author. He will never inspire them with hatred and aversion for one another, because such dispositions would ruin the essential duties of which His justice and truth are the principles and foundations. But He may command actions which nature forbids; prohibit others which nature requires; suspend its motions; and arrest its inclinations without causing any irregularity in the order and disposition of things which He has formed. God enjoys an absolute dominion over all His creatures; His wisdom and will determine the use to which He applies them; nor is it the business of man to set bounds to His almighty power.

Q. 18.—Does it not seem reasonable that the obligation of religious vows ought to yield to that of assisting our parents, since a vow is a free act, whereas the other is a necessary duty, and necessary things are to be preferred to such as are not so?

A. To this it is easy to reply, that the man of whom we read in St. Matthew was really obliged to bury his father; and that he was free to follow Jesus Christ or not, before the choice he should have made was determined by an express commandment. But as soon as our divine Lord had declared His will, that which was before indifferent, became a necessary duty. He required his attendance on His sacred person, and he was bound to obey. His obligation was then changed. To forsake his father's body for the sake of following Christ was a much more important duty than to neglect the divine call for the purpose of attending to its burial. That which otherwise would have been an impiety deserving of punishment became an act of piety worthy of recompense.

Abraham was at liberty to forsake his country, relations, and the house of his father, before the will of God was manifested to him, but from the moment that it was signified to him by these words, "Go forth of thy land, and leave thy kindred and thy father's house"(Gen 12:1), he was no longer free, but received a commandment which to disobey would have been a crime.

The same thing must be understood of those who are called by God from the corruption of the world. They are free before the Lord speaks to their hearts, but as soon as they hear His voice, they are bound to obey the call, and to consider that which before was to them indifferent, as now changed into a necessary state.

And to speak more clearly on the subject, the religious state is only proposed to all men in general as a counsel, but this counsel becomes a precept for every individual who is called to that state, and such persons are consequently obliged to embrace it. Therefore we ought to decide with much more reason, that those who are not only called to the religious state, but have moreover accepted the vocation, and ratified it by a solemn vow, that such persons are no longer free, and that they cannot fail in the accomplishment of what they have promised, without being guilty of a criminal prevarication. "That which before was an object of free choice," says Saint Bernard, "changes its nature, and becomes a case of necessity, as soon as we bind ourselves to keep it; and therefore we ought to consider ourselves henceforth, as being necessarily obliged to remain in the state which we have freely chosen."[56]

Q. 19.—As the religious state, according to the opinion of some, essentially consists only in the vows of poverty, chastity, and obedience, which may be equally observed in all places, does it not seem that nothing can oblige the members of that state to remain so constantly in their monasteries, since they can preserve the principle and essence of what they have promised in any place out of them ?

A.—The first thing that can be answered to this, my brethren, is, that those three vows are not so easily kept as some may imagine. Moreover, according to the opinion of the saints, religious persons never leave their

---

[56] *De praecepto*, PL 182:862 (1854) / *Treatises I*, 106.

monasteries, chiefly when they are induced by such things as are not connected with their state without being exposed to extreme dangers by reason of their commerce with the world, and the different forms they are obliged to assume amongst men, and by being entirely deprived of the means of defense they found in their retirement. It is beyond doubt that the greater number of those who live in sanctity while enclosed within the walls of their state, would find it impossible to observe their vows if they were separated from the discipline and regular exercises of the cloister.

The second and principal is that the religious state does not consist in the practice of the three vows of poverty, chastity, and obedience understood in a common literal way, but only when taken in all their integrity, extent, and perfection, as we have explained in a former place. [57] In this sense they suppose an attention to God so continual, a purity of heart so consummate, and a disengagement from all earthly things so entire and perfect, that it is impossible they should be able to exist in the midst of the affairs, customs, condescensions, and duties of a worldly life.

If any should tell you that religious persons are seen in the world on business relative to their communities, that they are even sometimes sent to places of considerable distance, and for a long time, it is easy to answer with Saint Basil,[58]

> In such cases they leave their retirement for the purpose of attending to the wants and necessities of their brethren, so they appear in the world as members and as a part of the body to which they belong, exercising such functions as are proper to their state. Thus they remain in their state, and receive of the divine goodness the same protection as he usually communicates to those who remain in the way in which he has placed them.

But the same saint continues and says:

> If a religious who is thus deputed for the affairs of his house, find himself too weak to resist the temptations which are too frequent, and too violent in exterior occupations, the superior ought to remove him from such avocations; and that there is no necessity which we are not bound to endure, though it should even terminate in death, rather than expose the salvation of any member of the community.[59]

---

[57] See Vol. I.

[58] Reg. fus.

[59] S. Basilius, Interrogatio XLIV, Quibus permittendae, *Fusius,* PG 31:1030 (1857).

That great doctor, who considered things with the eyes of faith, and saw them such as they really are, took particular care not to be deceived like so many others, who view them through perspectives which are not so just and true. He knows that temporal life deserves no attention, that the first thing he who engages in the religious state ought to do, is to expel the desire of preserving as well as the fear of losing it, preferring that of eternity, as the only object deserving all the affections of his heart, and all the attention of his mind.

Q. 20.—Is it not a divine precept to love and honor our parents, and is not the obligation it imposes consequently indispensable?

A.—Although we have already answered this objection, we shall here repeat, in a few words, that if there be a divine precept commanding us to love them, there is also one commanding us to hate them, and the latter deserves no less attention than the former. The same God who said, "Honor thy father and thy mother" (Matt 15:4), says again, "If any man comes to me, and hates not his father and mother, wife and children, brothers and sisters, and his own life also, he cannot be my disciple " (Luke 14:26). Saint Augustine says that Christians are commanded to hate their riches, their parents, and even their own lives, for the love of Christ.[60] This seems a contradiction; yet, it is easy to reconcile these two wills of God, which indeed are not contradictory, by distinguishing that which is immutable in the precept from what is not. It is clear that the precept of loving, honoring, and assisting our parents, always remains the same as to its essence and principle; nor will God ever destroy these natural affections in children towards their parents. But He may change the exercise of these affections and obligations. The various circumstances and occasions which occur by His divine appointments, and on which they depend, may require that He should suspend them for some time, or even make them stand unmoved for ever, if He sees it necessary for the interests of His glory.

Although the precepts of eternal truth are always in perfect harmony, and the love we owe to God is never hostile to that we owe to our parents, yet it sometimes happens that the exercise of these duties is incompatible, for the love of God may require and oblige children to perform actions contrary to those which the love of their parents demands of them. The

---

[60] S. Augustinus, Epistola CLVII, "Augustinus Hilario, Respondens ad illius quaestiones," *Epistolarum,* Classis III, PL 33:690-691(1845).

preference given in such cases to the will of God does not injure in the least the divine law by which we are bound to love our parents. I have said that they *seem* to oppose one another, because in effect they do not, since there can be no true charity where all things are not subject to the will of God, and obedient to His commands.

Thus we are taught to hate our parents, according to the language of the scriptures, when we forsake them for the love of Christ, or when, by the circumstances in which we are placed by our fidelity to His service, we are obliged to refuse them the assistance which the laws of nature and our own inclinations require. And though this exterior rigor is full of real charity, yet it is considered as a species of hatred, because it seems vested with the qualities of that vice.

Virtues cannot destroy one another; mercy and truth, according to the prophet, are always friends and inseparable companions; justice and peace embrace each other (Ps 84:11). Nevertheless, they oblige us to some actions, and to adopt modes of conduct which are in appearance opposite to one another. Moses lost nothing of his meekness even when he commanded so many men to be put to death with the sword. The Levites who executed his orders—or rather those of God, delivered by the holy legislator's mouth—dipped their hands in their parents blood without violating that eternal law which commands them to be honored and loved. And it can be said that they had these dispositions in their hearts at that time, but they were not allowed to evince them by their actions. The Lord himself was careful to justify their conduct, by giving the following testimony in their favor: "He who said to his father and to his mother, I know you not; and to his brothers, I am unacquainted with you; and who treated their children as strangers; these have kept thy word, O Lord! and preserved thy covenant" (Deut 33:9).

With much more reason ought children to remain in their cloisters, when they are called on for that purpose by the order of God, and fidelity to their promises; and refuse their parents the satisfaction of their persons and presence, even in their extreme wants, without fear of violating the integrity of the precept by such conduct. And more particularly since their monastery is, as we have already said, obliged to exercise these services in favor of indigent parents and to effect what the children can no longer perform.

Q. 21.—*Ought we not submit to the great number of doctors and casuists who maintain the contrary opinion?*

A.—The authority of those modern doctors cannot seem to be of more weight than that of Saint Basil, Saint Gregory Nazianzen, Saint Jerome, Saint John Climacus, Saint Bernard, and of so many other saints whose testimony we have adduced. They had received of God the spirit, character, and mission. The burning coal of the prophet had purified their lips as well as their hearts, and we may boldly consider them as the guides, masters and doctors of the world. But nothing of all this can be found in those new teachers, the greater part of whom having no vocation to treat of holy things have spoken on such matters in a mere human manner, giving us their own thoughts for evident truths. They have taken as much care to fortify the inclinations of nature, as the saints did to destroy them.

We should never finish, did we attempt adducing all the reasons which militate against the opinion of those who would open the gates of the cloister to religious souls whom the hand of Divine Providence enclosed in solitude for the whole term of their mortal life; and who endeavor to withdraw them from His power, or rather by violence to tear those chosen souls from His embraces, contrary to His will and commandments, and to replunge them in the impure feculence of a worldly life from which He had delivered them, so that they might offer a continual tribute of homage and service worthy of Him.

But though these reasons were not so numerous and considerable as they are in effect, the disadvantages arising from the opinion of which I speak, would be alone sufficient to prove, or at least to establish a well-founded doubt, that truth can hardly he contained in a source from which so many dangerous consequences flow.

First, it fills the cloister with confusion and disorder. It quite destroys the end of the religious life by depriving it of its principal support, peace, and repose. It changes the port and asylum into a tempestuous ocean, by subjecting those souls who have taken refuge therein to the necessity of leaving it, and exposing themselves again on the dangerous sea of the world from which they sought to secure themselves by flight. In a word, it murders those souls who are too weak to breathe the air of the world without being infected with its contagion, and who can only find their spiritual life and preservation in silence and retirement.

Secondly, the religious who returns to the world, not only exposes his own salvation, but also that of his brethren. For can anything be more natural, or happen more easily, than to behold this religious return to his monastery replenished with the evil maxims of the world, which he had quite forgotten, or perhaps had never known, and who, having forsaken the ways of a regular life, retains neither the spirit nor the regularity of the religious state. And now he exhibits nothing to his brethren but the empoisoned example of all the disorders he has contracted. Thus he may soon change an entire holy and well-regulated community into a house of scandal and confusion.

Thirdly, if the extreme indigence of a parent be sufficient to force a religious to go out of his monastery, he shall find many other reasons which require the same compliance. For why should not his extreme old age, the death of his wife and children, an important lawsuit, on the success of which his liberty or fortune may depend; why should not all this, I say, be of equal consideration, and oblige a religious to leave his monastery and go to the assistance of his parents? What reasons can be alleged to prove that the precept obliges him only in the case of extreme indigence, and that there is nothing to be done in cases less urgent? Who ever decided, that this commandment, which is so very extensive, ought to be confined to that of necessity alone, and that the words addressed by the Son of God to the Pharisees, supposing they refer to persons consecrated to God by vow, oblige them only when there is question of their parents lives? Who ever informed us that these words: Honor thy father and mother (Matt 15:4), supposes that a religious is free, provided he assists his parents in the above extremity, and not when by his care he may procure them some considerable goods, or preserve them from some great evils?

Fourthly, if religious persons are obliged to leave their monasteries, because there is a precept that commands us to honor our parents, ought they not to do the same for another, that commands us to love our neighbor as ourselves? And though the latter, in the order of charity be inferior to the former, who ever proved that this difference obliges them to behave with such disparity towards their parents and the rest of men; and that being indispensably obliged to assist the one, they may exclude the others from all help and assistance?

For if this duty of religious persons with regard to their parents alone be founded on the divine precept, the same reason stands good for their neighbor, and consequently ought to produce the same obligations. If it be established on the principle that we have received our lives and being from our parents, some amongst our neighbors may be found who have preserved the same lives and existence, with such particular circumstances of good will, knowledge, affection, and even dangers to which they have

exposed themselves for our sakes, as never animated our parents when we received the benefit of life by them.

Thus the different necessities of friends as well as of parents, serving as lawful motives for religious persons to leave their monasteries, the different classes of society shall soon be filled with erring members of both sexes, and the cloister will exhibit nothing but a scene of trouble and commotion. In fine, this opinion, by impeding all the fruit and effect of the retired life, is manifestly contrary to the designs of Jesus Christ, and by evident consequences destroys one of the most powerful means He has established in His Church for the sanctification of His elect, ever since He has been pleased to remove from it the sword of persecution, and the glory of martyrdom.

Whatever may be the motives which animate those who maintain this opinion, they, nevertheless, offend the Divine Majesty by withdrawing man from His service and by engaging him in that of creatures. These they place in his heart and give them a dwelling to which they have no right. They deprive God of a privilege belonging to His omnipotence, by which He can dispose of all things in an independent manner, and employ them in every service. They destroy piety under the pretext of preserving it; they establish a false worship in place of the true, and support their undertaking by the authority of the scriptures—an illusion common to those who endeavor to set off their own opinions under the appearance of real truths.

Hence proceed an almost infinite number of difficulties and dangerous accidents, the least of which are sufficient to convince a well thinking mind and to induce it to follow the sentiments of the saints in this important matter; and to conclude with them that a religious has nothing more to do with the world, that by his profession he is as much separated from it as he would be by a natural death; and to ask those who would force him into its anxieties and cares: "Why do you seek the living among the dead?" (Luke 24:5); that it is an illusion to expect vital actions of those who have lost the principle of life. In fine, every true religious ought to cry out with the apostle, Let no one disturb the repose of my solitude. The world has no longer the same claims on my person as it formerly had: "I am dead and I bear in my body the marks of my crucified Jesus" (Gal 6:17).

Although these truths are certain and possess every quality required to persuade, whether we consult reason, the sacred writings, or tradition, yet I fear they will not have sufficient force to penetrate the hearts of many who may read them. Parents will not, without much difficulty, renounce a privilege, which is, as it were, the only mark they possess of the authority they claim still to have over their children, even when they are consecrated to God. Nor will children consider a separation so rigorous less painful.

Worldly people will never admit a system so opposite to flesh and blood. Even amongst those who are distinguished for learning, piety, and discernment, very few will be found so entirely divested of those carnal sentiments as is necessary to relish maxims so disengaged and pure. Whatever some may think, the world is an inferior region, which is never without vapors, the air can never be found there entirely pure, nor is the firmament ever so clear and serene, as to present an aspect without clouds or shades.

As to the religious of our times, they for the most part contend with these truths, perhaps more obstinately than any other class of persons. For as nothing more clearly unfolds the sanctity and sublimity of their state, nor more widely discloses its depth and extent, so nothing can pronounce against them a more severe condemnation by making them evidently perceive the extreme disproportion that exists between their obligations and their works.

For if God withdrew them from all the cares of the world, it was for no other end but that they might be entirely employed in what concerns Him. He imposes duties on them in proportion as he dispenses them with regard to men. And it may be said with truth that the most holy employments are prohibited them, because they are connected with the world which they have forsaken. Those actions which sanctify people in society are so many iniquitous deeds to them. Their amusements, unprofitable conversations, agreeable visits, affairs and commerce with the world must be considered in their persons as so many criminal deportments and unjust profanations.

Therefore, we ought not to think it strange that this renunciation of children with regard to their parents is considered as an excess in Christian morality. When so many persons are induced to combat it by interest and various considerations, the multitude starts up and condemns those who defend it as persons who have imbibed inhuman principles. But in matters of evangelical maxims, the voice of the people is not that of God. The greatest truths are those which find less credibility and approbation amongst men; one of the most favorable testimonies they can have is that they are either little known or much opposed. Notwithstanding the clamors of sensual men—assisted by their flattering teachers—they still preserve their authority in the Church.

This renunciation has been at all times profoundly engraven in the hearts of all holy religious, and as they immolated themselves to God like so many whole burnt offerings, the fire of their charity leaving nothing in the victim unconsumed, so those souls purified from all natural affections, having once tasted the happiness of having a Father in Heaven, found no difficulty in forgetting that they had one on earth.

Those who give themselves entirely to God with the dispositions which a religious consecration requires shall find by experience the truth of what I advance. They shall discover so much advantage, and enjoy such consolation in this new alliance, that they will lose for ever all remembrance and sentiment of everything that might engage them again in the interests of men. As God will be the only object of their desires and thoughts, as He will fill the wide capacity of their hearts and minds, they shall behold and love in Him—by an anticipated beatitude—all those whom by His holy law He will not allow them to behold in the tumult of the world nor to procure their friends the perishable advantages it affords. Rather, they will employ themselves without intermission in obtaining for them of the divine goodness, true riches and eternal blessings. Hence, if the parents are real Christians, they will esteem it an invaluable happiness to have children, who are their protectors in the courts of the Lord, and will prefer the assistance they shall draw down on them from the throne of mercy to any advantages they might receive of them here on earth.

If it is objected that the Council of Gangres pronounced anathema against those who maintained that children might leave the world and forsake their parents, whatever might be their wants and necessities, it is no way difficult to reply that there is a great difference between the fact condemned by that assembly, and that of which we here speak. The council reprobated a heretic, who amongst many pernicious errors which he had disseminated in the Church, taught that persons who were free, under the appearance of a simulated piety might forsake their parents and leave them destitute of all assistance, whatever might be their distressed state or condition.

But we are far from insinuating anything of that nature. We speak only of those who—according to the disposition and will of God—have already contracted a holy and lawful engagement by the duties of which they are hindered from returning to the world. Besides we are persuaded that monasteries are obliged to assist the indigent parents of its members, if circumstances allow the concession of such assistance, and to comfort them in their wants, since the children can no longer attend to that duty.

To this we may add that if our opinion had been condemned by this council, Saint Gregory Nazianzen and Saint Basil would not have taught the contrary, for as they must have been well acquainted with the decision of a council held in their own country and in their own times, so they would certainly have submitted to it and have adopted it for their guide.

Q. 22—Are not, therefore, the advantages of retirement very great, since they preponderate over those important considerations?

A.— If religious persons knew the advantages they enjoy by living in an entire separation from men, either by reason of the dangers they avoid in this hidden life, or the abundant graces and benedictions which our Lord pours down on those who serve Him in solitude, they would prefer the happiness of living and dying in it to everything the world can bestow; and nothing less than a positive command of God could ever induce them to leave their sweet retirement.

This was Saint Basil's conviction, when having deplored the miseries of the world, and the dangers to which those are exposed who live amongst men, he said:

> It was to avoid the perils which everywhere abound, that I withdrew into the mountains, like a little bird who escaped the fowler's net. For this reason I live in the desert, as Jesus Christ lived in it. It was there the celebrated oak of Mambre is found. It was there the patriarch Jacob saw the mysterious ladder, whose top reached the heavens, and on which angels appeared ascending and descending. In solitude the people of God were purified, and received the law. Through the desert they were led to the possession of the promised land. There Mount Carmel is found, on which the prophet Elias retired by the command of God, and there reproduced the sacred scriptures which were dictated to him by the Holy Spirit. Retired in the desert the glorious precursor of Christ, Saint John the Baptist, lived on locusts, and preached penance to men. There Mount Olivet is seen, where the Redeemer of the world frequently retired to pray in order to teach us how to perform that holy exercise; there He demonstrated how much He loved solitude. There we find the narrow way that leads to life. In fine, the desert was the dwelling place of the prophets and of the masters of the spiritual life, when for the glory and service of the Lord they sojourned on mountains and in deserts, and lived in the holes and caves of the earth.

If you add all this, my brethren, to what we have already said of the sentiments of the saints concerning the monastic state, you will certainly conclude that our Lord considered the desert as a place of particular choice; that retirement is peculiarly attractive of His graces; that solitaries were His dearest favorites, the delight of His heart; that He reigned over them even in this life, as He reigns over the angels in His kingdom above; and that it was like a new Heaven in which He established His throne with singular content.

May we not truly say, my brethren, that the same things which are seen unfolding in Heaven, are likewise effected in monasteries where the spirit of Christ governs? For if the saints have only one employment in Heaven, which is that of contemplating, loving, and praising God by uninterrupted acts—"We shall see Him, love and praise Him," [61]says Saint Augustine—may we not say, that in like manner religious persons have no other occupation than to live in His divine presence; that amidst their various exercises they have only one end and desire, which is that of doing His will, and proving their love.

The prophet says that the saints are delivered from all wants and necessities, that they no longer suffer either hunger or thirst, or any other accident of times or seasons (Isa 49:10). And might we not almost be induced to think that solitaries had become impassible, when they were seen exposing themselves to wild beasts, to the fury of barbarians, and to the inclemency of seasons, without fear; more particularly when we consider that they were deprived of everything that seems necessary for the preservation of life.

The same prophet says that the saints shall dwell in a land where no grief, nor sorrow, nor mourning shall be ever heard, but joy and gladness shall abound, and shall be co-eternal with the source from whence they spring (Isa 65:18). This may be said proportionally of every holy community, for as all the members are united by the charity of Jesus Christ, as they have no particular interest from which dissension might spring, so they enjoy a profound and constant peace. From their purified hearts flows undisturbed tranquility and the consolations they enjoy are refreshed and renewed continually, by the joyful tears which are produced from the impressions they have of the divine mercies, as well as of their own sins.

In fine, my brethren, nothing on earth can more clearly prefigure the eternal repose of the elect in the glorious kingdom above than the life of

---

[61] Sermo CCLIV, *In Diebus Paschalibus* XXV, PL 38:1185 (1844).

a monastic society where the rules are carefully observed. There we find accomplished those words of the prophet Isaiah: "The Lord will change the desert into a place of delights, and the solitude into a garden pleasing in His sight; and joy and gladness shall be found therein, and it shall resound with thanksgiving, and the voice of praise" (Isa 51:3).

We must confess that those persons are really objects of pity, who, instead of loving those evident truths, or taking delight in them, instead of reading them to a profitable use, never raise their minds to anything that might assist them in appreciating the sublime grace of their vocation. Rather they evince by the whole tenor of their conduct that their hearts are possessed by the love of the world which occupies therein the place and rank which ought to be entirely filled with the love of retirement.

Q. 23.—*Are we to consider that retirement is as necessary for superiors as it is for their subjects ?*

A.—This question, my brethren, has been already sufficiently solved by what we have said concerning the vigilance and application with which superiors ought to attend to the salvation of their brethren. Hence, we shall only add here a few words, to show that superiors as well as their subjects are bound to live in retirement and in the silence of their cloister, unless they are induced to do otherwise by very pressing and lawful necessities.

First—Because in making their profession, they promised stability in their monasteries.

Secondly—They have the same obligations as their brethren, with whom they ought to be conformable in all things, and exhibit no distinction, but such as are annexed to their authority and to the place they fill.

Thirdly—They are bound to give good example, especially in those things which being more painful and difficult, are more subject to great temptations.

Fourthly—As they are more exposed to dissipation than their brethren, they have much more need than they, to repair in solitude the losses they suffer in the exercise of their ministry.

Fifth—They ought to communicate to their brethren the divine maxims and sentiments of Jesus Christ. Now it is in retirement that they can invoke that divine model, give ear to His words, and be replenished by Him.

Sixth—As nature supports the weight of retirement with more difficulty than any other duty (as Guy, general of the Carthusians remarks [62]) so is there nothing in which a religious has more need of being sustained by the hand of his superior. But the superior is entirely useless when he himself

forsakes his retirement, for the religious is tempted by his example. His words serve no purpose, and instead of being of any assistance, they lose all their influence by his conduct.

Thus, my brethren, having considered all things, retirement is more necessary for superiors than for those who are subject to them. The former flatter themselves, falsely, that they have an exemption, but for this they have no authority of God. On the contrary, they are bound by a double tie to live in their monasteries, since, as religious, they are obliged to it by their vow of stability, and as pastors they are bound to reside with their flock.

We read that Saint Benedict having promised to go to a certain place for the purpose of designing the plan and order of a new monastery, but being deterred from the journey by the love of retirement, God justified his conduct by a miracle. The saint appeared in sleep to the superior who had waited his arrival, and pointed out all things as if he had been corporally present with him.[63]

The same saint having founded Mount Cassino, made choice of that place for his abode, and lived there so exactly retired, that though he founded many other monasteries in Italy, we do not find that he ever went out of his own to visit them.

The same thing is abundantly confirmed by the life of Saint Bernard. Though he was replenished with light, yet he never went out of his retirement but by the orders of Heaven. Then he appeared in the world only as a brilliant sun to enlighten it, so that the most celebrated doctors and prelates heard his words in profound silence, as those of a prophet or an apostle. Yet he declared that he withdrew from God in proportion as he removed to a greater distance from his monastery. Writing to a cardinal who had requested him to favor him with a visit, he told him that if he did not comply with his desire, the cause was not sloth, but that he had made a resolution never to leave his monastery but when forced by some urgent reasons and important affairs. These reasons and important affairs were those of his order, a command of the legate of the holy see, or of his bishop, as appears by one of his letters.[64] Nothing is more edifying than the manner in which that great saint deplores his condition, when

---

[63] S. Gregorius Magnus, Caput XXII, De fabrica monasterii Tarracinensis per visionem ab eo disposita, *Vita S. Benedicti* (Ex libro II Dialogorum S. Gregorii Magni excerpta), *Sancti Benedicti Opera Omnia*, PL 66:174 (1847).

[64] Epistola XVII, Ad Petrum, PL 182:119 (1854) / Bernard, *Works*, 179.

he complains of those inevitable occasions which forced him from his retirement, and engaged him in the affairs of the world.⁶⁵

"My monstrous life," says this man of God, "and my uneasy conscience, cry aloud and demand your assistance: I am the phenomenon of the age, for I neither live as an ecclesiastic, nor as a layman, as 1 have quite laid aside its obligations, though I yet wear the habit."⁶⁶

This astonishing reproach of a saint inspired by God, ought to remove every pretext from those persons of his state, who might make an ill use of his example, by taking that for a rule which he did against the rule, or by following that as a law, which, to speak properly, was only a dispensing of the law. For the world abounds with persons who do that by the influence of their inconstancy and humors that which the saints performed by the inspirations of grace; and who endeavor to justify the impropriety of their conduct by the actions of the servants of God, which are no more than extraordinary dispensations of His providence, and the effects of their obedience. It is too frequently the case that the children of darkness imitate to their destruction what the children of light have performed for their sanctification.

Q. 24.—May not a superior go out of his monastery for the purpose of making visits ?

A.—He ought not. The making of visits is a subjection from which his state has delivered him. It is a duty the world no longer has a right to require of him, and which he ought not to pay. He has embraced a rule of holy liberty which disengages him from all creatures and binds him to Jesus Christ alone. Hence, he ought to consider visits as being of the number of those unprofitable things, the use of which is prohibited him during his future life. If he believes that they are necessary to secure the good will of his friends, or to acquire new ones, he deceives himself. He ought to learn that he never will be more esteemed by men than when he has less communication with them. For if his life be uniform in all things, if he be equally exact in every point of his rule as he is in this, all men will be edified and will esteem both his person and his conduct.

We find a most edifying example on this subject, in the history of the

---

⁶⁵ Epistola XLVIII, Ad Haimericum, PL 182:154 (1854) / Bernard, *Works*, 1:224.

⁶⁶ Epistola CCL, Ad Bernardum Priorem Portarum. PL 182:451 (1854). /*Works*, 2:732.

Spanish Discalced Carmelites,[67] which deserves a place here. Saint John of the Cross, being prior of a monastery at Grenada, was obliged at the request of his religious, against his own inclinations, to make a visit to the president of the city, and having in his complimentary address, requested to be excused for having delayed so long to perform that duty, the president answered, with a wisdom and clearness more becoming a father and doctor of the Church than a magistrate:

> Father Prior, we are much more pleased to see you and your religious in your houses than in our dwellings; because your reverences edify us when we have the happiness to see you in your retirement; whereas when you come to visit us, you only entertain us. A religious in his retirement charms and delights our hearts, and on the contrary, he who seeks to gain our affection by worldly compliments and polite ceremonies will never succeed in pleasing or edifying us.

The historian relates that this judicious answer so affected the saint that he immediately returned to his monastery without even going to the archiepiscopal palace, though when he left his convent he formed the design of visiting the archbishop.

Q. 25.—Is not the motive of instructing the faithful, sufficient to authorize a superior, when he leaves his retirement for that purpose?

A—By no means, for in the first place, monks are not appointed to instruct the faithful, but to weep for their sins. Unless God calls them to that employment by an evident extraordinary vocation, they ought not to engage in it.

Secondly—Our Lord has given the care of part of His flock to monastic superiors. It is true the portion is but small, but it ought to be so much the more precious to them, as they may consider it the dearest, most noble, and most favorite, says Saint Cyprian. [68]Hence, they ought to watch over it with a more faithful application, and a more tender solicitude. This is the end to which their persons, their time, and their care are destined by Divine Providence.

If they themselves initiate any other affair without being called by a clear and manifest call of God, they ought to be persuaded that they forsake the employment to which they were engaged by Him. They leave their own mission to undertake one foreign to their purpose, and thus they become an occasion of scandal and ruin to their brethren.

In a word, if superiors undertake the office of preaching and teaching of their own will, they become guilty of an unsupportable presumption. If they are invited to it, they ought to answer with Saint Bernard, "I have put off my robe, how shall I retake it? I have washed my feet, how shall I again defile them in the dust?[69] ... What you require of me is above my strength, and contrary to my state." [70] This was the true spirit of that great saint, who writing to a bishop who had sent him a person to the end that he might enjoin him a penance, tells him, "I am not disposed to undertake such functions as belong to bishops for it would be a strong presumption in me, who am so great a sinner, to interpose in affairs belonging to their ministry."[71]

The same sentiment prevailed in his whole order before the introduction of relaxed principles. We read in the ancient definitions of the general chapters that the proper dwelling of monks being the cloister, they ought not to serve in the chapels belonging to the order.[72] In another place the religious are forbidden to serve churches or chapels which are not of the order, or to engage themselves in the care of souls; and abbots allowing any such undertakings are to be punished.[73] Another statute of a general chapter enjoins that in future no religious shall accept any parish church. If an abbot should consent in this way, he is to be deposed without remission. If a private religious, he is to be expelled from his monastery without hope of being received into it again.[74]

Animated with the same spirit, Pope Eugenius III speaking to the abbots of Citeaux, and exhorting them to remain in their solitude, tells them, that their fathers and founders made choice of the retired life, while others applied themselves to ecclesiastical functions; that if the children of the world should endeavor to withdraw them from their solitude, and engage them in the direction of souls, from the repose of contemplation to the noise of employments and public affairs, they ought to remember the institutions of their fathers, and rather choose, like them, to be contemptible

---

[69] Epistola XXI, Ad Mattheum, PL 182:123 (1854). / Bernard, *Works*, 1:187.

[70] Epistola LXXXIX, Ad Eumdem [Oger], PL 182:220 / Bernard, *Works*, 1:319.

[71] Epistola LXI, Ad Ricuinum, PL 182:167b. / Bernard, *Works*, 1:242.

[72] Inst. cap. gen. disti. ch. 11.

[73] Lib. ant. def. dist. 4. c.3.

[74] Capit. gener. anni 1215.

in the house of God, than to dwell in the tabernacle of sinners, according to the words of the prophet (Ps 83:11).[75]

In fine, monastic superiors in general, who were animated with the spirit of their state, lived closely retired in their cloisters. They never interposed in any ecclesiastical functions; not only because such occupations were contrary to their state, and to that religious mourning which engages them, as Saint Bernard says,[76] to weep for their own sins, and for those of mankind in general but moreover, because they would have been occasions of dissipation to their brethren, would have fomented a disgust for their state, and under the specious pretext of exercising charity, would have excited them to desire the duties of a ministry which were by no means proper for them. In a word, it would have destroyed in them the spirit and piety of their holy state, there being nothing, as we have already remarked, by which private religious are more easily allured than by the practice of such things as they see their superiors both perform and authorize by their example.

Q. 26.—Before you conclude this instruction concerning retirement, tell us whether it is proper to invite the relations and friends of the religious to the monastery on the day of profession.

A.—Such a custom, my brethren, is not only improper, but we cannot be sufficiently astonished that it found access to the cloister, and more particularly, that there are yet persons who adopt and authorize such a practice. For we can discover no lawful reason to exhibit a religious to public view, on the very day he is going to sequester himself forever from the eyes of men, and to hide his life in that of Jesus Christ, according to the words of the apostle. But we find many reasons for secluding the world from those abodes of virtue at all times, particularly on the day of profession.

What! Shall that soul, who by the command of God has forsaken its father's house, be placed once more in the midst of those from whom it fled, like a dove from a bird of prey? Soft and tender as a young person is at the time of profession, and as yet susceptible of every impression, is there not reason to fear, that the view and conversation of his relatives will make a great many unfavorable impressions, very opposite to the perfect disengagement in which he ought to live when consecrated to God?

---

[75] Inter epist. S. Bernardi 384.

[76] Serm. de Magdelena.

The society of his acquaintances, perhaps of some who have been the accomplices of his former sins, will revive in his memory the ideas of many things which he ought to have buried in eternal oblivion. By what means shall he defend himself from the tenderness of a father, the caresses of a mother, even in the supposition that he may be proof against the attacks of his relations and friends? One tender look is sufficient to blow up a flame which no care or application is able to extinguish. The remembrance of the enjoyments, amusements, entertainments, and pleasures of their former life can be only by much difficulty banished, and regret is not far distant at a time when he is about to immolate them for ever.

The consequence is that one moment of false and transitory satisfaction may become the cause of sorrow and affliction for his whole ensuing life. That which is most deplorable is that, with the religious having now closed the door to every future entrance into the world, the evil is positioned to torment more acutely, the cause of which lies concealed within the soul. Thus it nourishes in itself the source of its misfortune and destruction, in the very place and condition wherein it hoped to find its repose and salvation.

But not to dwell on this inconvenience, which may seem extraordinary to some persons, let me ask, is it not an insupportable mode of conduct, that in the most important action of life, when a religious person has the greatest want of interior piety and the most animated charity; on an occasion when he ought to rouse and assemble together all the strength and powers of his soul, all the affections of his heart, and all the energy of his reason, to be then exposed to visits, conversations, or dissipating feasts, which may easily become even licentious; and to other circumstances so well qualified to destroy interior recollection, make him forget the presence of God, withdraw him from that divine object, ruin, or at least enervate, the good dispositions he might have acquired during the whole time of his probation, and thus make him enter into an engagement all over defiled, which requires a purity equal to that of angels?

It is certainly very strange that the day which ought to be to him a day of profound recollection, in which he ought to pour out his heart in the presence of his God in sentiments of peace, silence, and a lively contrition for his sins, and treat with Him alone concerning the great affair of his eternal salvation, is precisely that which is passed in dissipation, confusion, trouble, and commotion!

If (as you cannot doubt) what the ancient fathers and holy solitaries

16| ON RETIREMENT

of primitive times have said be true, that a religious who deprives himself of the presence of God willingly for a moment commits a spiritual fornication, in what a state must this soul be when coming from those familiar conversations and entertainments, he shall enter into the nuptial chamber, quite filled with a variety of thoughts and vain imaginations, perhaps divided by affections and desires, and even disfigured with secret infidelities that might have escaped his attention?

Is this the manner to prepare the soul for the sacred bed, and to make it worthy of the heavenly spouse, whose chastity, purity, and beauty are infinite. Do they not know that the spouse is a jealous lover? (James 4:5) This divine Lover is offended and provoked when He beholds his spouses taking any liberties. He considers all creatures as His rivals; He is offended when we stand an instant with them ; and we can give them nothing without committing an outrage against Him.

Nevertheless, as if all this were nothing, many are found who without scruple pass from the familiarity of men to the embraces of God. The desires of the world are gratified as much as they can, and those deluded souls pretend to ascend from the depths of the valleys to the summit of the mountains, and to be suddenly raised from the lowest parts of the earth to the highest point of Heaven. During the novitiate the soul may have been purified, but to no purpose, since it defiles itself again by profane and useless communications which should have been for ever excluded. He who washes himself, says the Holy Spirit, after having touched a dead body, and afterwards touches it again, makes his efforts unprofitable (Ecclesiastic. 34:30).

Another effect of this lamentable practice is the imperfect, defective, and impure preparation, or to say better, profane ornamenting of the novice when he is about engaging in a state the purity of which is equal to that of angels, thus giving birth to an uninterrupted chain of unhappy consequences, which are everything else except the happiness and blessings that were expected. The whole successive life is one continual complaint, because a state of holiness has been embraced without preparation or sanctity; the malady is perceived and felt, but the remedy is forgotten; the reason of which in general is, that the principle of the evil is not known, because the vice which is found in the engagement, spreads itself over the whole state, and covers all its ways with darkness and obscurity for such a person. The purest souls are like very clear mirrors; the least breath or vapor tarnishes them or destroys their brilliancy. There is, however, this difference, that the stains of mirrors are easily removed, they recover their first purity in an instant; whereas the stains of souls being spiritual, are more obstinate; they resist, and their impressions become proof against whatever pains are taken to remove them.

The same thing may be said of the mystical death that happens by a religious profession, as of the natural death effected by the extinction of the vital principle. A separation forever from the society of men is the consequence of the one as well as of the other. In both the goods of the world are renounced, but in our consecration to God we renounce willingly all perishable riches, we direct all our thoughts to the true riches of our heavenly country and attach ourselves to Jesus Christ, on whom all depend, and who is constituted by his eternal Father, the sovereign dispenser of every blessing. The words which the spirit of God puts into the mouth of those who die by vows, and those who die by the extinction of their natural life, are so synonymous, though the expressions are different, that the same sentiments ought to animate both the one and the other.

The man who in the world is going to expire by a natural death, committing his soul into the hands of Jesus Christ, he says to Him with confidence: "Into thy hands, O Lord! I commend my spirit." And thus entering into a state of unlimited separation, declares that his Redeemer holds the place of all things in his regard, and that he places all his hopes in Him alone.

In like manner, the man dying to the world by the death of grace, addresses himself to Jesus Christ, casting himself into the arms of His providence, and declaring that all things are come to an end in his regard, and protesting by a solemn declaration, that from his Savior alone he expects to receive his happiness, his salvation, and his life. "Receive me, 0 Lord! according to Thy word, and I shall live, and Thou wilt not allow me to suffer confusion in the expectation of the good things thou hast promised me" (Ps 118:116).

In fine, the man who desires to die the death of a good Christian, does not call together his relations and friends to be spectators of his death. On the contrary, he prohibits every access to those who might impede him in the affair. He closes the entrance of his house, remains alone, takes leave of his children, removes his wife from his view, lest the presence of those objects might produce any effects in him contrary to the entire disengagement from all things in which he desires to finish his life. He allows no person to remain with him but such as may assist him in his great passage, so that he may unite himself more immediately and more intimately to Jesus Christ, from Whom he hopes never to be separated.

Now a religious will not fail to observe the same mode of conduct, if he is affected with the spirit of grace. He ought to remove from his presence whatever might engage or distract him from his great object at the time of his mystical death, that is to say, at the time of his religious profession. And he will refuse himself to all so that he may give himself entirely to God. What has he to do with parents, relations, friends, or other persons of the world, since he finds within his solitude everything necessary for the accomplishment of his work? He is both the victim and priest of his sacrifice; his superior in the presence of his brethren confirms the holocaust; the saints and angels of the Lord are the witnesses.

In a word, my brethren, in whatever manner we examine this convocation of relations and friends on the day of profession, we can find nothing to recommend it. Whether we consider it in the superiors who allow it, in the relations who desire it, or in the novices who are the object of it. For the interest of superiors is to watch so carefully over the souls committed by our Lord to their charge that their purity be in no manner sullied; that of parents is not to disturb the repose of their children by proofs of an indiscreet and unseasonable friendship. And that of children is to contract this new engagement with such grace and preparation as may enable them to present themselves to Jesus Christ without having anything in them that might displease His divine Majesty.

Nevertheless, as if these considerations were mere chimerical ideas, superiors make no account of the sacred *depositum* with which they are charged on those important occasions. Parents forget the duty of procuring the happiness of their children, and the children themselves never reflect that they carry in frail vessels the most precious of all graces and treasures, that of a vocation to the religious state, and that they ought to avoid nothing more cautiously than whatever might diminish its fullness, or endanger its loss.

17 | ON SILENCE—CONTENTS:

QUESTION 1.—Ought the religious observe the rule of silence with great exactitude?   104

Q. 2.—Ought not this silence be perpetual?   105

Q. 3.— Would not a religious derive much advantage from the pious and edifying conversation of his brethren?   106

17

ON SILENCE

QUESTION 1.—*Ought the religious observe the rule of silence with great exactitude ?*

ANSWER—The same motives that induced Saint Benedict, my brethren, to establish a stability so unlimited, obliged him to prescribe rules for religious silence. Nothing was more reasonable than, by an exact separation, to afford religious persons the means of recovering the piety they had lost by indiscreet communications. And it is certain that the passions are nourished and cupidity entertained in retirement as well as in the world, unless entertainments and worldly conversations are excluded.

The man of vanity, who according to the disorder of his heart would display his talents and superior merit, will find sufficient means to gratify himself in the cloister, if he is allowed to employ his tongue. And a small number of brethren will be considered by him as a great assembly and a numerous auditory. The ambitious man will consider the offices of the monastery, however contemptible they may be, as considerable dignities. The busy and impertinent will form societies and parties with as much application and solicitude as if there were question of the fate of a kingdom. The angry man will have perpetual occasions of blowing the coals of his passions; the impure, of inflaming his wicked desires; the unsocial, of exciting murmurings and divisions; the detractor, of spreading his poisons; the babbler, of relating his fables; the complaisant, of forming particular friendships; in fine, every individual, of following the impulse of his passions.

For though these passions shall have changed the stage of acting, and shall be enclosed within a more narrow sphere, yet so far from being destroyed, they will become lively and inflamed; so that the only means best calculated to stem the torrent of all these disorders, is to cut off all communications, and to prohibit all commerce, by the observance of a strict silence; for nature being then deprived of all means and hopes of satisfying itself, will cease to request; its habits and inclinations will entirely subside, when they find nothing to fortify and support them.

Q. 2.—*Ought not this silence be perpetual?*

A. There can be no advantage extracted from silence in a religious community unless it is uninterruptedly observed. For conversations, though short and seldom, will be found, if allowed, equally noxious and dangerous. The moments will be carefully managed, and the brethren will soon discover the secret of saying a great deal in a little time. When they shall be forced to break off and leave their conversations imperfect, they will not forget to finish them at the next meeting. And as it is impossible that the desire of discoursing should not increase, so they will agree on the time and place to find out the means of satisfying themselves, without consulting either the will of the superior or the rules of the house, which would be in effect the ruin of discipline and the extinction of piety.

But if silence be perpetual, the brethren will consider its observance as indispensable, the most considerable advantages shall be derived from it, and it shall appear that nothing is better calculated to maintain good order, and promote the sanctification of the cloister.

First, having no communication with one another, and forming none of those familiarities which almost generally produce contempt, they shall behold each other with respect and their charity will suffer no alloy.

Secondly, if any should be found inclined to evil, his propensities shall be enclosed within himself, and all communication of the evil shall be prevented by the barriers of silence.

Thirdly, no factious or murmuring parties will be ever formed amongst the brethren, such an evil not being possible when there is no communication.

Fourth, the correspondence and intimacy which ought to exist between the members and the head, will be more connected, when not divided by any particular conversations or friendships.

Fifth, the superiors will never find any opponents, when they shall desire to make new arrangements, for the preservation of good order and the perfection of the community. And though a religious might not have the same ideas, yet he will not presume to make them appear, lest he should find no one amongst the brethren who would side with him.

Sixth, as the heart and interior man will find no means to diffuse and enervate its principles by vain and idle discourse, so recollection will be more uninterrupted, thoughts more pure, contemplation more sublime and lively, prayer more fervent and continual; and thus the soul will ascend to a union with God, so much the more intimate and holy, as it shall have renounced for his love all communication with men.

Q. 3.— *Would not a religions derive much advantage from the pious and edifying conversation of his brethren ?*

A. I allow it is possible that a religious might sometimes find edification in the conversation of his brethren, but it would produce so many inconveniences, and be followed by so many evil consequences, that the good and evil being well examined, the advantage of conversation must appear as nothing; so that a decision must be given in favor of silence without the least hesitation.

It is incomparably easier to keep silence, than to observe such just measures in speaking as not to offend in words.

However abundant water is, it may be restrained by banks, but if it find the least opening, it forces a passage, overflows with impetuosity, and bears away every opposition. In like manner, the tongue may be governed by silence, by making the observance thereof a necessary law. But as soon as the mouth is opened, and the barrier removed, the great difficulty of governing this member and regulating its operations is quickly perceived. The most exact and well inclined persons frequently fall into errors of this nature, of which they ought not, nor would not be guilty, if restrained by silence.

Even persons who make profession of piety, frequently treat of spiritual matters in a manner entirely carnal. They begin, it is true, by the motion of the Divine Spirit, but they continue and finish by those of nature. Self-love will lose nothing. It endeavors to distinguish its talents and to attract attention. The applause of the hearers is expected, victory is contended for, and nothing is more frequent than to see pious conversations change into disputes, or degenerate into idle babbling, and evaporate into vain and curious words. This is what made the royal prophet watch so carefully over the motions of his tongue, and induced him to abstain from speaking even of holy things (Ps 38:2).

Therefore, my brethren, silence cannot be too rigorously observed, nor can the members of a religious community be too far removed from the dangers resulting from conversation. For if they once obtain leave to speak, they will use the dangerous liberty in speaking of unlawful topics; they will transgress the bounds prescribed, if they perceive that they may speak, and entertain one another concerning things unconnected with their salvation; they will extend their conversations to everything without restriction; they will mutually unfold their thoughts, temptations, imaginations, pains, and discontents; they will establish a place of refuge in each others' breasts against future wants and affairs; they will link in the bonds of a false and particular charity, which is never constructed but on the ruins of that love which is and ought to be common amongst all the members. The words of Saint Bernard on this subject are well deserving notice: "What necessity can you have," says he, "to expose yourself to be condemned for speaking, since you may secure yourself by keeping silence. I have seen a great many fall by speaking, but never one by silence." [77]

It suffices, my brethren, to reflect that we are exposed to much danger every time we speak, that the government of the tongue is very difficult, that the most perfect souls are frequently overcome, and that the way of silence is the most secure. This, I say, is enough to convince us how much religious persons are bound to observe it, because they have retired from the world into their monasteries, as into so many secure havens, where they may avoid the rocks and tempests, as well as everything else that might expose them to danger in their voyage to a happy eternity. Therefore be convinced that the satisfaction which is enjoyed by private conversations is a thing of much less value than the great advantages flowing from silence strictly observed.

But as it is not possible to make persons submit to a yoke so heavy, unless they are willing to place themselves under it; and as there is no appearance of succeeding in subjecting them against their will to a law so rigorous, superiors ought to employ all possible means to enforce its utility and advantages, so that the brethren may esteem, love, and desire it. Without this they will never succeed in establishing its observance, and the brethren will always find a great many ways to render their zeal and vigilance abortive.

To succeed in this point, a superior ought to animate his zeal, labor in the way of instruction, and like a father in the midst of his children,

---

[77] *Tractatus de ordine vitae*, PL 184:569b

point out to his brethren the inconveniences of speaking, the advantages of silence, and above all, he should confirm his teaching by the authority of the holy scriptures, and the example of the saints. For how can the religious refuse to admit the necessity of silence, or remain in a state of indifference on the subject, when they shall be informed how severely the Holy Spirit condemns the improper use of the tongue. He tells us by the mouth of the wise man, "A lash of a whip raises welts, but a blow of the tongue smashes bones" (Ecclesiastic 28:21).

"Hedge up thy ears with thorns, that thou mayest not hear the discourse of a wicked tongue, and close up thy mouth with gates and locks" (Ecclesiastic 28:28). The same Divine Spirit teaches us by the mouth of his apostle, "The tongue is a fire, a world of iniquity, full of deadly poison, defiling the whole course of our lives, and no man can govern it" (James 3:6). Against this there can be no reply. How can you, my brethren, refuse to love silence, when you consider that the prophet tells us that silence, and tranquility—one of its principal effects—nourishes and cultivates piety? (Isa 30:15) To you these words of another prophet are addressed: "The solitary shall sit down in repose and be silent" (Lam 3:28); and in this silence you shall find your strength (Isa 30:15). Above all, remember what our Lord says, that for every idle word we speak, we must render an account on the day of judgment (Mt. 12:36).

This is enough to convince religious persons how necessary the observance of silence is, and to animate them to keep it with great fidelity. For, since the counsels of the gospel are become precepts to them, and as according to the designs of God they are obliged to tend to perfection, they are also obliged to avoid everything that may impede their progress, or put them out of the way, and embrace everything that may assist them in the acquisition. Now, as nothing is better qualified to effect both than silence, they must consider it as a necessary help, and as a principal obligation. From this divine source the holy fathers extracted the sentiments and maxims they have left us in their writings and examples.

Convinced of the necessity of silence, the holy abbot Nesteros told Cassian, by way of necessary advice, that if he wished to acquire the perfection of his state, he should bind himself to an eternal silence, attend with care and solicitude to the instructions of the ancients, keep his heart always open, and his mouth shut, and be more prompt and exact to practice what he had learned than to teach others. "For," added that great saint,

In teaching others divine truths there is danger of vainglory, but in reducing them to practice in silence, the fruit of spiritual understanding is acquired. Therefore, never take the liberty of speaking, unless when it is necessary to be informed of some truth the ignorance of which might be dangerous to you, or to acquire some necessary knowledge.[78]

It was from the same principle Saint Arsenius was so adverse to every sort of conversation, that even the presence and authority of his bishop could scarce draw a word from his mouth; and when asked the reason of such reservation, he answered that he found it impossible to converse with God and men at the same time.

The love of silence produced this remarkable saying from the mouth of Saint Pambo, who being reprehended for having let some persons retire without saying anything to them, though they came on purpose to speak to him, he replied: "If they have not been edified by my silence, they would not have been so with my words."

But who can help being feelingly affected with what we read in ecclesiastical history of the same saint, who going to visit one of the brethren in order to learn the meaning of some of the psalms, stopped at this verse: "I have said I will keep my ways, that I may not offend by my tongue" (Ps 38:1); nor would he hear any more, saying that was enough until he had learned and practiced it. Some years after, the same brother having reproached him for staying away so long, he answered, that he had not well learned by practice the first verse he had taught him.

Saint Ambrose, enlightened by the same Spirit, expresses his sentiments in the following words:

> The prophet kept a guard on his mouth, and you give unrestrained liberty to your tongue. If a prophet, whose mouth is the organ of the Holy Spirit, by which he announces his oracles, is nevertheless afraid to speak, how can you be secure, you who are so much exposed to fail in words?[79]

Saint John Chrysostom is admirable when he exclaims, on the same subject:

---

[78] *Collationes*, PL 49:967 (1846). / *Conferences* 2.14.9 (NPNF2/11:439).

[79] S. Ambrosius, *In Psalmum XXXVIII Enarratio*, PL 14:1091 (1882).

> Keep silence, my brethren, as a strong wall; for by it you shall surmount all your temptations; by it you shall be elevated, and from your high post you shall combat your enemies with advantage, and lay them at your feet. Keep silence in the fear of God, and the arrows of your enemies shall not wound you. Silence, united with the fear of the Lord, is a fiery chariot, by which we are carried up to Heaven; which was prefigured by the translation of the prophet Elias. O! silence, thou art the perfection of solitaries, the way to the kingdom of Christ, the mother of compunction, the mirror of sinners! O silence! which opens the source of holy tears, produces sweetness; thou art the inseparable companion of humility, the light of our souls, and the discernment of our thoughts!
>
> O silence! thou art the source of all good; our support in austerities, the bridle of intemperance. Thou teachest us the divine art of prayer, and the science of the saints; thou calmest our thoughts, and art a secure haven against all tempests. O silence! who destroyest all anxiety in our souls, thy yoke is sweet, and presents everything amiable; it refreshes and carries him who bears it, and replenishes our souls with heavenly consolations. O silence! thou dost regulate the motions of our eyes and tongue; thou art the death of calumny, the enemy of impudence, the mother of respect; thou dost repress our passions, and accompany every virtue; thou makest us love poverty; thou art the fertile field of Jesus Christ, that produces every sort of good fruit in abundance. O silence! who art joined to the fear of God, and dost serve as walls and ramparts for those who fight for the kingdom of Heaven.
>
> Purchase for yourselves, my brethren, this better part which Mary hath chosen for her inheritance; she is the model of silence, seated at the feet of our Lord, she gave herself to him without reserve.

The sentiments of Saint John Climacus were the same when having made an exact enumeration of all the qualities and graces which either spring from silence or accompany it, he says that the friend of silence draws nigh to God, enters in a hidden and secret manner into a holy familiarity with him, and his soul is illuminated with the rays of his heavenly brightness.[80]

Saint Benedict, who was well informed on this subject, and who considered it in the same manner, was so exact in the observance of silence, that he will not allow his disciples to speak, unless they are asked a question, or moved by some real necessity. He orders that the permission of speaking be only seldom granted to the religious, even to such as are perfect (that is, such as would not make any bad use of a necessary permission to speak),

though their words should be holy, and their subjects edifying.[81] In fine, that holy legislator makes the observance of silence a constant rule, which ought to occupy the attention of religious persons at all times.[82]

Saint Peter Damian says:

> It is by separation from the conversation of men, and the assistance of silence, we raise a temple for the Holy Spirit within our breasts; and as according to the sacred history, the temple of Jerusalem was built without any noise being heard in the house of God, either of hammers or of any other instrument, so the temple within us ought to be constructed in silence. The soul concentrating all her forces within herself, and carefully avoiding all effusion of words, shall attain the completion of a spiritual building. To this state she will advance with so much the more velocity and security, as she shall avoid all exterior communication, and confine herself within the limits of silence.

He adds:

> A solitary is raised above himself in proportion as he keeps silence. Enclosed within the protecting barriers of silence, man's spirit is raised to Heaven on the wings of vehement desire; being inflamed by the fire of divine love, like a living source it swells and portends, when it cannot flow by words, as by so many streams.[83]

Saint Bernard and all his brethren observed a silence so profound, that those who did not understand either the greatness or excellency of this secret, censured their conduct as being the effect of stupidity. The holy abbot, writing to Saint Peter, abbot of Cluny, tells him,

> I think that you will be more indulgent for the future, and not reproach me for my silence, giving it the epithet of stupidity, as you are accustomed to do. The prophet Isaiah gives it a name, much more expressive and agreeable to its nature, when he calls it the guardian of justice.[84]

In another place he says:

---

[81] *RB* 6.3.

[82] *RB* 42..

[83] S. Petrus Damianus, Epistola VI, Liber Septimus, Epistolae, PL 144:443(1853).

[84] Epistola CCXXVIII, Ad Petrum, PL 182:398a (1854)./ Bernard, *Works*, 2:653.

I have fled from the world, I have fixed my dwelling in the deep recesses of solitude. I am determined with the prophet to keep a strict watch over all my ways lest my tongue should betray me into sin, for according to the same prophet, the man who is fond of much speaking, shall not be blessed with a long life on earth. We read in another place of the scripture: Life and death are in the hands of the tongue. The prophet Jeremiah teaches us, that it is a great good to await our salvation of God in silence. To this silence that forms and preserves virtue, I invite you, not only you but all those who imitate you, and who desire to advance in virtue.[85]

The religious who were formed by that great saint, and filled with his spirit, were so zealous for this holy exercise and thought it so important that they instituted signs to treat of necessary matters, so that they might never be obliged to speak. *The practice of silence sanctified the whole Cistercian order.* The Carthusians followed their example, and obliged their lay brethren to observe it with rigorous exactitude; so much so, that they have kept it ever since with the same fidelity as the fundamental rule of entire solitude.

It is difficult to resist the force of these convincing truths. And a superior who applies himself to the duty of forming his brethren with them in a proper manner, must at last succeed in persuading them that the practice of silence is absolutely necessary for their sanctification and perfection. But his labors will be insufficient, unless he carefully removes every occasion of temptation from them, smooths the way to its practice, and makes the execution become easy.

The first thing to be done for that purpose is not to allow them the least communication with their parents and friends, to remove from them all knowledge of what passes in the world, to be careful that they never receive any information concerning state affairs, or those of the Church, or even those of their own order; and that they be satisfied with praying in general for public necessities without knowing them in particular, for it is impossible that amongst a variety of events, many things should not occur which make an impression on their minds, excite and animate desires, fancies, humors and other passions, which at best are only suppressed, but never entirely destroyed.

Secondly—Things must be disposed in such a way, that the brethren

---

[85] Epistola LXXXIX, Ad Eumdem, PL 182:217 (1854). / Bernard, *Works*, 1:319.

may be always employed, their time well filled up, and their days full; so that they may find satisfaction in the diversity of exercises, pass from the office to reading, from prayer to work, from labor to prayer; everything being so regulated that the long continuance of anything may not disgust them. The exercises must also be all performed in common, according to the true spirit of cenobites. Let them be always together at reading and at work, so that if they cannot discourse with one another, they may at least by their presence be a mutual support and consolation.

Thirdly—It is necessary that the brethren should sometimes have conferences, but they ought to be public. Let them be considered as regular exercises, and not as diversions and recreations, and let them be seldom and holy. They ought to be holy in the subjects and manner of holding them, without which they will produce more evil than good. And as the end of such assemblies ought to be to encourage, to inspire zeal and fervor, to dispel the anxiety and weariness which are sometimes the effects of uninterrupted retirement, so the matters treated of ought to be affecting, selected from those passages of the fathers which are most lively, animated and impressive.

The manner of delivering them ought to be simple and modest, divested of all affectation and self-seeking, so that those who are the least qualified may speak without embarrassment or fear before those who possess greater parts, and that the same simplicity may serve as a veil under which learning and ignorance may be equally concealed. But above all, no points of doctrine, curious questions, or theological difficulties ought ever to be spoken of in such meetings, nothing being more calculated to stimulate pride, disturb the peace or their minds, and provoke disputes, than such conversations.

Those conferences ought to be seldom, for if they were held too often, besides being contrary to the exact silence of which we make profession, so great an abundance of truths and maxims would soon exhaust the spirits, produce disgust, and make them become insensible to those things they ought always hear with as much avidity and pleasure as if they were entirely new. But the superior must in a particular manner animate them with his words, support them by his reflections, and enhance the reflections of his brethren; and in allowing them an unrestrained liberty of speaking take particular care that nothing should be uttered unbecoming the quality of persons who meet only to sanctify one another, and who are persuaded that where two or three are assembled in the name of our Lord, according to His promise, He is always present with them (Matt 18:20).

I think what we have said is quite sufficient, my brethren, to corroborate the respect and esteem I am persuaded you have for silence. Be convinced, that solitude is to no purpose, and that there can be no solid piety, nor true regularity in monasteries without it; and indeed it would be vain to close the doors of your cloisters, if you do not also shut your mouths. Nor would you be less exposed amongst your brethren without this holy practice than in the midst of worldly people. Therefore I desire, my brethren, with Saint Peter Damian:

> That the temple of the Holy Spirit may be raised more and more within you, and that the spiritual virtues, like so many heavenly stones, may be formed by the hand of silence into a holy building, in which the Divine Spouse, the object of all your love and affections, may repose with pleasure as in his nuptial bed. [86]

In these reflections and principles you will find sufficient resource to solve every difficulty that may arise concerning solitude and silence. As for our own part, we think we shall have entirely satisfied the design we proposed when we shall have related what Saint Guigo, that great general of the Carthusians, says to his brethren at the end of his constitutions: "We have said but little to you, my brethren," says that great man,

> Concerning the advantages of the solitary life, because many saints whose wisdom and authority are so great that we are not worthy to walk in their paths have already announced its panegyric. Besides it would be useless to tell you what you know better than we ourselves, for you have learned my brethren, both in the old and new testaments, that it was not in the noise and tumult of the world, but in solitude that God revealed his secrets to his servants. When they sought either to meditate more profoundly, or to pray with more liberty, or to raise themselves more sublimely above all earthly things, they always sequestered themselves from the society of men, and employed the advantages of solitude.
>
> There we find Isaac forsaking his tents and walking alone in the fields to meditate, which undoubtedly was not an extraordinary thing in him, but rather a holy custom. There we find Jacob sending his flocks before

---

[86] S. Petrus Damianus, Epistola VI, PL 144:444 (1853).

him, while he remains behind, contemplating God face to face, receiving his benediction, changing his first name into another more noble and glorious, and obtaining more favors of God in one moment, being alone, than he had received all his life in the company of men (Gen 32:23).

The scripture informs us, my brethren, with what earnestness Moses, Elias, and Eliseus sought retirement; that there they were favored by God with the revelation of His mysteries and secrets; that they were always exposed to extreme dangers when they were in the world; and that God took particular pleasure in comforting them in retirement.

Jeremiah, as we have already observed, remained alone, because he was terrified with the menaces of the Lord. He requests to have water given to his head, and a fountain of tears to his eyes, that he might weep for the loss of his brethren. He seeks a dwelling in solitude so that he might apply himself more uninterruptedly to that holy employment (Jer 9:1), because it was not possible to obtain it in cities. By this he gives us to understand how great an obstacle the world is to the grace of tears. That prophet, after having said, "It is good to await in silence the salvation of God" (Lam 3:26), adds, "It is good for a man to have borne the yoke of the Lord from his youth" (Lam 3:27). This is a consolation for us who have taken up his yoke while we were almost all young. He says, in fine, the solitary shall live in silence and repose, because he is raised above himself (Lam 3:28). By the word repose, he means solitude and silence, and the desire of heavenly things. He points out that which is most excellent in our state. In the following he informs us, who the disciples are that are formed in this holy school, saying, "He shall not turn away his cheek from him who strikes, he shall be filled with reproaches" (Lam 3:30). The first points out an universal patience, the second a perfect humility.

Saint John Baptist, who, according to the testimony of our Lord, was the greatest amongst men, proves by his example the security and advantages which are found in solitude. Although, according to the same oracles, he was to be filled with the Holy Spirit from his birth; though he went before the Lord in the spirit and strength of Elias, to all which graces and favors may be added the sanctity of his parents, yet all this was not sufficient to keep him in the world. He fled from the company and conversation of men as being dangerous, and concealed himself in the deserts, as in an assured dwelling (Luke 1:15,17). Nor did he know either danger or death while he remained in solitude. The glory of having baptized Jesus Christ, and of dying for the cause of justice, evince the virtue and merit he had acquired in his solitude, for he attained to such an eminent degree of both that he was found worthy to baptize Him who came to baptize the whole

world in His adorable blood; and to crown the measure of his greatness, he suffered prison and death rather than forsake the cause of truth.

Jesus Christ, our Lord and our God, whose sanctity could neither receive increase nor suffer diminution from the communication of the world, was pleased for our example to prepare himself in solitude by fasting and temptations for the divine functions of preaching and miracles. The scripture informs us that He withdrew from His disciples to the mountains for the greater facility of prayer, and that He left them a little before His passion for the same purpose, to teach us how necessary retirement is for prayer, since he would not pray even in the company of His apostles (Matt 4 and elsewhere).

Consider, my brethren, what progress the holy fathers, Saints Anthony, Paul, Benedict, Hilarion, etc. made in solitude, and you shall be convinced that it is by the means of retirement we find such sweetness in the psalms, affection for the holy scriptures, fervor in prayer, elevation in contemplation, and the gift of tears.

Be not satisfied with the few examples we have adduced to prove the excellence of your state. Seek others in yourselves in the experience you have of things present, and in the holy scriptures, though such enquiries are not necessary because its rarity, and the few who are called to it, sufficiently recommend it. For, according to the word of our Lord, the way that leads to life is narrow, and is found only by few. And on the contrary, that which leads to death is broad, and is frequented by many. So true it is that amongst religious institutes the most holy and most excellent are those which are least followed; and those which are more eagerly embraced and more numerously supplied, are generally the less perfect.[87]

Such was the manner in which that perfect lover of silence and retirement spoke to his spiritual children in order to replenish them with his spirit, and to give them a holy abhorrence for such commerce and communications as are never lawful for persons who are no more of the world, unless when by reason of some extraordinary accident or circumstance they engage therein, by a manifest appointment of God.

---

[87] Guigo I, *Consuetudines*, PL 153:757 (1854).

18 | ON ABSTINENCE AND AUSTERE FOOD—CONTENTS:

Q. 1.—Did the saints consider abstinence and austere food as things important to the religious state? 121

Q. 2.—Do not those examples seem rather singular—should they be proposed as rules and models for whole communities and entire orders? 122

Q. 3.—Why do some persons understand, in the 25th chapter of Saint Basil's Constitutions, which you have already cited, the word salt-flesh, instead of salt-fish? 133

Q. 4.—May we not believe that Saint Benedict allows the use of fowl, since by his rule, he only prohibits the flesh of quadrupeds? 135

Q. 5.—By what means shall we know that our fathers lived in this great austerity, of which there remains no longer any mark in the order? 144

Q. 6.—By what reasons were the saints induced to live in the practice of such great austerities? 147

Q. 7.—Are the advantages arising from the use of legumes, vegetables, and other such like food, so very important, that we ought to become singular, and to deviate from the customs generally received in that respect? 152

Q. 8. — Are the same rules and food to be observed and used in the reception of strangers? 156

Q. 9. —*Is it necessary that the superior should keep his table with the visitors?* 160

Q. 10.—*But can a point of the rule so expressly enjoined by Saint Benedict be neglected?* 162

18

ON ABSTINENCE AND AUSTERE FOOD

QUESTION 1.—Did the saints consider abstinence and austere food as things important to the religious state?

ANSWER.—The esteem of the ancient solitaries for the mortification of the senses, may be easily gathered from the rules and instructions they have left, particularly those which regards eating and drinking. Though mortification when destitute of the interior dispositions which enhance its value before God is of little advantage, yet they were convinced that when animated with the spirit—which gives life and sanctity to all exterior practices—it forms a necessary part of what is required to advance the perfection of the monastic state. Of this they have given many illustrious proofs. The history of the Church is replete with relations of actions and examples which have been considered as prodigies of penance. In a word, there is no religious order but was formed and preserved in the school of rigorous austerity.

Recall to your memory, my brethren, that great number of religious souls who lived in monasteries as well as in solitudes, who to retrace the astonishing penance which our Lord practiced in the deserts, fasted whole weeks, and entire Lents. My intention here is not to excite you to imitate what is indeed inimitable; but to convince you that God has awarded great helps and annexed great benedictions to this kind of penance, otherwise He would never have inspired His greatest servants with the desire and will of practicing it.

We shall therefore indulge the reflections of a few moments on the example of Saint Macarius, who passed an entire Lent in Tabenna, without eating anything but a few leaves of cabbages, and that only once every

Sunday. Saint Anthony remained three days without food, and in the end interrupted his fast with a little bread, water and salt.

Saint Dorotheus lived sixty years in a cave, taking nothing each day but six ounces of bread, a small quantity of herbs, and a little water; and to those who reproached him with impropriety, in treating his body so severely at an age so far advanced, he replied, "I will kill it, because it seeks to kill me."

Saint Marcian, who was a man of great birth and honored in the emperor's court, retired into the desert, and lived there on four ounces of brown bread a day, which he never took until after sunset. His disciple, Saint Sabin, lived on a little flour steeped in water.

Saint Macedonius never ate during the space of forty years either bread or legumes; his food consisted of a little barley, broken and mixed with water.

The great Saint James, bishop of Nisibis, lived on such things as the earth spontaneously produced. Saint Abraham, bishop and solitary, lived in the same manner; Saints Sabas, Acepsimus, Publius, Apharatus observed a similar austerity; Saint Mary of Egypt had only three loaves to feed on for seventeen years; and during the remainder of her life, which was thirty more, she lived on the wild herbs and roots she found in the desert.

Saint Simeon fasted uninterruptedly thirty whole Lents. In fine, the example of an innumerable multitude of men might be adduced, whose resplendent merit and consummate sanctity demonstrate how acceptable such mortifications are to God. Those eminent saints and holy fathers used no other food than a few ounces of coarse dry bread, a few legumes steeped in water, and some wild fruit; of which they only allowed themselves a small quantity, after long abstinence and severe fasting.[88]

Q. 2.—Do not those examples seem rather singular- should they be proposed as rules and models for whole communities and entire orders?

A.—It is certain, that what is proposed as a rule for a great number of persons, ought not to be extreme; and that more discretion is required in a general system than in the means which may be adopted and allowed in particular cases. But however discreet the saints may have been when they founded the different religious institutes, it is a fact that they have invariably introduced a penance so exact into their particular codes that their conduct has been censured by many as being excessive, though in effect they did not depart from the rules of proper moderation and discretion.

Yet it must be allowed that if we compare what is performed at present in most orders with what the saints practiced, and with what was observed in the beginning of each institute, we shall find, that the greatest and most rigid austerities of our times are no more than the shades and figures of those which the saints observed, so that we might with all propriety address to you these words of the *Imitation of Christ:* "Consider the lively examples of the holy fathers, in whom true religion and perfection was most resplendent, and thou shalt see how little and almost nothing that is which we do."[89]

This is a truth which will appear evident if you consult monastic history and take notice how great the austerity of the ancient solitaries was, particularly in what regarded food, manual labor and poverty. I speak not only of those incarnate angels, who being raised above the wants of nature, appeared in the deserts like so many brilliant stars; but also of those fervent cenobites who lived in communities and regular congregations.

As there were different institutes in the higher Thebaid, the same kind of penance was not uniformly observed by the holy monks who inhabited that solitude. But history informs us that their austerity was everywhere so great that a little dry bread, some herbs, legumes, and fruit, were the ordinary food both of solitaries and monks.

All the disciples of Saint Anthony observed this rule of abstinence, that is to say, all Egypt, since he was the father of all the institutes which were founded in that country.

Saint Pacomius, being instructed by an angel, assembled in the monasteries of Tabenna twelve hundred monks whose food was nothing more than herbs and legumes, and during Lent, they ate nothing prepared by fire. Many others were formed who observed the same kind of life, so that this great saint became the guide of three thousand solitaries and monks.[90]

Saint Basil and Saint Gregory Nazianzen inform us that true solitaries never eat any food, but such as is dry and weak, rejecting all succulent aliments, and taking only what may serve to support nature. They tell us that they eat but once a day as prescribed by their rule, and were so reserved as to everything relating to the necessities of the body that their consciences never reproached them with anything on that subject.

---

[89] L. 1. c. 18.

[90] S. Basilius, *Constitutiones,* PG 31:1322 (1857).

Nor can it be doubted that legumes and herbs were the common and ordinary food of the eastern monks of their times, for the same saints expressly tell us in another place if at any time it happened that the small portion of salt fish which the holy fathers thought might be used instead of other food, was put in the water, or among the pulse prepared for the solitaries, particular care was taken to extract and remove it as if it were flesh, lest under the appearance of a vain and singular piety more delicate and better food should be introduced. However, they made no difficulty in steeping their bread in the water in which that small quantity of salt fish was boiled. This they received with thanksgiving, because as there was so great a measure of water and legumes, so far from their diet acquiring any delicate quality, on the contrary, it gave evidence of the greatest and most severe austerity of those monks.

Saint Basil confirms the same in one of his letters, where he says, "When we are in good health, bread and water may suffice; to which some pulse may be added, if the weakness of the body requires that indulgence."

Nothing more clearly evinces the wonderful austerity of the monks of Asia than what happened between Cassian and the holy abbot Moses. For the former appeared much surprised when the abbot told him that there were solitaries in Egypt who lived entirely on herbs, legumes, or fruit, without any other addition, and that others contented themselves with two little dry loaves, each of which scarcely weighed a half pound, without anything else whatever. At this the abbot Moses began to smile, for he considered even that excessive, and declared to him, that he could hardly use one of those loaves at a meal.

Saint John Chrysostom, speaking of the sanctity of the monks of his time, says that some eat only bread, others added a little salt, sometimes a little oil, and the sick contented themselves with herbs and pulse.

Saint Jerome bears the like testimony, and says in many parts of his works that monks lived only on bread, herbs and legumes prepared with salt alone, and that to eat anything dressed by fire was considered as sensuality amongst them.

We learn from Saint Evagrius's history that about the fifth century the austerity of the monasteries of Palestine was so great that they had no money either in general or particular. Their food consisted of herbs and legumes; their labors were so excessive that they seemed more like dead than living men. They frequently fasted two or three days, sometimes four or five, and never ate anything but merely to support nature. In the holy monastery seated on the banks of the Jordan, in which Saint Zosimus retired by divine inspiration, the solitaries ate nothing but bread and water.

Saint John Climacus, tells us, that though the sanctity of the monastic state was much enervated in his time, yet the austerity of the ancient fathers of the desert was still preserved.[91]

Saint Nilus enjoins, that the religious who are in good health should live on pulse, the sick on esculent plants, but he allowed the use of a little flesh meat to such as were more seriously ill.[92]

It is true that this was an extraordinary lenitive, which the eastern solitaries never used. Among the accusations formerly leveled by the Greeks against the Latins one of the principal was that Saint Benedict in his rule allowed the use of flesh meat to the religious who were sick. This reproach they would certainly not have made if the contrary had not prevailed amongst them. And Cardinal Humbert, legate at Constantinople, in his apology, would not have forgotten to tell them that they ought not to find fault with what they practice themselves. However, instead of saying anything of the kind, he contented himself with vindicating the conduct of Saint Benedict on that subject, as being directed by charity, discretion and wisdom; and reproaching the Greeks for their rigor and unjust complaints,[93] which evidently shows that they observed abstinence from flesh without any dispensation, and with an inflexible rigor.

Now if the austerity was so great in the east as to the type of food, it was no less so with regard to the time and manner of taking it. For it is certain that the ancient monks never ate but once a day, their fast was almost continual, and according to the general rule, they never interrupted it before noon.

Saint Basil positively says that a religious ought never eat but one meal a day. The holy abbot Theonas assures us, that the indulgence which the solitaries of Egypt and Thebaid allowed themselves in Easter time, merely consisted in changing the hour of their repast from none to that of sext, and that even then the quality and quantity of their food was still the same, for they feared lest they might lose during the Paschal solemnities that purity of body and soul they had acquired during the fasting time.

---

[91] *Scala*, PG 88:1014(1864). / *Ladder,* 197.52.

[92] S. Nilus Abbas, *Philoni Episcopo,* PG 179:275(1865).

[93] Humbertus, *Adversus Graecorum Calumnias,* PG 143:970 (1853).

The same thing is confirmed by Cassian, who says that the Saturdays, Sundays and festivals on which the brethren have two meals, no psalm was said at sitting down to table, or at the end of the meal, because such a repast is extraordinary; so much so, that even the brethren do not appear, unless some strange religious should come to the monastery, or that they were obliged to it by indisposition, or some other particular reasons.

Saint Athanasius, in his book of virginity, gives the following rule:

> Let your fast be uninterrupted through the whole year, though you are not obliged to it by any necessity. Having persevered in prayer and in the praises of God, take your meal at the hour of noon, and let it be composed of bread, pulse, and a little oil, and remember, that the things you make use of for your food ought to be simple, and of such aliment as never had life. That great saint would certainly never have proposed such injunctions to simple women, if it had not been the common use amongst those who were consecrated to the service of Jesus Christ, and made profession of leading a penitential life.[94]

We find the following words in the rule of the holy abbot Isaiah: Eat only once a day, and never to satiety.[95]

The austerity of the monastic solitary life was not confined to the east; and though it has been more recently known in the west, yet it was no less successful in gaining admittance amongst the religious of this part, amongst whom it made great progress.

The rule of Saint Benedict, which has been always considered in the west as the principal by reason of its extent and fecundity, prescribes an exact fast from the feast of the Exaltation of the Cross to Easter; it prohibits the use of flesh meat, except in time of sickness and great debility. [96]It says that all shall abstain from the use of flesh meat except those who are very ill and weak. And again, the use of meat may be allowed to those only who are really sick and weak, but when they are recovered they shall abstain from flesh in the usual manner.[97] This rule allows no more than two different

---

[94] Lib. De Virginibus.

[95] Reg. Art. 56. / St. Isaias Abbas, *Regula ad Monachos*. In S. Benedicti Aniani Opera Omnia. PL 103:432D (1851).

[96] *RB* 39.11.

[97] *RB*. 36.

sorts of dishes at meals, and though the terms in which it points out the kind of food the religious are to use may be interpreted many ways, there is much reason to induce us to understand them in the literal sense, and that the word *pulmentum* signifies dishes made of pulse, esculent herbs, vegetable soup, and things of the like nature.

For, in the first place, in all matters of ordinance and regulation, words are to be taken in their proper sense, and natural signification.

Secondly, nothing can be more conformable to the nature of an institute formed in the bosom of humiliation and abjection—whose professional title is that of extreme poverty—than simple and abject food that may be procured without labor or expense. Nor is it reasonable to imagine that Saint Benedict would have allowed any other kind of food more delicate or costly to poor men, who ought to live by the labor of their hands. "Then they shall be truly monks, if they live by the labor of their hands, as our fathers and the apostles have done."[98]

Thirdly, the saints who founded the order of Citeaux, and who proposed to observe Saint Benedict's rule, according to the letter, understood the word *pulmentum* in the sense of which we speak, as is evident from the life they led in the beginning of this order, and from their constitutions.

Saint Columban ordains in his rule that the brethren are to eat only in the afternoon, their food ought to be poor, and even in its use they ought to observe temperance. He says, that food ought to be used as a means to preserve our strength, but not as an incentive of sin to our souls; that for ordinary meals, pulse, herbs, soup, and a little bread, ought to be considered as sufficient.[99]

According to the Carthusians' primitive constitutions they fasted on all Mondays, Wednesdays, and Fridays, on bread and water with a little salt; on Tuesdays, Thursdays and Saturdays, they used pulse, or something of that nature, which each individual prepared for himself. On those days a little wine was given them, and on Thursdays a little cheese was added, or something better than on the other days[100].

From the middle of September till Easter, they ate only once a day; the

---

[98] *RB.* 48.

[99] S. Columbanus, caput III, In *Regula de Coenobialis,* PL 80:210(1850).

[100] Guigo I, *Consuetudines,* PL 153:705 (1854).

wine that was given them was never pure, and salt was the sole ingredient employed in the preparation of their food.[101]

On Sunday afternoons all the brethren received pulse, herbs and salt, and such other things from the servant of the kitchen; and after supper a measure of bread for the entire week was given to each, as to the poor of Jesus Christ. This is what we learn from Saint Guigo.[102]

Fish was allowed for the sick only, and for those recovering from grievous infirmities.[103]

The lay brethren fasted on bread and water every Friday throughout the year. From the beginning of November to Easter they only ate bread made of oatmeal; and during the time of Advent and Lent a measure of wheat bread was given them as an allowance.

The order of the Camaldoli was founded by Saint Romuald, and that of Vallis Umbrosa by Saint John Gaulbert, on the basis of an almost equal abstinence.

No extreme penance could exceed that of the religious of Grandmont. Saint Stephen, their founder, prohibited the use of flesh in their sickness as well as in health. He forbade them to possess anything beyond their enclosure, commanded them to lead a poor life, so that they might be able to find their subsistence in their desert and garden, assisted by a little alms. That great saint said to his brethren:

> We have begun to live in eremetical poverty by the grace of God; we must therefore endeavor to conclude in the same by the assistance of His mercy. He who enjoyed ease and pleasure in the world, would certainly be very foolish, if in embracing a poor religious state, he proposed to himself anything else but the practice of poverty. Did he not indulge himself long enough in the use of delicate food and soft clothing while in his former condition? But if he had been poor, with what justice can he seek that in the desert which was out of his power to enjoy when living in the world?[104]

Saint Aurelian in his rule forbids the use of flesh, and allows it only to the sick; he enjoins that the ordinary food of the brethren be only esculent

---

[101] Guigo I, *Consuetudines,* PL 153:733 (1854).

[102] Guigo I, *Consuetudines,* PL 153:551 (1854).

[103] Guigo I, *Consuetudines,* PL 153:715 (1854).

[104] Stephanus de Mureto, *Regula Ordinis Grandimontensis,* PL 204:1157C(1855)

herbs, prepared with oil or cheese; he allows the use of fish only on certain festivals, and when the abbot will grant it by way of indulgence.[105]

Saint Fructuosus enjoins, that the food of his religious, be always esculent herbs and pulse; and allows them very seldom a few little fish, which may be taken from the sea or rivers.[106]

The rule entitled *The Rule of Solitaries*, enjoins the use of herbs and pulse, it allows cheese and eggs sometimes, and regards as a banquet the use of a few small fish.

We read in the rule entitled *Regula Cujusdam*, that two dishes composed of herbs, pulse, or herb-soup, ought to suffice for the food of the religious, independently of the fruit that may be added thereto.[107]

Saint Elredus, in the rule he composed for some holy women, says, that they are to reject white bread and delicate food, as the bane of chastity; he allows them only one dish of pulse, herbs, or pottage, to which may be added a little oil, butter, milk or small fish, with plain garden roots or fruit.[108]

All these examples, though so interesting, will not affect you, my brethren, so sensibly as the remembrance of the austerities practiced by the holy founders of the Cistercian order. The plan of life laid down by our fathers at the birth of this great order will place the dreadful state in which you behold it at present in the clearest light; and 1 doubt not, that when you shall have considered the almost infinite distance that exists between the father and the children, you will exclaim with Saint Bernard, "Oh! the monks of those times, and those of our unhappy days." [109]What a difference!

Those saints proposed, as we have already said, the literal observance of Saint Benedict's rule. Such was their end, and they were influenced by divine inspiration. Therefore they rejected every interpretation and meaning by which the severity of that rule might be alleviated or its purity altered. This same austerity they transmitted to their successors, as an obligation to which they called the attention of their minds and hearts,

---

[105] S. Aurelianus, *Regula*, PL 68:393A (1847).

[106] Fructuosus Brancarensis Episcopus, *Regula Monachorum*, PL 87:1102 (1863)

[107] Cap. 20.

[108] Aelredus, in *De Vita Eremetica*, in *S. Augustin Opera Omnia*, PL 32:1456D (1845).

[109] O monachi et monachi! –In serm. de S. Bern.

and commanded them to persevere in the hard and narrow way pointed out by the rule, unto the last moment of life. Such is the express injunction of the charter of the foundation.[110]

Now in order that they might live in accord with this duty, they would allow themselves no other food than pulse, herbs, roots and pottage; the sauce for which was nothing better than salt and water.[111] Their bread was brown and coarse, they drank wine but very rarely, and it never appeared on their table without being previously mixed with water. On

---

[110] In arcta atque angusta via quam regula demonstrat usque ad exhalatioem spiritus desudent.- Exord. Cistere. / F. Bertrand Tissier, ed. *Bibliotheca Patrum Cisterciensium* (Bonofonte, Renesson, 1660) 1.

[111] a) S. Bernardus, Epistola I, Ad Robertum, PL 182:78 (1854). / Bernard, *Works*, 1: 115-116.

b) Fastredus, Epistola CDXCI, PL 182:705 (1854).

c) Stephanus Tornacensis, Epistola LXXI, Ad Robertum Potiniacensem monachum, PL 211:362-363.

Editor: Mabillon sums up these passages wonderfully: "It does not seem necessary to explain in this place how austere and rigorous was the life of the Religious of Cîteaux or Clairvaux under Bernard, since that is shown with the greatest exactness in the letters and writings of Bernard, as well as in his Life, especially in B. I. 5, in which the first inhabitants of Clairvaux are said to have served God 'in poorness of spirit, in hunger and thirst, in cold and nakedness, and in many watches; frequently they had no food except the leaves of the beech tree boiled, and bread made of barley, vetches, and millet.' Bernard himself in his Letter to Robert (n. I.) says that the delicacies of the Monks of Cîteaux were 'vegetables, beans, pottage, and coarse bread with water.' Fastred makes similar statements in his Letter, which may be read among those of Bernard. Stephen of Tournay declares (Letter 72) that 'so great is their frugality in food that they use only these two dishes—either beans or pulse from the field, cabbage or vegetables from the garden. As for fish they use it so rarely that scarcely more than the name of it is known among them.' Many more details are given by the same author and by Peter of Celles. This austerity of the Order was kept up not only to the end of the twelfth century, as appears from Peter of Blois (Letter 82), but even beyond the middle of the thirteenth, according to James de Vitry, who says of them: 'Meat they do not eat except in severe illness, and they commonly abstain even from the use of fish, eggs, milk, and cheese.' (Hist. Orient. et Occid. c. 13) We see the same severity of life revived even in our own day in France in the pious monks of Notre Dame de la Trappe, and in those who have imitated them, who by the purity and austerity of their life, by their love of solitude, their silence, their labor, and other religious virtues, show that to be possible in fact, which we read of, but scarcely believe, of Bernard and his disciples." J. Mabillon, ed. *Life and Works of Saint Bernard.* (trans. S.J. Eales; London: Burns &Oats, 1889), 1:32-33.

days of two meals their supper consisted only of plain vegetables, except during the harvest time. [112] Eggs and fish were seldom known amongst them, except for the sick. They fasted according to Saint Benedict's rule, from the Exaltation of the Holy Cross to Easter, and from Whitsuntide to the middle of September on all Wednesdays and Fridays. On all fasting days of the Church they abstained from milk, butter and cheese, which abstinence they likewise observed during Lent, Advent, and all Fridays throughout the year, except during the Paschal time. The first three Fridays of Lent they deprived themselves of one of the two ordinary dishes, and the three last they had nothing but bread and water: though their labors were extremely hard, and their night watchings very long. Yet so great was their love of Jesus Christ, that their penance was very agreeable to them, and they even found pleasure and satisfaction in their sufferings[113].

Q. 3.— Why do some persons understand, in the 25th chapter of Saint Basil's Constitutions, which you have already cited, the word salt-flesh, instead of salt-fish?

A.—Although I have no intention to give an instruction on grammar, yet this subject appears to me so important, and militates so forcibly against the austerities of the ancient solitaries, that I feel convinced how necessary a full elucidation of it must be. Therefore I shall endeavor to remove every doubt that may be formed on this subject. Allow me then to observe that those who undertook to give us the meaning of Saint Basil's expression were not sufficiently attentive to the extent of its signification. Hence, instead of translating salt fish, they made it salt flesh, which is evidently adverse to the sentiments of that saint.

First, the austerities practiced by the solitaries of his time were so great, that we can scarcely find an example in all history of any individual amongst them who would eat flesh. For they considered it as an aliment so estranged from the life they led, that they would never have suffered it to find place in their food. Moreover, Saint Basil was too great a lover of penance to give them an advice so very opposite to what they professed by

---

[112] *The Ancient Usages of the Cistercian Order* (*Ecclesiastica Officia*), (Carleton, Oregon: Guadalupe Translations 1998), Chapter 84.12-15.

[113] Julianus Paris, *Usus Antiquiores Ordinis Cisterciensis,* in *Onomasticon Cisterciense seu Antiquiores Ordinis Cisterciensis Constitutiones* (Paris, Alliot, 1664), 190.

telling them they might, without any difficulty, temper the coarseness of their bread in the broth wherein salt flesh had been boiled.

Secondly, what reasons can be adduced for giving an equivocal and even a forced meaning to this passage of Saint Basil, since it bears one so natural and clear? Why is it not rather said that it is only intended to inform those amongst the solitaries, who abstain from the use of fish, and who live on pulse, that if a small portion of salt fish were put into their ordinary food, they ought not to reject it, as if the whole fish had been served up to them. Rather, they might and ought to imbibe their bread with the soup in which the fish had been boiled, eat with thanksgiving and consider such conduct as really austere. For, in effect, if only a small portion of fish had been boiled in so great a quantity of water, herbs and legumes, it could not produce even the same effect as a little salt, that is to say, give it a relish, which the most rigid and austere solitaries would have never condemned.

The sentiments of a man who speaks or writes are known by the words he employs to explain himself. These words are to be understood according to their natural signification, preferably to any forced meaning that may be given them. Now as the words of Saint Basil precisely signify salt-fish, to infer from thence that he allowed the use of flesh-meat to solitaries, is an assertion entirely unfounded.

To prove this more clearly, observe that Saint Basil employed two Greek words on the subject in question, the one is ταριχοτον or Taricaton, the other τεμαχος or Temacos, and though the first may sometimes be applied to all sorts of things salted, nevertheless, its proper and natural signification is salt fish.

As to the other, it is so exclusively intended to signify salt fish, that the dictionary expressly says it cannot be understood to point out flesh.
We read in Favorinus Camertes, who is one of the best and most correct, that the word signifies a piece of salt fish, and not flesh.

The great dictionary of Tussanus, Robertas, Constantinus, Marcus, Happenus, expressly says the same thing, which is also seen in an exact Lexicon, printed by Griffin, in the year 1545, Edit. Par. in quarto.

Julius Pallun, in his *Omastican*, points out, in two different places, namely, in the ninth chapter of the sixth book, and in the eighth chapter of the seventh book, that the word τεμαχος signifies a piece of salt fish.

The Lexicon entitled *Lexicopater Etymon in variis doctissimorum hominum locubrationibus, per Joannem Choradamum*, explains the word τεμαχος as signifying a salted piece, but remarks that it is to be understood only of fish, and that great fish salted are called τεμαχιταν. The Lexicon of Scapula says, that τεμαχος signifies in a particular manner a piece of fish.

Aristophanus, in his comedy of the clouds, and in that of riches, employs the word τεμαχος to signify fish, and Scholiast proves, by some examples, that it only can be understood of fish, and can never be used to point out flesh.

Hence you see, my brethren, that Saint Basil spoke only of salt fish. His design was to inform the solitaries that if any such thing was put in their ordinary food, they ought not to be scandalized, but receive it with gratitude and thanksgiving. In a word, this opinion is not only accords with austerities practiced in the east, but no other can be reasonably deduced from these words of this holy doctor.

Q. 4.—May we not believe that Saint Benedict allows the use of fowl, since by his rule, he only prohibits the flesh of quadrupeds?

A.—That thought, my brethren, is not new, but it stands on no solid principle. We must reflect that Saint Benedict addresses his rule to men whom he leads to the exercise of a poor, austere, penitent and laborious state; to a painful life, such as that of poor country people, who are employed in agricultural pursuits. Thus, whether he allows or prohibits them the use of flesh in certain cases, and for certain necessities, he does it in a manner conformable to their state and condition. A physician who prescribes or forbids the use of flesh to a peasant, is far from proposing chicken, capon, partridge, pheasant, or such like dainties, because the use of such food is already sufficiently proscribed, by reason of his indigent condition being unable to procure anything of the kind; and because they have neither proportion nor connection with the poverty of his life. But the same difficulty does not exist with regard to the more common sort of flesh, because it being his ordinary food, he may allow or forbid him to use it as circumstances may require.

This is precisely what Saint Benedict does in his rule with much wisdom and discernment. For when he taught the necessity of abstinence to his disciples, or allowed them the use of flesh, he did not think it necessary to propose such different sorts as have little or no conformity with the state of persons consecrated to God in a life of poverty and penance, but in order to explain his intentions in a more proper and natural way, he spoke only of the coarser sort, signified by the term of quadrupeds.

In effect, it is not reasonable to think that Saint Benedict, when he laid the foundation of a penitential life, and proposed the salvation of souls as the end to which a perfect mortification of all sensuality was to serve as a principal means, would have allowed the use of delicate meats, which are so well qualified to produce an opposite- effect, and unhinge all the system he established with so much care; and that he would give his followers the liberty to live like worldly people in softness, delights, good cheer, and in the research of everything that might gratify their passions.

Saint Jerome, writing to Salvina, spoke in the same manner:

> Banish from your table, says he, all fowl, such as pheasants, turtle doves, and the like, which cannot be had without care and expense; and do not figure to yourself that you live in abstinence from flesh, by confining your meals to the more common sort, as pork, hare, venison, and other four footed beasts; for herein we ought not so much consider the number of the animal's feet as the pleasure and relish enjoyed in the use of it.[114]

The author of the book on the contemplative life, attributed to Saint Prosper, speaking to those who abstain from the flesh of quadrupeds, tells them, that if they use pheasants and other fowl, or even delicate fish, they do not renounce pleasure, but merely change the object. By this they evince that in abstaining from the common and coarser sort of meat, the delicacy of their appetites has more influence on them than the love of virtue; and they seek to gratify their sensuality more exquisitely, by indulging themselves with food more expensive and delicate.[115]

This is just what Saint Benedict had in view, as appears from the 36th and 39th chapters of his holy rule. These were his sentiments, and whoever attributes any other to him proves thereby that he never knew either his spirit or intentions. The use of flesh meat may be allowed to those who are entirely sick and weak for the re-establishment of their health, but when they are recovered they shall all abstain from it in the usual manner.

The eating of the flesh of four-footed animals shall not be allowed, except to those who are very sick and weak.[116] Here it ought to be remarked that though the Holy Legislator removes from the sick the use of such things as deserve the name of delicacies and vicious superfluities, yet by allowing them the use of the flesh of quadrupeds, he has abundantly provided for all their wants; for in the use of such aliments, the most

---

[114] S. Hieronymus, Epistola LXXIX, Ad Salvinam, PL 22:729 (1845)

enervated and debilitated constitutions may find sufficient means to sustain their weakness, and those who are in a state of convalescence, a nutritious auxiliary, well calculated to facilitate a perfect recovery.

Hence, the distinction which some have formed on this matter is quite futile. They say that the coarser sort of meat has been granted to those who are very ill for the purpose of making strengthening soups; and that those who were less indisposed might use fowl, in order to complete their recovery. However, such a difference cannot be deduced from any passage of Saint Benedict's rule, nor do I conceive why the same kind of flesh may not suffice for the latter as well as the former; and abstracting from the rule, it would be more according to good sense to give the more delicate food to those who are most sick, and the coarser to such as are more recovered.

The advocates of the contrary opinion plead for it under the protection of two authorities, which they esteem considerable. The first is that of Theodemar, abbot of Mount Cassino, who writing to the emperor Charlemagne, told him that fowl was used in his monastery during the octaves of Christmas and Easter; and that those who acted in this manner did nothing contrary to the rule of Saint Benedict.[117] The second is extracted from the assembly held at Aix-la-Chapelle.

That the above abbot did write in the aforesaid manner is a fact. He manifested what was done in his monastery, and endeavored to justify it, but the proofs he employs for that purpose are so weak that I think they will never produce conviction in the minds of those who will read them with attention. Give ear to his own words. *Our father*, says he, replenished with wisdom, spoke with so much prudence in his rule, concerning the use of fowl, so that those who would use that food on certain occasions, might thereby incur no guilt.[118] But Saint Benedict speaks nothing concerning it. We find not one word on the subject in all his rule. It is a mere imagination, foolishly attributing a thing to him, of which there is not the least reason to believe that he ever had the most distant notion.

If Theodemar pretends to infer this permission from the silence of the saint, we can reply that there are many things concerning which he has given no explication, and, which according to that mode of reasoning would become lawful or indifferent though they are entirely adverse to

---

[117] Theodamarus Abbas 12 Casinensis, ad Carolum magnu Imp. In *Chronicon Casinensis Leonis Marsicani* (Paris: Drovart, 1602) 799A.

[118] Epist. Theod. Ad Car. Mag.

his spirit and rule, and if admitted, would become subversive of its real principles, and ruin its organization.

As to the abbots who assembled at Aix-la-Chapelle; we must remember that they found the evil custom of eating fowl so generally established through the whole order of Saint Benedict, that they thought it more proper to stem the abuse thereof, and repair the disorder, than to attempt its entire abolition. Hence they ordered that during the feasts of Christmas and Easter fowl might be served up to the religious, on condition that they should not consider such a permission as an obligation; and that the abbot and brethren might abstain from it if they thought proper.

It is necessary to remark that the assembly of which we speak was not convened for the purpose of restoring the rule of Saint Benedict to its primitive dignity. This evidently appears from its dispensing the religious from the obligation of fasting on the principal festivals, and that their food should in future be prepared with ingredients extracted from meat. All of this was a softening of the austerity of the rule, and therefore an authority of that nature can prove nothing against the opinion we defend.

A third authority is subjoined to the two foregoing, namely, that of Saint Hildegarde. That holy woman was persuaded she had been directed in all she wrote on Saint Benedict's rule by a special and divine light. Nevertheless she affirmed in her writings that our holy legislator did not prohibit the use of fowl, while he forbade the flesh of quadrupeds, and thus he allowed the free eating of the more delicate sort. To this it is easy to reply that such a revelation is not authentic, and that we are not obliged to believe it, by any authority, or even by rational proofs. Add to this, that though councils and popes have borne advantageous testimonies to the lights and sentiments of that saint, yet we are not to believe that they intended to canonize precisely all that she wrote.

It is moreover said, that if we pretend to infer the prohibition of the use of fowl from the silence of Saint Benedict, who while he allows the use of other flesh, says nothing at all concerning this: we should also conclude that he prohibits flesh, because he says nothing concerning it; but such reasoning is inconclusive: for Saint Benedict's intention was not to add anything to the ancient monastic rules; but on the contrary, to moderate them. He could not be at all disposed to prohibit the use of flesh, which was never forbidden, though the custom was very seldom introduced. But the same thing cannot be said of such animals as live on the earth, as in the air, because monks at all times abstain from them. No infraction or dispensation of this general rule having ever been known in the east, as appears from the complaints made by the Greeks against Saint Benedict's rule on this article.

Hence, we may conclude that our holy legislator having intended to mitigate the rigor of the primitive rules, allowed the use of the coarser sorts of meat, in cases of necessity, proper to the state and condition of poor people and penitents, such as his disciples were to be; but left the law in all its force with regard to the more delicate and delicious kind, which, properly speaking, serves no other purpose than to indulge pleasure and flatter sense.

There is another objection which is frequently opposed to our opinion; but it proves as little as the former. It is extracted from a miracle which is said to have been performed in favor of Saint Columban, for being in pressing necessity, God sent him an innumerable multitude of birds, on which he and his brethren fed for the space of three days. To this alleged miracle, we may oppose another, more favorable to our position. It is related that Saint Goutier, who observed the rule of Saint Benedict, being at dinner with Stephen, king of Hungary; that prince earnestly pressed him to partake of an Indian hen, without attending to the constant opposition he made. But the saint finding himself impelled by the king's entreaties, and being determined not to violate his rule, addressed a fervent prayer to God, who was pleased to hear him, and in a moment the bird disappeared to the great astonishment of all who were present. Now it is clear, that Saint Goutier would not have resisted the king's earnest solicitations, nor would Almighty God have wrought a miracle to deliver him from the difficulty in which he found himself, if the rule allowed him to eat fowl.

But abstracting from this wonderful event, would it be just to destroy a practice so much authorized, and so constantly observed to the great edification of the Church, on the sole influence of an uncertain fact? And supposing the event to be true, we ought not to have any doubt, but in such a case, God would have informed Saint Columban that He dispensed him in the observance of his rule at that time; and that He required him to make use of the gifts He sent him, as He formerly did by these words, *Arise, kill and eat* (Acts 10:13). Teaching him thereby that things which He permits and sanctifies are no longer to be considered as unlawful and unclean. This is no more than a personal circumstance from which we can only infer, that God exempted Saint Columban on that occasion from the observance of the general law.

There are some who say that Saint Benedict could not have reasonably prohibited the use of fowl, since he allowed that of fish. For there is as much sensuality and delicacy found in eating those large fresh fish, such as turbot, salmon, etc. as of using fowl of whatever kind we suppose.

To this we may without difficulty reply, that though Saint Benedict allowed his disciples the use of fish, yet he never intended they should have those delicate large fish of the above sort, or such as suppose any considerable expense. On the contrary, he testifies in every passage that the food of his religious should consist of nothing more than herbs, pulse, pottage, or at most, of small common fish, *pisculos* according to the term we find in some ancient rules. [119]Nor would he have failed to condemn that superfluity and excess as being contrary to the poverty, simplicity and penance which he required of his followers, in the same manner as Saint Bernard formerly did when speaking of the luxury and high living of the monks of Cluny.

In a word, Saint Benedict found abstinence from flesh generally established. He derogated from it by his rule in allowing the sick to use the flesh of quadrupeds. No person can reasonably admit the idea that what he allowed ought not to be understood in a strictly literal sense, nor that what he did not expressly permit ought not to remain prohibited, as it formerly was. Hence, the permission he gives is a restriction, not an abolition of the law. It is a dispensation that can extend no farther than it expresses, unless a meaning be given to it which it has not, nor of which it is not, strictly speaking, susceptible.

It would be futile to object to some, that the solitaries in the monasteries of Panes used the feet and extremities of some animals; for we know that there are some that may be used on fasting days of obligation appointed by the Church, without violating the law of abstinence, such as otters, sea ducks, beavers, tortoises, and the like.

But if we desire to know what the spirit of Saint Benedict is in this particular, we cannot address ourselves to more enlightened masters than the holy founders of the Cistercian order. Like so many new Ezras, they were chosen by God to re-establish the rule of that great saint, which was then no longer observed, and to revive his true spirit. For that end they resolved to take it in a purely literal sense,[120] and to establish its observance

---

[119] Fructuosus, *Regula Monachorum,* PL 87:1102 (1863)

[120] Integre, pure, et ad litteram.

according to the true end of its institution, as we have before remarked. Therefore they rejected every meaning and explication which were not conformable to its purity. They began by renouncing the use of flesh granted by the assembly of Aix-la-Chapelle; they established a rigorous and unlimited abstinence from all flesh, without distinction of quadrupeds or fowl.

It is declared in the fourth chapter of the institutes, that none but those who are very sick and infirm shall be allowed the use of flesh within the enclosure of any monastery of the order. This permission is also extended to servants or tradesmen who work for hire in the monastery.[121] This is absolute, and admits of no distinction.

This statute has been frequently renewed on several occasions, and we find it forbidden elsewhere under the pain of corporal chastisement, to all and every person of the order, to eat flesh in any place out of the infirmary, though he should be commanded to do so by the bishop.[122] And it is moreover enjoined that no abbot on account of recent bleeding, or any such like pretext, shall presume to eat flesh, unless he is attacked with a real malady, or fit of sickness.[123] And this is also absolute.

We find a similar prohibition in another place. Behold here a summary of what it enjoins. Let the injunctions of the rule, relative to the use of flesh meat, be inviolably observed, namely, that no member of the order shall eat meat out of the infirmary, under pain of excommunication, to be incurred, *ipso facto,* or by the very act. If the offender be an officer, he shall be deposed, nor shall he be reinstated in any charge or employment without permission being first obtained of the general chapter for that purpose. If he be only a private religious, he shall be deprived of the religious habit during two months for every offence. This is still absolute.

There is also a constitution of Pope Benedict XII, who having been a religious of the Cistercian order was perfectly well acquainted with its true spirit and observances, for he drew up the constitution of which we speak,

---

[121] S. Rainardus, *Instituta Cap. Generalis Ordinis Cisterciensis*, PL 181:1730 (1854).

[122] Nulla persona ordinis nostri extra infirmatoria nostra carnes comedat etiam jussu alicujus episcopi vel prelati. Quod si fecerit, pro singulis vicibus quibus carnes comederit, tribus diebus sit in pane et aqua ; et hanc poenam praecipienti dicat.— Nomast. Cisterc. 1. par. Inst. dist. 13. c. 1.

[123] Nulla etiam Abbas pro minutione aut solatio, aut aliqua alia occasione, nisi sit aegrotus, carnes audeat manducare.—Ibid.

and proposed it as a remedy against the relaxations which were introduced. He speaks thus:

> Let no religious or abbot, in future, presume to eat meat out of the common infirmary, or any food prepared with ingredients of the like nature, contrary to what has been so long established in the order. We revoke entirely the permissions which some abbots pretend to have obtained of the see apostolic, to use flesh meat, as privileges that produce only scandal.[124]

After this he enjoins that every time a religious, whether of the choir or of the lay character, infringes the above ordinance by eating flesh meat, or any food prepared with it or partaking of it, of whatsoever sort it may be, he shall be condemned to fast on bread and water three days, and moreover that he be enjoined a penance, with the regular discipline; and if the abbot neglects to enforce these injunctions, he shall fast on bread and water, as if he himself had eaten flesh.[125]

All the authors of the time, who have spoken of penance, inform us that they abstained entirely from all kinds of flesh, as we have it from Orderic Vital.[126]

William of Malmsbury writes that meat was served only to the sick.[127]

Cardinal Vitry states the same thing.[128]

All these relations are general, no distinction of quality, nature or sort of flesh is found in them. And those men were raised up by God to renew Saint Benedict's order, and appear to have been directed by the inspiration of His Holy Spirit in this undertaking.

Remember, my brethren, that the opinion we condemn, rests neither on the foundation nor basis of truth. It stands on no authority, but rather on a few private irregularities, which have been from time to time introduced

---

[124] Benedictus XII, *Bullarum diplomatum et privilegiorum sanctorum Romanorum pontificum Taurinensis Editio,* Tomus IV (Augustae Taurinensis, 1859), 338.

[125] Tribus diebus pro qualibet carnium vel pulmentorum cum carnibus decoctorum comestione jejunare in pane et aqua teneatur.— *Nomast.* p. 601.

[126] Ordericus Vitalis, *Historia Ecclesiastica,* PL 188:641 (1855).

[127] Willelmus Malburiensis Monachi, De Gestis regum Anglorum, PL 179:1289 (1855)

[128] Jacobus de Vitriaco, (Jacques de Vitry), John Frederick Hinnebusch, Caput XIII, *De Cysterciensibus in The Historia Occidentalis of Jacques de Vitry* (Fribourg: The University Press, 1972), 112.

into this order, than which nothing is better qualified to establish and maintain relaxation and licentiousness. Moreover, it is doing an injury to our holy father Saint Benedict to believe him capable of introducing such strange effeminacy into the monastic state that was unknown before his time. Nothing in effect, can less agree with the testimony given to that great saint by Saint Gregory, when he characterizes him with the title of an excellent master of a very austere life.[129]

Behold here more than sufficient to decide the difficulty; and I think that no person will hesitate to affirm, how unreasonable it was to admit uncertain conjectures, and imaginary reasons, against so many preponderating testimonies

Q. 5—By what means shall we know that our fathers lived in this great austerity, of which there remains no longer any mark in the order ?

A.—You shall receive every information by consulting the statutes of the order, and the evidences attested by writers worthy of credit. Both have carefully handed down to us the portrait of the austerities practiced by those perfect religious.

We read in the epistle written by Saint Bernard to his nephew for the purpose of inducing him to leave the congregation of Cluny and return to Clairvaux, the house where he first made profession, a description of the life observed in that celebrated monastery. "He who is really hungry," says that great doctor,

> Wants no seasoning to induce him to eat, a little salt is sufficient.... Hunger gives a relish to such food as is insipid of itself.... Herbs, pulse, legumes and pottage are disgusting to a man who leads an idle life, but they are dainties to one who lives in exercise and labor. If you labor as much as your state enjoins, you will eat every sort of food with pleasure.[130]

Saint Bernard endeavored by this letter to recall his nephew to his first monastery. He represented to him in a faithful manner what was done in it, and was certainly no way disposed to make the austerities appear more severe than they really were.

---

[129] S. Gregorius Magnus, *In Primum Regum Expositiones*, PL 79:245 (1849).

[130] S. Bernardus, *Ad Robertum* PL 182:77/ *Letters of St. Bernard of Clairvaux*, trans. Bruno Scott James (Collegeville, Minn: Liturgical, 1998), 8.

18 | ON ABSTINENCE AND AUSTERE FOOD

William of Thierry, in his life of Saint Bernard, relates that the monks of Clairvaux frequently ate the leaves of beech trees, served up for dinner in the refectory. Their bread like that of the prophet was made of barley and millet, or vetches; it seemed rather composed of earth than of flour; and the barren desert which they endeavored to cultivate with their own hands scarcely produced anything. Their food in general was so very bad, that nothing but hunger and the love of Christ could give them a relish for it.

Stephen, Bishop of Tournay, writes that their frugality was so great that they were satisfied with two dishes which consisted of herbs collected in their garden, or legumes gathered in their fields. And as to fish it was no more seen on their tables than it was heard mentioned in their refectory.

Cardinal Vitry, who wrote more than a hundred and thirty years after the foundation of the order, says that in his time monks very seldom used fish, cheese, milk or eggs; and if they sometimes used them, they considered such food as extraordinary.

The same austerity is seen in a letter written by Saint Fastredus, the third abbot of Clairvaux, to an abbot of the order, who had strayed from the common practices.

"Is that the mode of life," said he,

> Taught us by our father and predecessor, Bernard, of happy memory? Is it thus that abbots and monks of our order lived, who have taught us that our food ought to be no other than oatmeal bread, boiled herbs without butter or oil, or beans, even on Easter day, and you should remember, that this or the like austerity is at present observed in every monastery through the whole order.[131]

It is enjoined by the ancient statutes, that no white bread is to be made unless for the sick or strangers. The bread of the community must be coarse, the flour having been passed through a sieve, if of wheat, and through a searce or fine sieve, if made of other corn.[132]

It is forbidden by many constitutions to use flesh meat, or to allow strangers to eat it within the monastery, under pain of excommunication, deposition and other severe punishments.[133]

The use of fish was also prohibited to the religious when traveling; the

---

[131] Fastredus, Epistola CDXCI, PL 182:705.

[132] Julianus Paris, Caput XIV, De Pane Quotidiano, *Nomasticon* 250.

[133] Paris, Distinctio XIII, De victum et Vestitus, *Nomasticon,* 350.

same thing was forbidden to the abbots and religious on their way to the general chapter.[134]

And we read of some abbots who were obliged to do penance for having given a little cheese to some of their brethren on a Friday.

Now it is easy to conclude from all these proofs that what we have advanced concerning the austerities of the Cistercian order is a real fact. The relaxation in which they live at present cannot induce us to form any doubts of the primitive penitential spirit which animated the institute in its earlier times.

About an hundred years after the foundation of this order, a new congregation sprung up, which is thought to have derived existence from the Cistercian order. Though it did not extend very far, yet it gave great edification to the Church. It was called the order of the Cabbage Valley. Those religious men lived in forests, they never ate flesh meat, were content with one dish of legumes, with bread and water, which was their only food from the Exaltation of the Holy Cross, to Easter, and they wore a hair shirt continually.

During the last century, the reformed barefoot Carmelites of Spain were organized on the plan of an austere code, little inferior to the mortifications practiced by the ancient fathers. We read that the first religious of that observance lived on nothing but herbs, which they gathered in the fields, indifferently, and without choice; those which grew in their gardens seemed too delicate for their use. The only precaution they observed to discover whether the plants were poisonous or not was to give some of them to the beasts before using them. Their drink was only water; if sometimes wine was given them as an alms, or served at table, no one ever tasted it, because they considered it as unnecessary and unfit to meet the poor aliments on which they lived.

Some of them passed entire Lents on bread and water, others mixed wormwood with their poor food, in order to make it more disagreeable, and some ate nothing but oats and straw, and refused themselves the comfort of a few drops of water when parched with extreme thirst.

Q. 6.—By what reasons were the saints induced to live in the practice of such great austerities?

A.—It would be more reasonable to ask, my brethren, what reasons

---

[134] Paris, Caput XXIII, De Piscibus non Comedendis, *Nomasticon*, 310.

could have induced their successors to dispense themselves in the observance of them. Scholars may indeed reject their master's opinions in things merely natural and human, because they may have attained to a greater degree of light and knowledge. But in things relating to God, which ought to be founded on, and directed by His holy and unerring spirit, it is undoubtedly a great presumption in private individuals, or even in the generality of them to stray from the sentiments of the saints who were His heralds and ministers, neglect their maxims, and annul what they established and labored to preserve with so much piety and solicitude.

Now as monastic institutions are truly the productions of grace, the effects of the Divine Mercy; and as those whom it pleased God to employ in founding them were nothing less than the ministers by whom He announced His will to us, ought it not appear strange that their conduct should be now reprobated, and their holy practices which were then, and are at present, the edification of the Church, should be considered as human and unprofitable inventions?

But to return to your question, I will tell you, first, that as the saints were animated with a lively faith and an ardent charity, as they lived in the love and desire of heavenly things, and continually held the portrait of eternal punishments and rewards before their eyes, so they were careful to live each day as we would desire to pass the last of our lives. Those words of our Lord, "Do penance for the kingdom of Heaven is at hand" (Acts 10:13), sounded always in their ears, and were laid up in their hearts. And as they knew that the same divine master teaches that nothing less than a violent and continual war against ourselves can secure us an entrance into the heavenly kingdom (John 11:12), so did they consider the mortification of their senses, the crucifixion of their flesh, and the finding out new means to afflict and torment themselves as one of their principal obligations.

Convinced that whatever they could suffer in this life bore no proportion to the glory with which their labors are to be crowned in Heaven, they were inflamed with the most ardent love for the cross, and their desire of suffering increased in proportion as they tasted the excellent fruits of that tree of life. Their own inability and the will of God only could restrain their unlimited desire of suffering. Such was the spirit which animated the saints who were raised up by God to be the fathers and founders of monastic orders. Their children and successors who inherited their piety and faith, as well as their houses and names, persevered in the same dispositions.

And it is certain that while monks continued to be saints, they always loved penance.

Secondly—The most lively sentiments of gratitude and love always animated those truly religious souls, whose only occupation on earth was to imitate their Divine Redeemer, and to unite themselves to Him by the bonds of the most tender charity. They considered that the sacred repose they enjoyed in solitude was the fruit of His labors and sorrows; that the desert produced such abundant graces and blessings for them only because He had watered it with his precious blood. Hence they sought with a holy impatience every occasion and means to give Him proofs of their love. Already they had immolated all earthly things by forsaking them, but that sacrifice appeared imperfect until they had also offered themselves on the same altar.

For that end they ardently embraced fastings, watchings, fatigues, and all other exercises of a laborious penitential life. They renounced all things as much as is possible in mortal flesh, and denied themselves with pleasure the use of those things which a love less inflamed than theirs would have judged necessary for the preservation of life. If they sometimes allowed themselves a little, they did so because they thought that doing otherwise would be contrary to the will of God. They used them therefore to prolong their sufferings, and yet, however great their austerities were, those incomparable men found always reasons to be dissatisfied with themselves.

The cross of Jesus Christ held out such powerful attractions, and they were inflamed with such ardent desires of being fastened thereto with their heavenly master so that they might follow Him in His sufferings, that considering as nothing the greatest austerities, they condemned as a soft and effeminate life what the rest of men considered as excessive penance.

Thirdly—Can anyone doubt, my brethren, that the saints, who having a perfect knowledge of the essence of the religious state, and being inspired with a full conviction of their duties, should not be thereby led to walk in hard and difficult ways, and to seek those conditions of life which are most austere? They knew that they were indebted to God not only for the graces they had received, and for the sins they had committed, but also for the sins of the entire world, for which they considered themselves obliged to do penance. Men regarded them as their intercessors, by whom the Divine Mercy would be induced to be propitious to their crimes; and their state obliged them to nothing less than to endeavor to reconcile Heaven with earth by unremitting labors, tears and austerities.

If they considered themselves, the sublime ideas they had of the excellence of their state, and of the majesty of God whom they had offended, made them discover that no fault they committed was so insignificant but that it deserved to be expiated by great punishments. If they turned their eyes to view the state of the world, they beheld such a general desolation, such a deluge of evils, and an almost universality of crimes, that their charity became inflamed. Their zeal raised them above all measure. Nothing appeared too severe and rigorous, provided it was possible, to which those divine men did not expose themselves, in order to bear down the weight of the iniquities of the world before God, and to avert the just and terrible effects of His indignation from a guilty people.

Hence, they undertook severe fastings and austerities for those who lived in sensuality and excess. They passed their nights in watching and prayer for those who spent them in pleasure and sloth. They observed strict silence for those who lost themselves in the affairs of the world, and who by an ill use of their tongues, inflicted mortal wounds on themselves and on others. They endured poverty and contempt for those who sought riches and honors. They gave themselves up to all kinds of fatigues, pains and rigors for those who abandoned themselves to their criminal passions and unlawful pleasures. In fine, those true adorers, following the example of Jesus Christ, offered up to God a host of penance for the sins of men, and honored His sanctity by acts of piety and religion, contrary to the crimes and disorders by which they saw it so generally dishonored.

Fourthly—Those holy religious men knew that the state wherein their vocation had engaged them, required a perfect purity of life, and that the end of their vocation was nothing less than consummate virtue. And as they were not ignorant that our best designs are opposed by nothing so forcibly as by our concupiscence, that there is nothing so elevated or strong but lies open to its attacks; that the most constant resolutions are shaken by its violence and obstinacy; and that it frequently succeeds in casting those souls into disorder and scandal who seem to be most secure from its effects, so they omitted nothing that might impede its motions and repress its sallies.

They left nothing unemployed to destroy or to enervate that law of their flesh, of which the apostle complains, so that it might not disturb or prevent the operations of grace. For that end they labored without ceasing, like that great apostle, to bring their bodies into subjection by austerities and mortification of the senses, and by depriving themselves of everything that might foment their disorder or inflame their passions. And as they well knew the inconstancy and malignity of the human heart, so they were convinced that religious could neither acquire nor preserve the sanctity of their state without keeping close within the narrow way, restraining nature by exact penance, combating its inclinations, and resisting its propensities with inflexible rigor and constancy.

In fine, my brethren, whatever way a religious turns his eyes, he shall find too many motives and considerations to induce him to embrace a penitential life. If he consider the severity of God's judgments, there is nothing that he will not undertake to redeem by a few momentary pains those evils that will never have an end. If he contemplate the Divine Mercy, he finds all his consolation in endeavoring to efface whatever might impede or prevent its happy effects. If he view the fund of misery from which no mortal condition can be exempt, he sighs over the long duration of his banishment, and bewails his misfortune at finding his soul so long a stranger in a foreign land (Ps 119:5).

Hence, he is animated to embrace with fervor all the holy austerities he can to the end that he may innocently accelerate his deliverance. If he ascend in spirit and behold Jesus Christ reigning in glory amidst the splendor of His saints, his soul is immediately in raptures by its inflamed desires, and he exclaims with the prophet, "Deliver my soul from its prison, bring my soul out of prison, that I may praise Thy name; the just wait for me, until Thou reward me" (Ps 141:8). And he feels happy in finding so many innocent means in his state, by which the obstacles which stand between him and his happiness may be more quickly removed.

Therefore, we ought not to be surprised, my brethren, if the saints in former times lived in an apparently excessive penance. But we ought rather be astonished to find that in these our days religious persons are found whose intellects are plunged in such a state of blindness, so that they can neither see nor understand that the life of a monk ought to be the life of an austere penitent, that is to say, of a man who being entirely dead to the world, has no longer any other affair or occupation here below, but that of fastening himself to the cross of Jesus Christ, and of giving himself up without reserve to every species of pains, sufferings and mortifications.

Q. 7.—Are the advantages arising from the use of legumes, vegetables, and other such like food, so very important, that we ought to become singular, and to deviate from the customs generally received in that respect?

A.—When the singularity by which we distinguish ourselves from the ways of other men leads us nearer to the conduct of the saints, then it cannot be censured or said to be improper, particularly when we do nothing more than we have learned of our fathers and the saints. Singularity may be blameable when it is the production of our own minds, but when it is the work of the Spirit of God, and when a man is not as other men because he is either more virtuous or more holy, it is unjust to condemn him for such a happiness.

It is certainly no small matter to be like the saint in the practice of virtue; but the merit of such a state is much enhanced by the contempt or censures of men, for austerity is a distinction and separation of that which is pure from that which is impure. For this reason Jesus Christ, being sent by His heavenly Father to sanctify the world, declared that He came to unsheathe the sword of division and separation: "Think ye that I am come to bring peace on earth? I tell you not, but separation. I came not to give peace, but the sword"(Luke 12:51; Mt 10:34) . . . .

But to come directly to your question, I will tell you, my brethren, in the first place, that one of the motives which ought to influence those who desire to embrace this rigorous abstinence should be the advantages and consolation that are found in following the example of the saints, and chiefly in the practice of that penance, so much recommended in every age of the Church, both by the rules those saints have left us, and by their shining examples, as we have already demonstrated by a chain of tradition down from the time of the great Saint Anthony. But I am convinced you will feel more respect and veneration for this holy abstinence when I shall have shown that it can be traced to more ancient times, and, that its origin is found even in the lives of the holy apostles.

Although Saint John, the precursor of Christ, did not live on legumes and vegetables, nevertheless he may be considered as the model of all those who make use of that sort of food; since he drank only water, and his ordinary food was no better than locusts and wild honey (Matt 3:4). He abstained from wine, flesh, eggs, fish and butter; and therefore, he first set the example of that austerity which those holy monks rigidly practiced. Saint Jerome says that his manner of life was the beginning of the monastic state, and the sanctification of the desert.[135]

---

[135] S. Hieronymus, Adversus Jovinianum, PL 23:309B(1845).

18| ON ABSTINENCE AND AUSTERE FOOD

Saint Peter, according to the testimony of Saint Gregory Nazianzen, usually lived on small round beans. [136]

We learn from Saint Clement of Alexandria, that Saint Matthew lived on fruit, herbs, and legumes. [137]

Hegesippus relates in Eusebius's history, that Saint James, the brother of our Lord, never drank wine or cider, nor did he eat anything that had life.

We read that the first Christians who assembled near Alexandria in the beginning of the Church, and who having been instructed and formed by the apostles, were directed by their spirit, maxims and sentiments, lived in retirement, and in a perfect disengagement from all earthly things; that their food was only a little bread and herbs; that some of them fasted six entire days without taking any nourishment; and that they never ate nor drank before sunset. [138]

Secondly—As this sort of food has nothing in it that can excite the passions, it is easy to observe the rules of exact temperance. Hence it may be said of those who use it that necessity, not pleasure, induces them to eat. However, it is difficult to defend ourselves against the effects of more substantial food, because, as Saint Bernard says, "It pleases the palate, and inflames concupiscence." [139]

Thirdly—Vegetables and legumes are found without expense, and cooked without much labor. The service of the community is not attended with those perplexing embarrassments, which is unavoidably the case when the food is more delicate, and its preparation more difficult. Thus Martha can fulfill the duties of her ministry without trouble or confusion,

---

[136] S. Gregorius Nazianzus, Oratio XIV, De Amore Pauperum, PG 35:858.

[137] S. Clemens Alexandrinus, Quomodo Circa Alimenta..., PG 8:406 (1857)

[138] Philo, De Vita Contemplativa / Editor: Ryan's translation of a note by de Rancé: "Some persons in those latter times said that this passage of Philo is to be understood of the Essenians but St. Ephiphanius, St. Jerome, Cassian, Sozomen, and many others attribute it to the Christians. And it is to be remarked that Saint Denis calls them monks, Theraputes, which is the term used by Philo."

[139] "Palatum quidem delectant, sed libidinem accendunt" Epistola Prima, Ad Robertum, PL 182:77b (1854). / "Wine and fine flour, mead and fat things fight for the body, not the soul. With broiled meats the flesh, not the soul, is made fat. Many brethren in Egypt long served God without using even fish. Pepper, ginger, cumin, sage, and a thousand kinds of things pickled, delight indeed the palate, but inflame the passions." Bernard, *Works*, 115.

and there will be no reason to address her in those reproachful words: "Martha thou art troubled about many things"(Luke 10:41).

Fourth—Simple nutriment contributes much to the purity of the body. It moderates the ardor of the flesh, and stems its irregularities. In it nature finds all that is necessary for its support, but nothing superfluous that may be an excitement to excess. And as it is more quickly digested, so the vapors which arise after the use of such food are more easily dispersed, the mind is more disengaged, and consequently its thoughts, prayers, meditations, and all its other functions are more pure, more rational, and more holy.

Fifth—The use of this food removes every occasion of murmuring and complaining. Many religious who are naturally discontented and dissatisfied find something to contemn in every sort of food that is given them, however diversified it may be. Their delicacy in this point is such that neither the earth nor the sea can scarcely produce anything to satisfy them, as Saint Bernard says. But if they are induced by the spirit of penance to live on pulse and herbs, it may be said that they have at once surmounted intemperance, or at least so enervated its strength that the temptations arising from that passion shall in future be very few, and very weak.

Sixth—A monastery wherein this abstinence is observed may with a small revenue support a numerous community. Regularity will be more exact, discipline more rigorous, and the religious will live in tranquility, which can never be the case when a few persons are charged with the direction of a great diversity of offices and employments. In such a community God will be better served, His benedictions will be more abundant, the faithful will behold more powerful examples of every virtue, and the whole Church will be more edified.

Seventh—When a community lives in an expensive manner, the superiors together with those whom they govern are afraid to increase the number of members. They proportion their numbers to the revenues of the house, and refuse admission to all except such as are capable of producing some temporal advantage. The receptions are thus directed by human prudence and temporal interests. But when once this holy frugality is adopted, it enables a community to admit all who present themselves properly disposed. No person is rejected, and monasteries become safe harbors whose ports are always open to all who arrive from the stormy sea of the world. After being saved from shipwreck by the hand of Divine Mercy, they are led into solitude by the impulse of the Holy Spirit.

Eighth—Religious persons who live in the same manner as the poor, are always rich. Placed by their poverty in a state of real affluence, they want nothing. They deprive themselves of all superfluities and confine themselves to the use of simple necessaries. Thus they are enabled to communicate to the poor, whom they consider as their brethren in Christ, a part of the goods they have received of Divine Providence. And as their hands are always open to relieve the wants of those who are in distress, so God fills them with benedictions, and never closes His eyes on their particular necessities.

In fine, it is a means to avoid that dangerous rock, against which many who retire into the religious state unfortunately split, namely, that of discovering the secret of forming to themselves a soft, easy and sensual life in a state whose essential character should be composed of crosses, mortifications, and penance.

I feel convinced, my brethren, that you will subscribe to the justice and solidity of these reflections.

You will not only conclude that those who hear them attentively, who open their hearts to the truths they propose, and who follow in practice what they inculcate are guided in their choice by good reason; but also, that you will be astonished why those truths do not make the same impression on all persons consecrated to God in the religious state. Is it not really surprising that such forcible motives do not animate them; and that being obliged to perfection, they neglect means and practices so well calculated to assist them in acquiring it, practices, I say, which are recommended by the examples of the apostles, by the rules of the primitive holy solitaries, and by the whole line of monastic tradition?

Q. 8.—Are the same rules and food to be observed and used in the reception of strangers?

A.—Saint Basil says that religious persons ought to be very careful not to follow the example of worldly people, who being ashamed of the abjection which accompanies a life of poverty, endeavor to treat their visitors in a magnificent and sumptuous manner. "What have we to do with such ostentation?" says that great saint. A stranger comes to visit you, if he be a religious man of the same profession, he ought to find his accustomed fare in your house. If he be weary and fatigued, he ought to receive such refreshment as his case may require. If he be a man of the world, he ought to learn by your conduct what the spirit of the world cannot teach him, and he should find in our frugality the rule and measure to be observed in the use of food. Here he ought to find a just model of the Christian's table, and be informed, that he who endures privation, pain and labor for the love of Christ, knows not what it is to blush. In a word, if instead of being edified and affected with what he shall have seen, he turns them into so many subjects of scoffing and raillery, he will not importune us a second time.

Hear Saint Ephrem's sentiment on this subject: "If a solitary, or a secular come to visit you," says he,

> Treat him in no manner above your means or abilities, lest after his departure you may be obliged to complain to your brethren how much his visit shall have cost you; entertain him with what you have received of the divine bounty; for better is a repast of herbs, where joy is, than fattened victims and sadness therewith.

We read in the first constitutions of the Carthusians, that they admitted the persons only who came to visit them, but not their attendants; and that they gave no other food, nor other beds, but such as they reposed on themselves.[140]

Saint Benedict, who orders that the superior should always eat with the visitors, and requires for that purpose that there should be no separate kitchen for them, does not allow them any other food but that of the community. This is what the first religious of Citeaux, who were animated with his spirit, constantly observed. Their first constitutions, called the book of the *Usages*,[141] inform us that the brother who was appointed cook of the abbot's kitchen was to go into the garden after the office of prime, and there gather a sufficient quantity of legumes for the abbot and strangers, who may have come to the monastery.[142]

But nothing can better demonstrate how exact they were in this point than what passed at Clairvaux when Pope Innocent II came to visit that house. He was received by the monks in a manner so simple, and so religious, that his suite were no less surprised than edified. The bread, according to the author of Saint Bernard's life, instead of being made with pure white flour, was mixed, and the wine was also adulterated; vegetables

---

[140] Guigo I, *Consuetudines*, PL 153:671 (1854).

[141] *Usus Antiquiores Ordinis Cisterciensis* in *Nomasticon Cisterciense seu Antiquiores Ordinis Cisterciensis Constitutiones* (Paris, Alliot, 1664)./ *The Ancient Usages of the Cistercian order* (Ecclesiastica Officia), (Lafayette, OR:Guadalupe Translations, 1998).

[142] *Usus Antiquiores*, 227

appeared on the table in place of turbot, and legumes were served up at every course. A dish of fish by some chance was found and laid before his Holiness, more for the purpose of being seen by the assembly than of being eaten.

Nevertheless, those holy religious did not treat their visitors according to all the rigor of the common rules, for we find by their first statutes that the bread which was served to the strangers was white like that given to the sick. But whatever the mode observed in the reception of visitors might have been, they were careful that charity should never do any injury to regularity. Every part of their lives evinced their spirit of penance, and the whole tenor of their conduct affords us as great a subject of edification as does the simplicity of their table.

Hence, we must observe, my brethren, that although something of the regular austerity may be diminished in favor of strangers, and though we are to condescend to a more gentle observance in the entertainment of those who visit us than what we allow ourselves, since both charity and the example of the saints inculcate and require it, yet we ought to be guided in the practice of this indulgence by exact rules. And we need be convinced that there is no time, no circumstance, nor occasion in which monks ought not to remember how much they are bound to depart from the custom and manners of the world, according to this great maxim of Saint Benedict: "Monks should be entire strangers to the ways and customs of worldlings."[143]

But now, unfortunately, there is a strange subversion of order. Formerly the great ones of the world, princes and emperors, found the condemnation of their profusion and voluptuousness in the temperance and sobriety of monks, whereas in these our times worldly people find in the abundance of the claustral table a sufficient pretext to authorize their sensuality and love of pleasure. This is an evil which Pope Clement VIII endeavored to remove when he enjoined in a decretal that if any person of distinction should come to visit monasteries, whether from a motive of piety, or from any other, they should be allowed to dine in the refectory and be served only with the common food; and that the religious should conduct themselves on such occasions with so much propriety that religious sobriety and poverty might appear in all their simple and amiable attractions.

Now if monks were really impressed with the fear of God, and did

---

[143] RB 4.

but duly consider how many injustices they at once commit every time they depart from the true rules of conduct as to this particular, I think that the dictates of their own consciences would be sufficient to keep them within the bounds of duty. For, first, they change their monasteries, which, according to Saint John Chrysostom are houses of tears and mourning, into houses of joy and diversion, and instead of edifying the people of the world, as they are obliged, they become an occasion of scandal to them.

Secondly—They dishonor their state, and entirely efface its character of penance, which is its luster and principal ornament.

Thirdly—Impeded by the sense of their own excesses, they cannot reprehend those of others.

Fourth—They disturb the repose of their brethren, and as Saint Basil says, it is not necessary to ask who they are that come to the monastery when the visitors are persons of distinction, because the whole house is in commotion and agitation by reason of the diligent preparations which all are making to prevent the least defect in the food with which they are to be entertained.[144]

Fifth—Good cheer is an allurement to persons that love pleasure. Then conversation is indulged without restraint; and whatever good order may be prescribed, the precept of the apostle is seldom observed: "If anyone speak, let it be in a manner worthy of God" (1 Pet 4:11).

Sixth—The suffering members of Christ are deprived of the assistance to which they have a lawful claim, when that which is expended in one repast to please the rich ones of the world and to gain their esteem, might suffice to maintain two hundred persons. We ought to remember that to be generous to the indigent is to us a strict obligation, for as the prophet says, "The alms which are laid up in the bosom of the poor is the true seed of eternal justice" (Ps 111:9).

And now, my brethren, I feel convinced that we cannot give you better advice at the close of all these different reflections than that of following what Saint Basil teaches as a constant rule of conduct. He says that the end we ought to propose to ourselves in entertaining strangers ought to be the relief of their wants, and not the gratifying their passions. Nevertheless, at the same time, we may in general prepare for their use whatever may be provided without expense. Still it is necessary even in such cases to consider the dispositions and wants of the persons who are to be served, so

---

[144] S. Basilius, *Fusius,* PG 31:970 (1857).

that the more solid food may be given to those who are more fatigued, and that which is more delicate and of easy digestion to the sick. But, above all, care should be taken that everything be done with cleanliness, propriety and good order.

He adds, we have no money, well then, fortunately, let us not have any. Our granaries are without corn, what matter, since we live by the labor of our hands, and only for a day. And why should we foolishly waste the food given us by God for the wants of the poor, for no other purpose but to gratify the pleasures of voluptuous men?

As for our parts, my brethren, I will say that since, at present, religious persons have sufficient incomes and they no longer live by the labor of their hands, their possessions are for that reason more properly consecrated to pious uses, and hence they ought to be employed in a holy manner. And I will add that they cannot without sacrilege either dissipate or employ in superfluities those goods which the Church has at all times considered as the patrimony of the poor, the offerings of the faithful, and the ransom of the crimes of sinners.

Q. 9.—Is it necessary that the superior should keep his table with the visitors?

A.—Saint Benedict enjoins in his rule that the abbot's table should be always that of the visitors, as we have already said; and he has been induced to prescribe that form of practicing hospitality for many reasons.

First—Because the superior living in penance, to which he is obliged by his state, and consequently using only the common regular food, the strangers who come to the monastery cannot be the cause of much expense.

Secondly—Those who amongst strangers observe that sobriety in which a true Christian ought to live, shall find in the superior's table, an example by which they shall be confirmed in their good purposes; and those, on the contrary, who live sumptuously, shall find in the same the condemnation of their excess.

Thirdly—The presence of a superior will command respect, and prevent everything that might be contrary to that good and edifying conduct which ought to be observed in a religious house. And if, as Saint Benedict says, he ought to consider Jesus Christ in the persons of his visitors, they on their side, should consider Jesus Christ in him.

But, after all, though this practice was good and pious in the beginning, it has not been so in progress of time. For superiors, finding themselves out of the regularity of the cloister, and being no longer restrained by the presence of the community, or by the obligation of giving their brethren good example, allowed themselves many liberties which they would have never taken in their presence. They followed the impulses of a false charity, or rather the dictates of real cupidity, which bid them to entertain their visitors in a manner entirely opposite to the simplicity of their condition and the purity of their state.

This disorder produced a great many others. Superiors accustomed themselves to good living and lost the spirit of penance. Their unrestrained conduct being public, this in time destroyed their reputation and made them contemptible. Instead of inspiring reservedness, they on the contrary gave the example of licentiousness. Strangers no longer found any instruction in these repasts, as they formerly did when charity, penance and frugality made up their principal ingredients.

Entertaining topics were introduced, news and worldly affairs composed the whole subject of conversation, and edifying discourses were entirely banished. The example of the fathers was followed by their children. The former communicated their disorder to the latter, and this was followed by the extinction of piety, the destruction of religious houses, and the ruin of the goods which were destined to be the relief and comfort of the poor.

Q. 10.—But can a point of the rule so expressly enjoined by Saint Benedict be neglected?

A.—It not only can, but ought to be neglected. When the constitutions which have been made by the saints for the edification of the Church, the maintenance, the discipline and the preservation of morals produce opposite effects, they lose their authority. They are no longer to be attended to, and no reasonable doubt can be entertained concerning the lawfulness of forsaking the letter of the rules in all such cases, when it is incompatible with the spirit. Do not think, my brethren, that this is my own individual opinion, for many great men and eminent saints were of the same sentiments.

The assembly held at Aix-la-Chapelle, forbids both abbots and religious to eat with their visitors; it also enjoins that they be received and treated with all possible civility and charity in the common refectory.
Give ear to what Saint Peter Damien says on this subject: "It is true," says he,

> That the rule places the abbot's table with the pilgrims and strangers; and because there are some superiors, whose piety and devotion will not allow

them to observe the injunction for the purpose of suppressing disorders and removing those licentious dissolute repasts, you seek to depose and expel them from the places they fill, though they do nothing more than exactly comply with the intention of their holy legislator, without attending to the exterior of words. Nourishing their souls with the vital spirit that gives life, they tread under foot the straw of the letter that produces death. [145]

Saint Peter, abbot of Cluny, says almost the same thing. He, when speaking of superiors, says that while they drink pure waters, they present nothing but such as is troubled and filthy to the holy flock of Jesus Christ.[146] That is to say, while they are extremely careful of themselves, they neglect others. And because they have perverted the exercise of a precept which is good in itself, and thereby inflicted new wounds, it is necessary to bind themselves up with a new salve, and to change a rule which was formerly useful into another which is now more profitable. Therefore, in order to destroy by virtue a vice that springs from virtue itself—as it was the rule that drew them from the refectory to place them at the visitor's table—so we must employ right reason and charity to lead them back from thence to the refectory amongst their brethren.[147]

The religious of the order of Camaldoli maintain that Saint Benedict only gives the abbot a simple permission to eat with the strangers, and not a command, that it is not in any manner unreasonable to change such a point, since the same reasons which dictated it no longer exist, and that the fathers oblige the abbot as much as possible to eat with his brethren at the common table.

Saint Dunstan says that it was not contempt for the rule which induced our fathers to change this point, but the salvation of souls. This was the motive which led them to ordain by a synodical decree—which is at present exactly observed—that no abbot or religious should eat or drink anything out of the refectory, except in cases of sickness or infirmity.

Our Cistercian fathers, who undertook the most exact literal observance of Saint Benedict's rule, re-established this ancient practice. Though they took every precaution to prevent abuses, enjoining that legumes should be

---

[145] S. Petrus Damianus, *Probatio Ad Religionem...*, PL 145:378C(1853).

[146] Petrus Venerabilis, *Epistolarum Libri Sex,* PL 189:66 (1854).

[147] S. Petrus, Epistolarum, PL 189:133C (1854).

served up and should be common both to the abbot and to the strangers, yet their precaution with some was futile, as appears by a letter of Saint Fastredus, the third abbot of Clairvaux, to an abbot of that order who had abandoned its penance and discipline. "I have been informed," says he,

> By a person who has as much compassion for the maladies of your soul as you yourself have for those of your body, that you have completely effaced from your memory the obligation of living according to your rule, and of edifying your religious by your example; that you have separated yourself from the common table, ordering your food to be served up in the stranger's apartment even when there are no visitors in the monastery, for the purpose of having a more undisturbed opportunity of satisfying your appetite, and of gratifying your senses; and all this without being intimidated by the fear of the punishments with which the Lord menaces those who seek the consolations of this life, in the criminal indulgence of the senses. You are much more solicitous to imitate in your clothing and furniture, the magnificence of the rich man, than the poverty of Lazarus....
>
> If you are an abbot, and consequently the rule and model of those who are under your charge, how is it possible that you can order delicious food and delicate fish to be prepared and seasoned in a peculiar manner, and to be served up on your table with bread, made by women who live at a distance from the monastery.[148]

These and many such evils will always happen as long as superiors will allow themselves the liberty to withdraw from the common life, make no difficulty in having a particular table for themselves, and associate with their visitors in their repast. The reasons which are adduced against those undeniable facts are so weak that they deserve not to be refuted. In a word, if Saint Benedict lived at present and saw to what a pitch his intentions have been frustrated, he would change, not his spirit, but his opinion; and he would prohibit every intercourse of this nature between abbots and strangers in all succeeding times.

---

[148] Fastredus, Epistola CDXCI, PL 182:704.

19 | ON MANUAL LABOR—CONTENTS:

Q. 1.— Ought manual labor be numbered amongst the principal duties of monastic life? 167

Q. 2.— What induced the ancient solitaries to recommend manual labor so earnestly, and to make it one of their principal exercises? 182

Q. 3.— What answer can be made to those who say, that manual labor was necessary for monks, only while they were poor; but that it is at present quite useless, because the charity of the faithful has given them sufficient revenues, and provided for all their wants? 189

Q. 4.— Would it not be more useful for religious persons to employ their time in reading? 190

Q. 5.— Is there not reason to fear, that if religious persons do not study, they will fall Into gross ignorance, and from that into disorder? 191

Q. 6.—Shall not those religious who do not apply themselves to study be considered as persons useless to society? 197

Q. 7.—Are not religious persons to be considered sufficiently exempt from manual labor, when they apply themselves to the instruction of souls? 202

Q. 8.—Is it proper for religious to dispense with themselves *in point of manual labor, to the end, that they may have more time for prayer, and thus lead more interior and spiritual lives?* 202

Q. 9.—*May it not be said that manual labor was formerly a convenient employment far monks, when they were generally lay men; but that it can no longer be considered as such, since, they are now almost raised to the dignity of the priesthood?* 205

Q. 10.— *What are the works in which, religious persons ought to be employed?* 208

19

ON MANUAL LABOR

Question 1.—Ought manual labor be numbered amongst the principal duties of the monastic life?

Answer—There is no penitential exercise, my brethren, that has been more recommended or more practiced by monks than manual labor. It has been so universally esteemed necessary, that almost every regular congregation has enjoined it, and all the ancient inhabitants of the desert ranked it amongst the number of their principal obligations. But it is at present so universally abolished that there is scarcely the least trace of it preserved in many regular congregations. And some have succeeded in completely rejecting and despising it altogether, however commendable its utility. I have before remarked that its source is founded in the laborious life of Jesus Christ. It is justified, moreover, by the example of the apostles, the general suffrage of the doctors of the Church, and almost all the rules of the saints.

Now, as you naturally expect some proofs of what I here advance, I will tell you, my brethren, that the labors of our Lord cannot be unknown by any person, since the holy scriptures represent Him—during the whole time from the beginning of His public life to His death—going from province to province, and from city to city, day and night, on missions and journeys without intermission; and that he sometimes took rest, when wearied and fatigued.

As to the time He spent in His hidden life, before He began the functions of his ministry, there is every reason to believe that He employed it in the exercise of His reputed father's trade.

For, first, we find that the Jews, reproaching Him with his base extraction, called Him the carpenter and the son of a carpenter, undoubtedly because they had seen Him at work in the house, and at His supposed father's trade (Mark 6:3; Matt 13:55).

Secondly—Some of the fathers of the Church were of this opinion. Saint Justin says that while Jesus Christ conversed amongst men, He worked at making ploughs and yokes for oxen, teaching us by His example to live according to justice and to fly idleness. Saint Justin learned this opinion by tradition, and it seems credible, as he lived near the times of the apostles.[149]

Saint Basil says that as the parents of Jesus were poor, which appears from the place of His birth, and as they lived in piety and justice, so it is very probable that they lived by the labor of their hands; and that He gave them proofs of that subjection—which the scripture says He paid to them—by taking part in their labors, and in endeavoring to assist them in their wants.

Thirdly—As Jesus Christ was pleased to appear in the world under the form of a sinner, so it may be supposed that He was also pleased to bear the whole weight of our iniquity, and to take upon Him all the punishments of sin. As one of the principal and most humiliating is that of being condemned to labor, so there can be no reason why He would exempt Himself from it, particularly as He was born of a poor mother (Ps 87:16). Consequently He was, by choice, under a kind of necessity of reducing to practice the obligation which God imposed on all men, and of literally accomplishing that irrevocable sentence, "Thou shalt eat thy bread in the sweat of thy brow," etc (Gen 3:19).

This seems to be what the prophet would give us to understand by these words: "I am poor, and in labors from my youth" (Zech 13:5). Nothing, then, was more suitable to the poverty of Jesus Christ, nor more worthy of His charity, than to labor for His own subsistence and for that of His parents so that He might not be a burden to anyone; and moreover, to justify and sanctify manual labor, and thus to make it become commendable to His true followers.

Many great men of latter times have adopted this opinion. Cardinal Baronius, finding that Saint Epiphanius allows Saint Joseph to have been about eighty years old when he espoused the Blessed Virgin, infers that the Lord must have assisted his extreme old age by His application to manual labor.

---

[149] Justin, *Dialogus cum Tryphone Judaeo* PG 6:472.

Cajetan says, that Jesus Christ, during His private life until His baptism, worked at the carpenters' trade.

Denis the Carthusian, Estius, and many others say the same; and hence we may confidently say, that it is the most commonly received opinion.

As to the apostles, they worked with their hands, and amidst their multiplied solicitudes and uninterrupted application both for extending and governing the Church, they employed considerable time in manual labor; for so Saint Paul testifies of himself when writing to the Thessalonians, he tells them:

> You know, brethren, what pains we have taken and fatigues we have endured; and that while we preached the gospel to you, we labored with our hands also day and night, to the end that we might not be a burden to anyone (1 Thess 2:9).

The same thing may be said of Saint Barnabus, Saint Timothy, Saint Luke, Saint Silas, and Saint Silvan, since, having accompanied Saint Paul in his apostolic missions, there is no reason to doubt but that they imitated him as their master, and took part in all his pains. Cassian takes notice that the labor of this great apostle was hard, painful and fatiguing, and not merely a simple change of exercise to unbend his mind after the weariness he endured in his evangelizing ministry.

Saint Clement recommends labor both by the example of the apostles and by his own: "We who are employed in announcing the word," says he, "fail not to set apart some hours for manual labor, for some amongst us employ themselves in fishing, others in making tents and pavilions, and some in cultivating the earth."

Saint Gregory says that Saint Peter might have resumed his usual occupation after his conversion, namely, that of fishing, because it is an innocent employment.

Saint Isidore, in his rule, enjoins work, in imitation of the apostles.[150]

As to the fathers of the Church, all those amongst them who have spoken on this subject were of the same sentiments. They have also unanimously declared that monks are obliged to work, and that nothing is more suitable to their state than manual labor.

Saint Gregory of Nazianzen and Saint Basil require that the work which monks undertake should not oblige them to go out of their monasteries, so that they may not lose their repose and tranquility. Nevertheless they say, that if some pressing necessity forces them to labor in the open fields, that ought not to impede the holy philosophy of which they make profession. For an exact solitary, say they, who considers his body as the depository of his thoughts, and who governs the motions and actions of his soul, whether he be in the markets, public places, or assemblies, or on the mountains, plains, or in the midst of the world, he ought to be always enclosed in himself as in a monastery which nature has given him, and meditate on such things only as are worthy of the excellence of his state.[151]

They say elsewhere that a religious ought to employ himself in the lowest and vilest occupations with much zeal and fervor, knowing that whatever he does for God ought not to be considered small, but, on the contrary, that everything is great, spiritual, and worthy of eternity, and shall procure us infinite rewards when performed for God.[152]

Saint Basil teaches, from the words of Jesus Christ and the example of the apostles, that monks ought to work; and that we ought not to infer from our resolutions of leading a holy life that we may reasonably avoid labor and live in idleness. For, on the contrary, that consideration ought to be a motive to make us undertake the most painful labors, and the most difficult employments, in order that we may be able to say with the apostle: "I have served the Lord in labors, in fastings, and in watchings" (2 Cor 6:5).

"Be always employed," " says Saint Jerome, "that the devil may never find you idle. If the apostles who might have lived by the preaching of the gospel, labored with their hands, so that they might not be a burden on anyone, why do you not provide for your own wants?" He adds that the monasteries of Egypt admitted no religious without first obliging him to manual labor, not only on account of their poverty, but also for their salvation. "We must labor," says the same saint, "lest our hands ceasing to clean the fields of our hearts, they may be overgrown with the briars of evil thoughts."[153]

Saint Augustine wrote a whole treatise in which he proves the obligation of manual labor for all who are engaged in the monastic state; and he refutes all the reasons which are adduced by those who would exempt them from it. "If a rich man," says that great saint,

> Embraces the religious life, he shall never taste but little of Jesus Christ,

---

[151] S. Basilius, *Constitutiones,* PG 31:1346 (1857).

[152] S. Basilius, *Constitutiones,* PG 31:1410 (1857

[153] S. Hieronymus, Ad Rusticum Monachum, PL 22:1078 (1845).

unless he is first persuaded that nothing can contribute more to heal the tumors of his former pride, than to labor with humility, in procuring for himself such things as are necessary for the preservation of life, after having retrenched all those superfluities which had, previous to his retreat, excited in him the mortal heat of concupiscence. If he who embraces the monastic state had been poor, let him not think that in laboring, he does more than what he formerly did when in the world, because he has changed his motive, so, that what he then performed for money, he now does for the love of Jesus Christ.[154]

"O! solitaries," cries out Saint Ephrem, "labor during the winter, in the evil days, so that, having entered the harbor of eternal life, you may possess everlasting rest and joy."[155]

Cassian relates that the solitaries of Egypt, regulating their conduct according to Saint Paul's injunction, would never allow the religious to be idle, particularly those who were young. Moreover, they judged of their good dispositions, and of their advancement in the virtues of patience and humility, from their fervor in manual labor. They not only would not allow them to receive anything for their subsistence, but they even found sufficient by their industry, to entertain the brethren who came to visit them. Moreover, they sent large sums to Libya, where sterility and famine were most prevalent, and to cities afar off to relieve those who suffered in the horrors of prisons[156]

The same thing is confirmed by Rufinus, who says that on the confines of Arsinoe there was a priest named Serapion who governed ten thousand monks who all lived by the labor of their hands. They deposited in the care of this priest the greatest part of what they earned in the harvest time so that he might distribute it amongst the poor. He adds that it was a general custom amongst all the monks of Egypt to hire themselves to farmers during the harvest, and that what they gained was so considerable that they were obliged to send it to distant countries, because there were not sufficient poor in Egypt to consume it.[157]

---

[154] S. Augustinus, De Opere Monachorum, PL 40:547.

[155] Ephraem Syrus, Ad Imitationem Proverbiorum, (Cologne: Quentely,1616), 509.

[156] *Institutione*s, PL 49:388b (1846) / *Institutes* 10.22 (NPNF2/11:274).

[157] Tyrannius Rufinus, *De Serapione Presbytero,* PL 21:440 (1849).

Saint Bernard declaims against nothing more vehemently than against the idleness of the monks of his time. He was so convinced that manual labor was necessary to the religious state, that when he would teach us in what it consists, he ranks work amongst its principal obligations: "Labor, retirement, and voluntary poverty are the titles of honor which belong to religious persons: they are the ornaments of the solitary life."[158]

"We are obliged by our state," says he, in another place, "and by the example of our fathers, to live by our labor, and not by the altar." And in one of his sermons, having continued too long, so that he was overtaken by the time of work, he said to his brethren whom he was instructing: "Behold the hour has arrived which calls us to manual labor, to which we are obliged, as well by our rule as by our poverty and indigence."

These sentiments of the fathers have been adopted in practice by all holy solitaries, and the rules they have left us are so many standing monuments which attest their fidelity in the observance of this holy practice.

The following words are found in the first of all monastic rules, which is that of Saint Anthony: "Humble yourself to labor with your hands, and the fear of the Lord shall dwell in you. Be continually attentive to these things when you are retired in your cell, namely, manual labor, meditation on the psalms and prayer."[159]

Saint Isaias gives the following advice: "Love manual labor and affliction, that your passions may be weakened." Having said that we have learned the above from Saint Anthony, he also adds, "Do not flatter yourself with the idea of becoming like your fathers, unless you imitate them in your labors."[160]

The following injunction is found in the rules of Saints Serapion, Paphnutius, and Macarius: "Let the brethren be employed in spiritual things, from the hour of prime to tierce; and from tierce to none they shall apply themselves to such labor as shall be commanded them, without murmuring or complaining."[161]

According to the rule of the holy fathers, everyone ought to work, from

---

[158] *De moribus*, PL 182:833(1854).

[159] S. Antonius, *Regulae ac Praecepta*, PL 103:426,427 (1851).

[160] S. Isaias, *Regula ad Monachos*: IV, XI,LXV, PL 103:432D (1851).

[161] *Regula Sanctorum Serapionis, Macarii, Paphnutii*, PL 103:435 (1851).

the second hour until none and do what is enjoined, without delay or repining, according to the precept of the apostle.[162]

The same thing is found in a second rule of the holy fathers, and in that of Saint Macarius of Alexandria.[163]

It is written in the rule of Saint Pacomius that after morning prayers, the septenarian shall ask the superior of the monastery what occupation he thinks most necessary for the brethren, and what number of religious is to be sent to labor in the fields. And in another place it is enjoined, that nothing shall be cooked out of the kitchen; but when the brethren shall go to the country to work, they shall take with them vegetables prepared with vinegar and salt.[164]

Manual labor is enjoined by Saint Basil's rule, as we have already taken notice.

Saint Benedict makes it a principal obligation. "*Idleness*," says he, "*is the enemy of the soul; therefore the brethren shall be employed at certain times in manual labor.*"[165] He requires that they should work at the harvest, and in bringing home the corn, when the necessity or poverty of the place require it; and he exhorts them to do it with pleasure; because, says he, "They shall be then truly monks; when they shall live by the labor of their hands, as our fathers and the apostles have done."[166] And it appears by many passages of his rule, that he considers manual labor as one of the most important practices of the religious life.

The rule which appears under the name of an uncertain author, says, that the brethren shall work from the morning until sext. . . . And after dinner they shall labor until night, in the garden or in any other place that necessity may require it.[167]

Saints Paul and Stephen, who were famous solitaries, exhorting their brethren to manual labor, tell them that the rule they gave them on that subject is much mitigated, and that there is as much difference between

---

[162] Reg. Patr. c. 7. and in alia reg. c. 10/ Ephes 4:28 /1 Thess 4:11.

[163] In 3 Reg. 6. 11. 25.

[164] S. Pachomius, *Regula,* in *S. Hieronymi Opera Omnia,* PL 23:67 (1851).

[165] *RB* 48.1.

[166] RB 48.8.

[167] *Alia Regula Incerti Auctoris,* Caput II, in *S. Benedicti Opera Omnia,* PL 66:997.

what it prescribes and what Saint Paul practiced, as there is between that great apostle and them; for he commanded manual labor to be exercised in such a manner as to produce sufficient means to assist the poor in their wants; whereas you labor only for your own subsistence. That great apostle suffered hunger, thirst, cold and nakedness, laboring day and night to find a living for those who accompanied him, as well as for himself.

They, on the contrary, receive abundantly from the house of God everything necessary for their food and clothing. Hence, they should carefully avoid idleness and in perfect union labor according to their strength. Let everyone, say these two great saints, cast off sloth and quickly embrace every kind of labor, for it is written, thou shalt not despise painful labors, particularly agriculture, which has been commanded by the Lord, so that we may have by means of our work everything necessary for life in abundance, that we may receive in a proper manner those who make us visits of charity, and be enabled to assist those who are in distress.[168]

We read in the rule of Saint Cesarius, that the brethren are to be employed in spiritual reading until tierce, and afterward labor, in doing whatever they shall be commanded.[169]

The rule of Saint Aurelian enjoins manual labor during the whole day, without any interruption for meditation, which, nevertheless, they are to nourish in their souls continually.[170]

According to Saint Fereol's rule, the brethren are to employ the first part of the day, until tierce, in spiritual things, and the remainder in manual labor, as it shall have been commanded. Those who during the harvest time shall be ordered by the abbot to go to work early in the morning, shall not be obliged to observe this rule.[171]

It is enjoined by the same rule that if a religious passes a day without doing any work, he shall not be allowed to eat, according to the words of the apostle: "If anyone will not work, neither let him eat" (2 Thess 3:10). This rule removes every pretext with which religious persons are accustomed to

---

[168] SS. Stephanus et Paulus Abbates, *Regula ad Monachos,* Caput XXXIII, PL 66:956.

[169] S. Caesarius, *Regula ad Monachos,* Caput XIV, PL 67:1100.

[170] S. Aurelianus, *Regula ad Monachos*, Caput XXIV, PL 68:391(1866).

[171] S. Ferreolus, *Regula ad Monachos,* Caput XXVI, PL 66:968 (1847).

cover sloth, for it proportions the labor to the strength and dispositions of each individual.[172]

Saint Columbanus says in his rule, that a religious ought not to pass a day without fasting, praying, reading, and working.

The rule of the monastery of Tarnat obliges the religious to labor from prime to tierce; after tierce, to resume their work until sext; from sext to none, to remain in repose, and apply themselves to reading; and after none, to work in the garden, or in any other part of the enclosure until night.... Those who have particular employments, were not obliged to observe this distribution of time, because their exercises were continual.

Saint Isidore, bishop of Seville, enjoins in his rule that the religious are to be employed in manual labor, and other such occupations. He requires that during the summer, they should work from the morning until the hour of tierce. From tierce until sext, he allows them reading, and from sext to none, he permits them to rest, and after that office, they are to work until evening. In every other season, the brethren are to read from the morning to tierce, which being said, they work until none, after which dinner, lecture, work, and meditation.

Saint Fructuosus lays down the following order for manual labor during the spring and summer. Prime being said, the deans shall receive orders of the prior concerning the work, which they shall communicate to the brethren, and all having taken the necessary implements, and having prayed together, shall proceed to work in good order until the hour of none, which office being said, they shall return to work, if necessary, until midday.

In the rule entitled, *Of the Master*, there is a chapter which regulates the order of the work, and the hours the religious are to employ in that exercise.[173]

The holy Priest Grimlaic in his rule for the solitaries, enjoins daily manual labor. "The holy apostle," says he,

> Who announced the gospel, would not eat his bread gratis, but lived by his labors and fatigues. With what assurance can we expect to eat ours, if we fold our arms and remain idle, we to whom the preaching of the divine word is not committed, and who are charged only with the care of our own

---

[172] S. Ferreolus, *Regula*, Caput XXVIII, PL 66:969 (1847).

[173] Auctor Incertus, *Regula Magistri*, PL 88:943; *The Rule of the Master*.

souls? We must therefore labor with our hands, so that we may provide our necessary subsistence, and find means to assist the poor. [174]

Saint Caesarius, and Saint Aurilan, bishop, enjoins in the rule they composed for nuns, manual labor. Aleredus, who also composed a rule for women, commands the same occupation.

The same injunction is found in a rule, the author of which is not known; this rule is entitled *Regula cujusdam,* or, the rule of a certain person.[175]

The Carthusians were strictly obliged by their first constitutions to employ a part of their time in manual labor. During winter they worked from tierce to sext, and in summer from prime to tierce; and that they might more effectually sanctify that exercise, they were commanded to interrupt it by short and frequent prayers. After dinner they returned to the same occupation, and employed therein all the time between none and vespers.[176]

Saint Francis enjoins manual labor in his rule: "Let the brethren," says he,

> Who have received of God the gift of knowing how to labor, perform their work with fidelity and piety, that thus banishing idleness, which is the enemy of our souls, they may preserve the spirit of devotion and prayer.

[177]This point seemed so important to that great saint, that he confirmed it by the will he left his brethren. "We were," said he,

> Nothing more than simple people, subject to every one. I have worked with my hands, and I will yet work; I will also have my brethren absolutely to employ themselves in such labors as are not against decency. My intention is, that they must learn trades, if they are unacquainted with any; not indeed that they may earn money, but to avoid idleness, and give good example. [178]

---

[174] Grimlaicus, Caput XXXIX, *Regula Solitariorum,* PL 103:629.

[175] *Regula Cujusdam Patris,* in *Sancti Benedicti Opera Omnia,* PL 66:987(1847).

[176] Guigonis I, *Consuetudines,* Capitulum XXIX, PL 153:699 (1854).

[177] S. Franciscus, De Modo Laborandi, *Regula Fratrum Minorum,* Caput V (Paris, Rigaud, 1653), 31.

[178] *Regula et Testamentum S.P.N.S. Francisci.* (Cadomi: Typis Pagny, 1872), XIV, XV.

We read in the life of Saint Albert that the religious of Vallumbrosis were so exact in observing the rule of Saint Benedict in what regards manual labor that they afflicted their bodies with fatigue and weariness.

Saint Peter Damien writes, that the religious of Camaldoli worked with their hands; some spun, others made nets, cords, hair cloth, spoons, and such articles.[179]

The monks of Saint Victor, formerly worked every day. Each one was employed according to his strength, and when they were prevented by bad weather from laboring outside, they were occupied in the monastery at something proper and convenient.[180]

The Celestines had also their regular labor, as appears by their ancient constitutions, from which none but the sick were exempt, or those who had necessary offices and employments in the monastery.[181]

Saint Albert, founder of the Carmelites, enjoins manual labor, so that, says he, "The devil may find you always employed, and that your idleness may give him no entrance into your soul."[182] The Discalced Carmelites of Spain, at the beginning of their reformation resumed this observance with exactness; each one labored according as the diversity of places and the facility they found in selling their productions served their purpose.

1 have expressly omitted to speak of the monks of the Cistercian order. I have taken them out of their rank, in order that seeing them alone out of the crowd, you may view them more attentively, and take notice how great was their fervor and exactitude in manual labor. Those admirable men bound themselves to a literal observance of their holy Father's will, and to reject every gloss and interpretation that might oppose his true intentions. For this reason they considered manual labor as a principal obligation, nor was any thought too difficult. They cut down the corn in the harvest, broke up uncultivated lands, hewed wood in the forest to erect monastic

---

[179] S. Petrus Damianus, *Vita Sancti Romualdi,* PL 144:976 (1867).

[180] In const. c. 31./ Liber ordinis Sancti Victoris Parisiensis.

[181] Cap. 111./ Constitutiones monachorum Ordinis Sancti Benedicti Congregationis Coelestinorum (Bononiae: Rossium, 1590).

[182] *Histoire des Carmel, dechaus. de l'Espagne./The Rule of St. Albert,* Chapter 20, http://carmelnet.org/chas/rule.htm, accessed 5/19/2018 / see also Bede Edwards, *The Rule of St. Albert* (Carmelite Book Service, 1973).

buildings, built themselves houses, carried manure on the land, made hay, sheered sheep.

The monks of their time, jealous of a sanctity so resplendent and edifying, failed not to decry their conduct and to exhibit those actions, so holy and exemplary, in an unfavorable manner, making them appear as novelties, indiscretions, and excess. "Where has anyone learned," said they, "That God takes delight in beholding men tormenting themselves? In what part of the Scriptures are we commanded to overcharge and kill ourselves with excessive labor? What kind of religion is it to dig the ground, hew wood in forests, carry out dung on fields ?" [183]

But those solitaries were inspired by God; and meditating continually on His judgments, they gave themselves no anxiety about the injudicious reflections of those men. They pursued their way with a steady even pace, like men who continue their course without stopping at the noise of children who cry after them, when surprised at beholding their great and rapid motion.

Saint Bernard considered manual labor so important and so necessary that he obtained of God by his fervent prayers both the necessary skill and facility to reap the corn and work at the harvest. And when the brethren were employed at labor that required more strength than he had, he compensated for his inability by digging, carrying wood on his shoulders, and applying himself to other humiliating employments of the monastery.[184]

The time they employed in this exercise may be learned by consulting the rule of Saint Benedict, and by their first constitutions. In general, they labored during the summer from the end of the chapter, or daily assembly (which met always after prime), until tierce, and from none until vespers. In winter, from the conventual mass until none, and during Lent until vespers. During the harvest, when they worked at the farms, they said prime, the conventual mass, and tierce without interruption, so that they might apply themselves to their work without impediment during the rest of the forenoon. They frequently said the divine office in the same place

---

[183] "Quando delectatur Deus cruciatibus nostris? Ubi praecepit scriptura quempiam se interficere? qualis religio est, fodere terram, silvam exscidere, stercora comportare." S. Bernardus, *Epistola* I, PL 182:73 (1854).

[184] In ejus vita, lib. 1.c.4. / *Vita S. Patris Bernardi Claravallensis Abbatis Primi Melliflui Ecclesiae Doctoris,* Caput IV (Bamberg: Hoffling, 1678), 40.

where they worked, and at the same time that their brethren at home sung it in the choir.[185]

"How happy is their poverty," said an eminent contemporary author,

> Which, though it reduces them to the necessity of suffering hunger and cold, yet does not oblige them to a degrading mendicity, or to gratify the great ones of the world with base condescensions. They find sufficient for food and clothing by their labor, imitating the holy apostle, who, though he could live by the functions of his ministry, chose rather to labor for his subsistence than to make his preaching become oppressive, or himself a burden to any person.[186]

In fine, their zeal was so great for this penitential exercise, as well as for every other, that, according to the testimony of those who have written on the subject, they invented for themselves new crosses and torments so that they might procure the health and salvation of their souls in the affliction and sufferings of their bodies.[187]

Behold what labors our fathers endured. Behold the effects of that holy hatred they had of themselves, so much recommended in the sacred writings. Behold what the mortification of those great men was, who were dead to all things, and who seemed to have life and sentiment only that they might suffer evils and pains for the love of Christ. Divine Providence made them flourish, to be our models as well as our progenitors. We ought therefore be their imitators as well as their descendants. But if — notwithstanding all your efforts—you only retrace imperfectly a penitential life so eminent, be at least affected and confounded at the great disparity you find between your life and theirs. Let it animate you to beseech our

---

[185] a) RB 48; b)In usibus c. 75. 84 / *Usus Antiquiores Ordinis Cisterciensis,* Caput LXXV De Labore; caput LXXXIV Qualiter Se Agant Fratres in Aestate. In *Nomasticon Cisterciense* seu *Antiquiores Ordinis Cisterciensis Constitutiones* (Paris, Alliot, 1664) / *The Ancient Usages of the Cistercian order* (*Ecclesiastica Officia*), (Lafyette, OR, Guadalupe Translations, 1998).

[186] Stephanus Episcopus Tornacensis, *Epistola LXXI, Ad Robertum Pontiniacensem Monachum,* in *Epistolae*. PL 211:361 (1855).

[187] Importabiles corporibus suis pro animarum remedio com miniscuntur cruces. Guillel. Malmerburg. *Hist Anglica*. l. 4. / *Willielmi Malmesburiensis, Rerum Anglicarum Scriptores Post Bedam Praecipui* (Frankfurt: Wechlians, MDCI), 71.

Lord to give you the grace of compensating, by your humility and tears, for what your inability will not allow you to perform.

Q. 2.— *What induced the ancient solitaries to recommend manual labor so earnestly and to make it one of their principal exercises?*

A.—The same reasons which made the ancient solitaries so rigorous in the observance of fastings, abstinence, watching, and like practices, induced them also to apply themselves to manual labor. It cannot be doubted that the love of penance, the desire of immolating themselves for Jesus Christ, like so many victims, of washing away their sins with their sweat as well as with their tears, the design of chastising their bodies and bringing them into subjection, thus to prevent their irregularities, and make them become more pure and worthy of their holy state, made them embrace labor and find delight in the most humiliating and most laborious employments. But as we have spoken already of these motives when treating of their austere abstinence, we shall content ourselves here with adding a few particular considerations which are more immediately connected with manual labor.

One of the principal reasons which induced the solitaries of former times to apply themselves to manual labor and to lay down such rigorous and general rules for that exercise was so that their whole time might be employed, that there might be no empty space in their lives, and to prevent the fatal consequences of sloth and idleness. They were well persuaded that as soon as they would cease to be employed in holy occupations, it would be impossible for them to avoid being engaged in evil ones. For inaction opens the door to every vice and closes it to every virtue. Hence the ancient solitaries of Egypt used to say that the religious who worked was tempted only by one devil, whereas he who spends his time in sloth and idleness is attacked by a great number, all of which combat against him in diverse ways.[188]

As sloth destroys all the vigor of the soul, extinguishes that holy fervor which is the principle of its motions, so it binds up its faculties in the links of dispirited affections, and obstructs its active powers, so, that the heart can produce no good affection, nor the spirit form any good thought. Hence, when the passions are irritated, and temptations take up arms, the religious is no way prepared to resist their united efforts. The invisible enemies taking advantage of his disordered and impotent state, attack him

---

[188] Cassianus, *Institutiones,* PL 49:393a (1846) / Institutes 10.23 (NPNF2/11:274).

furiously, and carry him a resistless captive where ever they please. And this unfortunate soul fails not to rush into every snare they lay, for he may be considered as a man without defense, and exposed to all the darts of his malicious and cruel enemies.

When this vice becomes master of the soul, says Cassian, it either engages the solitary to remain in his cell in a state of inaction without doing anything for his spiritual advancement, or it drives him forth and makes him wander from place to place in a constant round of instability. Becoming incapable of any good, he may do nothing more than run from one cell to another, from monastery to monastery, on pretext of visiting his brethren; but in effect, being led on by no other motive but that of finding a good repast, for the slothful are frequently influenced by the care of what they shall eat.[189]

Behold the true state of such persons; thus they go on, until they find some man or woman in the same slothful and effeminate dispositions, in whose embarrassing affairs they engage themselves without scruple. Thus they undertake the most dangerous occupations without scruple, and by little and little they yield themselves up to the serpent's folds, from which they cannot extricate themselves. Hence they no longer enjoy that liberty, so necessary to labor in attaining the perfection of their state.

The holy fathers, whose rules we have before cited, were of this opinion, nor had Saint Benedict any other, for he takes express notice in his rule that one of the motives which induced him to enjoin manual labor was to secure the brethren from idleness, which he considers as a cruel enemy of souls.[190] This was also the opinion of the holy Abbot Paul. This great anchorite, who, having labored with great assiduity, burned all his work at the end of the year, because he lived so remote from all society that he could not send them to any market.

The second reason that induced the ancient solitaries to recommend manual labor so earnestly was that they thought it unbecoming for persons who made profession of the solitary life to eat that bread which they had not gained by the sweat of their brow. They understood that sentence of the holy scripture as being literally addressed to themselves: "Thou shalt eat thy bread in the sweat of thy brow" (Gen 3:19). And they believed that nothing was more agreeable, nor more conformable to the condition of

---

[189] Cassianus, *Institutiones,* PL 49:370a (1846) / *Institutes* 10.6 (NPNF2/11:268).

[190] *RB* 48.1

penitents, who by their vocation were charged with the sins of men, than to bear the punishment which God was pleased to inflict for their sins.

They were persuaded that the prohibition addressed by Saint Paul to the Thessalonians, "If anyone will not work, neither let him eat" (2 Thess 3:10), was a precept which obliged all monks; and that the sentence which the same apostle made no difficulty to pronounce against those who were engaged in secular concerns, was with much more reason addressed to those who renounced it by being consecrated to the exercises of a poor and penitential life.[191]

This was the reason why Saint Abraham made the following reply to a solitary, who boasted of living by the alms which were given him by his relations:

> It would not, my son, be difficult for us to obtain the same assistance from our friends; but we have preferred the poverty in which you behold us to their riches. We have chosen rather to live by our own labor and fatigue, than to depend on their assistance; and we value much more this painful and laborious poverty, than all those unfruitful meditations on the holy scriptures of which you have spoken. You may be convinced, that it would be very easy for us to imitate your conduct, if we could learn from the example of the apostles and the instructions of the fathers, that it is the most proper; but let me tell you, that you do yourself an injury in thus accepting those alms, you who are strong and healthy, which properly belongs to persons who are weak and infirm.[192]

Manual labor was an exercise common to all the solitaries of the east as long as the religious state was preserved there in its purity and simplicity. Saint Benedict revived it in his time in the west. Many congregations that lived under his rule observed it, and amongst others the religious of Citeaux adopted it with literal exactitude. Besides what we have already related on this subject, behold here what we find in one of their primitive statutes:

> The monks of our order ought to live by the labor of their hands; for that end they must apply themselves to agricultural employments, to feeding cattle, etc.; hence it is lawful for them to possess lands, ponds, forests, vine-

---

[191] Cassianus, *Institutiones*, PL 49:379a (1846) / *Institutes* 10.12 (NPNF2/11:271)

[192] Cassianus, *Collationes*, PL 49:393a (1846) /*Conferences* 3.24.18 (NPNF2/11:539).

yards, all of which should be remote from the common recourse of worldlings....

But what is most of all remarkable is that like the ancient solitaries, who, by their industry and work were enabled to feed whole countries and provinces, so those latter of whom we speak were enabled by their great labors to assist pilgrims, comfort the poor, and entertain the strangers who came to visit them. Indeed, the cardinal of Vitry had reason when he compared them to oxen, who having threshed the corn contented themselves with the straw, leaving the grain for their masters. [193]

A third reason made the primitive solitaries so zealous and fervent in manual labor. Animated by the instruction of the great apostle who commanded the Ephesians to work for the relief of the poor, their charity became ardent, they recognized Jesus Christ in His members. They considered their necessities as their own, and esteemed themselves happy when He was pleased to accept in the persons of His servants the fruit of their labors and pains. This is what Saint Basil would inculcate when he said that labor was useful not only to macerate the body, but also to furnish means to exercise charity towards the poor. By it God employs our ministry to assist our infirm brethren, in the same manner as is prescribed in the Acts of the Apostles by these words of Saint Paul: "I have given you the example that you may work, and thus find means to assist the infirm in their necessities" (Acts 20:35).

The fourth reason is example. Monks ought to be living rules. The divine truths of religion ought to be exemplified in their conduct. Every time they appear in view of worldly people, their aspect ought to be such as to exhibit a condemnation of every vice and a perfect model of every virtue. Their separation from the world may be an inducement to conclude that they have despised all its vanities as soon as they forsook it. And their retirement is an apparent proof that they have judged it unworthy of their attachment, affection or esteem.

But all this is too general, and speaks in a language too undetermined, since it too frequently happens that their lives present a portrait of such inconstancies as are inconsistent with the first great step they made, and are so many open retractions of what they have done. They must necessarily either fail in the accomplishment of the duty which obliges them to give

---

[193] de Vitriaco, *Occidentalis,* 113.

good example to the rest of men, or point out to their view by particular dispositions, and by a detailed line of action what they ought to avoid or embrace.

Their chastity, as we have said before, condemns luxury; their abstinence, intemperance; their obedience, self-love; their humility, pride; their patience, anger; their poverty, covetousness and envy both together, for he who is truly poor desires nothing. But as all this is insufficient to destroy those seven principal sources of all disorder and excess. They must, moreover, condemn sloth by their assiduity in working and teach men to fly idleness by their laborious lives. And it seems right to conclude that they are so much the more obliged to this latter, as inaction alone is capable of replunging a soul who has the happiness of being emancipated from the slavery of bad passions, into the bondage of every vice. "The ways of the slothful," says the Spirit of God, "are filled with thorns" (Prov 15:19); that is to say, he who is given up to sloth is attacked and at last overcome by every vice.

Therefore, every religious ought to give that example and edification in this point, as well as in every other to which he is bound by his state; and to live in such a manner as not only to be exempt from every suspicion of sloth, but also to inspire a horror for that vice, and hold out such a constantly laborious conduct, as may be qualified to induce those who desire to examine it closely, to embrace a life of labor and pain. Above all, let him call to mind frequently the fate of the fig-tree in the Gospel which was cursed by our Lord, because He could not find thereon the fruit He sought (Matt 21:19).

The example of the apostles may also be considered, and added to the preceding motives which oblige religious to embrace manual labor, as Saint Benedict teaches,[194] as well as many other saints whose testimonies we have already adduced. There is nothing more just, nor even more necessary for those who are obliged by their state to imitate the apostles in their sanctity, than to imitate them also in their laborious exercises. And how can we tend to the perfection of those glorious disciples of Christ, if we do not propose to ourselves the same means, and walk in the same ways which led them to it?

Therefore, monks ought to propose to themselves the holy apostles of Jesus Christ as their models, since as St. Bernard says, God will

---

[194] *RB* 48.

examine them according to the perfection of those great men. And as they undoubtedly worked with their hands, and as many of them gained their subsistence by their industry, with what reason can monks pretend after this to exempt themselves from doing what the apostles did, or from exemplifying the same conduct in their lives? [195]

If monks should say that the actions peculiar to the apostleship are not proper for them, that the preaching of the word, missions, and the care and instruction of the faithful, are duties which do not belong to their state, there would be reason in their assertion. But to pretend that the actions, exercises and duties which are conformable to their state, such as fasting, watching, penance, poverty, manual labor, of which the apostles have given such remarkable examples, are practices indifferent for them, is what they will never be able to persuade those who know that the life of religious ought to be a representation and a retracing of the apostolic life.

Cassian insinuates a reason which is not less important than the foregoing. He says that monks ought to obliterate from their minds the pleasures and vanities of the world, and acquire humility of heart by the humiliation and pain of manual labor.[196]

Saint Dorotheus confirms this thought. Labor, says he, humbles the body, and the humiliations of the body produces that of the mind. It is evident, as the same saint affirms, that our hearts assume dispositions according to the different circumstances in which we find ourselves. The sentiments of a man who is seated on a throne are different from those of another who is on a dung hill. He who is clothed with rich and sumptuous robes has thoughts very different from him who is covered with poor and torn garments. Therefore actions which are mean and humiliating are well calculated to destroy our ideas of glory and ambition, and are consequently proper for monks.

This motive, independently of all others, should be sufficient to inspire religious persons with the love of manual labor, and animate them in an exercise so capable of preserving them from all dispositions contrary to the sanctity of their state. It humbles those who were of considerable fortune and rank in the world, by placing them in the same state with such a great number of persons whose poor condition makes them appear

---

[195] *Sermones de Diversis*, Sermo XXVII, PL 183:613 (1854). / Monastic, 153.

[196] *Institutiones*, PL 49:81(1846). / "That he may also forget the pride and luxury of his past life, and gain by grinding toil humility of heart." Institutes 2.3 (NPNF2/11:206).

contemptible in the eyes of men, and thus effaces from their minds what they had been before their conversion. As to those who have nothing either of birth or fortune, it keeps their poverty continually before their eyes, preserves them from being puffed up with pride, and nourishes in them a constant remembrance of their former late condition.

Thus, my brethren, we may with justice conclude by asserting, that religious persons who are assiduous in manual labor shall find in it a powerful means to acquire and preserve humility; and that if they fulfill that obligation with a true spirit of piety, it will serve them as a strong defense against all vain things, and securely maintain them in the modesty and simplicity of their state.

Q. 3.— What answer can be made to those who say, that manual labor was necessary for monks only while they were poor, but that it is at present quite useless, because the charity of the faithful has given them sufficient revenues and provided for all their wants?

A.—As manual labor has been instituted amongst religious persons, not only on account of their poverty, but also for many other motives which make it useful and necessary, it ought not to be inferred from this that they ought not to work, because they have sufficient means of subsisting without it. The intention of those who gave them the property they enjoy was not to enervate their virtue, but to strengthen it. And God, who raises up men to found and establish monasteries, requires an acknowledgment from monks which they can only give Him by the fervor and exactitude with which they fulfill the duties of their state.

Hence, if necessity no longer forces them to embrace manual labor, they ought to be induced to adopt it by the love of regularity, the authority of the holy fathers, the spirit of penance, the mortification of the senses, the avoidance of idleness, and all the disorders it produces. They should be decided in favor of this holy practice, too, by the obligation of giving good example; and in fine, by the desire of imitating the great apostle, who, instead of living by the gospel (Acts 20:34; 1 Cor 4:12; 1 Thess 2:9), as he might have lawfully done, according to the rules of strict justice, rather chose to work with his hands, not only that he might not be a burden on any person, but also to remove every occasion of scandal from the faithful, and for the edification of the whole Church.

Thus, my brethren, you see that the obligation which binds religious persons to manual labor stands on the basis of so many solid and important reasons that it cannot cease to exist, though that of poverty may be entirely removed. As the apostle by laboring would deprive himself of what was lawfully due to him, so that he might not deprive his brethren of anything, so religious persons must labor, and distribute amongst the poor what they may save of their incomes, by the help and assistance of their work and industry.

Q. 4.— *Would it not be more useful for religious persons to employ their time in reading and study than in manual labor?*

A.— The first thing that can be replied to this question, my brethren, is that the most useful employment for religious persons is undoubtedly that which is most conformable to their state, most connected with the designs of God, and most agreeable to His will. Now it is certain, as we have already shown, that monks have not been appointed for study, but for doing penance. Their condition is to weep, and not to teach, for the designs of God in establishing solitaries in His church was not to form doctors, but penitents.

If some of them have been as eminent for learning as for virtue and sanctity, nothing more can be inferred from this particular fact than that it was a singular conduct of Divine Providence, Who being the sovereign Lord of men, employs them in His service as He thinks proper, without binding Himself to the observance of common laws. And it may be said that when He called monks from obscurity, silence, and retirement to employ them in the affairs of the Church, to defend the faith and instruct the people, His will in such extraordinary cases was to make use of persons who by their state and condition were simple and contemptible, according to the world, and to confound the pride and vanity of human wisdom (1 Cor 1:27).

Therefore, though it be true that there have been some solitaries remarkable for learning, yet, as it was uncommon and above their profession, it ought not serve as an example. Nothing would be more unreasonable than to abolish on that pretext the exercise of manual labor that has been enjoined by all monastic rules, and practiced so religiously by all holy monks. Such a conduct would be condemned by all antiquity, because it would substitute what was never considered as a rule by monks, for that which held a principal rank amongst their most essential practices. It would, of course, be foolish to imagine, that such a reversion of order could be more productive of blessings and advantages.

There are few members of the cloister qualified to undertake and succeed in extensive studies, and it would be difficult to find religious persons who could employ all their time in lectures, if they were not employed in manual labor. Study would unavoidably become disgusting. It would be a loathsome exercise, full of bitterness. And it would come to pass that though such an occupation would be given them as a means to preserve them in the sanctity of their state, yet it would procure a quite contrary effect. For either they would be weighed down by an insupportable burden, and be induced to unbend their minds, and reanimate their spirits by diversions incompatible with the purity of their state, or give themselves up to dejection and sloth, which inevitably destroys the piety of the cloister.

This is undoubtedly what the Synod of Verneuil would teach us, the fathers of which complaining to the king of the ruin and desolation of the monastic state said that the monks had strayed out of their way and were lost in the holy places by means of study and sloth. As if they would thereby signify, that the religious had forsaken manual labor, penance, and other regular occupations, on pretext of applying themselves to studies, and that by such a disorder they were fallen into effeminacy, idleness and sloth. [197]

Therefore, to think that study can supply the exercise of manual labor is an illusion. And to imagine that the leisure moments which are found in the lives of religious persons who do not work can be usefully employed in literary pursuits is an error already condemned by experience.

Q. 5.—*Is there not reason to fear, that if religious persons do not study, they will fall into gross ignorance, and from that into disorder?*

A.—This fear is certainly very ill-founded. Monks will never fall into disorder so long as they will remain invariably attached to the duties of their state, faithful in the exact observance of their rules, and careful to walk in the ways which their fathers have traced. Therefore, my brethren, to pretend that religious persons can lose the true path because they do not apply themselves to classical studies, though they fulfill all the duties of their state, is really nothing less than the effects of mere imagination. For study, as I have already taken notice, is an employment foreign to their purpose and has nothing in common with their profession.

Nor is there reason to believe that monks will become ignorant if they do

---

[197] In locis sanctis, hoc est in monasteriis, alios studio, nonullos desidida, a sua professione deviare comperimus.—Sub. Serg. 2. Can. 3. anno. 844. / Karoli II Concilium in Verno Palatio, Canon III, PL 138:541 (1880).

not occupy their time in literary pursuits. And though we have sufficiently elucidated this truth when speaking of the duties of superiors, we shall here add, my brethren, that a religious cannot be considered ignorant when he knows what his state obliges him to know. He shall have all necessary information, when he understands how to love our Lord Jesus Christ, and in what manner he ought to take up his cross and follow Him in the perfect accomplishment of His adorable will.

This is a science not to be acquired by study. Jesus Christ is the master and doctor who teaches it, and from Him alone we can learn it. Whatever may be our application, we shall never acquire this necessary knowledge, unless He himself engraves it with His finger, that is, by His Holy Spirit in the midst of our hearts. The means which a solitary ought to employ for obtaining a gift so precious are submission of the mind, docility of heart, and perfect exactitude in the accomplishment of his duties. It cannot be doubted, then, that if he observe with zeal and fidelity all that his rule points out, or rather what God Himself prescribes by His holy legislator, he shall acquire this science of sciences. By it alone saints are formed, and every other acquisition of learning or knowledge which may be possessed by the most enlightened doctors, when compared with this, is but mere ignorance and obscurity.

But if the saints were unwilling that monks should apply themselves to study, yet they were very careful to instruct and to assist them in everything relative to their state, that might excite in them its sentiments, and enforce its maxims. For that end, they appointed certain portions of time for spiritual reading, which they placed amongst the number of regular exercises, and Saint Benedict enjoins it as a principal occupation.

Indeed the subjects which are to engage our attention, and to form the matter of this exercise, so far from being curious or capable of exciting the least dissipation, ought to be no other than the holy scriptures, the works of the holy fathers, their lives, actions and spiritual conferences. In these we shall find abundantly everything necessary to inflame our affections, animate our fervor, excite our compunction, exercise our contempt for the world, and fortify our souls in the desire of death, and in the hope of eternal good. The saints, our predecessors, had their time so diversified, and their days were regulated with such order, that everything found its place without confusion, so that there were no empty spaces of time left unemployed; and it may be truly said that their whole lives were spent in singing the praises of God, in meditating on His law, in reading pious books, and in manual labor.

Here then you may judge, my brethren, whether religious persons who employ themselves in these occupations and studies may be justly accused of gross ignorance, or whether there is the least danger of their falling into a state of disorder if they do not apply themselves to other studies and pursuits. Divine Providence has provided for all their wants. Then there is no necessity to seek out extraordinary means. Everything required for their sanctification is contained in their rules. The only thing therefore that remains to be done—in order to prevent disorder—is to oblige them to observe them exactly, and to live according to the true spirit of their state. This will not only preserve them from error, but will also lead them into the right way, if they have unfortunately strayed from it.

Be convinced, my brethren, that the application to learning is an enemy to the spirit by which the conduct of a solitary ought to be animated. Though there have been many holy monks of eminent erudition who have done great service to the Church by their learning and doctrine, yet, to make these examples serve as a general rule, and to conclude from them that study is to be considered as one of our regular exercises, would be directly opposing the spirit of our holy state and introducing a system never approved of by the saints.

If learning is the cause why men frequently become proud, as the apostle teaches, how can study be an exercise for persons who ought to live in continual abjection and in the practice of uninterrupted humility? How can it be expected that simplicity, meekness, compunction, and recollection, which ought to reign in the cloister, can be compatible with the curiosity, vanity and contention which are found in the schools?

We know very well how useful and necessary learning is; we are well convinced that the greatest evils of the Church have sprung from the ignorance of its ministers. But we also know that Jesus Christ committed the care of instructing the people to those whom He is pleased to call to the functions of the ministry. It belongs to them alone to carry the light of truth and knowledge where it is wanted by the preaching of the Word. They have received of God the key of learning. They are obliged by their state to know the various questions of divinity, and to penetrate the sacred dogmas of faith and the depth of tradition. Called by God to a ministry that requires a complete knowledge of ecclesiastical affairs, and being constituted by Him the masters and dispensers of sacred learning, He is attentive to preserve

them, when faithful to the grace of their vocation, from the inconveniences which generally defile the purity and merit of learning, even in those who possess its largest stores.

As to solitaries and monks, it is not by study and learning that they are to edify the Church, but by silence, retirement and penitential labors. Every time they forsake these paths, unless when obliged by an evident divine command, and by some urgent necessity, they are doing no better than tempting God, and are of course unworthy of His protection. So in like manner, there is no disorder with which they are not threatened, nor evil into which they do not deserve to fall.

The ancient fathers who were filled with these sentiments never allowed solitaries any time for studies. Saint Benedict, as we have already said, enjoins reading to animate the brethren's piety, but not for the purpose of acquiring learning. You will not find in any of the ancient rules that any notice has been taken of studies in the distribution of time.

Saint Basil forbids teaching children destined for the monastic state anything but what regards the end to which they are destined. He requires that they be taught to express themselves in terms taken from the sacred writings. And that instead of speaking to them of fables and profane stories, they should be entertained with the sacred histories, with the remarkable events which are found in them; and that sentences should be selected from the Proverbs, to instruct and lead them to the practice of virtue.

The same saint, when asked whether it is necessary to learn many things of the holy scriptures, answers that there are two sorts of persons, the one to direct, and the other to submit and obey. The first ought to learn and know everything contained in the sacred books, that they may be qualified to teach each individual both the commandments of God and his particular duties. But as to those who live in obedience, they ought to remember those words of the apostle: "Not to be more wise than it behoveth to be wise; but to be wise unto sobriety" (Rom 12:3); and to apply themselves to learn and practice such things as are proper for them, without disturbing themselves about matters unconnected with their state.

There has been nothing more remarkably said on this subject than what we read in Saint John Climacus:

> Penitents rest on sackcloth and ashes, but doctors are seated on chairs of honor.... Solitaries will not be examined at the judgment seat of Christ as to the depth of their knowledge of the mysteries of theology, but whether they have sufficiently wept for their sins.

Saint Peter of Damien, consoling a religious who was afflicted because he found himself deficient of acquired knowledge, pointed out to him the vanity of such learning, and showed that he who has received the gift of understanding by the grace of the Holy Spirit, discovers all things by the vigor of the spirit which has been given him, and no longer has any need of rule or method to become learned.

To confirm this truth, he cites the examples of the three children who were cast into the fiery furnace, of Daniel, of Saint Benedict, of Saint Hilarion, and of Saint Martin, who had never studied. In fine, he says that they who seek God and imitate His saints with pure intentions, want no help of strange light to contemplate that which is true, for true wisdom comes willingly to those who seek her; that God alone is our true science; that He ought to be the only object of our interior motives, the subject of all our meditations, in whom we ought to fix our eternal repose.

There never, perhaps, was a religious more employed in worldly affairs by Divine Providence, than Saint Bernard. Men of every state and condition applied to him in their doubts and difficulties. He was considered as the oracle of the Church. He supported it both by his doctrine and sanctity, yet he everywhere testifies that nothing but the appointment of God could have induced him to leave the bounds of his state, that the duty of a monk is to live in silence and retirement. He tells one of his friends who had complained that he wrote a letter much shorter than he expected: That what he desired of him was both above his strength, and beyond the limits of his condition; and that the duty of a monk (of whom he had only the appearance, but of a sinner he had the real character), was to weep and not to teach; that an ignorant man was not qualified to be a master; that a monk ought not to presume to undertake it, nor a sinner entertain the desire.

"Believe me," says the same saint,

> For I know it by experience, that you will learn more in forests than in books; the trees and rocks will teach you more than all the masters in the world. If you desire to possess Jesus, you will much sooner obtain Him by following Him than by reading of Him.[198]

"You deceive yourself," says he in another place,

---

[198] Epistola LXXXIX, Ad Eumdem [Oger]. PL 182:220 (1854).

If you believe that the doctors of the world can teach you the science of the disciples of Jesus. That is to say, those who despise the world learn of Jesus alone that science which is not acquired by reading, but by the unction which the spirit gives (not the letter), and which we cannot acquire by study, but by obedience to the commandments of the Lord[199].

In another of his epistles, speaking of a hermit who pretended to have the right and liberty to preach, he says that he ought to know that the duty of a monk is to weep and not to teach, that he ought to consider the city as his prison, and solitude as his paradise.[200]

From all these reasons it is easy to infer that it would be neither just nor prudent to abolish manual labor, and thus to deprive the religious state of the advantages it may derive from an exercise so holy, to substitute in its place the study of science, which at best is only an extraordinary occupation, and is frequently no better than a temptation and a stumbling block in the monastic state.

Q. 6.—Shall not those religious who do not apply themselves to study, be considered as persons useless to society?

A.—Such a thought cannot stand much examination, for it derives its existence from the weak faith of men, and from their usual custom of judging all things by human prudence. Since they are not otherwise informed, they do know not how to value the free access and influence which the saints acquire with God by their penance. As they cannot understand that those who are sequestered from society assist it by secret ways, and by means unknown to men, so they undervalue the services they receive by the mediation of religious men.

A religious appears in public, gives himself up to preaching, composes volumes, and frequently with very little fruit; he is considered as doing wonders. Another in the deep recesses of solitude supports by his fervent prayers and holy life, the truths of faith and the glory of the Church. He preserves whole kingdoms and states, and yet no person takes any notice of him, because the connections which unite those great events with their causes do not appear. Nevertheless, whatever men may think of this matter, it will be no less true that while monks perform their duty in the world, while they keep themselves in the way in which they have

---

[199] Epistola CVI, Ad magistrum Henricum Murdach, PL 182:241 (1854).

been placed by God, and fulfill their rules with that piety and devotion to which they are obliged, they will be so far from being useless to the world, that on the contrary, it may be said that no other persons do more for its preservation, and consequently, that there are none to whom the public are more indebted.

You ought to know, my brethren, that all the obligations of a religious, particularly of those who are solitaries, may be reduced to three principal ones. The first is that they are bound to bear the sins of men before the justice of God, and to do penance for those who do not think of doing anything of that kind. The second, that they sanctify the world by their example. And the third, that they intercede for the world with God without interruption, so that they may obtain of His infinite goodness all the graces and blessings which are necessary for the good of society.

These are the real helps and advantages which the world has a right to expect and require of solitaries. And solitaries will fulfill these duties with regard to the world, not by their learning and talents, but by their penance, sanctity and prayers. Hence, the assistance which monks are obliged to give to the world, does not depend on their studies and knowledge; and it is no less than a popular error to imagine that they are useless to the public, because they are not learned.

In effect, my brethren, what assistance has not the world received of monks and solitaries while they assiduously aspired to obtain the spirit and perfection of their state, while they were faithful to keep their vows, and to preserve the purity of their rules? They were the refuge and salvation of sinners. Their extraordinary penance penetrated and softened the most obdurate hearts. The almost incredible labors and austerities they undertook peopled Africa, Asia, and finally almost the then known world, with innumerable penitents. They vanquished pagan incredulity and reduced their idols to dust. Nor was the life they led on earth of less edification and glory to the Church, than the blood the martyrs poured forth in defense of the faith.

Here we behold Saints Anthony [201] and Julian Sabas leaving their deserts by the command of God; the one appearing in Alexandria, and the other

---

[201] S. Athanasius, *Vita Sancti Antonii Abbatis,* In Heriberti Rosweyde, S.J., *Vitae Patrum.* PL 73:127 / Richard Challoner. *The Lives of the Most Eminent Saints of the Oriental Deserts* (NY: McLoughlin, 1841), 39.

in Antioch; both triumphing over the pride and insolence of heretics, by the sole reputation of the sanctity they had acquired.

The same Saint Julian having been informed that Julian the apostate had formed sanguinary resolutions against Christians, offered up fervent prayers to God during the space of ten days, to avert the persecution with which the Church was menaced. At the end of that time he heard a voice that told him that that execrable and cursed monster was no longer in the world.[202]

Saint James, bishop of Nisibis, who had been an anchorite, by his mediating prayers drove the whole Persian army from before the city of Nisibis, when they were just about taking it; he deprived the impious Arius of his life by the force of the same means.

Saint John of Egypt, whom Theodosius the Great consulted as a second Elias, gained battles by his prayers, and won victories after he had prophesied them.

Saint Bernard by his prayers threw the army of Roger, king of Sicily, into disorder, and put him not only to flight, but also completely overthrew him, after he had espoused the anti-pope's cause.

About the end of the last century, Saint Catherine of Cordona knew in spirit what passed on the memorable day of the battle of Lepanto; she decided the success of that happy event by the tears and prayers she poured forth before God. Her prayers changed the winds in favor of the Christians; and it may be said with truth, that she had a greater part in that glorious victory than those who contributed to it by their strength and valor.

How many times have those visible angels been seen causing rain to descend from Heaven to fertilize the sterile land? They calmed tempests, appeased the fury of the elements, arrested the arm of divine justice when lifted up to strike the earth. They healed the most inveterate maladies, raised the dead to life, expelled devils from those who were possessed. In a word, there is no kind of assistance that men have not received from God by the mediation of those holy solitaries, and the same thing may be said of them as was said of their Divine Master, that they filled the countries and places where it had pleased the Divine Providence to establish them with blessings and graces.

All those wonders, my brethren, were the effects of the sanctity of

---

[202] Theodoret, *Philotheus,* Caput II, Julianus Sabas, In Heriberti Rosweyde, S.J., *Vitae Patrum*. PL 74:20.

solitaries. Study and learning had no part in them, and they wrought all these prodigies by their humility, penance, simplicity, love of Jesus Christ, and by the purity of their faith.

But take notice, my brethren, for your instruction, that just as the piety of holy monks has been the salvation of many, so the impiety of bad religious has been the scandal of the world and the destruction of the monastic state. The one by virtue and penance continually pray down the mercy of God, while the others never cease to provoke His wrath. If, then, if to the former all the blessings and prosperity given by God to men may with so much justice be attributed, there is no less reason to impute to the latter, many of the calamities and evils which afflict the world.

We learn by sacred history that the sin of Achan (Joshua 7), though it was personal, and seemed to be nothing very criminal, yet it cost three thousand persons their lives, and God was disposed to punish it by the destruction of all His people. The sins of the sons of Heli the high priest, caused the bloody defeat of the same people, the capture of the ark of the covenant, and the sudden death of their father (1 Kings 4).

When these events are well considered, it will be easy to discover that nothing is more capable of drawing down the indignation of the Lord on whole empires than the disorder of monasteries, and the licentious conduct of monks. For where impiety is once entered into the sanctuary, when the temple of the Most High is become the retreat of His enemies, and when those whom He had set apart to serve as vessels of honor, for the glory and sanctity of His house, dishonor it, then it is that He pours down His vengeance in a more rigorous and terrifying manner.

For when those who ought to cover the sins of the people by the innocence and merit of their lives, and stand between them and the justice of God, have themselves become objects of His wrath, then there is nothing more to solicit and move His compassion, or to stem the fury of His vengeance. Then it is, that the accomplishment is seen of these terrible menaces which He announced by His prophet: All the arrows He shall let fly against His enemies shall make deep wounds; His sword shall be inebriated with their blood; and He will seem to measure His punishments with the extent of His power (Deut 32:41).

This is what made the saints of the primitive ages, who knew perfectly the ways of God, declare that the excesses, crimes and disorders of those persons who are particularly consecrated to Him are the real causes of the evils which happen in the world. The desolation of states, the persecutions

of the Church, and the ravages of infidels in every Catholic country are the unhappy consequences of their infidelities to God.

Q. 7.—Are not religious persons to be considered sufficiently exempt from manual labor, when they apply themselves to the instruction of souls?

A.—Saint Augustine proposes to himself a similar observation, and answers it by saying that if some religious are employed in teaching in monasteries, they are not all in the same case, nor in the same functions. And that even those who are applied to it, so far from being able to say with the apostle, that they filled all the country from Jerusalem to Illyria with the gospel, and that they are commissioned to maintain the peace of the Church in all the barbarous nations of the east, they are for the most part assembled in communities where they pass their time in inaction and sloth.[203]

Your question, my brethren, according to the sentiment of that great doctor regards only the mendicant religious, who are sometimes employed by bishops in the functions of the ministry, but not those who are monks in the strict sense of the word, destined to live in retirement, and therefore, not concerned in the care and direction of souls; though the former ought to secure to themselves some part of their time, if possible, so that they may sanctify themselves in the exercise of manual labor.

Saint Basil was of the same opinion when he said that even those who are usefully employed in monasteries for the glory of God, ought nevertheless apply themselves to manual labor with all possible care and affection.

Q. 8.—Is it proper for religious to dispense with themselves in point of manual labor, to the end, that they may have more time for prayer, and thus lead more interior and spiritual lives?

A.—That reason, my brethren, will have no weight, except in the minds of those who do not know that though religious persons have generally laid manual labor aside, yet they have not become more spiritual or more holy. On the contrary, so far from leading a life more perfect and sublime, they for the most part have suffered themselves to be carried away by the grossest vices, or by passions, which, though more concealed and delicate, are no less contrary to the sanctity of their state.

"I wish to know," says Saint Augustine,

> How those monks will employ their time who will not labor? Undoubtedly they will say, that they apply themselves to prayer, reading, and to medita-

tions on the word of God. I allow that such a life is agreeable and laudable: but how can we remain so without interruption? Shall we take no time for eating; preparing what is necessary for life? And if necessity oblige us to give some time to those exercises, why shall we not find some to obey the apostle's precept?

"The prayer of a man," continues the same saint,

> Who obeys the law of God, is sooner heard than ten thousand prayers of his who despises it. Prayer may be employed, and the divine praises sung, while manual labor is attended to: we may console ourselves in the one, at the same time we are employed in the other.... And what can hinder the servant of God from meditating on His holy law, while his hands are employed at work, and to raise his voice in praising His holy name? [204]

Saint Bernard speaking on the same subject says that we ought to be careful not to neglect exterior things. Nor are we to imagine that he who does not exercise himself in corporal works becomes immediately spiritual, since on the contrary spiritual virtues, which are the most excellent, cannot be acquired without much difficulty, nor even at all, unless by the penitential exercises of corporal mortifications. Saint Paul teaches similarly when he says, that no one begins by the spiritual (1 Cor 15:46), but that the corporal precedes, and is followed by the spiritual. As the patriarch Jacob did not first espouse the beautiful Rachel, who was the figure of the spiritual contemplative life, until he had first been united with Leah, who was the sign of the active life; and that the excellency of the religious life consists in embracing the one and the other with discretion and wisdom.[205]

We find a remarkable thing in the works of Saint Peter, Abbot of Cluny.[206] The religious of that institute pretended to follow the spirit of Saint Benedict's rule (who so expressly enjoins manual labor to avoid idleness) by giving, as they said, all the time destined for that exercise to reading, study, and meditation. But Saint Peter, who had been of the same mind, as appears by his twenty eighth letter, soon changed his opinion, for we find by his statutes that he enjoins manual labor, which had been

---

[204] S. Augustinus, Monachorum, caput, XVII. PL 40:564 (1841).

[205] *Apologia ad Guillelmum*, PL 182:908 (1854).

[206] S. Petrus Venerabilis, Liber I, Epistola XXVIII, PL 189:112 (1854).

rejected in his congregation. [207]He assures us that he found by experience how pernicious such a change was.

For example, the greater part of the community, particularly the lay brethren, were so given up to sloth that—except very few who employed their time in reading and writing—the whole were seen asleep, leaning against the walls within and without the cloisters. Moreover, they spent their time from morning to night, and sometimes until midnight, in vain and useless conversations when they could do it without fear of being reprehended. And frequently these discourses were nothing less than real detraction and calumnies. It is deserving of notice, that the saint published his statutes only after having consulted with the most ancient and wise of his brethren, of those who were most penetrated with the fear of God, and by the consent of the general chapter of his order.

All this evidently proves that the cessation of manual labor is by no means the way to arrive to perfection; and that those who reject the occupations of Martha, do not find the repose of Mary in exchange. Indeed, my brethren, if things were not so, the holy monks of antiquity would have been strangely mistaken, and those who succeed them in latter times would prove themselves much more enlightened and wise. For the primitive solitaries, who proposed to themselves nothing more than Christian perfection—to which they desired to lead their successors also—enjoined manual labor by such express rules, and placed it amongst the principal regular exercises. On the contrary, our modern religious have rejected it as a useless occupation that may be supplied by other practices more advantageous, as they claim.

Now, although there was nothing to decide the difference but experience, that alone is sufficient to remove every doubt on the subject. For it is a fact, well known by all, that monks were never more holy, nor more esteemed, than during the time they were animated with the spirit and simplicity of the gospel, and exercised themselves in manual labor. Neither is it less true that since they have forsaken this exercise, they have fallen into a wretched state of inaction that has made them the scorn of men. Though there have been some who have enlightened the Church by their piety and learning, yet it is too true that the monastic state is quite disfigured. Its beauty has lost the principal features which made it so amiable, and without saying anything of those religious who live in public disorder, the others may well

---

[207] S. Petrus Venerabilis, *Statua Congregtionis Cluniacensis*, PL 189:1023(1890).

employ all their efforts to set themselves off with false merit. To gain the esteem of men they will scarcely ever be even the shades of those who preceded them in the monastic life.

Q. 9.—May it not be said that manual labor was formerly a convenient employment for monks when they were generally lay men; but that it can no longer be considered as such, since they are now almost all raised to the dignity of the priesthood?

A.—That such an assertion might be well founded, it would be first necessary to prove that religious priests are dispensed from labor by the laws of the Church, or that they are exempt by monastic rules, or finally that they have employments in their monasteries compatible with that exercise.

The first of these three positions is without any foundation, for the apostles labored with their hands, and the Church has enjoined that priests, and even those who have the care of souls, should learn trades for the purpose of employing their time in manual labor, as we learn from the fourth council of Carthage. In the fifty-first canon it is said that however skilled an ecclesiastic may be in the holy scriptures, he ought to live by his work.[208] And in the fifty-second, that an ecclesiastic ought to find his necessary food and clothing by the help of some decent trade, or by means of agriculture, without doing any injury to the functions of his ministry.[209] And in the fifty-third, that all the ecclesiastics who are able to work, must learn trades, besides applying themselves to study.

The second stands on no better ground, for the rules given us by the saints equally oblige all monks to manual labor, without exception or distinction. They were so very far from having even the idea of excepting those who would be engaged in holy orders, that on the contrary, Saint Benedict does not allow the least dispensation in that point to the priests who should embrace his rule. He binds them in the same manner as others to all the exactitude of regular discipline.[210] He requires that they should assist at and partake in every common exercise, that they should go before

---

[208] "Clericus quantum libet verbo Dei eruditus, artificio victum quaerat.".

[209] "Clericus victum et vestimentum, sibi artificiolo vel agricultura absque officii sui detrimento paret."

[210] *RB* 60.2.

their brethren and become their models in humility, and every other virtue.[211]

As to their employments, they have no particular exercises, unless they are charged with the care of souls. And in that case they are more strictly obliged to become models of every virtue, and to animate their brethren by their good example. If it be objected, that priests ought to possess a more extensive degree of learning and information, the answer is not difficult. Let them carefully employ their time appointed for *lectio* by the rules, without losing the least part of it, and they may be certainly assured that they shall acquire every necessary qualification, and become eminent doctors in the science of the saints.

Therefore, to claim that because monks are raised to the dignity of the priesthood, they are therefore exempt from manual labor, is mere imagination. Were it said, that they forsook that exercise, when they were indiscriminately promoted to the sacred character, there would be truth in the assertion; but it would not follow that they had proper reasons to claim such an exemption, or to infer that they were no longer concerned in a rule so general, so important and so much authorized.

Saint Thomas also, who is most favorable to dispensations from manual labor, nevertheless exempts none from it but such religious as are employed in the instruction of the faithful, in ecclesiastical functions, or in other employments by which they render public service to the Church; but not solitaries who have no such employments, and who profess rules obliging them to work.

Be not astonished, my brethren, to find so many difficulties on this matter, for however evident a truth may be, there are always a great many false reasons which oppose it. Flesh and blood, says Saint Augustine, employ every effort to corrupt holy things, and to obscure those which are clear and evident.[212]

And in effect, there can be no other cause found for this opposition so general, which religious persons everywhere manifest for labor. For although some persons may be dispensed from it for very just and holy reasons, chiefly at such times as the Church is pleased to make use of their ministry, nevertheless to banish this exercise entirely from the cloister is to expel the piety of monasteries, to introduce idleness amongst those who

---

[211] *RB* 60.5.

[212] Augustinus, *De Opere Monachorum*, Caput IX, PL 40:556 (1845).

dwell in them, and with it every species of disorder and licentiousness. Concupiscence alone is the cause of those pernicious effects. And if anyone will only take the pains to trace them to their source, they will be found to be the natural productions of pride, sloth, and effeminacy.

Monks would no longer give themselves to a mean contemptible occupation, which requires a virtue they no longer possessed. They became weary of an exercise that filled up all the empty spaces of their lives and left them not one moment of dangerous leisure. This act of uninterrupted penance, this mortification of sense, seemed to them an insupportable subjection. And that they might deliver themselves from a yoke they were disposed to carry no longer, they adopted the pretext of studies, lectures, and the meditation of holy subjects. They said that they could employ the time destined for manual labor more usefully in the exercises of interior piety.

But some had not even a thought of employing themselves a single moment in that manner; others may have begun to do something of that nature; but as there are only few who are capable of interior functions, chiefly when they are great and continual, so the consequence was that they were soon disgusted and entirely relinquished that employment. Hence, not being supported either by the occupations of the mind, or the action of the body, they fell into a state of idleness, and into all the vices and excesses from which the saints endeavored to preserve themselves by the pursuit of manual labor.

Finally, my brethren, give no ear to the discourses of men when they are contrary to your duties. Remain steadfast in the tradition of your holy fathers; observe inviolably the rules they have given you; say to those who tempt your faith and obedience what the sons of Jonadab said to Jeremiah, "We will obey the voice of our fathers, and observe their precepts" (Jer 35:8); and be assured, that the Lord will reward your piety, by giving you a part in the blessings he announced to that faithful race by the mouth of his prophet, "Because you have obeyed the precept of Jonadab your father, and have kept all his commands, and have done everything he enjoined to do. Therefore, thus, says the Lord of hosts, the God of Israel, there shall not be wanting a man of Jonadab's family, the son of Rechab, to stand in My sight for ever"(Jer 35:18).

Q. 10.— What are the works in which religious persons ought to be employed?

A.—Saint Basil says that it is difficult to point out in what trades or exercises monks ought to be employed, because they formerly made choice of different works and occupations, according to the diversity of countries and commerce. Nevertheless, he requires that those be adopted which are of such a nature as not to disturb the peace and tranquility which ought to reign in a religious community, and such as may be disposed of when done, without much difficulty, or without engaging the religious in a communication with persons of both sexes; and, on the whole, that modesty and simplicity be attended to. He enjoins that the brethren must never be employed in such works as are calculated to gratify the bad passions of men, and that care must be taken never to occupy their time or persons in operating such things as the lovers of vanity seek with so much ardor and curiosity.

He comes to particulars and says, that if for example, the brethren make linen, it ought to be such as serve for necessary use, but not such as might become dangerous to young people, who are already too much inclined to sensuality and levity. He gives the same advice to shoemakers, he allows them to work only for common use and necessity. He approves of carpenters', joiners', and masons' trades, as being proper for solitaries; also, that of working in brass, and agriculture, as being very useful employments, and very necessary for life. These occupations ought to be encouraged (says the saint), unless they cause disturbance and confusion, for in that case, they must be banished from the monastery, and others substituted in their place, which do not hinder recollection and the presence of God, dispositions which we ought to cultivate continually; so, that our occupations ought never be able to deter us from the divine office, prayer and other exercises which are peculiar to those who profess a regular life and an exact piety.

Above all he recommends agriculture, because it produces everything necessary for life. Moreover it preserves those who employ themselves in it from the necessity of going from place to place, and traveling to distant parts. He supposes that such an exercise produces no confusion or tumult in the neighborhood, nor within or without the monastery.

Ecclesiastical history informs us, that the most ordinary employment amongst the ancient solitaries of Thebaid, and other parts of Egypt was making baskets, ropes and mats, and during the harvest, as we before observed, they hired themselves to save the corn, and to do other work proper to that season.

Palladius relates that in the monastery of Saint Pacomius the monks were employed in diverse sorts of labor. Some worked at agriculture, others in the garden, some at the mill, some at baking, some were smiths, others were fullers, tanners, shoemakers, writers and basket makers. In the deserts of Porphyrion and Calame the solitaries applied themselves chiefly to agriculture and the care of flocks.

Saint Ephrem, relating the different employments at which solitaries labored in his time, says that some were occupied in the different offices of the community, others wrote books, others made linen, some made baskets, mats, purple colored paper, and such like.

Saint Isidore of Seville, requires that the brethren should do all their own necessary work, repair all that may be wanting in their furniture, clothing, and in all the necessary utensils of the monastery.

We find the same thing, or nearly the same, in Saint Benedict's rule. By it the brethren are shown reaping, saving the harvest, working in the garden, bakehouse, kitchen, and in general employed in everything necessary for the service and advantage of the house.

We read that when King Clotair asked Saint Junian if he wanted anything, he told his majesty that he was a monk and superior of a monastery; that they lived according to Saint Benedict's rule, as exactly as they possibly could, but that they could not observe it entirely, because they lived in a place which, being too confined, prevented them from laboring as the same rule required. At these words the king granted him a piece of ground sufficiently large to furnish the religious with proper means of employing themselves at manual labor, and the saint built a monastery on the place.

The Cistercian monks were not less exact in observing this part of the rule than they were in every other; but it is useless to repeat here what we have already said of their great and various labors.

As for you, my brethren, who are obliged to perform many duties from which the ancient solitaries were exempt, you are bound by the Church offices, prayers and other exercises which she did not expect from them. If you cannot imitate them in their great labors, endeavor to imitate them at least in the spirit and affection with which they applied themselves to them, so that you may not lose all the advantages and profit they produce. Follow them as closely as you can, though you cannot overtake them in the way. This you may expect to accomplish, if you employ at manual labor all the time that intervenes between the different offices in which you are not occupied in pious reading, and in the other exercises prescribed by the rule.

If you perform in your house what those religious who have rejected manual labor effect by the hands of daily laborers, or by servants; and to speak more in detail, if you prepare the necessary food of the community, if you wash your own clothes, clean your own stables, manure and cultivate your own lands, prepare and dress your own gardens without any exterior assistance, with care and fervor, in such a manner as that you may derive your principal subsistence from them; if you make your own linen, spoons, baskets, shoes and such other like works, without calling in, or having recourse to exterior tradesmen; in fine, if you neglect nothing of those things which are necessary for the service of your house, and embrace with joy the lowest and most contemptible employments, I say, if you persevere in doing all these—as your holy rule enjoins—you will sanctify yourselves, give glory to God, and great edification to the Church.

20 | ON NIGHT WATCHINGS—

Q. 1. —By what reasons were the ancient monks induced to be so rigorous and exact in the observance of night watchings?   213

Q. 2.— These are sentiments indeed which prove the inimitable zeal and fervor which animated those great men; but we request that you will propose something more proportionate to our weakness.   216

20

ON NIGHT WATCHINGS

QUESTION 1.—By what reasons were the ancient monks induced to be so rigorous and exact in the observance of night watchings?

ANSWER.—As the ancient solitaries desired nothing more ardently than to correspond with the grace of their vocation, and to accomplish the will of God, by continually aspiring to the perfection of their state, so were they particularly attentive to avoid every obstacle that might impede them, and to seek every means that might assist them in prosecuting their designs. As they thought that night watchings might contribute much to their purpose, so they diminished the time of sleep as much as they could, and allowed themselves no more time for rest than what they could not refuse to the wants and pressing necessities of nature.

First, they found a particular happiness in conforming to the example of our Lord in this respect, who having employed the whole day in the duties of His mission, and in instructing the people, He spent whole nights in retirement and prayer (Luke 6:12).

Secondly, they imitated the examples of the holy apostles who, following that of their Divine Master, sang the praises of God at the hours in which others were accustomed to take their rest, as we read in Acts.

Thirdly, solitaries were induced by the spirit of piety which animated them to embrace this holy practice so much recommended to the Christians of the first ages of the Church. These assembled at night for common prayer, and to comfort themselves in reading the holy scriptures and in singing devout hymns and pious canticles. This they did either because the day seemed too short to satisfy their ardent zeal and love, or because they desired to keep themselves always ready, prepared for the second coming of our Lord, according to the opinion they entertained that He would come to judge the world in the middle of the night. They inferred this from His own words: "A great cry was heard in the middle of the night, behold the spouse cometh; go ye forth and meet Him" (Matt 25:6).

Fourth, those divine men whose conversation was already in Heaven, and who had entirely forgotten the earth, could not well avoid loving night watches, for they considered sleep as a real waste of time. In it the spiritual action of man is arrested, and as he loses his noble and excellent qualities during that suspension, he is leveled to a similarity with the brute creatures, over which God has given him such great advantages.

Fifth, those great saints—being endowed with a truly evangelical purity—were extremely afflicted at the idea that during the time of sleep the temple of the living God, that is, their bodies, were without their usual guards and abandoned to their enemies. These found free access into them, became in some degree masters there, filled their imaginations with illusions and their minds with every kind of vain thought, reviving in their memories the ideas of those things which ought to be entirely effaced, extending their power and malignity over the senses, and casting the whole man interiorly and exteriorly into a state of confusion and disorder.

They continually sighed at beholding themselves in a subjection so grievous. Nor did they ever close their eyes but with fear and trembling. For though they knew that the majesty of God was only offended by the consent of the will, nevertheless, as they considered themselves as the guardians of His sanctuary, as they loved the beauty, honor and glory of His dwelling above all other things (Ps 25:8), so they could not behold without horror what passed within them, lest it might oppose His sanctity and divine presence, whether it was voluntary or not.

Sixth, they knew that watchings cooled the heat of concupiscence, as a great saint formerly said. They expel evil dreams, produce penitential tears, soften the heart, make us vigilant and exact in the choice of our thoughts. They allay the ardor of our passions, stem the indiscreet liberty of the tongue, dispel the obscurity of the mind, disperse the illusions which tarnish the beauty of the soul and disturb its repose.[213] In a word, they knew that it is in evening and night prayer that the religious soul lays up all its treasure of virtue, and the riches of heavenly knowledge.

They knew that on the contrary sleep and the immoderate love of

---

[213] *Scala*, PG 88:939d (1864) / *Ladder*, 162.5

rest extinguishes all the vigor of our souls, fills our minds with darkness, hardens our hearts, dries up the source of tears, extinguishes piety, banishes the presence of God, dissipates the mind in prayer, foments the irregularity of the senses and produces insensibility for heavenly things. Sloth, love of good cheer, disgust for instructions and pious reading are all its effects. In fine, they knew that the carnal man is nourished and strengthened in the softness of sleep, that by it his inclinations become more ardent and wicked, that the soul is enervated by sleep, loses its vigor, its light, and its strength.

Therefore, they found pleasure in mortifying their bodies and in subjecting their senses, as well by privation of sleep as by fasting. And if they allowed themselves some hours of repose during the night, it seemed as if they did it more for the purpose of suffering the pain of interrupting it than for the pleasure of enjoying it, or so that preserving the victim by some momentary indulgence, their sacrifice might be longer, and their martyrdom more protracted.

Such are the motives, my brethren, which induced the ancient monks to be so rigorous in the practice of night watchings, and so reserved in the use of sleep. It was this that made Saint Arsenius spend whole nights in prayer, and say that one hour's sleep should suffice for a true solitary.

This it was that induced the great Saint Anthony, after having passed the whole night in continual prayer, from the beginning to sunrise in the morning, to exclaim, when the first rays of that luminary beat on his eyes, "Oh sun, how importunate art thou? Thou hast deprived me of my true light." [214]

Animated with the same sentiments, Saint Dorotheus never willingly closed his eyes. It frequently happened to him that being overcome with weariness, when taking his scanty meal the bit fell from his mouth; and when some persons endeavored to convince him that it was necessary to take some rest on his mat, he did not hesitate to say that a solitary who desires to advance in virtue would be disposed (as far as possible) to vie even with the angels in avoiding sleep.[215]

Saint Pacomius seeing himself pressed by the continual attacks of the devil, besought the Almighty to give him grace to overcome sleep, so that he might fight his enemies, day and night, according to the words of the

---

[214] In *Vitae Patrum,* PL 73:848. (1849).

[215] Palladius, *Historia Lausiaca,* PG 34:1013 (1860).

prophet: "I will fight against my enemies, and will never give over until they are all overcome"(Ps 17:38).

Q. 2.— *These are sentiments indeed which prove the inimitable zeal and fervor which animated those great men; but we request that you will propose something more proportionate to our weakness.*

A.—I grant, my brethren, that we cannot presume to imitate such examples. But if it may be said that the recollection of them is a just cause for the shame of our times, as well as for the glory of the past ages, we may

also affirm that there are other examples in antiquity itself which, though more temperate, yet furnish matter of great instruction.

Saint Basil used to say that sleep caused great loss and watchings produced great advantages;[216] that he who sleeps knows not even whether he is alive or dead; but that he who watches may raise himself to God by meditation and prayer; that a solitary ought to pray at the beginning and middle of the night; and that the light of day ought never to surprise him in bed.[217] Moreover, in a letter to Saint Gregory he says that the sleep of a solitary ought to be light, conformably to his abstinence, and that however short it may be, he ought to endeavor to interrupt it by his solicitude for the great things with which his heart is replenished.[218]

Cassian relates that the solitaries of Africa immediately applied themselves to manual labor after the night prayers, or divine office. They paid particular attention to that exercise, so that they might better resist sleep, lest the devil should make use of it to lay snares for their souls, destroy the fruit of their prayers, and tarnish the purity they had acquired by singing the divine praises. Or lest he should overcome those by sleep who had vanquished him by watching. When on great solemnities they began the office at the vespers of the evening before and continued it the whole night, they then allowed themselves only one or two hours sleep to prevent nature from being exhausted.[219] There was scarcely ever a monastic order that did not adore the Lord in the obscurity and silence of the night.

---

[216] S. Basilius, *Brevius,* Interrogatio XLIV, PG 31:1110 (1857).

[217] S. Basilius, *Fusius,* Interrogatio XXXVII, PG 31:1014 (1857).

[218] S.Basilius, *Epistolae,* Epistola II, PG 32:223 (1857).

[219] *Institutiones,* PL 49:101(1846) / *Institutes* 2.12 (NPNF2/11:210).

Saint Benedict, who restrained whatever appeared too severe in the ancient observances, nevertheless did not fail to leave us in his rule injunctions which are both exact, painful and useful; painful because nature must do violence to itself when there is question of interrupting sleep in the middle of the night.[220] This rule is not only useful because such a practice—including the pain that is felt in the sacrifice of our rest, but also the mortification of the body—becomes very meritorious before God; but it is moreover very profitable, because prayer when offered to the Lord in the darkness of the night is more pure, more ardent, and more animated. For the mind not being distracted by a variety of sensible objects, the attention is more undivided and the praises which are offered become more acceptable to His Divine Majesty. The time of night, says Saint Jerome, offers a very favorable occasion to those who desire to entertain themselves with the Lord in devout prayer; and it is no less profitable for those who watch because it introduces them into the presence of God, after having been purified from the thoughts of all earthly things.[221]

Here you see, my brethren, of what utility night watchings are in the monastic state, and though the saints instituted them from very solid reasons and holy considerations; though they are replete with a variety of graces and benedictions, nevertheless you will derive no advantages from them, unless you support them with the necessary dispositions. In a word, as vocal prayer is to no purpose, unless it be accompanied with the prayer of the mind, so it will be of very little advantage to watch with the eyes, unless you do it also with the heart. Your senses will be unprofitably awake if your souls are languishing in drowsiness and sleep, for the prayers we address to the Lord in the night can contribute to our sanctification only in proportion as they are accompanied with fervent zeal, with sincere piety, and with such pure devotion as may render them worthy of being heard.

21 | OF POVERTY—CONTENTS

Q. 1.—*You have already spoken of the excellence and extent of religious poverty, but we now request that you will show us in detail, the manner in which we ought to practice it.* 221

Q. 2.—*Does it not hence follow, that a religious ought not to have his cell adorned with curious and neat furniture, like that which is found in the chambers of worldly people?* 222

Q. 3.—*Is it proper for religious persons to have rich and magnificent church ornaments?* 226

Q. 4.—*Are religious persons obliged to give much alms?* 229

Q. 5.—*When a religious is allowed money for his use, can he in conscience keep any of it in reserve, on condition of giving his superiors an account of it, when they require he should do so?* 235

Q. 6.—*Is it reasoning justly to say, that any religious may be allowed the use of money, since there is no difficulty made, in placing money in the hands of the housekeeper, or in allowing the same to a religious, who is sent to some considerable distance from the monastery?* 241

Q. 7.—*Is it lawful for religious persons to increase their property by making new purchases?* 243

Q. 8.—*Tell us also whether money or some temporal emolument may be required of those who desire to embrace the religious state.* 249

Q. 9.— Why do you condemn the custom of requiring money for receptions?   250

Q. 10.—A third reason remains yet to be known—in what manner has the Church explained herself on this subject?   256

Q. 11.— Which are the monasteries that may, therefore, be considered poor, and what regulations ought they observe?   261

Q. 12.—One of the first reasons opposed to your opinion is, that in those stipulations which you condemn, the contracting parties have no design to exact money as the price of a spiritual thing; it is only considered in the secret of the intention, as a simple condition, or as a motive.   262

Q. 13.—For a second reason it is said, that in those receptions, the spirituality of religion is not the thing which is given for the money received, but only that which is temporal in religion, such as the food of the person who is admitted.   263

Q. 14.—In the third place, some pretend, that if poor communities may exact money for receptions, without incurring the guilt of simony, those that are rich may do the same, and that in such cases the conduct of the one is not less innocent than that of the other.   264

Q. 15.—Some religious who are lately established, pretend that they may exact money of the persons they admit, on pretext of building large mansions and magnificent churches.   265

Q. 16. —*In fine, some persuade themselves that this practice is approved of by the Church, since she knows it exists, and yet does not prohibit it.*   216

Q. 17.—*Is it improper to require presents for the church, or money to provide feasts?*   266

Q. 18.—*Your sentiments are supported by so many reasons, that it is difficult to resist the conviction they enforce.*   268

21

OF POVERTY

QUESTION 1.— *You have already spoken of the excellence and extent of religious poverty, but we now request that you will show us in detail, the manner in which we ought to practice it.*

ANSWER.—To what I have already said on this subject, I will add, my brethren, that a monk is not truly poor, if, when he is deprived of all the necessaries of life, he does not believe himself to be really happy in being in the way of imitating the poverty of which Jesus Christ has given us the example. And if he does not enter into the same dispositions as the poor man of the gospel, who being almost ready to die of hunger at the unmerciful rich man's gate, deserved by his persevering patience in the greatest extremities to be transferred from a kingdom of peace to a kingdom of glory. But as it is almost impossible, according to the present order established in the Church, that any religious can be in a similar state, I will tell you something more adapted to your position. When monks are poor in the manner they ought to be, they will not only remain destitute of the gifts of fortune, and of the riches of this world, but they will even love their condition in being deprived of them, and live with content and pleasure in their poverty.

Saint Bernard says that it is not poverty alone which makes the truly poor religious, but the love of poverty. To this we may add, that as the joy of the covetous man consists in finding out means and expedients of becoming rich, so the satisfactions of one evangelically poor, consists in never losing an occasion of becoming still poorer than he is. His love of poverty flows into all his actions. That virtue is in his heart like a living and abundant spring that diffuses its waters on every side. He is poor in all things and at all times. He is poor in his clothing, in his food, and in his furniture. He demonstrates it by his charity to the poor, by his unwillingness to acquire new possessions, or to undertake disorderly affairs to increase the revenues of his community. In fine, he testifies on every occasion a perfect disinterestedness and an entire nakedness of all the goods, superfluities, curiosities and advantages of this world.

Q. 2.—Does it not hence follow that a religious ought not to have his cell adorned with curious and neat furniture, like that which is found in the chambers of worldly people?

A.—A religious has undoubtedly renounced everything that retains any likeness to the luxury and vanity of the world. He is obliged by his state to be satisfied with the use of simple necessaries, and consequently everything contrary to exact poverty is to be retrenched.[222]

Saint Basil says that whatever is more than necessary is to be condemned as vain curiosity; and therefore he prohibits by those words every motive of place or decorum.

The Council of Trent prohibits all superfluities in the necessary furniture of religious persons, and enjoins that superiors are not to permit the use of any which does not agree with the poverty they have professed,[223] They have made themselves poor, not from the motive of hatred for the possessions they have left, since there is nothing naturally bad in them, but that they may overcome their passions, without which, such things are scarcely ever possessed. It is certain, that nothing can make it lawful for such persons to love and possess what is capable of reviving in them that which they should have proposed, and really did intend to destroy by the poverty they vowed.

Now as this affected neatness, this curious and studied furniture, such as pictures, paintings, vessels, watches, cabinets, and even crosses, medals, or holy water fonts, all which being precious either in the matter or form in which they are made, have no other end than that of gratifying self-love, flattering concupiscence, and nourishing luxury. We must agree that all these, and such like, are things which a religious has renounced by his vows, and consequently they ought to be numbered amongst those he is bound to reject.

When a Christian who lives in the world, and who, according to the gospel ought to be interiorly poor, does not observe this poverty in his furniture, train, and exterior conduct, he excuses himself on account of his condition, the decency and necessity that obliges him not to separate

himself entirely from the general mode adopted by those with whom he is compelled to live. And he is sometimes right. But for a monk to allege the same pretexts is unreasonable, because he cannot have any well-founded reasons of the like nature. For his state, as we have already said, is nothing less than a public profession of an humble life. "Our order is abjection; it is humility and voluntary poverty," says Saint Bernard.[224]

Hence, it is impossible to put on the garb of pretended decency, because that which most becomes a man who is poor by his state and profession, and whose happiness consists in poverty, is to evince this evangelical virtue in all the actions and circumstances of his life. And as for human approbation, though it were even lawful to seek such a phantom, it is certain that the surest way to attain that object (at least amongst the wiser sort of men) is to keep invariably within the limits of his state. Thus, my brethren, we may truly say that a religious who seeks these vain curiosities and worldly amusements cannot be induced to do so by any good motive; that the esteem he shows for them evinces the disorder of his heart and points out his want of self-denial; that it is an effect of the spirit of the world, by which he is governed, and of the contempt which he has for that great precept of Saint Benedict, by which he enjoins all monks to seek their pleasure and satisfaction in such things as are most vile, poor, and humiliating. [225]In fine, as the having poor furniture in the palace of a prince can never find approbation in good sense, so neither can reason enlightened by faith ever approve of precious ornaments in the cell of a monk.

But to show you more clearly that a religious ought to retrench all ornamental, curious, and superfluous commodities, I will relate a very remarkable case on this subject, which we read in the history of the Spanish barefooted Carmelites. Some years before the foundation of the house of Valladolid, these are the words of the history,

> The greater part of our religious had adopted the custom of carrying a pewter crucifix on their breast, after the example of Saint Catherine of Cordona, who had practiced the same, as we find by the history of her life. A little after her happy death, some began to wear crucifixes made of brass,

---

[224] "Ordo noster abjectio est, humilitas est." Epistola CXLII, Ad monachos alpenses. PL 182:297c (1854) / "Our order is lowliness, humility." /Bernard, *Works,* 1: 440–441.

[225] RB 7.49

wrought by excellent masters, and placed on crosses made of ebony; others who were still more curious had their crucifix gilt, and added to the end of their ebony crosses, small pieces of gilt brass, which were neatly set in. All that was not enough, for some fathers who were often employed in the office of preaching, provided themselves with crucifixes much larger than the others, in order that by showing them in the pulpit, they might affect their congregation and move them to compunction.

One of these latter, who outdid the rest in this passion, allowed himself to be so far led away by his curiosity, that he purchased an ivory crucifix of great value, which was sold to him, as to a friend at a very cheap rate, though it cost him no less than five hundred reals, which was given him by a devout friend. I am sure the image was made of ivory, and the cross of ebony; its length was two or three palms, and if I mistake not, the embossing was of silver. I will not name the person, that I may spare the honor of one of the most celebrated preachers our reformation possessed at its rise; neither will I conceal his weakness, that we may learn to what excess curiosity insensibly led some of our fathers, who otherwise made profession of a very exact poverty and austere penance.

Now the disorder was silently introduced little by little into this house in the space of five or six years. God however provided a remedy by means of our father Jesus Maria, who generously eradicated this abuse from our monastery; and afterwards from every other house of the reform. That great man having assembled the general chapter of Valladolid in the year 1587, at which time I had already made profession in this house, was informed that the above mentioned preacher kept his crucifix in his cell; and that amongst the capitulary fathers, some of them wore the like on their breasts, which were almost as valuable. In consequence of this information he commanded every one to lay his crucifix before him in his cell; and having severely reprimanded them, as such an abuse deserved, he deprived them of all their crucifixes, leaving the greatest and most valuable for the tabernacle of the church, with some others for the novices' oratory, ordering the prior to distribute the rest amongst the benefactors of the house.

And in order to prevent any future relaxation on the subject of poverty, he regulated the form and matter of the crucifix which was to be worn, ordaining the proper size, as has been ever since observed, without being enriched or adorned in any manner; and that the crosses should be quite simple, and made of common wood. This law has been inviolably observed ever since amongst us; and some having learned wisdom by this example, would have no crosses but such as were made of two small pieces of very common wood, which they continue to wear, according to the custom of the order, that they may gain the indulgences granted by several popes for that purpose.

This holy simplicity has been a just punishment for the superfluity of those curious members, and a very profitable instruction for religious souls, who ought not to form their devotion according to the inclinations of sense, but on the contrary, should seek that which is solid, and live in purity of spirit. In the same assembly it was forbidden to use girdles of leather with the hair unstripped, because some were found who, by a secret vanity procured for themselves girdles made of curious rare skins, giving thereby occasion of scandal to worldly people, who considered it as a mark of pride.[226]

Here you see, my brethren, that vanity springs from piety itself, and that concupiscence nourishes itself with devotional pretexts, when piety is not regulated according to good knowledge.

Q. 3.—Is it proper for religious persons to have rich and magnificent church ornaments?

A.—Before I make any reflections on this question, I will lay before you Saint Bernard's sentiments on the subject. That saint, speaking of the evil customs which were introduced into the order of Cluny says:

> I come now to the greater abuses, but which seem the lesser, because they are now common. I will say nothing of the immense height, the great length, and the vast breadth of their churches; of the sumptuous embellishments, and curious paintings which are there seen in every part, which, attracting the eyes of those who pray, distract their minds from prayer, and bring to my remembrance, in some manner the ancient form of the Jewish religion. I allow that the whole may be done for the honor of God; but may not I speak as a religious to religious, and use the words by which the poet reprehended the idolatrous priests, saying like him: Tell me, pontiff, to what purpose have you placed gold in the sanctuary?
>
> May I not say, tell me, you who are poor, if indeed you are so, to what end have you introduced this gold into the churches of your order? for there is a difference between the cathedral churches of bishops, and those of religious. Bishops are debtors to the wise and the ignorant, as Saint Paul says, and by those exterior ornaments they may excite the devotion of the carnal people, which they cannot move by spiritual exercises. But we who have left the society of men; we, who have all forsaken the riches and splen-

---

[226] Seconde part. de l'Hist.d.Espag. Carmel. lib 5. c.14.

dors of the world for the love of Christ; we, who have cast away as filth and dung whatever might flatter the senses; such beautiful objects, music, perfumes, and all this to the end, that we may gain our Lord Jesus Christ. Whose devotion do we intend to excite by this magnificence and splendor? What other fruit can we reap? To what purpose are those crowns, or rather wheels, all resplendent with precious stones, in the temples of religious persons? Candlesticks are no longer employed, but trees of brass with many branches, which shine more by the diamonds and pearls that are set in them, than by the torches and wax candles that stand burning in them. To what end are those things directed? Is it to excite sentiments of sorrow and compunction in penitents? or rather pleasure and satisfaction in the beholders?

O vanity! O folly! the church shines and smiles in its edifices, while it mourns and is desolate in its poor members. It covers the stones of the temples with gold, and leaves its children quite naked! The curious find enough to feed their eyes, but the miserable want bread to satisfy their hunger! What connection is there between those superfluities and persons who have vowed poverty? Persons who are called religious! spiritual men![227]

Here you behold the principal points of the saint's complaints. He adds,

I have abridged this discourse, because 1 had rather say a little with peace, than much with scandal; and I wish that even the little I have said may be received without emotion or scandal; for I know that while I am reprehending the disorders, I offend the persons disordered. Nevertheless it may happen by an effect of grace, that those whom I fear to offend may not be offended; but that cannot be the case unless they cease to be disordered.

Now, what you are to infer from this, my brethren, is that the churches may be richly and splendidly adorned which serve for the use of the people, because they being generally carnal and led by the senses, and their devotion being either dead or languishing, they have need of being excited by exterior things. But as for monks who have been separated from this carnal world by a particular choice of God, who are no longer inhabitants of Babylon, but citizens of the holy city above, the heavenly Jerusalem, their faith ought to be more lively, their piety more pure, and their worship more animated. Hence that sensible beauty, that pomp and magnificence

---

[227] Apolog. c.11.

either in the ornaments of the church or in the structure of the buildings, in the paintings, singing, musical instruments, etc. are not conformable to the purity or sanctity of their state.

Those things are good in themselves, and are proper in such cases as I have cited above, but for persons of our condition they only become as so many occasions of dissipation. They help to revive in our minds the remembrance of what ought to be forever entirely expelled. They invite the world into our solitude, and tend to disturb the peace and repose of our retreat. In a word, it frequently happens, as Saint Bernard says, that by a false and unintelligent piety things are given to the inanimate temples of the Lord which are useless to them, while necessaries are refused to the poor, who are the living temples of the Holy Spirit!

This sentiment of Saint Bernard was that of the whole order of Citeaux while it maintained its primitive spirit; and we find by many standing memorials, what an aversion those holy monks had for everything that could injure the simplicity or poverty of their state.

The history of this celebrated order informs us, that lest there should be anything in the house of God (in which they proposed to serve Him), that might have the smallest appearance of worldly vanity or superfluity, or be in the least degree adverse to the poverty they had vowed—which they esteemed as the guardian of every other virtue—they directed that the crosses which were to be used in their churches should neither be of gold or silver, but merely of painted wood, that there should be only one iron candlestick, one thurible, of brass or iron, that the chasubles should be of woollen or linen cloth, without gold or silver; that they should never use copes, or dalmatics; the chalices should be silver unadorned, or at most silver gilt, but not of entire gold, that the stoles and maniples should be without gold or silver. [228]

By a general chapter of the order was forbidden under the menace of considerable punishment to use wrought altar cloths.[229]

By another it was appointed, that the chasubles should be simple, of only one color, and without gold or silver embroidery.[230]

---

[228] *Exordium Coenobii et Ordinis Cisterciensis,* Caput XVII. In *Nomasticon Cisterciense seu Antiquiores Ordinis Cisterciensis Constitutiones* (Paris, Alliot, 1664).

[229] Anno 1199.

[230] Anno 1134.

By another general chapter all carvings and paintings were prohibited in the churches of the order, and even in the places appointed for work in the monasteries, because the fathers considered that such things when made the object of too much application hinder the advantages of more sublime meditation, and injure the observance of religious discipline. It was also forbidden to use altar fronts painted with diverse colors—they were allowed to be painted only white.[231]

We find again, in another general chapter, an injunction given to the abbot of Royamount to remove the carvings, paintings, and pillars, adorned with the figures of angels, and the images he had lately placed around the high altar, and to reduce things to the ancient simplicity of the order. Namely, that the glasses of the windows should be simple, without paintings; that there should be neither gold nor silver on the books to be used in the divine office; that the bells should be small, so that one man alone might ring them, and that the steeples should not be of an excessive height, nor should towers be made of stone, but simply of wood, conformably to the spirit of the order. It was likewise forbidden to all the abbots of the order to use carpets when they officiated.

This detail appeared to me of such consequence, that I persuaded myself that the perusal would be of service to you, my brethren. Knowing what the spirit of your fathers was in this point, how much they cherished holy poverty, and what care they took to transmit to you proper rules for your conduct, that you may observe such a holy and religious moderation in your lives, as will entirely remove you from the least fault in a matter of such consequence. Also that you may conceive and nourish in your hearts a real separation, together with a sincere aversion for everything that presents the least appearance of the vanity, luxury, and superfluity of the lovers of this world.

Q. 4.—Are religious persons obliged to give much alms?

A.—There was nothing in which the piety and zeal of the ancients were more conspicuous, than in the solicitude with which they always endeavored to assist the poor.

They undertook everything possible to relieve them in their wants.

---

[231] *Instituta Capituli Generalis Ordinis Cisterciensis*, Caput XX, De Sculpturis et picturis, et cruce lignea. In *Nomasticon Cisterciense seu Antiquiores Ordinis Cisterciensis Constitutiones* (Paris, Alliot, 1664), 251.

Some of them gave up even their garments for that purpose, according to the injunctions of the gospel, and reduced themselves to a complete nudity. Others sold *themselves,* and forfeited their liberty for the sake of the suffering members of Christ. That was extraordinary, but the usual conduct of the holy monks of former times was to provide for the relief of the poor by their labors, and to feed them by the sweat of their brow. And we have already said that the solitaries of the higher Thebaid sent immense alms to Egypt, where not finding sufficient poor to consume the entire, they sent the remainder to more remote and distant countries of Africa. Their faith and charity were both equally animated. Every word of our Lord Jesus Christ, every signification of His holy will inflamed their piety. It was their consolation when they found occasions and means to prove by their actions what the love of that divine Master had engraved in their hearts.

Those perfect disciples of an incarnate God, knew that it is written, "Alms-deeds efface sins as fire is extinguished by water" (Ecclesiastic 3: 33); that to hide our alms in the bosom of the poor is to sow our seed in a land of blessings and abundance, and that a true Christian's ambition is to lay up immortal treasures.

But that which most affected them was the consideration of Jesus Christ in the person of the poor. They viewed Him under those old clothes and tattered garments; they saw Him pressed with hunger, parched with thirst, and overwhelmed with misery and fatigue. Such was the liveliness of their faith that all those objects became present to their minds, made them undervalue all their cares, time, labors and pains, provided they could relieve those who held the place of Jesus Christ. And their happiness would have been complete, if they could have sacrificed their lives for Him who had poured out the last drop of His blood for them.

There is no precept necessary to excite generous souls to the practice of alms-deeds. Faith is sufficient, since we believe that it is Jesus Christ who suffers, that it is He who extends His hands to crave assistance. How is it possible to be a Christian and to refuse, and thereby deserve this terrible reproach:

> I have been hungry, and you gave Me not to eat; I have been thirsty, and you gave Me not to drink; a stranger, and you did not take Me in; naked, and you clothed Me not; sick and in prison and you came not out to visit Me. Verily, I say to you that as often as you did not these things to the least of those who believe in Me, you have refused to do them to Me.

The primitive monks gave alms of their poverty, and those of our times ought certainly do the same out of their superabundance. The former were as poor themselves as those whom they relieved. They had no other means to assist them but their great and assiduous labors; but as to the latter, the incomes they have received from the piety of the faithful place them in the capacity, and under the obligation of comforting the distressed. The one gave because their faith was great. The others, besides being bound by the same reason, are moreover obliged to it by a new title, which is the will of their founders, who left them a part of their property only that they might disengage themselves of this twofold duty, by laying it on them, namely, that of employing themselves continually before God for the expiation of their sins by prayer and alms-deeds.

Therefore, monks ought to consider themselves as being bound to this duty by the will of their founders. They should consider themselves as the executors of their will, the dispensers of the property they have in their hands, the application of which has been committed to their care. And lest they should consider themselves as masters and proprietors of what they enjoy (since they only have the administration of it), or imagine that they fulfill their duty in this point provided they support a certain number of religious to sing or perform other common services, let it be known, and frequently considered, that monasteries, according to the intention of those who founded them, ought to be not only houses of penance and prayer, but likewise public and uninterrupted sources of charity and alms. This is so evident by the titles and acts of the foundations of monasteries, and by so many ecclesiastical testimonies and monuments, that it cannot be reasonably doubted.

William, Duke of Guienna, declares in the foundation of Cluny that he requires and wills during his life and after his death that abundant alms be given to the poor and to pilgrims in proportion to the property possessed by that house.[232] Many like expressions are found in other foundations, and particularly the following, regarding the property of the monks, and the patrimony of the poor, and again, provision for the monks and the poor.[233]

---

[232] In testament, tom. 24. con.gen.

[233] "In substantiam monachorum et alimoniam pauperum"; "in stipendio monachorum et pauperum." Exempla gratia: *Charta domni Alberici episcopi.* In *Joannis Monachi Chronicon Besuense.* PL 162:876 (1854).

Saint Urban I calls the revenues of churches the vows of the faithful, the price of sinners' offenses, and the patrimony of the poor.[234]

We find the following passages in a council held at Verneuil, under Charles the Bald, king of France. Addressing the king, the council says:

> We behold the anger of God ready to fall on us, and on your royal person as well, by the violent usurpations and other enormous crimes which are committed every day, for the churches are stripped of their goods in favor of worldly people though these goods had been consecrated to God by kings and by the faithful for the support of the sacred ministry, and for the relief of the poor, as also for the comfort of strangers, the redemption of captives, and for repairing the temples of the Lord. This is the reason why the servants of God are become a prey to hunger and thirst, the poor are deprived of their accustomed alms, pilgrims are neglected, captives are forsaken, and our reputation is so justly stigmatized. Truly, if pagans were the authors of these outrages, the Church might bear them patiently; but as we are oppressed by our own children, that is, by those whom we, or our predecessors have regenerated in Jesus Christ, who have received the sublime character of Christians by our ministry, the fear of their eternal ruin produces in our minds an inconsolable affliction. It is certain that no person can reasonably question the proper use and destination of Church property, because it is evidently the patrimony of the poor, the offerings of the faithful, and the price of the redemption of their souls. How is it possible, therefore, that some have been so bold as to take from God what others have consecrated to Him? How could they have the presumption to deprive the poor of their inheritance, and how can they be induced to lose their souls for the same goods by which others have secured their eternal salvation.[235]

Pope Alexander II says in one of his constitutions that to feed the poor with ecclesiastical goods is offering a tribute of divine praise to God, and applying a most profitable remedy to the necessities of the living and dead, because such property has been offered as a satisfaction for their sins. He says that to apply what has been left to the Church by the faithful for the salvation and repose of their souls to any other use but that for which they

---

[234] Vota fidelium, pretia peccatorum, et patrimonia pauperum. - Urban. 1. ep. 2. tom. 1. concil.

[235] *Canones Concilii Verenesis*, in *Nicolai I, Pontificis Romani Epistolae et Decreta, Opera Omnia.* PL 119:618A (1852).

have been left is an injustice and a kind of sacrilege. Therefore, as the relief of the poor is the principal end of such donations, such persons as do not employ them in that way, are guilty of that grievous crime.

All the saints have followed those holy maxims in practice ever since monasteries have received permanent revenues. Some have distributed even the bread which was intended for the religious, such as Saint Germain, abbot of Saint Symphronius of Autun, Saint Columban, Saint William. Saint Hermenold, abbot of St. George's in Sweden, distributed all the corn he had in the granaries, without reserving anything for the religious. Saint Adalart frequently borrowed money to relieve the poor. As soon as Saint Gregory, abbot of Utrecht, had received any money of his abbey's income, he gave it to the poor. Saint Odilon sold even the sacred vessels and the golden crowns the emperor had given to his church and distributed the whole amongst the poor in the time of necessity.

Saint Aelred, disciple of Saint Bernard, says that goods which have been given to monasteries ought to be administered by proper persons, and that what remains after the necessary subsistence of the brethren ought not to be put in reserve, nor shut up in coffers, but employed for the nourishment of strangers, pilgrims, and poor persons.

An infinite number of examples extracted from the lives and writings of the saints, might be adduced on the subject; but what I have cited is sufficient to prove that almsgiving is an indispensable duty for the monks of our times. To this they are bound both by the sanctity of their state and the intention of their founders. The conclusion therefore is that the poor ought to have a part of the goods and revenues of their monasteries. They ought to divide their bread with them; their charity ought to know no other limits than impossibility alone. They can do no better than to follow the advice of blessed Lanfranc, who says that religious persons ought to give alms, either of themselves, or by persons of known piety, and that they ought carefully to seek out the poor, the sick, and the infirm; that they are bound to assist them, comfort them, and give them every relief their indigent state may require.[236]

Above all, my brethren, monks ought to avoid all superfluous expenses, and everything they find contrary to the will of God, and the intentions of their founders. Let them remember that they shall one day give an

---

[236] In decretis pro ordine Sancti Benedicti.

account to our Lord Jesus Christ, even to the last farthing, of everything his Providence has placed in their hands; and that it is to them, as well as to ecclesiastics, that these words of St. Bernard are addressed, words so capable of striking terror into the hearts of all those who enjoy church livings:

> The poor afflicted with hunger and nakedness complain and cry out, you are unprofitably squandering away what belongs to us, you cruelly tear away from us those goods which you do not employ in a lawful and proper manner.[237]

Q. 5. *When a religious is allowed money for his use, can he in conscience keep any of it in reserve, on condition of giving his superiors an account of it when they require he should do so?*

A.—Poverty is so essential to the monastic state, and it obliges all religious so invariably, that it can be said with truth that they are not less obliged to be poor than to be chaste. Every dispensation given in this matter is abusive. It equally binds the consciences of those who give them, and those who receive them; and they are both undoubtedly linked in the same condemnation.

Saint Benedict's rule, conjointly with every other rule, obliges those who profess it to a dispossession so entire that it allows only a small number of things, necessary for the preservation of life, which are to be expected from the superior's charity. Nor can anything be more contrary both to the spirit and letter of that rule than to allow the brethren the use of money in any manner whatever.

The constitutions of the Church have always been so exact in this point, that it is easy to see how much she enjoins the practice of perfect poverty, and unlimited dispossession to religious persons.

The Council of Lateran, held under Alexander III, forbids all religious the possession of anything, or the use of any money whatever. It declares:

> If anyone be found retaining any sum of money, unless he has received it of the abbot for the purpose of executing some commission with which he has charged him, he must be separated from the participation of the holy mysteries; that he who shall be found possessing any money at the time of his death, shall be deprived of the prayers of the community, and

---

[237] *De moribus*, PL 182:815d (1854).

of religious burial; and that the abbots who shall neglect to enforce the execution of this statute are to know, that by the same, they shall deserve to be deposed from their dignities.[238]

Innocent III made a similar constitution. "We forbid," says he,

By virtue of obedience, and under pain of incurring the judgment of God, any religious person or persons to possess or have anything, and if it happen that any such persons have anything, they must instantly give it up; if afterwards anything be found in his possession, and that he will not amend, after being regularly admonished, let him be expelled from the monastery, never be re-admitted, unless he does penance for his sins according to the discipline of the monastic state; and if anything be found after the decease of a religious, and is proved to have been his property, let it be cast into the dung outside the monastery, in testimony of his condemnation.

In concluding the chapter, he adds:

Let not the abbot imagine he can dispense in matter of property, because the renunciation of all things, as well as the preservation of chastity is so essentially annexed to the monastic state, that the Pope himself cannot dispense in it[239].

The Council of Trent enjoins the same prohibition, and will not allow religious persons of either sex the possession of any goods, either moveable or immoveable, either in their own name or in that of their community. It permits superiors to allow their religious the use of such furniture only as is necessary, on condition that it is conformable to the poverty of their state, and is exempt from all superfluity.[240]

Clement VIII says that the Council of Trent, intending to make religious persons more exact in the observance of poverty, forbids any of the brethren, even the superior, to possess any private property, either moveable or immoveable; money, income, profit, alms, either in his own name, or in that of the community; whether he acquires it by preaching, teaching, officiating in his own or in another's church, or by any other title or cause whatsoever; though it might have been given him by his relations,

---

[238] Canon 10.

[239] Decreta lib, 3. de stat, monach, tit. 35. c. 6.

[240] Sess. 25. c. de reform.

or willed to him by pious persons. All these and such like things are to be given up to the superior in order that they may be incorporated and mixed with the money and other property of the house, from which the brethren may receive in common whatever is necessary for their subsistence.

He likewise forbids all superiors to grant their brethren the least possession of any immoveable goods, though it were only the usufruct, under the title and pretext of administration, guardianship, or deposit. Moreover he requires that no religious shall possess, use, as being his own property, any of those things which are granted to him for necessity. In fine, he declares that those who shall have violated any of these prohibitions not only incur the punishment already assigned by the Council of Trent; but that superiors can moreover enjoin other penalties still more severe, if they judge proper; and that no dispensations granted by superiors, can justify any religious in the possession of any moveable or immoveable property, or prevent him from deserving the punishments decreed by the Council, whatever authority superiors may pretend to have to give such dispensations or permissions; in which we require, says that Pope, that no person believe or admit, whatever they may allege to prove their unfounded pretensions.

Fagnano, a celebrated canonist of our times, who seems to be perfectly informed in these matters, writes that the congregation of the council of Trent having been consulted by the general of the Carmelites, declared in their answer that regulars cannot possess, even with the permission of superiors, and dependently on their will, and for their own use, any furniture more than what is necessary and conformable to religious poverty. Elucidating the doubt whether religious persons with the pope's permission might possess lands, revenues, and other superfluous goods, moveable or immoveable, the same congregation replies in the negative; and that the religious, who by the dispensation of their superiors possessed such goods, could not be excused from sin, nor secure from the punishments decreed and contained, *ipso facto,* by the prohibitions; and in fine, that no credit is to be given to superiors, who pretend to have authority for granting such dispensations.

From all these convincing and decisive authorities we may justly deduce, my brethren, what I have already pointed out so many times, namely, that a true religious in consecrating himself to Jesus Christ renounces and forsakes all the goods of this world, without exception. He embraces a state of perfect nakedness. Heaven becomes so entirely his inheritance that he reserves nothing to himself on earth; with this difference, that he ought to reject forever, by an unlimited abdication, everything that is not conformable to his state, or that might impede him in advancing to that purity to which he is called by God. As for such things as are indispensably necessary, he should depend entirely on the goodness and charity of his superior and hope to be supplied by him, with the same confidence as if he lived under the immediate direction of God Himself, being sincerely disposed not to have anything even of what he necessarily wants, without the consent and appointment of his superior.

Now it is certain that amongst the things which a religious has renounced forever, those of which the enjoyment is most hurtful are to be considered as the principal objects of his renunciation and the real matter of the vow of poverty which he has promised. Hence, as the possession of money has a particular malignity, and frequently tempts and seduces the purest souls and as it has been always considered as the root of all evils, because there is no evil but may be committed for acquiring it, or by means of it, so, consequently, it cannot be doubted but that money ought to be the chief and principal object of our renunciation when we embrace a state of religious poverty, that we ought to cast it from us as a dangerous allurement, and withdraw ourselves both from the possession and management of it. Hence the superior cannot dispense in an engagement so important and positive, nor can he touch what is contained in a vow so essential. It is a point to which his authority neither can nor ought to extend.

Secondly, if a religious may have money, and use it because his superior has given him permission, and if he is always ready to give it up when proper authority requires him to do so, it must be allowed that if by this means he is authorized to keep small sums, he may by the same have larger sums of money, since it is said that such a permission can justify the use of them. Consequently, why may he not by the same authority and on the same grounds possess houses, inheritances, and lands? And as such a liberty may be as well given to many as to one, it follows from these principles, and by necessary consequences, that an entire community may be delivered from the obligation of keeping the vow of poverty they had promised to God. In such a case, the brethren will be poor in name, but rich in effect. They will enjoy every kind of goods, and each individual in particular will have his riches and treasures. But what is all this but a contempt and transgression of the rules of the Church, a violation of the vow of poverty, and a manifest ruin of the piety and essence of the monastic state.

Thirdly, a superior has no more authority over the vow of poverty than he has over that of obedience. As nothing could be more extravagant than to attempt emancipating anyone of his religious from the bonds of subjection (with which he freely and by choice bound himself by his vow) and make him again the master of his person and conduct, in like manner nothing can be more opposite to good sense than to imagine that a superior can lawfully unbind the engagement a religious has contracted of living in a perfect separation from all things, and to give him the possession, management and use of the very things he had solemnly renounced by his profession.

Fourthly, how can the conduct of a superior who allows any of his religious the use of money be reconciled with the obligation by which every superior is bound to assist his brethren by all possible means in attaining to the perfection of his state? For instead of providing him means, he puts impediments in the way, he lays snares, opens pits, and lulls the unfortunate soul into a state the best adapted to revive in her those very passions and disorders from which the religious flattered himself to be delivered by forsaking the world. Is the superior so uninformed, or can he be ignorant that the love of money, according to the apostle, is the root of all evil, the source of every crime and excess (1 Tim 6:10), that it is difficult to have money and not to love it, and particularly when it is possessed against the appointment of God?

Cassian says that he who loves money has no horror of lying, perjury, or theft; that he violates his faith without any difficulty, becomes furious when things are not according to his expectations, and that he fears not to exceed the limits of decency and Christian humility. Money, says he, is his god, as good cheer is that of so many others, which made the apostle say that it was not only the root of all evils, but that the love of money was a real idolatry (Col 3:5).

Notwithstanding all this, the superior of whom we speak exposes his religious to all those disorders, leads him into them, sets before him everything that may tempt him to fall, and in a word, he could scarcely do more were he as much bound to destroy him as he is to save him. In effect, what could be thought of a superior who would allow a religious to live in the midst of the most luxurious fruits, the most delicious liquors and delicate food? Nothing less undoubtedly, than that he wished him to become intemperate. What would be said if he obliged, or permitted, any of his brethren to live in the company of depraved young persons of the other sex? Nothing else could be said of him, but that he laid snares for their chastity. Now is there not sufficient reason to believe that he seeks to destroy at once both their temperance, chastity, and every other religious virtue, since he inspires them with the love of money, which is the source of all vice, either by permitting them to possess or enjoy it?

Here let me ask such a superior whether the religious to whom he gives the permission of having money has solid virtue or not? If he has no virtue, how can you entertain the least doubt but that he will fall a prey to every temptation that attacks him, and commit all the evil he can? If he be virtuous, is it thus that you watch over him, both to assist him in persevering in his virtue and improving it? Is it thus you prepare yourself to render an account of all the souls committed to your care? Do you not know that David, holy as he was, fell into adultery and murder? That a man is frequently chaste, only because he is not exposed to the sinful occasions of the opposite vice; that the heart being so penetrated with iniquity and impelled by its own weakness, finds all the means that God has given it scarcely sufficient to keep itself in His fear and love?

Moreover, is there a shorter or a more assured way to destroy the very foundations of a community, however exact and regular it may be, than that of dispensing those religious who are the principal and chiefs, whether by their age or virtue, from the severity of the most essential rules, instead of making them bear all the rigor of discipline, and of giving example to the younger, the less perfect and the weak, so that they may encourage them and at the same time labor for their own sanctification?

If we examine the motives and considerations, by which superiors are induced to grant those liberties, nothing can be found more worthy of indignation and punishment. For example, a religious is allowed to have money, because he murmurs if he be not gratified with some indulgence. But they do not reflect, that this condescension is only casting oil into the fire, that it nourishes ill humor, and makes it become more acrimonious and lively than it was before.

Again money is given for the purpose of clothing, and it is alleged that thus superiors are delivered from the care of providing in detail for the necessities of individuals. But if the superior will not descend to such particulars, why does he not rather commission some person of the community to do it in his name? How can he for such a futile consideration, expose his brethren to such great evils, and dangerous temptations?

The same liberty is granted to spare the property of the monastery, as it is pretended, because the religious manage things better, and spend much less when they have the care of providing clothing for themselves. But allowing all this to be true, can anything be more injurious to the sufferings of Jesus Christ than to prefer an insignificant advantage, a mere temporal interest, to the salvation of a soul that cost that Divine Savior so dear? Does not such a superior deserve rather the name of a destroyer, of a ravenous wolf, than that of a pastor and protector of the sacred flock of Jesus Christ?

Q. 6.—Is it reasoning justly to say that any religious may be allowed the use of money, since there is no difficulty made in placing money in the hands of the housekeeper, or in allowing the same to a religious who is sent to some considerable distance from the monastery?

A.—The prior is an officer, a religious of the monastery, authorized and approved by the Church, who is lawfully commissioned to direct and superintend the affairs, goods and revenues of the community. Now, as when a hand receives money touches and secures it, the action is attributed to the whole man, of which the hand is the agent and member. So a community being considered as a body, having its members and parts, the abbot is the head, the prior is as the hand which he employs in his necessities, and everything he does is so natural, proper, and necessary for the community that he is in every sense only its agent and minister.

The same thing maybe said of a religious, who is sent to some considerable distance to transact business for the monastery, for as the house is obliged to provide him everything necessary for his subsistence, and as this cannot be done from the nature and quality of those necessary things, it follows of course, that money must be given him, so that he may procure them for himself; so that he acts, as it were, a steward in that respect, and performs in his own favor what he would do for another were he commissioned to provide for his wants.

But as to the religious who obtains the use of money, without being in like circumstances, he is in a personal condition, his state is a forced one and peculiar to himself. It is a singularity which draws him aside both from his state and his rule, separates him from the community, and makes him become a real proprietor.

I will conclude this question, my brethren, by telling you that the superior who allows his religious the use of money, or precisely determines the manner in which he is to employ it, or leaves him at liberty to do what he pleases with it, whether it be for things really necessary, such as food, clothes, such a superior, I say, cannot be excused from sin, because he ought to give his brethren those things in quantity and kind, and not in value, unless it be impossible to avoid doing so by some insurmountable difficulty which intervenes. But the religious who makes use of the power thus given by his superior against his own inclinations and desires is exempt from sin. If the superior enjoins that the money is to be employed in vain and superfluous things, he not only sins thereby himself, but the religious also who complies with such an injunction, or makes use of such a permission. And if he leaves him at liberty to spend it as he thinks proper, without determining for what purpose he is to employ it, he makes him a proprietor. In such a case, the dispensation of the superior neither preserves the religious from living in a violation of his rule, nor prevents the superior from committing a real prevarication, so that both the one and the other incur the punishment decreed by the Church to correct those who may be guilty of such crimes.

These truths and reasons, my brethren, are clear, ancient and constant, and you ought not to consider them as containing anything new. They only place before your eyes, and re-establish what has been religiously observed by all holy religious, and which the disorderly monks of latter times have scandalously destroyed. Far from being seduced by the opinions of those who endeavor to enervate them, in order to make them bend to the common practices, be persuaded, my brethren, that such persons prevent the designs of the Church, trifle with her ordinances, and unjustly abuse her authority, in favor of a disorder and a licentiousness which she has always condemned.

Consult the spirit of God, the essence of your state, the maxims and examples of the holy fathers—that exact poverty in which they lived—and give no ear to the discourses of modern relaxed teachers. And so that you may have neither pain nor difficulty in adopting sentiments opposite to those they inculcate, remember, that a great saint writing to Saint Teresa on the subject of religious poverty, declared to her, how much he was astonished that she listened to the advice of learned men on such matters as do not belong to their profession; and that when there is question of the laws, or of cases of conscience, it is proper to consult lawyers and divines, but when the question is to take resolutions concerning the direction of morals, and of embracing a life of perfection, none but those who have made some progress in that state are qualified to give proper advice on the subject, because those only, in general, who practice perfection can

communicate its sentiments, and point out the way to those who, like themselves, desire to walk in it.[241]

Saint Teresa evinces the same sentiments: "I wrote," says she,

> To the religious of Saint Dominic's order who assisted us, and he answered me, by sending two sheets of paper full of theological reasons quite opposite to my thoughts, for the purpose of making me take another course, telling me that he had perfectly well studied this matter, but I replied, that I would not employ theology when there was question of my vocation, and of perfectly fulfilling the poverty I had vowed, as well as the counsels of Jesus Christ; and I entreated him to pardon me if I did not embrace his doctrine, nor yield to his sentiments.

This ought not to astonish you, my brethren, since our Lord informs us that He frequently reveals to the humble and simple those truths and mysteries which He conceals from the learned and wise of the world. "I thank thee, O Father! Lord of Heaven and earth, because Thou hast concealed these things from the wise and prudent, and hast revealed them to little ones; yea, Father, for so it was pleasing before Thee" (Matt 11:25).

Q. 7.—Is it lawful for religious persons to increase their property, by making new purchases?

A.—It is not to be doubted, my brethren, but religious communities may make new acquisitions, and that just reasons may induce them to increase and extend their property. They may lawfully acquire more extensive possessions when this is necessary to place them in a more exact regularity, to furnish them with sufficient means for serving God with more tranquility and peace, or to remove an occasion of scandal, or a cause of disputes. And it must be allowed, that Saint Benedict could have lawfully purchased the inheritance of that wicked priest who endeavored to sow disorder amongst his brethren;[242] and that Saint Junien could accept the lands which he obtained of King Clotair's piety, for the purpose of furnishing his brethren with the means of exercising themselves in manual labor.[243]

But if religious persons may increase their property by these and such

---

[241] St. Peter of Alcantara's letter to St. Teresa— *History of the Spanish Carm. Reform*, 1 part 1, 2. c. 8.

[242] S. Gregorius Magnus, *Vita S. Benedicti*, PL 66:146 (1847).

[243] Letaldus Miciacensis Monachus, *Vita Sancti Juliani*. PL 137:782 (1879).

like considerations, they ought to remember that it is not lawful for them to make new acquisitions for no other motive but that of aggrandizing themselves, and of possessing a more ample property, and more extensive revenues.

For first, if they are religious in spirit and piety, and not merely such by their habit and profession, they will love poverty and seek means to become still more poor than they are. Now this desire is incompatible with that of unnecessarily augmenting their property.

Secondly, if they purchase, they must either employ for that purpose what is necessary for their subsistence, or what they find superfluous. The first is fixed according to the appointment of God, and ought to be expended in providing for the necessary wants of the house. The second belongs to the poor of Jesus Christ; it is their inheritance, and to employ it in making new acquisitions would be to increase their property and to become rich with that which belongs to another. It would be taking from the children by a cruel injustice, what was given them by the providence of their Father to comfort them in their miseries and to rescue them from the arms of death.

Thirdly, these sorts of acquisition are contrary to the spirit of the saints, and to that of the Church, since, as we have already shown, we learn by the doctrine of the saints, of popes, and of councils, that what remains of monastic revenues, after the wants of the community are supplied, belongs to the poor, and consequently cannot be lawfully applied to other uses.

Fourthly, the religious who increase their finances, unless by manifestly lawful necessity, scandalize the world. Some are offended at beholding such avaricious conduct in persons who make public profession of an exact poverty; and others are much rejoiced to find their unjust craving desires of wealth openly authorized by the example of monks.

These were the views and thoughts which induced Saint Stephen of Grandmont to prohibit all possessions beyond the limits of the desert where his religious dwelt. That apostolic man, speaking to his brethren, said:

> We forbid every sort of land possessions beyond the confines of the place where you dwell; for being strangers on earth, you should have no attachment to any temporal property, but your treasure should be in Heaven; and having forsaken all things here below, when you entered this solitude, you ought to direct all your thoughts and desires to futurity. Sufficient ground for a sepulcher is enough to satisfy a man when dead; and it would be a

thing unheard of, if, when laid in his grave, he endeavored to deprive another dead man of the place he occupied near his tomb. You are really dead, my brethren, to all worldly affairs, according to the apostle, who says, we must die to sin, that we may live only to God (Rom 6:11).

Is it not sufficient for you to possess as much ground as is necessary to make an enclosure: by enclosure I mean all that by which the wood is encompassed which has been given you for your habitation. Here you may erect the necessary buildings, and employ yourselves in manual labor, lest you should pass your time in idleness. Now, you must know, my brethren, that you cannot purchase any lands beyond the bounds of your desert, without doing the same violence to those who possess them, as one dead man would do to another, if he attempted to drive him out of his tomb. You are not ignorant what stench is exhaled from a dead body, when drawn out of its grave. Now, however insupportable this infection maybe, it is nothing in comparison with that moral infection which you would diffuse through the world, if you should ever depart from the spirit of your state, and the laws of your institute, by purchasing lands and possessions. For worldly people will take occasion from such conduct to blaspheme the name of the Lord, and to say, behold those who retired into solitude by an affected humility, how they begin to raise their heads (Rom 2:24).

You have willingly forsaken the lands which you possessed in the world, because they kept you at a distance from Jesus Christ; and have we not reason to fear, that since you could not keep your own hereditary property without doing yourself an injury, you cannot purchase those of others without displeasing God. For as Saint Jerome says, very well, it is not humility but pride that animates us with the desire of possessing the goods of this world. But if you resolve to have as much land as you think you ought to have, because you possess none beyond your enclosure, you will find, that as the different parts of land hold to one another, the least division you can purchase will excite you to desire that which is contiguous, and thus your cupidity will never be satisfied. Therefore, leave the earth, my brethren, that God may draw you to Himself, and give you His heavenly mansions for your inheritance.[244]

The Carthusians observed the same conduct in the beginning of their order, as appears by the statute made by Saint Guigo. In order, says he, that we may remove from ourselves and from our successors as much as possible, with the divine assistance, every occasion of covetous and restless desires,

---

[244] Stephanus de Mureto, *Regula Ordinis Grandimontensis,* PL 204:1140D (1855).

we enjoin by this present constitution that the inhabitants of this charterhouse shall possess nothing beyond the limits of their desert, neither fields, nor vineyards, nor gardens, nor churches, nor places of interment, nor offerings, nor tithes, nor in fine, anything of the like nature.[245]

The same spirit of disinterestedness induced the holy founders of the Cistercian order to renounce by the first and most authentic of all their statutes, possession of tithes, churches, chapels, offerings, parishes, villages, estates, etc. They were satisfied with the possession of some fields, far distant from the society of men, for the exercise of manual labor, with a few meadows for the use of cattle, with some rivers and ponds, not that fish was their usual food, but because their monasteries being for the most part situated in deep valleys, and in the midst of watery plains, fish was one of the natural products of their deserts. They had moreover vineyards, because they could not absolutely do without wine, though its use was very rare amongst them.

Saint Bernard's sentiments on this subject cannot be disputed. That man, so holy and disinterested, was far from approving the conduct of those religious who made new acquisitions, and aimed at enlarging their possessions without motives of real necessity, so much so, that he was always ready to yield to others the property belonging to himself. He gave up to the religious of the order of Premontre the ground on which they built their first monastery, and made over to them another place called Saint Samuel, with a thousand crowns of gold which were left him by Bandorun, king of Jerusalem, for the purpose of building.

He wrote to the Duke and Duchess of Lorraine, informing them that both he and his brethren were disturbed about the passage of a river which their Highnesses had made over to them, adding that if they did not make the disorder cease, both he and his brethren were disposed to render to Caesar what belonged to Caesar; and that they employed all possible means so that they might not be a burden to any person. That their desires were so very far from tending to any immoderate acquisitions, he enumerated ten or twelve monasteries, or places prepared for building them, which had been taken from him, either by deceit or violence, because he would not dispute the right he had to them, choosing rather to *lose* what belonged to him, than to *gain* by means of disputes and unpleasant contentions.

---

[245] Guigonis I, *Consuetudines*, PL 153:719 (1854).

The monks of Citeaux, conformably to the sentiments of their fathers, declared in a general chapter held in the year 1191 that in order to set bounds to cupidity, and to secure themselves from the reproaches which the religious who make new acquisitions of property draw upon themselves, they prohibited every person of the order to purchase any lands. And in the year 1215, they enjoined that no religious of whatever sort or dignity he might be, should presume to purchase any arable lands, vineyards, mills or ovens. But as this simplicity was forgotten soon after, they made another ordinance in 1229, though less rigorous; the terms of which are as follow: so that we may provide a security for the consciences of our brethren, and secure the regulation of the order for the future, the general chapter expressly forbids all persons of the order to purchase any immoveable goods, either in their own name or in that of other persons, unless they have a right of feudal tenure on such property, or some other rent, service, etc. Pope Innocent III made a similar prohibition in the council of Lateran, addressed to all monks in general.

All these reasons evidently prove that it is not lawful for religious to purchase or increase their property for no other end but that of living more at their ease, or of becoming more affluent; and that they are only authorized in such acquisitions by real necessity, such as we have explained above, where we have said nothing but what is founded on real truth, which will still appear more forcible when we reflect that when, instead of exhibiting a mode of conduct perfectly disinterested, and pure from all immoderate desires, we suffer ourselves to be hurried away by a willingness to multiply our revenues and increase our property, we then stray from the sanctity of our state, from the spirit of the saints, and from the intention of the Church; we withdraw ourselves from the appointment of God; in fine, we contract and diminish our heavenly dwelling above, in proportion as we extend and increase our earthly possessions; we fall under the malediction fulminated by the Lord against those who, without reason or scruple, join estate to estate, and extend their possessions, as if the world were made only for them, and as if they pretended to dwell in it alone, by excluding the rest of men. "Woe to you that join house to house, and lay field to field, even to the end of the place: shall you alone dwell in the midst of the earth" (Isa 5:8).

Q. 8. —*Since we are on the subject of religious poverty, tell us whether money or some temporal emolument may be required of those who desire to embrace the religious state.*[246]

A.—The saints have willingly accepted the offerings of those who consecrated themselves to God in monasteries. They did not think it improper to allow them to sacrifice a part of their riches at the same time that they immolated their persons to the divine love, but they never required it as a condition. They were very careful not to make a vocation so holy and divine depend on human considerations and temporal interests. As they well knew that God calls to His service the great and the little, the poor and the rich, they admitted both without distinction. They required of them only a pure heart, upright intentions, and a sincere will to die to all created things, in order to live only for Jesus Christ.

It was in this perfect disinterestedness that so many religious communities were formed. As vocations were then pure, as they had nothing human in them, and as God was the only principle and motive of the design and accomplishment, so nothing was found in the soul that could impede the operations of His grace. His Holy Spirit communicated Himself with full plenitude; and it may be affirmed that cloisters were then so many sanctuaries, and that the souls who there consecrated themselves to Jesus Christ were by their eminent virtue, and the purity of their lives, the principal ornaments and beauty of His house.

This state, so immaculate, became in time defiled, its splendor became tarnished (Lam 4:1). Amidst the great variety of disorders which disfigured it none was more pernicious than the love of wealth, the desire of acquiring and increasing possessions. Money was exacted of those who presented themselves in monasteries, particularly in communities of women. Receptions became venal; certain sums were fixed as conditions, without which no person could be admitted. Thus was this angelical state perverted and changed into a shameful traffic. The spirit of God having forsaken it, the united assemblage of as many scandals and profanations soon emerged

---

[246] Vincent Ryan: In order to make a profitable use of what our venerable author says in this and the following questions, concerning receptions and professions, it is necessary that the reader should remember, that as religious communities in Ireland and England have no fixed and determined revenues like the numerous monasteries in the Abbe de Rance's time, so, it would be neither just nor reasonable to make an exact comparison between them, and apply to the one what he wrote concerning the other.

from its center as made a lamentable contrast with the examples of sanctity and edification by which it was formerly dignified.

Q. 9.— Why do you condemn the custom of requiring money for receptions?

A.—I condemn it, my brethren, first, because it is contrary to the law of God; secondly, because it is against the example and doctrine of the saints; thirdly, because it is condemned by the rules and ordinances of the Church.

As to the first reason, I will tell you, my brethren, is that simony, as every person well knows, is condemned by the divine law, as no one can doubt, unless their eyes are willfully closed to a truth that shines both clear and evident. Those who make stipulations, who require money or temporal things for the reception of those persons whom they admit as professed members of any religious community, by this conduct violate the holy law of God and act contrary to His divine precepts. For simony being nothing less than a will to purchase, or to give a spiritual for a temporal advantage, it follows that the favor of admission to a religious profession, which is purely spiritual and holy, can never agree with any pecuniary stipulations or conditions of temporal emolument. On the contrary, every such contract is an action pregnant with the character and malignity of simony.

Secondly, you know, my brethren, that the saints always walked in pure and disinterested paths; and nothing could be more exact and perfect than their conduct in this matter. Indeed, it must be granted that they would not deprive the faithful of the consolation they found in giving some of their property to Jesus Christ, but at the same time, those great men were persuaded that such offerings ought to be voluntary. They accepted them as testimonies of the piety of the donors, but never exacted them as stipulatory conditions..

Saint Augustine says that receptions in monasteries ought to be pure; that virtue alone ought to be required of the persons who present themselves for admission; and that the poor are to be received as well as the rich. He tells nobly born women that when they bring their worldly goods to the convent, they are not to boast, as having been benefactresses to the house. He also teaches those who were poor in the world not to be puffed up because they have embraced a state which provides them with necessary food and clothing, and ranks them on a level with those who were above them by the advantages of birth and fortune. He adds that neither the one nor the other should acknowledge either advantage or glory, but such as result from the sanctity of their state, and the happiness they enjoy in being consecrated to Jesus Christ. [247]

Saint Benedict shows that the poor and the rich are all alike to be received into monasteries.[248] Pointing out the manner in which children of the wealthy are to be received, he says that the parents shall promise on oath that neither they nor any persons commissioned by them shall ever give any of their property to the child, or even any occasion or means of possessing it. But if they desire to offer anything as an alms to the monastery, by way of acknowledgment, they may make a donation of property to the house, reserving to themselves the usufruct during their lives. He requires that everything should be conducted in such a manner that the child may never have any cause of temptation on that subject, which might be to him the cause of destroying his vocation, as was sometimes the case.

Saint Isidore of Seville, enjoins in his rule, that those who forsake the world to engage by a holy and salutary humility in the service of Jesus Christ, should begin by distributing all their goods to the poor, or make them over to the monastery. He recommends to those who have given their property to the monastery to beware of becoming elated, but on the contrary, to humble themselves, and to fear lest their donations might be the cause of their destruction if they become proud. And as to the poor, he advises them to take care of boasting that their state makes them equal to persons who were considerable in the world; and that nothing would be more shameful, if in those places where the rich humble themselves by divesting their persons of all worldly glory, the poor should suffer themselves to be led away by vanity and pride, instead of preserving a continual remembrance of their poverty and lowliness. [249] The same saint says, in another place, that religion opens its asylums not only to persons of a free condition, but also to slaves, peasants, laborers, and tradesmen; and adds, that to exclude them would be a great crime.[250]

We find a very remarkable statute on this subject, in a rule drawn up

---

[247] S. Augustinus, *Epistolae,* PL 33:960 (1845).

[248] *RB* 59.

[249] S. Isidorus, *Regula Monachorum,* PL 83:871 (1850).

[250] S. Isidorus, *De Ecclesiasticis Officiis,* PL 83:801(1850).

for nuns, amongst the works of Saint Jerome. "Let your congregation," say the author of this rule,

> Be seized with horror at hearing this detestable heresy of simony only spoken of in which religious women, impelled by the malice of the devil, are accustomed to fall. Let the punishment of Giezi, and the impiety of Simon, fill you with dread, And let your ears continually resound with those terrible words pronounced against that imposter by Saint Peter, the vicar of Jesus Christ: Let thy money perish with thee, because thou hast believed that the gift of God could be purchased with money (Acts 8:20). For your parts, my sisters, admit gratuitously those who present themselves to become spouses of Jesus Christ. Prefer piety to riches, seek holiness of life and not nobility of blood, nor any temporal advantage. Let not the purity of your intentions in this point be sullied by any contracts or perverse thoughts. Wisdom declares aloud that he is happy whose hands are pure from gifts, who despises profit, and who does not trust in money, which usually corrupts the understanding. If any sister desires to assist the convent out of her abundance, let her place her worldly goods at the sisters' feet in an apostolic manner, so that divesting herself of all worldly things without reserve, she may become as one of the last of her companions.[251]

He forbids the rich who have given some property to the house to be elated on that account, and declares to such that if they become more proud from such a motive, the poor who had nothing to give but a sincere desire of possessing nothing made a more ample and a more acceptable offering than they, with all their wealth. On the other side he tells the poor that they ought to be so much the more humble as they had no means to assist the community like their sisters; and that they ought to thank the Lord for having called them to religion, where they are provided with all the necessaries of life, which they could hardly find when in the world, and are subsisting on their sisters' labor, as well as the rich, who might have lived at ease on their abundant property.

The cardinal of Vitry relates that at the time the Cistercian order began to appear, and to be established in the Church, the religious orders of women were fallen into so great a relaxation that women who desired to forsake the world did not dare to enter into them, because they knew that such a step would expose them to fall into disorder, and that they could find no security in such places. Amongst the greatest reigning disorders he

---

[251] Hieronymus, *Regula Monacharum*, PL 30:409

enumerates the liberty adopted by religious women of publicly exacting money for admissions and receptions into their convents, without having the least scruple of committing the detestable crime of simony, or of changing the house of prayer into a place of business and traffic.

He says also that they were all proprietors and thought nothing of keeping something privately; and these drew on their heads the terrible chastisement with which God formerly punished the sin of Ananias and Saphira. He adds that it was at that time that the order of Citeaux became as numerous as the stars of the firmament; that religious women, those who were married, together with the unmarried, and widows, flocked to it from every quarter; that noble and wealthy ladies of the world forsook all things to seek refuge in it, and that they chose rather to have the last place in the house of the Lord than to dwell in the tabernacle of sinners.[252]

According to some ancient constitutions of the Carthusian order, superiors and priors of their houses were forbidden, under the most severe penalties, to exact anything of the monks, either for clothing or for any other purposes. It was likewise enjoined by the same that no vicars, prioresses, or communities of women should admit more subjects than they could support, and that they should be careful never to receive any presents for such admissions, lest they should fall into the sin of simony. This constitution is related by Denis the Carthusian.[253]

We read in the life of Saint Edmund, Archbishop of Canterbury, that he feared to place his sisters in a convent of nuns for the sole purpose of being educated, because the community refused to receive them without money. This was a thing he much dreaded, lest it might contain something of the malice of simony. That great saint addressed himself to God by fervent prayers, and having discovered that there was a convent of poor women who lived in great perfection, and in an exact observance of their rule, he went thither, and his sisters were received with extraordinary circumstances which evinced how much his conduct was pleasing to Almighty God.

Give ear to the sentiments of Saint Thomas on this subject: "It is not lawful," says that holy doctor,

> To ask or to receive anything as a condition for being admitted into monasteries; but if a house be so poor that it cannot provide for so many persons,

---

[252] Vitriaco, *Occidentalis,* 116.

[253] Dion. Carthu. lib. de Simonia, art. 16.

those who present themselves may be gratuitously admitted and something may be received of them for their subsistence, as the community is incapable of providing everything necessary for them. It is also lawful in such circumstances to testify a greater facility for receiving those who demonstrate more sincere piety by their more abundant alms. It is even permitted to excite others to piety by some temporal benefits, so that they may be induced to embrace a religious life; but it is never lawful to give or receive anything by way of stipulation or contract, for admission into monasteries.[254]

Saint Bonaventure is nearly of the same opinion as Saint Thomas; he speaks in the following manner in a book that he wrote in defense of his order:

> There are four ways of admitting novices to their religious profession. The first is when it is not for money, nor with money, that they are admitted, but only in the view of pleasing God. This manner is most pure, both before God and men.[255]
>
> The second is when they are received with money, but not for the sake of money, so that if they had nothing to give, they would be received equally the same for the love of God. This is pure before God, but it ought to be done with precaution before men, that no cause of scandal may be given them, and lest they might think that the hope of gain excites avaricious sentiments in our breasts.
>
> The third is when a person is received, not indeed for money, but nevertheless, so, as that the community would not receive the postulant without it, because the house being poor, could not provide for their corporal necessities, the property of the monastery being barely sufficient for the maintenance of those who are already received, which is the only reason why any difficulty is formed in the reception of the person in question, lest thereby he might become burdensome to the existing members, and so deprive them of what is necessary. This mode of acting, is not yet an improper one, provided that the community is so disposed that they would receive the person without money if the house were rich, or sufficiently provided with common necessaries.
>
> The fourth is when a member is received for money, in such a way as that if the money could be received without the person, there would be no

---

[254] *Summa*, ii-ii. q. c. a. 3, ad. 4.

[255] *Libello Apologet.* Quaest 18.

regard for the person himself, but he would be positively rejected. That is to say when they receive him merely for the sake of receiving his money, this is real simony, because the money is the cause why the person is received. Therefore, it is simony to receive a person into a monastery for money only, for in that case, a spiritual thing, which is the association to a spiritual fraternity, is bartered for money, which is a temporal thing. This is what they are frequently guilty of, who being poor, desire that some persons might present themselves with money by which they might be delivered from their distress, find means to pay their debts, purchase more property, or raise new buildings. These are they of whom the wise man speaks, when he says that poverty has made many fall into sin; but as to those who receive money only by reason of the persons, and who are otherwise really disposed to admit them if they had none, if the house were sufficiently supplied for that end, it seems that such persons are free from the guilt of simony, provided that the exterior conduct agrees with the intentions.

We find, by the works of Saint Teresa, how great her disinterestedness was in this point, and how undefiled her conduct was in all matters of this nature. "Be not afraid," says she to her sisters,

> That you shall want anything; and therefore, provided that you are satisfied with the disposition of those who desire to become religious, fear not to receive them if they are rich in virtue, though they are poor as to the things of this world. It is enough if they come well decided to serve God in the best manner they are able. He will provide for your wants by some other more profitable way. I speak by experience, and He is my witness that I never refused any young woman because she was poor, when I was satisfied with her other qualities. The great number I have received purely for the love of God, as you know, is a proof of what I say. And I can assure you, with truth, that I did not feel so much inclined to receive the rich as the poor, because the former gave me some reason to fear, whereas the latter affected my heart so sensibly that I often wept for joy.
>
> Now if, while we conducted ourselves in this manner, having neither house nor money to purchase one, God so wonderfully assisted us, how can we be excusable if we do not behave in the same manner at present when we have sufficient means to live? Believe me, my daughters, you shall lose by endeavoring to gain. If those who present themselves have any property which they are not obliged to give to others who may be in want of it, I think you may accept it as an alms; for otherwise it seems to me, that they would testify but little affection for you.

But take care that those who are received dispose of their property according to the advice of learned persons, and for the glory of God. Without these conditions we could accept nothing of them, and it is of much greater consequence to us, that they should serve God in the most perfect manner they are able, since that ought to be our only desire[256].

And in another place the same saint writes thus:

Believe me, father, it is delightful to me when I receive any young woman without property, because then I know she is received purely for the love of God. My greatest joy would be never to receive any other; but at least I never remember to have refused anyone who satisfied me in everything else, and who had all that I wish for but property[257].

Q. 10.—*A third reason remains yet to be known—in what manner has the Church explained herself on this subject?*

A.—The Church never failed to testify her indignation against lucrative receptions, every time she had occasion to do so. She considered such conduct as detestable; and neglected nothing in the decisions of her councils, or by the decrees of her popes, which might convince the faithful how much she abhorred it.

The second Council of Nicea, held under Pope Adrian, first condemned such receptions in these terms:

The crime of avarice is come to such excess amongst the pastors of the Church that some even of those who make profession of piety, whether men or women, having lost all memory of the commandments of the Lord suffer themselves to be deluded by admitting for money those who present themselves for holy orders, or to the monastic state. Hence it is that the beginning of those engagements being vitiated, all their consequences, as the great Saint Basil says, ought to be rejected, because it is not lawful to engage or enter into the service of God by the way of money and riches. Hence, if anyone be found guilty of this disorder, whether he be a bishop, an abbot, or any other ecclesiastical person, he must amend his conduct, or be deposed according to the rules established by the holy Council of Chalcedon. If any abbess fall into this sin, she must be expelled from her convent, and transferred to another, where she shall be condemned to live

---

[256] S. Theresa, *Foundations*. Trans. John Dalton (London: Jones, 1853), 170.

[257] S. Teresa, *The Letters of St. Teresa,* No. XIX. (London: Baker, 1902), 91.

in obedience. An abbot, who is not honored with the sacerdotal character, must be treated in the same manner.²⁵⁸

The Council of Frankfort, under Adrian I, in like manner condemns this abuse. "Being informed," says the Council,

> That some abbots, being influenced by the spirit of avarice, exacted presents from those persons whom they admit as members of their communities, we enjoin that in future no money shall be exacted for any receptions in the holy societies of the religious state; but admissions shall be granted to all who seek it according to the rule of Saint Benedict.²⁵⁹

The Council of Melphe, under Pope Urban II, enjoins, "No abbot, on any pretext whatsoever, shall require money of those who present themselves for admission into monasteries."²⁶⁰

The third Council of Lateran, under Alexander III, enjoins:

> No religious is to be admitted for the sake of money and if it be found that anyone has made any stipulation for that purpose, he that will have given it shall not be admitted to holy orders, and he who shall have received it shall be punished by being deposed from his dignity.²⁶¹

The Council of London, under Innocent III, and the fourth Council of Lateran, under the same pope, renewed the same injunctions and prohibitions. The Council of London speaks of this abuse in the following terms:

> Simony having infected religious communities, particularly those of wom-

---

²⁵⁸ Concil. Nicaen. 2.Act. 8. Can. Eccles. 19. anno 787 / Schaff, Philip, and Henry Wace, eds. "The Canons of the Holy and Ecumenical Seventh Council." In *The Seven Ecumenical Councils*, (NPNF2/14:567: New York: Scribner's 1900).

²⁵⁹ Conc. Frank. Sub Adrian I, Can. 160, anno 794. / Benedicti XIV, Tomus Undecimus, De Synodo Diocesana (Prati, Aldina, 1844), 410.

²⁶⁰ Conc. Melph. Sub Urban II. Can. 7. anno 1090./ Caesaris S.R.E. Card. Baronii, *Annales Eccclesiastici,* Tomus Septimusdecimus 1046-1093 (Parisis, Palme, 1729), 47.

²⁶¹ Conc. Later. Sub Alex. III, c. 10. anno, 1179 / Henrico Denzinger, Conc. Lateranese III 1179, Cap. 10, De Simonia. In *Enchiridion Symbolorum Definitionum et Declarationum de Rebus Fidei et Morum* (Fribourg, Herder, 1908), 174.

en, in such a manner, that scarcely one can be found who will admit subjects without money, which crime they endeavor to cover under the pretense of poverty. We prohibit all such exactions in future; and we enjoin, that if any religious shall be found guilty of this iniquity, she who shall be admitted, as well as the superior who shall have received her, or even any other, whether superior or private nun, shall be expelled from the convent, without ever being received again; and those who shall have been thus punished, shall be enclosed in a convent of a more strict and austere observance, that they may do uninterrupted penance for their sins; and as to those women who may have been thus received before this statute of this present Council, we ordain, that they shall leave the convents in which they shall have rashly engaged, and be placed in other houses of the order. If the great number of sisters cannot allow this to be done, they shall be received again by dispensation, and shall remain in their first convent, but shall be ranked in a place inferior to those which they formerly held, lest they should be exposed to stray about the world, to their own condemnation.[262]

"We enjoin," says the Council of Lateran, "that the same statute be observed with regard to monks and other regulars; and to the end, that they may not allege their ignorance or simplicity as an excuse, we command all bishops to publish it every year in their respective dioceses." [263]

The Council of Sens, under Clement VIII, speaks in the following manner on the same subject:

We command, with the approbation of the sacred Council, that all things be done in the house of God with so much purity and sincerity, that every suspicion and appearance of evil may be prevented, and for that end, all prelates, abbots, and abbesses, as well as all other ecclesiastical persons, shall apply themselves to fulfill the charge committed to them by God, with all possible care and diligence, without any views of pecuniary interest or temporal emolument, lest the Lord should one day seek at their hands the blood of the souls committed to their care. Therefore, we command and enjoin, conformably to the decrees of the same councils and fathers, that they shall keep their hands pure and undefiled, according to the injunctions of the common law, abstaining from all exactions, notwithstanding

---

[262] Conc. Londin sub Innoc. III. capit 14. anno. 1200.

[263] Conc. Later. 4. sub Innocent III, capit.. 64. anno 1215.

the contrary customs or statutes already introduced or that may be introduced hereafter.[264]

The same council enjoins in the twenty-eighth decree, that as many members shall be received in convents as may be commodiously supported with the property of the house, without exposing the community to any necessity, reserving withal the unavoidable expenses of repairs which shall be wanting in the church, the enclosure, or other places, necessary to religious regularity; that no stipulation shall be exacted from those who may present themselves for admission or profession under pretext of custom or for any other reason whatsoever. If, nevertheless, some person or persons request to be received, though the number is already complete, we do not prohibit the concession, provided that they are able to pay a reasonable pension, which may enable the house to provide for their subsistence with the other sisters; and when anyone of those who are kept on the property of the house shall die, another, without property or pension, shall be received in her place.

The council of Treves, under Paul the III, enjoins that the religious are to be gratuitously admitted to profession, without money or stipulation; and it expressly prohibits the contrary, under the pretext of poverty.[265]

Pope Urban II prohibits all stipulations and pecuniary contracts to be made by abbots in the reception of novices.[266]

Pope Alexander III testifies by the following decree, that he was animated with the same sentiments:

> Having been informed by a priest that came to us, that the abbot and religious of the monastery of N. would not admit him to make his religious profession unless he promised to give them the sum of thirty crowns, which, having given to them, the following day, after having received the habit, the same religious again required the sum of thirty crowns, the abbot ten, and all the house twelve, for a feast, assuring him that it was the custom of the monastery; and because this action, says that pope, appears to us pernicious and of dangerous consequences, we command you, that in case that this fact is found such as it has been represented to us, you shall oblige

---

[264] Conc. Senon. Sub Clemente VII. decret 2. morum. anno 1527.

[265] Concil. Treviren. sub. Paulo III.. Decret. 11. anno. 1549.

[266] In decret. Gratiani. 2. part. causa. 5. ques. 2. cap. 30.

the aforesaid abbot and religious to restore the money to brother N. which they took from him in such an unworthy manner: besides which, you shall suspend both the abbot and ancient religious from the exercise of their authority for a crime so detestable; and command the said brother N. to retire into another monastery, that he may serve God in the religious habit.[267]

We find a similar decree of Pope Clement III:

You have desired to consult us, says he, concerning the regular canons or monks, who have been received by means of simony, and with their own knowledge of the fact. But as there are a great many definitions on this subject, we shall answer nothing but what has been already decided, namely: that they must leave the place where they have made profession, and retire to other monasteries or solitudes, where a more austere rule is observed, so that they may uninterruptedly bewail the detestable excess they have committed.[268]

Pope Innocent III condemns the same abuse. In one of his decrees addressed to the Archbishop of Canterbury, he speaks in the following manner:

You have discovered that the crime of simony is so generally diffused through religious communities, that many persons who should have been received gratis, and even excited to embrace a religious life, are admitted only when they will pay a certain sum of money; and you doubt whether the great number who have fallen into this disorder, ought not to be considered as a sufficient motive to relax something of the rigor of discipline. In answer to your question, we declare, that if you find any such cases, wherein persons are canonically accused before you, and that the crime shall be proved according to the order of justice, you shall not fail to punish both parties according to the canons; the party who have given money, and those who have received it. If you have undoubted assurance of the fact by private researches, you shall oblige those who have been received by simony into monasteries to leave them, and compel them to enter into other houses of a more austere life, there to do penance for their sin. And, as to abbots, abbesses, priors, superiors, and other officers, you shall enjoin them a penance proportioned to their crime, suspending them from the

---

[267] Decretal. Lib. 5. de simonia, titulo 3. c. 19.

[268] Decret. Lib. 5.de simonia. tit. 3. cap. 25.

exercise of their functions until they shall have accomplished it. In like manner, you shall enjoin, that all your bishops shall enforce the observance of this injunction in their respective dioceses. Nevertheless it shall be lawful to accept whatever is offered gratuitously, without stipulation or exaction.[269]

From all these reasons and evidences, you may learn, my brethren, first, that the saints never exacted anything of those who presented themselves to embrace the religious state, but only accepted what the charity of such persons moved them to offer. Secondly, that opulent monasteries, that is to say, those that can support a greater number or subjects than there are in the community, cannot, without sin, exact, stipulate, or even ask anything of those whom they admit to the religious habit; that the councils and fathers always detested and abhorred such conduct, and considered it as simony. Thirdly, that when monasteries are poor and incapable of receiving any person beyond their number, it is lawful for them to receive, and to ask, provided that it is done without stipulation or contract; with all the circumstances of purity, which exclude that shameful bartering which the Church has always condemned in a manner so rigorously and uninterruptedly.

Q. 11.— *Which are the monasteries that may, therefore, be considered poor, and what regulations ought they observe?*

A.—That a monastery may be considered poor, it ought to be unable to support more subjects than it already has; and this poverty must not have been either caused or maintained by unnecessary expenses, such as good cheer, entertainment of strangers, buildings, acquisitions, embellishing churches, precious ornaments, or such like things. This being premised, the monastery must be careful not to admit more subjects than it can support.

Nevertheless, some extraordinary cases may oblige it to act contrary to this rule, as for example, if by some accident, a part of the property belonging to the house were lost, and that the number of persons were at the same time so notably diminished, that they could not perform the divine service, nor fulfill the other regular duties. Again, if a person requested admission, who appeared to be really called, in these cases, my brethren, the house should candidly manifest its inability to the person, declaring how

---

[269] Innocent III, Decret. lib.5. de simon. tit. 3, c. 30.

willingly the community would receive him, if circumstances could allow it; observing, that if he could give something annually for his maintenance, they would readily consent to admit him.

If this postulant then promised, either by words or writing, to give what is required for his subsistence, there is nothing in it against the law; but the community must be disposed to admit the aforesaid person to profession, though it should happen that by some accident he may find it impossible to accomplish his promise. In this case, the monastery ought to consider the privation of that assistance in the same manner as if it happened after profession, or as it considers all other temporal losses.

To do otherwise, independently of the inhumanity which would appear in refusing to admit a subject who is found properly qualified after his novitiate, and who by the same would be exposed to lose his vocation, the rigor with which the profession would be made to depend on the actual and effectual execution of the promise, would be visibly tending to simony. It would evince the spirit of that crime, and produce the scandal annexed to it. But when the conditions we have laid down are carefully observed, there is no danger, because they demonstrate a sincere disinterestedness, and a conduct entirely exempt from all sordid contracts and stipulations.

Q. 12.— One of the first reasons opposed to your opinion is that in those stipulations which you condemn, the contracting parties have no design to exact money as the price of a spiritual thing; it is only considered in the secret of the intention, as a simple condition, or as a motive.

A.—It is very easy to judge, my brethren, that this apparent reason is nothing better than a mere evasion, and a wretched excuse that deserves not to be heard. For if this were admitted, who would be guilty of anything? All men would be innocent, if private views were sufficient to exculpate them. There is no crime that would not be justified by men, if secret intentions were enough to cover them. But men are not judged only for their thoughts, but also for their actions, and as this appears with strong marks of simony, it cannot be designated by any other name. To be a simoniac, and to be reputed such, it is not necessary to believe that money is a real price for a spiritual thing, nor that it can be equivalent to the gifts of the Holy Spirit.

It suffices to behave in the same manner as those do who are infected with that error. This is precisely the conduct of all those religious who will not receive their novices to profession, unless they purchase it with money; who for that purpose make contracts and stipulations, and who judge such conditions to be so necessary, that they are not ashamed to exclude those who cannot accomplish them. For to speak properly, a man is guilty of simony, and sells spiritual things, when he only grants them in exchange for those that are temporal.

Q. 13.—For a second reason it is said that in those receptions the spirituality of religion is not the thing which is given for the money received, but only that which is temporal in religion, such as the food of the person who is admitted.

A.—This reason has nothing solid. It has been imagined only to palliate the abuse, cover iniquity, and calm the anxiety of consciences by a deceitful security. For simony not only consists in buying or selling a spiritual thing, but moreover in doing so by a temporal thing, when it is annexed to a spiritual one. Now there is nothing more closely annexed to the reception of a religious in a rich monastery than his food and subsistence. As soon as he is received into a community, he becomes one of its members. It takes upon itself the charge of him, owes him its care, and is obliged to give him everything necessary for his maintenance, and the preservation of his life.

Therefore, by an undoubted consequence that no subtlety can destroy, the persons who take money of those whom they admit to their religious profession, in the view of that maintenance, which they oblige themselves to give them, commit a real simony, and consequently an action damnable in the judgment of God, whatever care they may take to disguise it before men, simony being according to the opinion of all divines, an effective will to give or receive something spiritual, or something annexed to a spiritual thing for a temporal interest.

Q. 14.—In the third place, some pretend, that if poor communities may exact money for receptions, without incurring the guilt of simony, those that are rich may do the same, and that in such cases the conduct of the one is not less innocent than that of the other.

A.—This pretension is no better than the former, for though it be true that poor monasteries may lawfully require money for admissions, that can furnish no precedent in favor of those that are rich. An indigent community, that is to say, one that cannot support more subjects than are actually within its pale, may declare its poverty and incapacity to those who seek admission, as we have already shown, and the desire it has to receive them if circumstances would allow it. The superior may explain that if those postulants could bring in something, the community then would be in a proper state to provide them a subsistence. Besides which, this community, being assured of the postulant's vocation, by the usual probationary rules, must be sincerely determined to admit the subject to his profession, though by some extraordinary accident he may find it impossible to keep his word, and to give the pension he promised, for, if the reception depended on the stipulation, however poor the monastery might be, it could not be exempt from the sin of which we have spoken.

Secondly, to speak correctly, temporal goods are not the objects this community seeks or desires; and it may be said, that it has in view only the salvation of the person, and the accomplishment of the designs of God in his regard.

Thirdly, it is evident, that in this case the reception depends not on the stipulation, and therefore it cannot be considered as being a species of simony.

Fourthly, this annuity as required in the above case, is according to circumstances a charity or an alms, rather than an exaction, or a real contract.

Now, we not only do not find any of those conditions in the conduct of rich monasteries, but we find quite the opposite.

First, they have means to receive those who seek admission.

Secondly, the foundation on which they place the pretext of exacting money is unjust. It is a cloak for their simony, a palliation of their avarice, for the subsistence of a religious is inseparable from his profession, as we have shown. It is due to him from the moment he is admitted. It belongs to him as a member of the body to which he is associated.

Thirdly, the reception of the religious is not an object proposed in those monasteries, but the temporal interest or advantage which may be derived from such reception. For the truth is that they would not have the person without money, as Saint Bonaventure says, but they would accept the money very freely without the person.

Fourthly, these and such like stipulations can be considered only as vending contracts, for the most exact rigor is observed in them; each party takes securities and precautions; each looks only to his profit and advantage. Whatever marks of a vocation the postulant may manifest, they will not receive him unless he fulfill all the conditions of such simoniacal contracts.

Here then, you may perceive, my brethren, that there can be no solid reasons adduced to justify, from the practices which absolute necessity forces upon the poor monasteries, this conduct in opulent communities. Their dispositions and conduct are entirely opposite to one another. The one does innocently, without either violating the law of God, or dishonoring its profession, what the other never does without sin and scandal.

Q. 15.—*What of some religious who are lately established, who pretend that they may exact money of the persons they admit, on pretext of building large mansions and magnificent churches?*

A.—If religious persons be conducted by the spirit of Jesus Christ, and influenced by enlightened piety, they will never yield to such thoughts. They will understand that God does not require, nor is He pleased, that altars should be erected to His honor with impure hands. His house, which is holy, ought not to be constructed by any other means save those that are just and virtuous. He rejects the sinner's offering, and regards with horror the holocausts of rapine and injustice.

To conclude that we may violate His holy law, despise the commands and injunctions of His Church, and tread under foot the decrees of His sovereign vicegerents on earth, would be to dishonor His sanctity and draw down on ourselves this terrible reproach which He addresses to the wicked by the mouth of His prophet: "Wretch, hast thou believed, that I could become an accomplice in thy iniquity, and partake of thy injustice. I will chastise thy sin, and thy crime shall turn against thee" (Ps 49:21).

Q. 16.— *Yet do not some persuade themselves that this practice is approved of by the Church, since she knows it exists, and yet does not prohibit it?*

A.—To this I reply, that the Church has prohibited it at all times, and in every manner she possibly could. She has condemned it by her councils, by the organ of her chief pastors, by the mouth and writings of her saints. And her decisions (which are nothing less than so many confirmations of the divine law), so very far from being enervated by any opposite practices, have been on the contrary renewed in these latter times. This we find not only by the council of Sens,[270] but also by that of Trent, which enjoins that regular communities shall be re-established on the basis of their primitive institutes, and the observance of their ancient discipline.[271] Nothing can

---

[270] Concil. Senonense decret 2& 28. motum.

[271] Concil. Tridentin sess. 25. cap. 1. De Regularibus.

certainly be more opposite to those holy rules than a traffic so base and scandalous.

Moreover, can anything be less warranted than to judge that the Church approves of a thing because she does not punish it? Is it not well known that she forbears, when she has due reason to fear that by endeavoring to remove abuses they might become more dangerous than they are, that she awaits a more convenient time when she may do it more successfully, and that she frequently enjoins and prohibits without any effect, because the execution of her injunctions is not in her own hands, and that when she beholds disorders which she cannot remove, she contents herself with sighing and weeping over them?

But to say that what the Church tolerates, she approves, is a false principle, from which frightful consequences may be deduced, and against the sanctity with which she is always adorned. For there is no excess which may not be authorized with impunity by alleging such an approbation, and all those religious who live in public disorder throughout the world may, according to this maxim, justify their licentiousness by the silence of the Church.

Q. 17.—Is it improper to require presents for the Church, or money to provide feasts?

A.—According to the reasons already adduced, it must appear that such exactions are undoubtedly prohibited. The maintenance of the person received being the only lawful motive for receiving anything, whatever is not necessary for that end must be unlawful. As the above demands have no such object, it follows that they are improper, vicious, and such as cannot be justified. To make the reception of a person who desires to consecrate himself to God depend on such motives and conditions, is to fall precisely into the case the Church has condemned.

Urban V published a decree on this subject, by which he declares that being informed in what manner many religious houses of both sexes, of different orders and countries, committed this detestable abuse, already condemned by the sacred canons, namely, of exacting from those persons whom they admitted to the religious profession, repasts and feasts for the community, obliging them to make presents of money, jewels, or ornaments to their churches or superiors, on pretext of custom or rule; this practice he reproves as a corruption and the poison of religious orders, calling it the ruin of monastic sanctity, and a plan which shuts the entrance of that state to virtuous persons.

To remedy so great an excess, and to punish those who shall be guilty of it, he prohibits, with more severity than had been done by any former pope, that no abbot, prior, abbess, or any other superior of whatsoever order they may be, shall presume to ask, either directly or indirectly, of any person or persons of either sex, who seek admission into the religious state, either before or after reception, feasts, repasts, money, jewels, or anything else, though it were to serve the church, or for other pious uses.

He then enjoins that receptions shall be gratis, and performed with entire purity, that whatsoever shall be given as alms by the persons who are admitted shall be thankfully received, but it must be offered freely, without stipulation or contract; and that whoever will act contrary to this injunction, shall incur excommunication, as well those who give money as those who receive it. If an entire community prevaricates in this point, it shall be punished with suspension, which chastisement of excommunication and suspension can only be absolved at the hour of death, unless an express permission is obtained of the Holy See for more indulgent measures, etc.[272]

This decree has been confirmed by Pope Gregory XI, by another to the same effect; so that after so many authentic declarations and express prohibitions, it is impossible to doubt that those stipulations and contracts for dinners, feasts and church ornaments are abuses injurious to the sanctity of the religious state, contrary to all ecclesiastical constitutions, and that no reason can justify such practices, or make them innocent.

I have said nothing of the opinion of many eminent doctors who maintain our sentiments, because I am convinced it would be superfluous, and that nothing can make a more forcible impression on your minds than the authority of the Church, and the doctrine of the saints.

Q. 18.— Are not your sentiments supported by so many reasons that it is difficult to resist the conviction they enforce?

A.—It is certain, my brethren, that we have proposed a constant and evident truth. But though our reasons were not stamped with all that evidence and certitude which, in effect, they really are, at least it must be allowed that they are more than sufficient to overcome the contrary opinion, make it appear very uncertain, and afford well grounded motives of fear in those who adopt it. This being the case, my brethren, how is it possible that those who ought to have no desire in this world but that

---

[272] Urban V. Extravag. Commun. lib. 5. cap. 1 de simonia in sexto decretal.

of pleasing Jesus Christ can—in a matter of such importance—align themselves with the most unfavorable party? That is to say, how can they expose themselves to commit an action so much detested by Jesus Christ, and so frequently condemned by His Church? Is it a sign that they truly love Him? Is it proving their love when they willingly adopt such things as may at least outrage Him? And do they not become unworthy of His friendship, as soon as they are willing to live in danger of losing Him for ever?

Some may say, perhaps, that they feel no anxiety on this matter, that they act without fear or scruple. But the question is to know whether this assurance is well founded or not. For when security is false, it can be of no advantage for the justification of a sinner. He who commits evil without scruple, when he ought to have it, is not much less criminal than he who does it against the testimony of his conscience.

Now, is it not sufficient to have a doubt of any such mode of conduct, and to suspect it is bad, when we hear it condemned by the saints, and reproved by the Catholic Church as a detestable practice? And is it not true, my brethren, that if those souls who have the honor of being united to Jesus Christ as spouses, had nothing now before their eyes but His glory and their own salvation, the very thought of such a sin would fill them with fear and terror, and they would chose rather to suffer a thousand deaths than to expose themselves, by uncertain ways, to commit so many crimes, and to be for ever excluded from His divine presence?

If to all these considerations you join the inconveniences which arise from those impure contracts, you shall more easily discover their corruption and deformity. Consider that they are the cause of an almost infinite number of scandals and murmurings. They dishonor the monastic state before those whose esteem and approbation it ought to attract. They make religious persons appear odious under the character of covetousness and self-interest. They furnish reasons to conclude that the spirit of God is no longer amongst them, and that the cloister is governed by as much cupidity as could be found in worldlings.

Consider, I say, that by means of those infamous negotiations interest alone is that which decides vocations, opens and shuts the gates of monasteries, that virtuous persons abhorring those detestable practices—as a certain holy pope [273] remarked—do not dare to engage in them. Thus many are admitted who are not called. Instead, then, of presenting to Jesus Christ spouses who are chaste and pure, others are offered who are equally unworthy of His sanctity and His love.

Hence, by an inevitable consequence, his sanctuary becomes a place of disorder and profanation. It was for the purpose of remedying such terrible evils that the Church made constitutions and published decrees. She exerted all her authority to banish the love of money from those houses consecrated to God. But that passion having got entrance, has now become inflamed. The fire is kindled in spite of all her care—the conflagration has become so great and universal, that all her power is not able to extinguish. it.

---

[273] Urban V

22 | ON PATIENCE IN SICKNESS AND INFIRMITIES—CONTENTS:

Q. 1.—What dispositions ought a religious have in time of sickness? 272

Q. 2.—Is it proper for a religious to consult physicians, and to use remedies in the time of sickness? 272

Q. 3.—Is it not lawful for religious persons when sick to ask remedies, and attend to whatever may be necessary for the recovery of their health? 281

Q. 4.—Does not charity oblige a superior to employ every sort of means and remedies for the recovery of his religious when they are sick? 285

Q. 5.—Ought not the discipline and penance of monasteries be relaxed when the religious die frequently; and is not the fear of not being able to persevere, a sufficient reason to diminish the austerities of religious orders? 287

Q. 6.—What answer can be made to those who say, that it is unlawful to embrace austerities which shorten life7 Can they support such an assertion? 294

Q. 7.—Does not Saint Basil recommend great moderation and prudence in the practice of austerities? 300

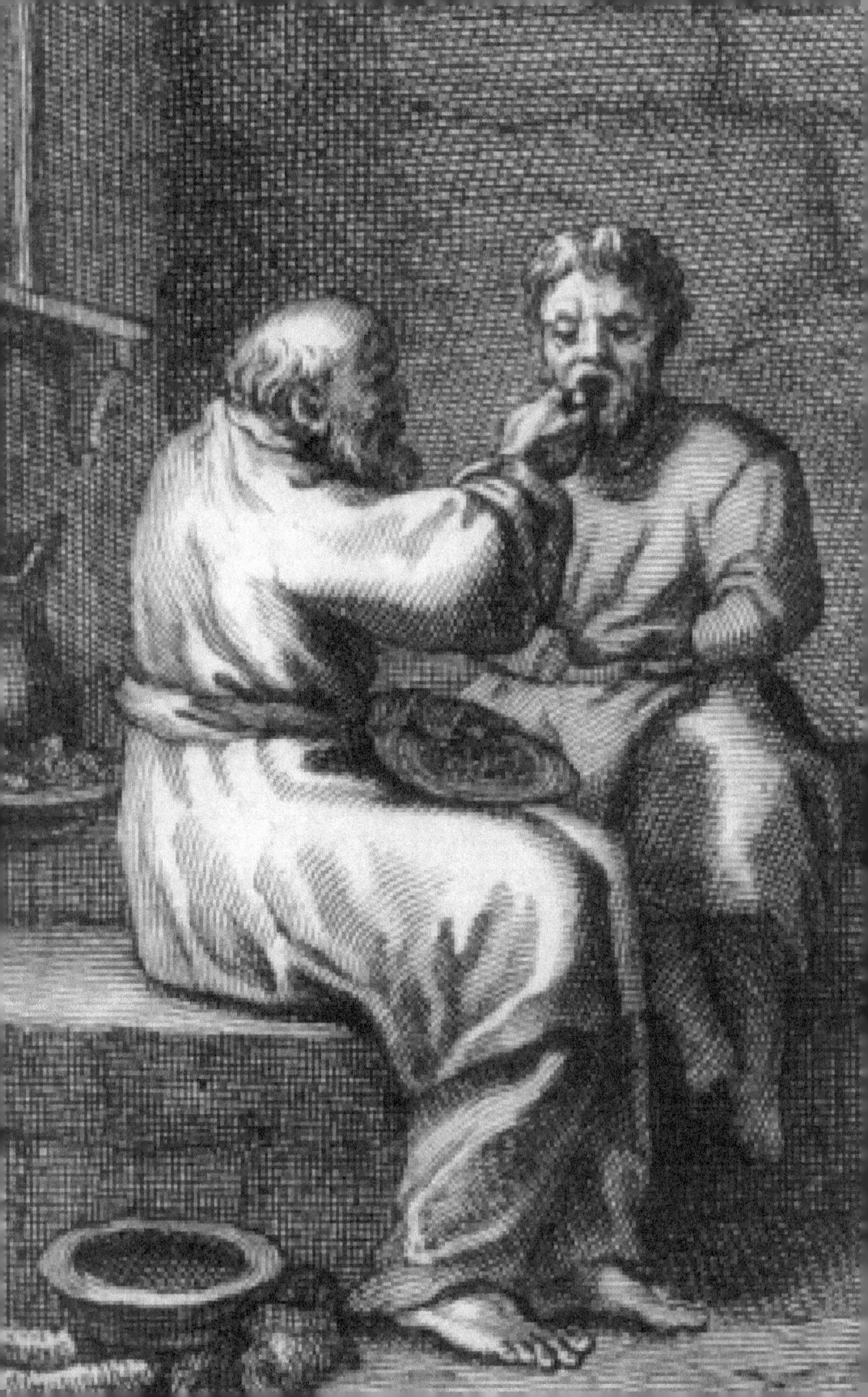

22

ON PATIENCE IN SICKNESS AND INFIRMITIES

QUESTION 1.— *What dispositions ought a religious have in time of sickness?*.

ANSWER—A religious, when attacked with sickness, ought to enter into the secret intentions of God. He ought to endeavor to discover the designs of His providence in his regard. The divine goodness has visited him with this sickness, so that in his afflictions he may imitate our suffering Redeemer in His sorrowful passion and in the torments He endured on the cross, and by a just conformity with that divine model, may become more pure, more perfect, and more holy. Therefore, he ought to receive the sickness and all its circumstances, not only with resignation, but also with thanksgiving, considering that the pains he endures are the remedies with which the heavenly physician labors to heal the disorders of his soul.

Hence, penetrated with gratitude, he should say with the prophet, "I will take the chalice of salvation, and I will call upon the name of the Lord" (Ps 115:13). These are the means by which he shall prevent the unmodified desires, anxiety and vexations which, instead of assisting, are frequently the cause why many lose the advantages of their sickness, and when restored to health, are more subject to their passions, and more miserable than they were before.

Q. 2.—*Is it proper for a religious to consult physicians, and to use remedies in the time of sickness?*

A.—In order to answer your question I will tell you, my brethren, that the primitive solitaries lived in so great an independence of creatures, and placed themselves so unreservedly in the hands of God that for the most part, when sick, they only sought their recovery from His Divine Providence. Animated with a lively faith, to which they united a contempt of all earthly things, and fervent desires of being united to Jesus Christ, they rejected all human assistance and left to Him alone the decision of their life or death.

This is what we learn by the actions and instructions of the saints. Saint Theodore, a solitary of Tabenna, being afflicted with a most violent headache, besought Saint Pacomius, his superior, to obtain his deliverance from that affliction by his prayers; but that great saint, who knew how profitable it was for him to suffer, answered him in these remarkable words:

> Believe me, my son, we are never afflicted with pains or afflictions, but by the permission of God. Bear your present pains with humble patience, and He will deliver you when it shall please His holy will. If He think it more proper to try you a longer time, give Him thanks for it, after the example of the most perfect man, Job, who, in the midst of so many torments, always blessed the Lord, so that like him our Lord may increase your consolations. For, though abstinence and perseverance in prayer are very meritorious, yet a sick person merits much more when he supports his sickness with patience.[274]

The same saint, going to see one of his brethren who was ill, and who by hard labor had torn his hands, to which he applied a little oil as a remedy, but this, instead of relieving him, only increased the pains caused by the wounds, and made them insupportable, the saint spoke to him in the following terms:

> Do you think, brother, that this oil can heal you? Why did you work in such a manner as to be now in a condition which induces you to have more confidence in this visible remedy than in God? Is it not in His power to cure you? Does He not know our infirmities? Does He want to be informed of them by us? By no means; but considering our spiritual advantage, He permits us to be afflicted for a time, that He may crown our patience with eternal rewards. Let us, therefore, place all our confidence in Him, and He will deliver us from our sorrows.[275]

---

[274] *Vita Sancti Pacomii Abbatis Tabennensis*, Caput LI, *Vitae Patrum*. PL 73:269C.

[275] *Vita Sancti Pacomii Abbatis* PL 73:270C (1849).

22 | ON PATIENCE UNDER SICKNESS AND INFIRMITIES

Saint John Chrysostom, speaking of the solitaries of his time, says:

If any of them fell sick, no tears or mourning were seen among them; they did nothing more than renew their supplications to their heavenly physician. He adds, Faith alone frequently removed their maladies, independently of any human assistance; and if sometimes the physicians of the world were called on to exercise their skill in favor of those great men, their conduct was dignified by an extraordinary wisdom and patience.[276]

Saint Diadocus says:

Solitaries who live in deserts and solitudes far remote from the society of men, either alone or in the company of two or three brethren, under the same rule, ought not to do anything more in their sickness than address themselves to God with a lively faith, who can heal all evils and infirmities. Next to God, their solitude ought to supply every other consolation.[277]

Saint Macarius says, "To use remedies is unworthy of a solitary." To the objection that God has created medicines and annexed virtues and remedies to plants for healing human infirmities, he answers:

Since we became subject to sickness and death by the disobedience of our first parents, God, moved by His infinite goodness, would not allow the sinful race of men to be suddenly destroyed by the many infirmities to which they are exposed in punishment of their rebellion; for which end, He granted the remedies of medicine to the weak and incredulous, to those who are attached to the world, and strangers to His holy law and covenant; this He also allows to the faithful who have not sufficient courage to place themselves entirely in the hands of His providence. It is true the use of these remedies relieves, and sometimes even cures, corporal infirmities.

"But you, O! solitaries," says he,

You who live remote from the society and conversation of men, you who are associated to Jesus Christ, who desire to be the children of God, and to be regenerated by a spirit superior to human nature; you who await the

---

[276] Homil. 14 in 1 ad Timoth. / St. John Chrysostom. *Homilies of St. John Chrysostom, Archbishop of Constantinople, On The Epistles of St. Paul the Apostle to Timothy, Titus, and Philemon* (NPNF1/13:457).

[277] Diadochus Episcopus Photices, *Capita Centum de Perfectione...*, PG 65:1183.

effects of promises more extensive and sublime than those made to Adam, even when he was yet immortal; you, in fine, who are preparing without interruption for the coming of the Lord, and who consider yourselves as travelers and passengers in this world, you ought to have a more lively and generous faith than other Christians, and your lives ought to be more spiritual and disengaged from the senses than what is found amongst them. [278]

We read that Saint Fulgentius being ill in the Isle of Circine, whither he had retired with some religious, to prepare himself for death, and the physicians having proposed the use of the bath as a remedy for his distemper, he asked them whether the bath could hinder a mortal man from dying who had finished his course. "Why do you endeavor," he asked, "to persuade me to relax at the end of my life that severity in which I have lived so long?"[279]

But nothing is more deserving our notice, than what was practiced in a convent in the lower Thebaid, where the great Saint Euphrasia lived. The austerity was so great in that house that when the nuns fell sick, they gave thanks to God as for a particular favor. Nor would they use any remedies, because they sought their cure from God alone; and the sanctity of their lives made their prayers so acceptable to God that they frequently recovered their health in a miraculous manner.

This austerity was not general among solitaries, nor did the ancient Cenobites observe that great rigor. We, then, may securely affirm that monks may use remedies during their illness, for this appears quite conformable to the examples and instructions which the saints have left us; but with these restrictions, namely, that they are not to be attached to them, nor to have confidence in them; that they ought to consider God as the only source of health; that the remedies are to be common, such as may be procured without much labor or expense; that the whole process be so entirely dependent on their superior's will that the religious never anticipate him either by desire or anxiety; and in fine, that they do nothing more in it than submit and obey.

Saint Basil says that the use of medicine is lawful and that God has given natural properties to roots, leaves, flowers, fruits, and juices of plants and herbs, minerals, and other things which are found in the earth and sea

---

[278] S. Macarius Magnus. De perfecta fide in Deum, PG 34:811 (1903).

[279] S. Fulgentii Episcopi Ruspensis Vita. PL 65:149A (1847).

for the purpose of healing our bodies; that men may use them, but that Christians ought to endure all remedies which cannot be procured without much trouble, expense, anxiety and research, and which do not engage them in a continual embarrassment, taking up their whole time in the care of their bodies.[280]

According to that saint when we are obliged to employ the assistance of the medical art, we are to take care not to consider it as the entire cause of our health or illness; nor when we are deprived of that help, that we cannot be cured without it; but on the contrary, we ought to be persuaded that God will not suffer us to be tempted above our strength; and as our Lord sometimes healed infirmities by the application of sensible remedies, so He has cured others in a secret way, by the sole operation of His divine will.

The same saint adds that sickness is sometimes the punishment of sin, and then the sick ought not to employ natural remedies, but should endure their infirmities in peace and silence, imitating him who said, "I will bear the anger of the Lord because I have offended against Him." They should earnestly apply themselves to remove the cause, amend their lives, reform their conduct, and to produce worthy fruits of penance, remembering those words of Jesus Christ, who having cured the sick man, said to him: "Behold thou art now healed, take care and sin no more, lest something worse happen to thee" (John 5:14).

The saint continues:

> God permits the devil to tempt the faithful, that his pride may be confounded by their patience, as it happened in the person of Job. Sometimes he afflicts them with sickness that the constancy with which they endure violent pains until death may serve as an example to those who cannot support the least anxiety. This is what may be seen in Lazarus, who, though covered with ulcers, yet desired nothing of any person for the relief of his infirmities.

In all these cases, Saint Basil says that a sick person ought not to seek any assistance from men, lest he should pervert the designs of God, and withdraw himself from the appointment of His holy will.

Saint Diadocus says that the use of medicine is lawful in the state of sickness, but that we ought to hope for our recovery of Jesus Christ alone, who is our Saviour and true physician. Here he directs his discourse to

---

[280] S. Basilius, *Fusius,* PG 31:1043 (1857).

those religious who live in cities or in great communities, because they are exposed to many accidents which hinder them from supporting themselves, and from constantly acting by the principles of a lively faith and charity; besides singularity would expose them to vain glory, and to the temptations of the enemy.[281]

We find that the primitive Carthusians used remedies very seldom, their principal applications consisted in the use of issues and letting blood.[282]

Let us now consult Saint Bernard's sentiments on this subject. Undoubtedly you will have no difficulty in assenting to them:

> What do you say, you who consider the qualities of food, and neglect purity of manners? Hippocrates and his followers teach how we may preserve this mortal life; Jesus Christ and His disciples teach us how to lose it; which of the two will you take for your guides and masters? He evidently evinces under whose direction he wishes to live, who discourses on the natural qualities of aliments, and who says, this injures the eyes, that the head, the other the stomach. Have you read any such differences in the prophets or in the writings of the apostles? Undoubtedly it was flesh and blood that revealed this wisdom to you, and not the spirit of the fathers.
>
> For according to the true physician of Christianity, the wisdom of the flesh is pernicious, and mortal, and an enemy to God. Nor do I think it my duty to propose to you the sentiments of Hippocrates and Galen, or those of Epicurus. I am a disciple of Jesus Christ, and I speak to disciples of Jesus Christ. I would be criminal if I taught you any other maxims but this; Epicurus labors for pleasure, Hippocrates for health, but Jesus Christ, my divine master, commands me to despise both the one and the other. Hippocrates employs all his solicitude to keep the soul in the body, Epicurus seeks everything that can entertain it with pleasure and delight; but our Lord teaches us to lose it, saying, he that loses his life shall find it; namely, by forsaking it like a martyr or afflicting it like a penitent; though it is in another sense, a sort of martyrdom to mortify the unruly passions of the soul.
>
> To what purpose is it to cut off pleasures and delights, if we employ all our care in comparing the difference of complexions, and in examining every day the nature of the various sorts of food? It is said, that legumes produces flatulence; cheese loathes the stomach; milk makes the head ache; the chest cannot endure pure water; roots and herbs nourish melan-

---

[281] Diadochus, *de Perfectione,* PG 65:1183.

[282] Guigo I, *Consuetudines.* PL 153:715 (1880).

choly; fish taken out of muddy water disagrees with my temper. What, is it not possible to find anything you can eat in the waters, fields or gardens? Consider, I beseech you, that you are a religious and not a physician, and that you shall not be judged by your complexion, but by your state and profession.

If it be said that the apostle Saint Paul ordered Saint Timothy to use a little wine, by reason of his stomach and frequent infirmities, it should be attentively considered, first, that the apostle did not allow himself that indulgence, nor did the disciple ask it for himself. Secondly, that this command was not given to a religious but to a bishop, whose life was very necessary to the infant church. It was given to Timothy—give me then another Timothy, and I will nourish him with potable gold and amber if you choose. But it is you that grant this dispensation to yourself; you are yourself the dispenser and dispensed; you call it discretion, but I really suspect, that the prudence of the flesh conceals itself under the specious name of discretion. It seems, that since we became religious, we have all found the way to have weak stomachs.[283]

The same saint, writing on this subject to the religious of Tre Fontane Abbey, near Rome, tells them:

Your venerable abbot requested something of me, which I do not approve: in this I think, I have the spirit of God, and that the counsel I am going to give you comes from God. I know that you live in unwholesome air, and that many of you are infirm, but be mindful of him who said: I will glory in my infirmities, that the power of Christ may dwell in me, for when I am weak, then am I more strong (2 Cor 12:9) I compassionate, I certainly feel much for the infirmities of the body, but those of the soul are much more to be feared. Therefore, it is neither expedient for your state, nor for your salvation, to seek remedies for the preservation of your health. The use of herbs may sometimes be tolerated, such as the poor are accustomed to procure in such cases; but to buy drugs, consult physicians, and take medical draughts, is unbecoming the religious state. It is contrary to the purity, and chiefly adverse to the modesty and simplicity of our order.[284]

---

[283] *Cantica,* PL 183:938d (1854) / *Canticles,* 1:360.

[284] Bernardo da Pisa, afterwards Pope Eugenius III. / Epistola CCCXLV, Ad fratres de Sancto Anastasio. PL 182:549d (1854) / Bernard, *Works,* 2:884.

Something like this may be seen in a letter written by Saint Fastredus, abbot of Clairvaux, and disciple of Saint Bernard, who seemed animated with his spirit. Writing to an abbot of the Cistercian order, who, on the pretext of infirmities had forsaken the common austerities. "You allege," says that holy man,

> That being subject to headaches and disorders of the stomach, that the common food is unwholesome for you, but you are really much deceived if you think that a religious may adopt the regimen of health which physicians prescribe for worldly people. For we have entered religion in order to make our bodies suffer more inconveniences, and not to provide pleasure and satisfaction for them.
>
> Believe me father, I have often seen Saint Bernard make great difficulty to take a liquor composed of flour, honey and oil, which was given him to warm his stomach; and when I accused him of being too austere, he answered me, My son, if you knew what the obligation of a religious is, you would not eat a morsel of bread, or take any food, without first watering it with your tears: for we have come to religion to weep for our own sins, and for those of the people; so that it is not enough for a religious to say he is sick, for our fathers made choice of low and wet valleys to build their monasteries in, that the religious being frequently sick, and having death before their eyes, they might always live in the fear of the Lord. If then the saints sought that which might cause infirmities, how can you be so studious in seeking what may contribute to health? [285]

Peter of Blois reprehended the delicacy of the monks of his time, in words almost similar: "If it happen," says he,

> That a religious perceives his pulse beating a little more quick than usual, or his appetite somewhat diminished, he consults physicians, seeks medicines, makes electuaries, eats nothing but what is prepared with cloves, cinnamon or nutmeg. What a shame for a man who ought to raise himself continually to the contemplation of heavenly things to be thus groveling amidst those of the earth!
>
> It must be allowed that such a religious is not a disciple of Jesus Christ, but of Epicurus. This, says he, is bad for the eyes, that is not good for the stomach, the other injures the liver; butter corrupts, beer produces wind, cabbage nourishes melancholy, leeks excite the bile, peas give the gout,

---

[285] Fastredus, Epistola CDXCI, In *S. Bernardi Opera Omnia*, PL 182:706A (1859).

beans make one costive, lentils injure the sight, cheese is good for nothing at all. Meditation when long, debilitates the nerves, fasting disorders the brain, watching dries up the body.

But after all, we do not find all those distinctions, either in the gospel or the prophets. The rule of Saint Benedict speaks nothing concerning them; but flesh and blood have revealed them to the relaxed monks of our times.[286]

Saint Teresa speaking to her daughters in the same spirit, says to them:

It seems to me, that some amongst us have come into religion for no other purpose but to find out means of never dying. Each individual labors to attain this point as well as she can. But be convinced, my sisters, that you should have come hither only to die for the love of Jesus Christ. For the devil puts that doctrine into our minds, persuading us that when we do so, it is only that we may be able to support ourselves and observe the rules and constitutions of the order. But the consequence is we set ourselves so much on keeping the rules by taking such exact care of our health, that the end of life arrives before we have kept them for one month, or perhaps for a single day. These two things do not well agree together, to be poor and well treated. In certain small evils patience ought to be exercised without going to bed and killing everybody with our importunities.

Let us call to mind the holy fathers, our ancestors, whose lives we pretend to imitate. How many pains and infirmities must they not have endured in their solitudes? How much from heat, cold, hunger and thirst, without having any person to whom they might complain, except God alone. Do you think they were of iron? No, no, they were clothed with mortal delicate flesh as we are; and on the whole, be convinced, my daughters, that when you begin to subdue your bodies in earnest, they will not be so importunate.

Unless we are determined to swallow down the loss of health, and even death itself at one blow, we shall never do anything. Endeavor not to fear the enterprise, and place yourselves in the hands of God with entire resignation. What matter whether we die or not? How many times has not this body deceived us? Shall we not in our turn be indifferent to it? Believe me this resolution is of the greatest consequence; for in so doing, we shall, by little and little become complete mistresses of it..[287]

---

[286] Petrus Blesensis, *Compendium in Job*. PL 207:803 (1904).

[287] *The Way of Perfection*. Ch 10.

Here you can see, my brethren, with what care, and on what conditions the saints allowed religious persons the use of medicine. You behold how far they were from permitting anything that was not conformable to the simplicity of their holy state. Their indulgence was limited to the use of such medicines as were inexpensive, common and agreeable to the condition of the persons who were bound to live in exact poverty.

You find how much they condemned the anxiety for medicines which could not be had without much labor and expense and how much they censured the confidence that religious persons placed in them; and their avidity in keeping themselves engaged and employed in everything that regards the nourishment and treatment of the body. You discover that they required religious persons to live in an entire disengagement from life, and that at all times—in sickness as well as in health—they should nourish in their souls the same sentiments and spirit of penance and austerity. In a word, that there are some infirmities in which they ought not to seek any medical assistance at all.

Now, if these rules and maxims are carefully observed, monastic discipline will suffer no injury by the use of medical remedies. Nor will regularity be at all enervated by the assistance granted in the time of illness, particularly if the religious do not interpose in what concerns them, when in the state of sickness; but placing all in the hands of the superiors, leave to their prudence and charity the whole direction of every necessary arrangement.

Q. 3.—Is it not lawful for religious persons when sick to ask remedies, and attend to whatever may be necessary for the recovery of their health?

A.—The religious can accept the remedies which are presented to them by their superiors, but they ought not to ask or desire them. For, as by their vows they have renounced the claim they had to their own persons, they have no longer any power over their own bodies. "For they no longer have any power over their own bodies or wills," says Saint Benedict.[288] Since this is the case, they ought not to have any care concerning themselves, but should entirely depend on the will of him to whom they are subjected according to the appointment of God, and this is of duty at all times and in all things, but chiefly in the time of sickness. For then it is that temptations are more to be feared, and that discretion becomes more necessary.

---

[288] *RB* 33.

Nature is then anxious, self-love excited, the soul becomes more enervated by reason of actual pain, so that, unless a religious is supported by solid and constant virtue, he will be entirely occupied with himself. He will consider himself only as a sick person, forget that he is a penitent, attend only to what his sickness and pains require, but will give no ear to what the sanctity of his state requires. The consequence will be that if left at liberty to guide himself in that state, he will never be satisfied with physicians and remedies. He will violate every rule of his state, and forsake without scruple the care of his soul for the comfort of his body, to the great scandal, perhaps to the destruction of discipline amongst his brethren in this most essential point.

Secondly, if a religious consider himself in the manner he is obliged; if he judge himself as severely as he is bound; if he cultivate such dispositions as Saint Bernard had when he considered himself as a carnal man and a slave to sin; that is to say, if he be a true religious (unless he is only so in his own ideas, if he does not look upon himself as a sinner, certainly, really, and in effect), he will be so far from desiring remedies when he is afflicted by the hand of the Lord, or thinking about his recovery, that he will receive his sickness as a punishment which he has deserved, and as the chastisement of the sins he has committed, not only remaining in silence like Lazarus, with regard to men, but also being careful to address himself to God like another Job. He will say to Him in the fullness of his heart: "Let it please Him to finish what He has begun. If He strike me with all His strength, and reduce me to dust, it shall be my comfort not to contradict His holy will." Thus believing himself unworthy of any human assistance, he will never anticipate his recovery either by his desires or anxiety; and he will have no other thought but that of keeping himself in an entire submission to God, of being guided by the motives of His Divine Providence, and of expecting purely of Him a change of his present condition.

Thirdly, the Son of God who came down from Heaven to open for us the gates of that eternal kingdom, found no way more effectual to accomplish His merciful designs than those of crosses and sufferings. Into these He freely entered that He might hold up to our view a model for our imitation, excite us by His example, and obtain that our sufferings might—by being united to His—become an acceptable sacrifice to His heavenly Father for the expiation of our sins. For this reason, He delivered Himself up to unlimited confusions, to unmitigated torments, and preferred a sorrowful ignominious death to all the joys of this world (Hebrews 12:2). By His violent martyrdom He broke down the barriers that opposed our entrance to eternal life, opened the gates of His everlasting kingdom to share with us the joys of His bliss. He now carefully furnishes us with the means of discharging the duty that binds us to imitate His laborious penitential life by the different pains, distempers, afflictions, and sorrows, which He is pleased either to send or permit to us.

Let persons who lack faith and light, and who consider those temporal afflictions as misfortunes, and as the unpleasant sports of fortune, let them grieve on such occasions as much as they please, and employ every possible means to avoid them. For your part, my brethren, who live by faith, nourished by the word of life, and enlightened by the sacred truths which the Son of God received of His heavenly Father, you, who by a special privilege annexed to your state, are consecrated to His cross, and who may say with the apostle: I bear the marks of the sufferings of Jesus Christ in my body (Gal 6:17) can you, I say, consider those accidents in any other view, but, as so many precious occasions of purifying your love, as the effects of that vigilance and paternal solicitude with which He watches over His elect? Is it possible that you should not be animated to bear them, not only with resignation, but even with a lively joy and sincere gratitude?

The glory of all Christians is that of Christ, and as He knew no other in this world but that of offering Himself incessantly to His eternal Father as a victim for the honor of His holy name, so ought we to seek no other but that of immolating ourselves with Him, in the same spirit and for the same end.

He has made the felicity which He has prepared for those who shall live and die in His love and service to depend on their fidelity in the exercise of penance. He requires that they partake of His pains and labors, and that they should begin in time that blessed conformity which they are to have with Him for all eternity. Hence, our infirmities, distempers, and afflictions are at once the remedies of our sins, the effects of the judgments of God, the marks of our reconciliation with Him, and the pledges of our eternal crowns.

From all this you may easily gather what the dispositions of a true religious ought to be when he is visited by God with sickness and infirmities. He should remain in a passive state before that heavenly guide, submit to his illness, because such is the holy will of God, and be calmly resigned to the effects of His justice and goodness. He should fear going astray, by making the least step towards his recovery, accept what is given him by his superior as coming from God Himself. Thus the remedies he applies to his disorder will be only so many acts of obedience, but never the consequences of his particular inclinations.

Certainly, nothing is more insupportable than to behold a religious, who ought to be no longer numbered amongst the living, taking every means, and employing all possible solicitude to avoid death. He is by his state no longer of this world, and yet he finds it as difficult to leave it as if he were plunged in its pleasures and affairs. He lives only to prepare for death, and yet he is disturbed with fear when it appears, and exerts every faculty to protract the moment.

He ought to love nothing here below but God; He should be the only object of his affections, and yet he cannot resolve to go to Him when He calls. He strains every nerve to defer the journey; he flies from His presence as a criminal before his judge; and appears only with regret when he is forced and can no longer avoid it. What kind of love is this for Jesus Christ, says Saint Augustine, to fear lest He should come; we say that we love Him, and yet we fear to see Him. [289]

According to the sentiments of the saints, all Christians, as well those who are engaged in the world as those who are not, ought to meet death with joy, and consider sickness as the necessary harbinger that precedes the coming of their Creator. Nevertheless, if those who live in the world evince any weakness in that respect, they are certainly more excusable, for they may say, "I have bought a farm, I have purchased five yoke of oxen, I have married a wife, and therefore I cannot come" (Luke 14:19). These are pretexts that have some color and appearance. But as to monks, who have been delivered from that slavery by Jesus Christ, and placed by Him in the happy liberty of His children, they can no longer allege such reasons.

The love of life, the desire of remedies, the uneasy solicitude in seeking what may prolong their days, are no better than the defects of their disordered consciences and corrupted hearts. They are the marks which prove that their faith and charity are quite dead, and that hence the crown laid up, according to the apostle, for those who love the coming of Jesus Christ, is not for them.

Q. 4.—Does not charity oblige a superior to employ every sort

---

[289] S. Augustinus, *Enarratio in Psalmum* XCV, PL 37:1235 (1845).

of means and remedies for the recovery of his religious when they are sick?

A.—Charity obliges a superior to employ such means and remedies only, for the recovery of his religious when they are sick, as are conformable to their state. That virtue obliges him to measure all things, not only according to their wants, but also according to their salvation and the edification of the community. He must remember that he governs men who have forsaken the delicacies of the world in order to live in austere penance, under the rules of severe discipline, and hence he must be careful not to allow them anything that might injure the integrity and perfection of their state.

All monastic rules oblige the superiors to have a particular attention, vigilance and charity for the sick; but there are none which oblige him to conduct himself with such mildness and condescension as to cease to contribute to the salvation and perfection of their souls. As he would do wrong in not granting without difficulty whatever is allowed by the rules to comfort his brethren in their sickness, in like manner he ought to be inflexible in refusing those which are forbidden. In a word, he ought to act with much prudence and discernment, lest too much severity should terrify his brethren, or too great mildness might lead them to relaxation.

Nevertheless, as we find by experience, the easy conduct of superiors, and the immortification of monks, have filled the cloister with disorder and abuses, and that as soon as a religious is ill, he thinks himself exempt from every observance, and entitled to ask medicines and remedies as he pleases, and assume a full independence. It is necessary that those who govern monasteries should, as much as possible, resume the primitive exactitude, cut off all abusive liberties, be firm in maintaining discipline. They ought to re-establish in the infirmaries proper regularity, and keep continually in their minds this remarkable advice of Saint Guigo, namely, that a monk ought not to be less different from worldly people in the time of sickness than during his health, and that it is not lawful for him to desire in the desert what he could scarcely have found in cities.[290]

Call to mind also, my brethren, that holy and solid advice addressed by Saint Ambrose to all Christians, when he says that the precepts of physic are contrary to the documents of heavenly science, for they condemn fasting, will not allow watching, turn away the mind from the labor of meditation;

---

[290] Guigonis I, *Consuetudines,* Capitulum XXXVIII, PL 153:714 (1854).

and therefore, whoever gives himself up to physicians, renounces all right to himself.[291]

Remember that our lives are measured, that all our moments are numbered by God, and that as it is written, we cannot by all our cares add anything to our natural stature, nor change the color of a hair on our heads, much less can we prolong our days beyond the limits prescribed by the author of our existence, that all men must die as Moses did, by the command of the Lord, for they cease to live when it pleases Him. Remember that the remedies He allows us to use (while we live in this state of incertitude regarding the limits He has prescribed) have no other force or virtue but what He is pleased to give them; and therefore those who use them ought to remain in a profoundly tranquil submission to the dispositions of His adorable will. Consider that nothing is more worthy of a religious man whose faith ought to be apostolic, than to separate himself from all dependence on creatures, and place himself unreservedly in the hands of God, so that He alone may decide his death or life.

Consider, my brethren, that the infirmities which attack us in this mortal life, are as it were, the instruments of the punishment due to our sins; they are true crosses to which the justice of God attaches us, and that we must remain thereon so long as He pleases, awaiting His command to descend. Leave therefore medicines to the lovers of the world, let them seek assistance in the creature, for besides their imperfect faith, their anxious love of the present life excites them to seek everything they imagine to be conducive to their health, without judging whether they are worthy of it or not.

But you who are separated from the world, you who are retired in a monastery, not for the purpose of seeking a long life, but a happy death, you who are already immolated to Jesus Christ, as so many victims, and whose only ambition is to imitate Him in His labors and sufferings, be always indifferent as to the assistance of human means, which so easily wound that confidence we ought to have in the providence of God. The poverty and abnegation of our state, as well as the respect we ought to have for the precepts of the gospel by which we are commanded to hate our life, and despise our flesh (Jude 1:23) oblige us to this.

If, however, obedience to your superiors, joined to the fear of being too singular from the rest of men, oblige you to adopt some measures

---

[291] S. Ambrosius, *Expositio in Psalmum* CXVIII, PL 15:1519 (1845).

contrary to these maxims and to condescend to their desires, be careful at least to preserve the purity of your hearts. Never suffer the least desire to be formed there that might tarnish its beauty. Preserve it from every weakness, nourish the will in a fixed determination of suffering more, even at the time when they allow you some medical assistance in your afflictions and pains. Thus the exterior remedy, having nothing of your own will, cannot injure your first resolution. Your fidelity will preserve its merits before God, and will not fail of being eternally rewarded by Him.

Q. 5.—Ought not the discipline and penance of monasteries be relaxed when the religious die frequently; and is not the fear of not being able to persevere, a sufficient reason to diminish the austerities of religious orders?

A.—First, being come to religion not to seek a long life, but to prepare for a happy death, monks, as we have said many times, ought to be neither astonished nor terrified if they behold frequent deaths. They came to seek the salvation of their souls, and not the preservation of their health and life. Hence, if by the exact performance of their rules, they should finish their course in the fear and love of God, it may be said that they arrive at the end of their wishes and labors. Though the time might seem short, yet being filled up with the practice of virtue and perfection, it is equivalent to a great many years, according to these words of the Holy Spirit, "Being made perfect in a short space, he fulfilled a long time (Wisdom 4:13)."

Secondly, if the kings of the earth gained as many victories, and took as many cities, as they lose soldiers, would anyone think of complaining of the number of those who perished in such a war? What reason can there be then in the conduct of those who, at the expense of everything important in religion, endeavor to spare the lives of the soldiers of Christ who immolate themselves for His love, by the arms of penance, since according the sentiments of the saints, and according to truth, Jesus Christ gains so many victories over the powers of hell, as He saves men? And the delivery of a soul from the rage of the infernal spirits, which is always the case when the elect consume themselves by their penitential labors, is for our great King, and for the conquest of a real kingdom.

Thirdly, the same thing may be said of the sufferings of monks as is said of the sufferings of martyrs. The tears and sweat of the one as well as the blood of the others make the Church become fruitful. As Christians are never more increased than by the violence of persecution, so monks are never more abundantly multiplied than by the greatness of their austerities. It is easy see that monastic orders were never so much extended by any other means as by the reputation and fame of the penance, austerity and sanctity in which their members constantly lived. The prudence of the flesh says that religious persons must relax their ancient severity and descend from their elevation, if they wish to increase or even preserve themselves; but the wisdom of God, on the contrary, says, that they must bind themselves up, and walk by the narrowest paths. The spirit of Christ breathes in those congregations where exact discipline is maintained, but the prudence of the flesh in such as are relaxed.

Fourthly, those frequent deaths which alarm men so much, are either signs of the anger, or merciful visitations of God. Now if He punish because He is angry, is it not by penance we are to appease Him? Have we ever learned by the examples or writings of the saints, that the means of satisfying His divine justice consists in making our lives more soft and sensual? The men of Nineveh covered themselves with sackcloth, proclaimed a general fast, which was observed even by children and beasts, in order to avert the punishment with which a prophet of the Lord threatened them. Shall there then be found anyone so unreasonable as to maintain that publicly professed penitents, such as all religious of our order are, shall be obliged to cast away their usual austerities when the Lord is offended, and makes men feel the weight of His indignation?

But if God by an effect of His goodness, diminishes the number of members in a community, calling them from this place of banishment to crown their labors, is it the way to acknowledge the blessings He bestows on His servants, and the means to induce Him to continue the same effusion of His heavenly graces, to forsake the penance and mortification by which they were made worthy of those favors, and to relax the austerity of their lives, rather than increase it if possible? Would it not be more reasonable to declare the necessity of being at least faithful to their first obligations from such a consequence?

In fine, if the fear of non-perseverance could have attracted the attention of the ancient holy monks, they would not have so earnestly applied themselves to form all those religious observances which were so austere and holy, and were from time to time the glory of Jesus Christ, the ornament of the Church, and the edification of the world. They well knew that there is nothing stable here below, that those works which are effected by the intermediacy of men, however holy they may be, are subject to inconstancy, that there is nothing permanent under the sun, and that the perpetual motion of creatures who succeed one another, renders, as it were, a continual homage to the eternal immutability of God, who is alone always the same, and knows no change or vicissitude. I am the Lord and change not: with whom there is no change, nor shadow of vicissitude (Mal 3:6; James 1:17). But they were very far from giving ear to a reason so feeble, or believing that they ought to forsake or interrupt a good thing, because it was not to last eternally, or because its duration might only be for a time.

Ecclesiastical history informs us that there was scarcely any religious order, monastery or congregation, that did not fall into a state of defection or enervation in a short time after its institution.

Saint Pacomius saw in spirit the ruin of Tabenna, which happened soon after his death; and even during his life a great number of his religious revolted against him.[292]

Scethe, that began during the combats of Saint Anthony, was so changed in the time of Saint Arsenius, that that great saint said, weeping, "Scethe is lost by the great number of its solitaries, as Rome was by that of its inhabitants."[293]

The sanctity of Sinai was not of long duration; and though in the time of Saint John Climacus, many solitaries of eminent virtue lived there, yet that saint testifies that though in his days some of the penitential practices and austerities of the saints were there preserved, yet the place was full of pride and hypocrisy; and that neither the purity nor simplicity of the ancients could be found amongst them.[294]

That so celebrated laura of Saint Euthymius fell into disorder after his death, and Saint Sabas was obliged to leave it. A little time after he founded another, and immediately sixty of the brethren joined in a great conspiracy revolted against him, and separated themselves from his government.[295]

The great order of Saint Benedict fell into relaxation in the second century after its foundation, and though almighty God always preserved some men of virtue, who employed all possible means to prevent its entire

---

[292] Ernest A. Budge, ed. *The Paradise or Garden of the Holy Fathers* (London: Chatto, 1907), 1:294.

[293] *Vit. Patr.*

[294] *Scala*, PG 88:1014 (1864). / *Ladder,* 197.52.

[295] Vita Patrum

destruction, or to repair its ruins, yet, according to the testimony of a celebrated abbot of the same order, corruption did not fail to spread itself, and become almost universal.[296]

The Carthusian order, though it maintained itself longer than others, yet found the effects of the common inconstancy. This is proved by the insurrection which happened in the great charter-house in Saint Bernard's time, by means of the relaxations which was introduced there after the death of Saint Guigo, and which more evidently appears by the life of Saint Anthelme[297], who being ordained prior in the Chartreuse De Portes, and finding there a great abundance of money, corn and such things, which ought not to be found amongst solitaries of such consummate disengagement and sanctity, distributed a thousand crowns of gold amongst the monasteries of his own order and other indigent religious houses, threw open his granaries, distributed the corn to the poor, and removed all the unnecessary church ornaments. [298]

The order of Grandmont degenerated and fell forty years after its birth.

Saint Bernard was no sooner taken out of this life, than this order of which we have the happiness to be members declined into such weaknesses that it was easy to behold in its members the harbingers of its general dissolution. For though it maintained discipline and austerity in the beginning of the second century after its foundation, yet it is certain that it lost much of its perfection and sanctity in the first. The reproaches which were addressed by Pope Alexander III to the religious of Citeaux, a few years after the death of that great saint, are such convincing proofs of this assertion, that we think it much to the purpose to insert a few words thereof in this place.

"We feel much regret," says that great pope,

> In being obliged to tell you, that, though you have not strayed away in every point from the sanctity of your order, yet there are many of you who no longer observe a great many things belonging to your rules; thus having quite forgotten the sanctity of their origin, they now possess villages, parishes, feudal tenures, honoraries, justices . . . . For which reason we exhort

---

[296] Trithem. Abb.

[297] Vita S. Anth.

[298] Epistola CCLXX, PL 182:473 (1854). / Bernard, *Works,* 2:765.

you to consider the state in which you are, and to confine yourselves within the limits of your foundation; for if you are determined to forsake your primitive institute, and arrogate to yourselves the rights of other monasteries, you must also expect to be treated henceforth as others; for as you live in the common way, it is not just that you should enjoy particular distinctions and privileges.[299]

The facility with which they yielded to the menaces of the king of England, and allowed Saint Thomas of Canterbury to leave the monastery of Pontigny, show that their disinterestedness and charity were not the same as in the time of Saint Bernard, who would not have failed to oppose himself as a wall of brass against the violence of that king. But we ought not to pass over in silence what Louis VII, king of France, said when he was informed of the saint's egression from the above monastery: "O, Religion! O, Religion! Where art thou at present?" exclaimed the prince,

> Since those whom we considered as being dead to the world, are yet intimidated by the fear of the world; and who, to preserve a little of its perishable goods, which they profess to have despised for the love of Christ, forsake the works of God, which they had happily begun, by expelling from their house a saint, exiled for the cause of justice.

Then addressing his discourse to the person who brought him that news, he said,

> I am much grieved to find, that persons who seemed to love and fear God alone, are terrified at the menaces of the king of England, and fear to assist the Bishop of Canterbury. Assure that prelate, on my part, that though the world, and even those who seem to be no longer of the world, forsake him, yet I will never abandon him.

Baronius says that this expulsion caused a great scandal in the Church.[300]

The divisions which were provoked by the first abbots of this order, about one hundred years after its foundation, evince that it was then deeply wounded, and much estranged from its primitive purity and simplicity.

---

[299] Decret. lib. 3. de stat. monas. c. 3.

[300] Baronius anno 1167.

Those disputes were so great that Pope Innocent III was obliged to write to them in the following terms:

> We have been informed by unpleasant rumors that this pure and excellent gold is finally tarnished, its color lost, and its substance changed into dross, for now you dispute about authority: thus seeking your own interests, and not those of Jesus Christ, you evidently show that you have forsaken the true road, and abandoned your primitive simplicity.

Then having exhorted them to persevere in their original purity, and to remove every occasion of scandal, he tells them to beware of becoming the fable and mockery of the world, like the monks of Grandmont.[301]

The order of Saint Francis fell soon after its foundation by the restless and ambitious spirit of brother Elias.

The famous Carmelite Monastery of St. Joseph of Avila in which Saint Teresa had by her care established the practice of the rule and an eminent perfection, a few years after fell into so great a relaxation that the transgression of the rule was considered as lawful and necessary. The evil would have been incurable if the saint had not applied a proper remedy by her presence, prayers, and zealous endeavors.[302]

Moreover, if we run through the history of all the orders which have been formed in the Church, we shall find that there was scarce one that did not degenerate in a short time after its birth, from the spirit, virtue, and sanctity of its founders.

Now, my brethren, I have placed these examples before your eyes to convince you more evidently that if those great saints inspired by God, and directed by His Holy Spirit, founded congregations, orders and monasteries in such rigorous and severe penance, though they were soon after to lose the essential fidelity to their primitive obligations, and fall so low from their original fervor; and if the Lord Himself did not fail to send workmen into His vineyard, though He knew it would be soon laid waste, we must from these facts infer that we ought never forsake the work of God, nor enervate it when perfected, for fear it would not last long nor maintain its original perfection. On the contrary, if it were ascertained that

---

[301] Innoc. III. Epist. ad Abb. Cist. an. 1202, & 4 prim. abb.

[302] History of the Reform. Carm. p. 570. 2 part, book 5, c. 21. [as given by dR: Hist. Des Carm. Refor. P. 570, Seconde Part. Lv. 5, ch. 21.]

this destruction were near at hand, we should then excite our zeal, fervor and piety, so that by such exertions we might give to God so much the more glory and honor, as we should be certainly convinced of its impending ruin, and of its becoming for ever useless to His honor and service.

Monasteries and religious institutes are of the same condition as the life of man. God has regulated their duration, and prescribed their limits, beyond which they cannot subsist. A man ceases to live, the reasons and causes of his death are anxiously sought; but if we ascend to the source, we shall see that the real cause of his death is no other than as I have already said, because God is not pleased that he should live any longer. The same may be said of a religious order. It perishes as soon as it has attained the limits prescribed for it by the divine wisdom.

In a word, my brethren, a monastery is an ark of salvation. In it God encloses a small number of His elect in order that they may be preserved from the deluge of corruption which causes so great a desolation throughout the world. He guides this ark and protects it as long as it serves the purpose for which He designed it. But when His designs are completed, when His elect are safely arrived in the port and His eternal views are accomplished, He retires, and forsakes those who neglect the duty to which He called them. Then by a just punishment, this frail vessel being left to itself without helm or pilot in the midst of the tempest, is tossed about by the fury of vices and passions as by so many impetuous winds and waves. It strikes, breaks, and is at length destroyed by a total submersion.

To this we may add, my brethren, that though almighty God foresaw the future infidelity of the angels and of man, yet He created both in charity and justice. And if men find a resource in the mercy of God, through Jesus Christ, the revolted angels find none; and yet their creation was not a less effect of His infinite goodness. How much ought we not praise this same infinite goodness for the institution of so many religious orders which fell only when they had produced so many elect of the glorious city above? And may we not hope that God has still reserved a time, known only in the councils of His providence, when He will renew the effusions of His first graces, a time, I say, like that in which He prepares for His formerly chosen people, when, according to His promise He will gather them together from all parts of the world after a dispersion so long and general.

Q. 6.— *What answer can be made to those who say, that it is unlawful to embrace austerities which shorten life? Can they support such an assertion?*

A.—Though you may find the solution of this question without much difficulty in what we have already said, yet I will here add, that if such a proposition be admitted, we must, of course, condemn a great number of eminent saints who shone like so many brilliant stars in the Church throughout every age since the beginning. Those whom God held up to the world as objects of continual admiration, would become the subjects of its censures. The holy conduct of the Pauls, Anthonies, Palemons, Pacomiuses, Hilarions, Simeons, Marcariuses, and of so many others, who, like them, walked through hard and rigorous ways, would be considered as so many excessive and rash enterprises.

For though they had not precisely the intention to put an end to their existence by the austerities they practiced, yet their mode of life did not fail to produce that consequence. And it cannot be doubted that when they undertook it, they preferred the purity of their bodies and the sanctification of their souls, to the hope of protecting their lives. Those incomparable men who had learned of Jesus Christ the necessity of hating their lives in this world, in order to preserve them in the next, were persuaded that they could not make a better use of the life they had received of God than to lose it for His glory by becoming martyrs of penance and mortification, in order to be delivered for ever from the horrors of the second death.

If those who are willing to persuade themselves that it is not lawful to undertake austerities which may enervate health and shorten life, did only reflect how many conditions in human society are subject to the same inconvenience, and which, nevertheless, cannot be condemned without extravagance, they would soon change both their sentiments and manners.

Let them but consider those persons, for example, who labor in the mines, or those employed in purifying metals and minerals, or smiths, or glass-blowers, *etc.* who live, as it were, in the midst of burning fires, and are constantly surrounded by its flames, which continually diminish that natural moisture which is so necessary to the principle of life; so much so, that every person agrees that they cannot enjoy a long life in employments so adverse to its duration. And yet nobody ever thinks they are to be condemned for engaging and persevering in these works.

In like manner, the man of letters weakens himself by his continual application to study, which, though profane is yet necessary for human life, for he proposes to himself either the acquisition of extensive learning or to become useful to the public by his elaborate compositions. The zealous missionary consumes himself in the study of the word of God, and in announcing to men the knowledge of salvation.

The lawyer who distinguishes himself at the bar by his deep study and eloquent discourses, and by so many other labors, clearly perceives that his constitution is changed. He feels that such occupations injure his health. His debilitated system appears evident by the paleness of his emaciated face, the weakness of his breast, by his frequent sleepless nights, and by many such unconstitutional sufferings, which are the effects of an industrious, sedentary life, and of excessive application. Yet he feels no anxiety about it, nor does anyone ever think of making it a scruple of conscience for him.

Others embrace the profession of a military life, and at the same time engage themselves in an almost infinite number of inevitable dangers, as well by sea as by land, to which they are continually exposed by the many accidents incident to them at every step. Their health is threatened not only by the dangers of fire and water, but also by the excessive labors and fatigues which are inseparable from their condition. Here they may be seen exposed to all the inclemencies of the weather, scorched by the burning heat of summer, and again frozen by the chilling cold of winter. They sometimes endure all the extremities of hunger, thirst and cold; they pass whole nights exposed to wind, rain, snow and frost; they lie indifferently on the ground, sometimes in mud and dirt, etc. In a word, thousands of them fall victims to the hardships they endure, so much so that those who are well acquainted with the rigors of that state are at a loss to know how anyone can outlive such perilous hardships.

Though this delineation falls short of the horrors of war, and though it is a fact that all these evils and sufferings are inseparably attached to the military life, nevertheless it is praised and extolled. Men consider it as the theater of their honor and glory. What person ever maintained that it is not lawful to bear arms, or to go to sea or to war?

This being so, my brethren, can we not affirm that if without doing any injury to the laws of conscience, men may embrace the employments of the world, the duties, functions, and exercises of which lead to death by almost inevitable consequences, then with much more reason shall it be lawful for Christians—who are more sensible than others to the obligation which binds all to bear the cross of Jesus Christ—to embrace voluntary austerities so that they may retrace His sufferings in themselves, honor His sacred passion, and at the same time subdue their own flesh, subject their bodies, repress their senses and passions, and so make themselves more agreeable to and worthy of Him to whose service they are exclusively consecrated. Would it not be an extreme injustice to condemn as imprudence, rashness and indiscretion a conduct which is the result of their faith, piety and charity, grounded on the doctrine and example of Christ and His saints?

This evidently appears by the abundant graces with which it pleased our Lord to crown those men of benediction, who, in every age, undertook and practiced those austerities for His sake, and by the particular care He took to justify that which carnal men could neither bear nor understand.

Amongst those holy penitents who undertook to chastise their bodies or to subdue their passions, some were found who passed several days, and even entire Lents, without eating. Others, that they might not die of hunger, used a few wild herbs. Some deprived themselves of bread; others lived on lentils steeped in water; some on a little bruised barley. Some deprived themselves of the use of water, and only took a little to prevent their being consumed at once by the violence of a burning thirst. Some were seen who macerated themselves by almost continual watchings. They remained standing all night, and when they took a little rest, they were content to lean against a wall.

Still others remained in the open air, on the tops of high rocks, day and night, winter and summer, suffering all the inconveniences of the seasons, without refuge or covering: others, that they might crucify their flesh by new inventions of penance. Still others put themselves into wheels, or shut themselves up in such narrow holes and caverns that they were obliged to keep themselves continually folded, as it were, and thus obliged themselves to endure all the pains which accompany a position so distressing.

In a word, millions might be recounted who treated themselves with similar severities. And although it might seem that such austere practices would carry them on rapidly to their end, and that to practice them seemed incompatible with long life, yet God declared in their favor, and evinced, by many public testimonies, that He was sensibly affected with the affliction of His servants, and that He received the sacrifice of their penance. For either He prolonged their lives beyond the usual limits, and made them attain an extremely advanced age, as we see in Saints Paul, Euthyemius, Theodore, John the Silent, Queriacus, Zosimus, and so many others who lived more than a century. Or He exalted their names, making them famous throughout the world, and giving them an immortal reputation.

His ears were always open to their prayers; their petitions pierced the clouds, and brought down every blessing. In a word, it seemed as if He had placed his almighty power in their hands, for He performed so many wonders by their ministry that they appeared on earth like the supreme masters of all nature.[303]

From all this it may be safely inferred that it is lawful to undertake austerities which may be injurious to health and shorten life, since God cannot approve or authorize sin. This truth, so unchangeable, appears in almost every monastic rule, for the most famous and holy rules, written by the finger of God, propose such austerities, mortifications, and penitential exercises that are almost impossible to be observed with exactitude for any considerable time, and still preserve health and life.

This will be clearly proved by a serious examination of Saint Benedict's rule, which has been always esteemed as the dictates of divine wisdom and discretion. It ordains that a religious must always endeavor to keep the imagination of death present to the eyes of his mind, and never lose the memory of it. That he must be mindful of the commandments of the Lord, meditate on His judgments and on the rewards He promises to those who are faithful in keeping His holy law. [304]

It enjoins that the religious shall, at all times, evince the humility of their hearts by proper exterior signs in every place, whether at work, in the monastery, in the church, in the garden, traveling in the fields, or in what position soever they may be. Standing, sitting or walking, it requires them to keep their eyes cast down, and that acknowledging themselves guilty of many sins, they should believe themselves always ready to be summoned before the dreadful tribunal of Christ.[305] Thus they should weep and say with the publican of the gospel: "I am not worthy to lift up my eyes to Heaven" (Luke 18:13). It recommends to love and study perpetual silence, prohibits all idle and jesting expressions, and condemns them with as much severity as if they were so many blasphemies.[306]

So that all pretext for transgressing this important statute may be entirely removed, it will not even allow those who are perfect in virtue the

---

[303] Those celebrated heroes of primitive Christianity and religious perfection were Saints Simeon Stylites, Alacaine, James of Nisibis, Mary of Egypt, Acepsiumus, Macedonius, Eusebius, Dorotheus, Thebain, Thalassus, Thalelus the hermit, Auxentius, Marcien, etc.

[304] RB 4 and 7.1.

[305] RB 7.62-66.

[306] RB 6.8.

liberty of speaking even on pious and edifying matters but very rarely.[307] It places them in such a dependence on their superior that they can dispose of nothing relative to their own person or wills. [308]To this it joins a fixed and constant stability in the monastery, [309]painful labors,[310] long watchings, great fasts,[311] and perpetual abstinence.[312] At that time when a fast was observed, nothing was taken beyond one meal, which was always at the hour of none, and this was the proper fast of the order; this hour was about three o'clock in the afternoon, and later on fasting days of the Church.

This rule fills up the time with regular exercises and employments, so that no moments can be found for recreation, or unbending the mind. Now, everyone will grant that a life so painful and laborious cannot, morally speaking, last long, and that nature must sink under the pressure of such a constant and connected succession of interior and exterior mortifications. Great labors and fatigues may be overcome when they are not continual, and when necessary repose is afterwards supplied.

This, however, is a state that knows no rest; it is an engagement that allows no relaxation; and therefore, he who desires to fulfill exactly and piously all that this rule enjoins must live in constant motion, never interrupting his vigilance. He must successively pass from prayer to reading, from reading to work, from work to the divine office. He must carefully watch over himself, and never stray from himself by dissipation.

In sum, joining to all this fastings and watchings, his life is a real crucifixion that points out death, hastens its approach, and makes him desire it. But this is not because he is weary of his sufferings, but because his soul being purified, his love for Jesus is so inflamed, that, though he endures everything with pleasure, and says with the prophet: "For thy sake, O sweet object of my love, I live in the embraces of continual sufferings, and we appear like so many victims destined for the slaughter" (Ps 43:23).

Yet he receives no consolation nor refreshment, except in anticipation

---

[307] *RB* 4.

[308] *RB* 33.

[309] *RB* 58.

[310] *RB* 42.

[311] *RB* 8.

[312] *RB* 41.

of that boundless ocean of delights, which await him at the close of his career. It is undoubtedly true, however, that He for whose love all this is undertaken sweetens those bitters with His interior consolations, and alleviates those crosses with the delightful unction of His heavenly grace.

Notwithstanding all this severity and constraint, this holy rule has received the approbation both of God and men. It has been adopted by the greater number of the western monks, and has produced inexpressible fruits of grace and benediction.

Here it must not be alleged that those are the excesses of past ages which can find no supporters in these days, for we behold even now the Carthusians, who form one of the most holy and celebrated monastic orders of the Church, keeping an abstinence so rigorous and inviolable that they never interrupt it in whatever danger of death they may be. The whole Church approves their conduct. Divines who justify it say that they ought to be more attached to the law that binds them to abstinence than to the law of nature which obliges them to preserve their lives, because this rigorous austerity produces more public edification than could even result from the preservation of the life of any individual. And though this inflexibility may be the cause of shortening life, yet death is not an infallible and necessary consequence of it, for it is absolutely possible to live without the use of flesh-meat.

It is thus, say they, that a man may expose himself to the danger of pestilence; that a sick man may, without injuring his conscience, remain where he is though physicians assure him that the air is mortal and that he cannot live unless he change his abode; that he may refuse very precious and costly medicines, delicate food, and even a softer bed when he feels induced—by the spirit of penance and a desire of being more pleasing to God—to seek a more disagreeable, painful and difficult situation.

Animated by these and the like sentiments, the great Saint Martin, being near his death, and his disciples having entreated him to place himself in some more tolerable position, he answered them in these remarkable words: "It does not become a Christian to die in any other manner than on ashes. Were I to leave you, my brethren, any other example, I would thereby offend against my duty."

Therefore, learned men of the Church conclude that when those actions are continued during life, and extended to death, they produce incomparably greater good in the Church than ever could result from all the care that could be employed to preserve a few moments of life; and therefore, that there can be no doubt but that such things may be lawfully undertaken, and safety practiced.[313]

To all this we may add, my brethren, the example of Saint Charles Borromeo, who having undertaken a severe penitential rule of life which injured his health a great deal, and evidently abridged his life, resisted all the advice of his friends who endeavored to persuade him to soften even a little of its austerity. Nevertheless, he yielded to the orders of the pope in that respect for some time, by which he showed that obedience might induce him to relax something of his usual severity, but not the fear of offending his God by so rigorous a course, or the fear of doing anything against his duty, though he should persevere in the austerity he had embraced even at the expense of his life.

Q. 7.—Does not Saint Basil recommend great moderation and prudence in the practice of austerities?

A.—It is true, Saint Basil declares in many parts of his writings, that we ought not to treat our bodies with too much severity, nor reduce them to a state which might disable them from fulfilling the duties to which monks are obliged. He condemns indiscreet austerities, and shows that they are productive of much evil when they are excessive. However, Saint Basil never condemned a life which, though it leaves the body sufficient strength to fulfill the duties and rules of its state, nevertheless prescribes austerities and penitential exercises sufficient to produce consequences injurious to the health of the body, enervate its strength, relax its principles, and in fine, totally undermine it by indispositions, which are sometimes quick, and sometimes slow and imperceptible.

These were so undoubtedly his sentiments, that he teaches the necessity of corporal austerity in the clearest terms, saying that true solitaries ought to live on dry aliments, or such that are less nutritious and merely sufficient to support their strength, that they ought to be content with one meal a day, and that when the hour of refection calls them to this abstemious repast, they ought to conduct themselves with such temperance in giving

---

[313] Editor: Although Prospero Lambertini (Pope Benedict XIV, 1675–1758) wrote after the time of de Rancé, he assembled a great number of authors who support this opinion. See *Heroic Virtue: A treatise of Benedict XIV on the Beatification and Canonization of the Servants of God,* Volume I (London: Richardson, 1850), 366.

the necessary attention to nature that they may never feel disturbed by any well grounded anxiety of conscience.[314]

In another place he says that bread and water ought to be sufficient for a solitary in good health, and that the weak might use esculent roots; that he ought scarcely spend one hour in the day at his repast and in the service of the body; and that all the rest ought to be employed in everything that regards the soul; that his sleep ought to be very light, proportioned to his abstinence, and that he ought to endeavor to interrupt it, however short it may be, by his application to spiritual concerns, which ought to replenish both his heart and mind.[315]

Now, although it is possible to maintain this religious exactitude, we may without difficulty decide that according to the usual course of nature it is not possible to preserve vigorous health, and to live long in the observance of such austerities. Therefore, we infer that Saint Basil disapproved only of those excessive rigors, those extraordinary deprivations, those uninterrupted fasts of several days, those excessive abstinences, either as to the quantity or quality of food; specifically, the indiscretion of those who being impelled to undertake those practices by their own spirit, and not by the spirit of God, refused that nutriment to their bodies without which nature cannot subsist. His design was to propose a more moderate rule of conduct, such as might be adopted and observed by many persons without danger of giving in to those excesses.

In a word, there is a great difference between doing an action with the real design to put an end to one's life, and that of engaging in actions and states which may only lead to it, or accelerate that term. The former was never allowed, the latter was never prohibited. A prince, for example, commands his soldiers to cast themselves down from a tower into the depth of a pit: in that case, they are not bound to obey him. However, if he orders them to swim across a rapid river, to ascend a breach lined with soldiers, and all on fire, they are obliged to obey and execute his orders. The difference between these two injunctions is this, that in the first death is present and inevitable, whereas in the second, though the danger is great, yet it is not entirely certain, and it may be possible to escape.

Those who would dispense monks from the obligation of living in great austerity persuade themselves that by so doing they would deliver them

---

[314] S. Basilius,, *Constitutiones,* PG 31:1322 (1857).

[315] S. Basilius, *Epistolae,* PG 32:219 (1857).

from a yoke which they are very unwillingly bear. However, they do not perceive that they do no less than wrest from them the only plank on which they may be saved after shipwreck; that the only consolation they enjoy in this world is to revenge on their persons by the sacrifice of their lives the injuries they have committed against the Divine Majesty, and to testify their unlimited sorrow by this unbounded renunciation.

Penetrated with the sole view of their misfortune in having offended a God so good, they are ardently excited to desire the end of life, not only that death may punish their guilt, but also that they may find an assurance by it of never offending Him again. Thus they consider all their penitential actions as the avenging instruments of chastisement, to which they have willingly condemned themselves.

Those souls who have preserved their innocence may indeed entertain more moderate sentiments, but as to those who have unfortunately lost that treasure, or who as monks and penitents hold the place in the Church of Christ of those who have violated it, there are no austerities but what they should embrace with gladness. And when they consider that men usually err much in their judgment and estimation of things, they fear nothing more than that their actions should be much inferior to their obligations, and may perhaps be found unworthy of any attention on that terrible day when they are to be so rigorously examined. Yet when they compare the pains they endure with those they have deserved, the terrifying disproportion that appears between both moves them to adore the infinite goodness of God, who is pleased to remit eternal chastisements for so inconsiderable a reparation.

Another consideration that ought to fortify the love of sufferings in a religious is that he has contracted a twofold obligation of imitating the life of Jesus Christ, first, by his baptismal vows, and secondly, by those of his religious profession. He should remember, too, that the predestination of the elect made by the Eternal Father before all ages, cannot be completed in Heaven, except in proportion as they are made conformable to His Divine Son on earth.

Now as a good religious finds it impossible to retrace exactly in his life the uncommon sufferings of his Redeemer, namely, His bloody scourging, painful crowning of thorns, dolorous crucifixion, together with the shame, ignominies and other horrors which accompanied His bitter passion, so is he persuaded that the least he can do is to condemn himself to every mortification of body and mind, to watchings, fastings, labors, and to everything else that the will of God and his holy rule allow him to practice, lest at any time it should happen that by diminishing the weight of the cross which he has undertaken to bear after his suffering Lord, he should lose its merit and crown.

If those who presume to come forward and stop penitents in their course—by prescribing such narrow limits to their austerities—did only reflect on the disorders that may result from such improper advice, they would be reserved in giving it. Did they reflect, I say, that they oppose the honor which is given to God by the penance of a sinner, when it is true and sincere; that they impede Jesus Christ in triumphing over the powers of hell, afflict the Holy Spirit, deprive the Church of the edification she would receive, and the sinner of the fruit and advantage he would derive from it. If it is written that the penance of a sinner fills the heavens with joy (Luke 15:7), can it be doubted that he who prevents it from being as extensive and entire as it ought to be, causes such sorrow and grief in the abode of joy and consolation as is compatible with its unchangeable eternal bliss.

If the greatness and number of sins and the secret dispositions of those who commit them were known; if we could penetrate the judgments of God, and the severity of His justice, then we might speak with more light concerning those who live in penance, and say that they keep within just limits or go beyond them. However, since those things are all concealed from us, and since God has reserved to Himself the knowledge thereof, a penitent will always have reason to fear, whatever may be said, or whatever he may do, that when his sins are put in the balance with the works he shall have done to expiate them, these words may still be applied to him: "Thou art weighed in the scales, and art found of little weight" (Dan 5:27).

Therefore, he ought not to give much attention to those who tell him he does too much, who censure his penance as an excess that deserves to be condemned; and especially in these times of dissolution, in which the use of penance is so rare, and so little known, even amongst those who seem to think of their salvation more seriously than others. For it may be said, with truth, that so much care has been taken to level the ways, to tear up the briars and thorns, that from whatever country people desire to return to Jesus Christ, they find nothing but pleasant fields and agreeable plains. They have not yet thought it proper to combat the necessity of bearing the cross—the words of Christ are too explicit—but at the same time they make no scruple to enervate its signification, to elude its obligation by the explication they give it.

Here, as in almost every state and profession, the secret has been discovered of making this duty agree with the enervated system of a soft, commodious and relaxed life. So we ought not be astonished if everything above the common practices and ordinary ways of men seem to be considered as a sort of enthusiasm and vicious singularity.

It is true that Jesus Christ offered Himself to His Father as a victim for the reconciliation of the world, but the favors He bestowed on it, in consequence of the prayers and death of that Divine Mediator, do not exempt men from the necessity of endeavoring to render themselves deserving of the application of His merits by their own personal sufferings. The sentence pronounced by God after the fall of our first parents has not been revoked. Jesus Christ has only changed the nature of the punishments then inflicted, and sanctified them by His own infinite merits.

Instead of being the stigmas of the malediction and proofs of the anger of God, they are now become, as it were, so many decrees by which men are enabled to raise themselves to the felicity which their divine Savior has merited for them by His bitter passion, and the effusion of His most precious blood.

Though Jesus Christ took on Himself the punishment of sin, yet He did it in such a manner as not to exempt men from suffering for it also. He drank the chalice to make us worthy to drink it after Him. He has decreed that it shall pass from His mouth to those of all sinners, according to the words of the prophet, "All sinners without exception shall drink of it" (Ps. 74:9). Let it be only remarked that He reserves the most severe part for those who are more particularly dear to Him, and consecrated in a special manner to His love.

Hence, we deceive ourselves, if we pretend to obtain the possession of eternal glory without partaking of His sufferings—we certainly deceive ourselves. Such a pretension would lead to unhinging that plan so holy, necessary and adorable, which He has been pleased to establish in the world by His own example. It would destroy the divine correspondence which should exist between the head and the members, instead of producing that similitude by which we may truly say with the apostle: "We bear the mortification of Jesus Christ in our bodies" (2 Cor 4:10); that is to say, instead of fastening our irregular desires and unruly passions—together with all the inclinations of corrupt nature—to the cross, with the nails of penance and mortification.

Behold, my brethren, your lot. Whatever men may say, this is your inheritance, your dignity, the distinctive mark by which God has been pleased to sign you, when He predestined you to His immortal glory, and called you to the society of His saints (Col 1:12).

These are the truths which we have learned from the adorable lips of Jesus Christ; truths which He has confirmed by His own example and signed with His precious blood, truths which have been preserved in the Church by the fidelity with which His servants have practiced them, and that have been transmitted down to us through the pure channel of tradition. If in succeeding ages the faithful will look back to our times, and from there to the origin and source, the monuments which preserve the lives and actions of the saints will clearly show that nothing has been more evidently conspicuous in all their conduct than the love of the cross, mortifications and sufferings.

Behold, my brethren, the true principle by which you ought to solve the difficulty you have proposed in your question. As to what regards yourselves in particular, if it should ever happen that anyone shall attempt to attack the moderate life you have embraced, and claim that it prescribes excesses and extravagances from which it is really exempt, you may without difficulty reply that you are not the shadows of so many saints and religious men who are gone before you, and who served our Lord Jesus Christ in hunger, thirst, in cold and nakedness, in labor and fatigue, who persevered with unshaken constancy in watchings, fastings, prayer, meditation, and in an almost infinite number of long and painful afflictions.

The edifying history of their lives must be either declared unlawful or its perusal forbidden, if they require that you should not endeavor to retrace, at least imperfectly, something of a likeness to it in yours. In effect, to what purpose do you read them? Is it merely to learn your own confusion? And never to have the consolation of imitating their holy examples?

Tell them that your founders were saints, that you are obliged at least to imitate them, and yet so far from practicing their heroic virtues, you are still very far from observing the holy instructions they have left you, though you endeavor to make them the invariable rules of your life. It is certainly true, that we endeavor to observe the same fasts as were observed in the times of Saint Benedict, but we are far from possessing the same fervor and charity. Saint Bernard, and all the primitive Cistercian fathers, observed the same, and never took any food during the time of the regular fast, that is, from the fourteenth of September until Easter, before the office of noon. They labored in the fields, cut the corn, and occupied themselves in painful agricultural employments, and yet they were exact in observing this rule. Their food was usually legumes, vegetables, and esculent roots, which were prepared with water and salt: one pound only of coarse bread was allowed each day, and if anyone had not sufficient for supper, a little more was given but made of unsifted flour. The sick arose every night at the same hour as the community, and remained barefoot on Good Friday, like the rest of the brethren, so that you may affirm, that they were in many things more austere than we are at present. Hence, so far from deserving to be accused of excess, we feel that we are much inferior to our fathers and founders in that respect.

If it should be objected that the brethren die very frequently, and therefore that some would infer the indiscretion of our austerities, you ought not to be uneasy on that head. Their objections shall not be able to produce any disturbance in your minds when you reflect that those whom the Divine Providence has called to a better life closed their career in a penitential state, and under a rule approved of by the Church. They found in the monastery that tranquility and holy consolation which they came to seek, and they expired in the embraces of their amiable and beloved companions.

To this you may still add, that those who shut themselves up in the cloister by the will and appointment of God are not induced to do so by the desire of a long life, but by the motive of preparing for a happy death; and that banishing from their hearts the love of all created things, they ought to be exclusively employed about those which are eternal.

This was the spirit which animated our holy father Saint Bernard, when he refused the monks of Saint Anastasius the use of medicines, as we have already observed, though the unwholesome air of the country in which they lived produced many infirmities in their community. He only allowed them some of the common plants and herbs which were used by the poor, telling them that he was persuaded that the spirit of God was the author of what he advised, and what induced him to decide on that subject, and that he was confident he spoke by His divine influence, when he informed them that those who follow the maxims of the flesh cannot please God, that spiritual things are to be purchased with spirituals; that they would do much better to desire such draughts as would assist them in acquiring humility, and say to the Lord with fervor, "Heal my soul, 0 Lord, for I have sinned against thee " (Ps 40:5). This, said he, is the health you ought to seek with all possible solicitude, but that which comes from men is vain (Ps 107:13).

How solidly that great saint was confirmed in this thought is evident from his writings, but it more clearly appears by what Saint Fastredus testifies, as we have seen above, who declares that he heard him say these words which cannot be too frequently repeated:

> It is not enough for a religious to allege his infirmities, for our fathers and holy predecessors made choice of low swampy valleys to build their monasteries in, that the religious being often sick, and having the image of death always before them, they might continually live in the fear of the Lord.

Therefore, my brethren, we may conclude that the objection of those who imagine that it is not lawful to embrace austerities which shorten life does not agree with the opinions of the saints. That the holy fathers indeed observed a just discretion in their penitential exercises is certain, but they were very far from confining them to the narrow limits of our modern dictators, for they esteemed their salvation as a thing much more precious than their lives, and they walked in the royal highway of the cross with a great good will and a dilated heart.

To conclude, if your life be neither liked nor approved by the greater part of men, let it suffice for your consolation that it bears every mark and character necessary to convince you of its being directed by the Holy Spirit. It is neither new nor singular, nor can it be condemned by any solid reasoning, since in your conduct you do no more than follow the maxims of those whom Jesus Christ has appointed to be your fathers and guides.

23 | ON MITIGATIONS—CONTENTS:

Q. 1.—As the religious life is a state of such extraordinary penance and eminent perfection, how can any religious remain with an assured conscience in a mitigated observance? 310

Q. 2.—Is not the superior of a monastery to be considered as a living rule, and therefore authorized to modify the rule as he thinks proper? 310

Q. 3.—Can the truths, of which you have just spoken, be opposed by any solid and convincing reasons? 318

Q. 4.—Can it be safe to follow the example and conform to the practice of so many religious, who live according to the maxims so contrary to the primitive rules? 324

Q. 5.—Is it possible to be saved in these mitigations? 325

Q. 6.—What are the mitigations you call lawful? 327

Q. 7.—What can be said of a certain manner which is found in some observances, that make profession of being reformed, and which may be considered as a spiritual mitigation. 330

23

ON MITIGATIONS

QUESTION 1.—*As the religious life is a state of such extraordinary penance and eminent perfection, how can any religious remain with an assured conscience in a mitigated observance?*

ANSWER—To give you a clear solution of this question, I will tell you, my brethren, that the mitigation of an order being a softening, a modification or an altering of the statutes, this mutation may be effected either in small matters or in important articles, for as to the essential constituent parts, they ought to be immutable.

Now, whatever alteration is made in any, even the smallest matters belonging to rules, it is never exempt from sin, if effected by those who are not invested with proper authority for that purpose. As Saint Bernard very well remarks, the least point of the rule when violated with advertence and determination becomes a sufficient cause of guilt. If those who have authority make any alterations without proper motives and solid reasons, they sin more grievously than others, because superiors are more strictly obliged to preserve and maintain the observance of rules than those who are placed under them.[316]

Nevertheless, in either case, a religious may live in security of conscience in a mitigated state, for the mutilated points not being of an essential consequence, he still finds therein the necessary means to attain the end of his vocation, which is his perfection and sanctification.

---

[316] *De Praecepto,* PL 182: 877, 878, 880, 884 / Bernard, *Treatises I,* 127, 128, 132, 137.

Q. 2.—Is not the superior of a monastery to be considered as a living rule, and therefore authorized to modify the rule as he thinks proper?

A.—I answer that he cannot modify the rule as he pleases, and to undertake it would be an abuse.[317] He is subject to the rule as well as his brethren, and even more than his brethren. Saint Benedict enjoins that his rule must be observed by all without distinction, and with an uniform exactitude.[318] Give ear to his words, which I here select as an example: "In all things everyone shall observe the rule as the mistress and guide, nor shall any presume to deviate from it in anything." The superior has no authority but to enforce the observance of the rule, and to preserve it entire; and he is bound to employ his words, his solicitude, but much more his example for that purpose. He is called a living rule only because the dead letter ought to appear more animated and conspicuous in his conduct than in that of his brethren.

Saint Benedict requires that the superior should instruct his community more by the example and sanctity of his life than by his words.[319]

Saint Basil teaches, that the superior should instruct his community more by the example and sanctity of his life than by his discourses.[320]

Again, Saint Basil teaches that his conversation ought to be so correct, his manners so grave and dignified, that they may serve both as a law and rule to all his community.[321]

The same holy bishop says that a superior ought to be raised above those who are under his direction by the prudence, gravity, exactitude and regularity of his life, so that the virtues which shine in his conduct may reflect on those who have chosen him for their model, and have proposed to walk in his footsteps. Therefore, it is only when a superior is endowed with those qualities that he ought to be considered as a living rule, and not when he is degraded by contrary dispositions; when he maintains his rule amongst his brethren, not when he destroys it; in brief, when his life

---

[317] *De Praecepto*, PL 182:865./ *Treatises I*, 11

[318] *RB* 3.

[319] *RB* 3.

[320] Tract. 2. *de Inst. Monast.* cap. 2.

[321] Serm. 2. *de Inst. Monac.*

is so regular and exemplary, that as Saint Benedict says, he performs in the monastery what Jesus Christ Himself would do were He visibly present.[322]

This clearly shows that the above maxim, by which so many religious communities are lulled into a false security, is ill understood, and that the sense attributed to it is nothing better than the effect of a deceitful imagination that serves to no better purpose than to authorize the improper use that some superiors make of their authority, and the licentiousness of those who are subject to them.

Now, as to mitigations in considerable points, and important practices: Let us suppose that they have been introduced by the libertinism or licentiousness of monks; or by the sloth, negligence, or false prudence of superiors; or by the authority of the Church. In the two first cases they are to be considered only as infractions of the rule, and transgressions of the law; and neither length of time, approbation of superiors, or the consent of individuals, can ever make them more lawful or less criminal. They are nothing better than means of corrupting the monastic state, as we have said above.

They conceal destruction under specious pretexts; they are shameful prevarications that no longer make the actors blush, because they are accustomed to them. But as truth always subsists in itself, adverse customs can ever destroy it. Crimes, then, however frequent and public do not annul the law, for nothing would be more extravagant than to pretend that it has lost its force because infractions are multiplied with impunity, so as to exculpate the guilty, because the number of accomplices are great.

The rule is now in itself what it was in the beginning; non-observance has not revoked it; oppositions do not deliver those who have professed it from the obligation which binds them to keep it; and therefore it must be granted, that these sorts of mitigations are abuses; that those who first introduced them became thereby guilty of error and sin, and that those who now follow them cannot continue these infractions with a safe conscience. They live in a continual prevarication. It is only by the effect of a groundless assurance and a deplorable infatuation they can persuade themselves that they are safe in the port at the very time they are involved in the wreck.

It is a constant truth, my brethren, that religious persons are obliged to observe their rules, unless they are annulled or changed by lawful

---

[322] RB 2.

authority. Nor can the statutes and practices of an order be transgressed, as we have already advanced, without a considerable sin and an offence which, according to Saint Bernard, deserves the epithet of a crime that produces death. [323]

That the matter may be more clearly understood, let us take Saint Benedict's rule for an example, which is at present the most extended, and by which the greater number of regular observances have been formed in the Church. There we find the abstinence from flesh quite abandoned, as well as the austerity of fastings, watchings, hard beds, manual labor, retirement, silence within and without the monastery, the estrangement from all secular communications and affairs, expressed by Saint Benedict in these words: "To become a stranger to the manners of the world"[324] by poverty, simplicity, humiliations, interior and exterior, mortification, submission to superiors, stability in the monastery, and many other such like practices.

Now, if all this mutation has been effected by the influence of degenerate superiors or the libertinism of monks, it is a manifest corruption, which by no means prevents the rule from still subsisting in itself. If it has been done by the ministry of regular monastic superiors, they had no authority for that end and therefore their conduct can only be considered as a presumptuous or an unjust enterprise. For although superiors can dispense in the observance of particular points, when they are induced thereto by just reasons and pious considerations, it ought only to be done in some cases, for some persons, and for a time, unless the same necessity that induced them to grant the dispensation should by its uninterrupted duration oblige them to continue it.

However, to change all the practices to which we have been just alluding would be overstepping their authority. It would be abolishing a regular observance, and depriving it of that which forms and preserves it. Nevertheless, it cannot be lawfully destroyed by any authority but by that which first established it. I mean that of the Pope, or the Church.

Yet, though all this might be within the sphere of monastic authority, still superiors cannot use their dispensing power unless they are induced to it by a real necessity, from motives of charity, and the good of the Church,

---

[323] *De praecepto,* PL 182:862.

[324] *RB* 4.20.

as Saint Bernard teaches. Does it not appear most just that whatever was established on this basis of charity should on the very same principle, when a lawful occasion requires it, be omitted or interrupted, or changed into something of equal or greater importance or advantage? Therefore, he who is invested with competent authority may dispense in such cases for the benefit of the Church, as necessity sanctions the alteration of the law.[325]

Now this is what cannot be found in the greater part of the mitigations of which we have some knowledge. For if charity were their moving principle, they would propose to themselves the glory of God, the sanctification of their members, the edification of the Church, and their own salvation. So far from being able to discover any of those pure motives, everything we behold seems qualified to persuade us that they had quite opposite views. For in all places where those mitigations have been introduced, the disorders which are committed in them furnish the enemies of God with arms to attack the glory of His holy name. They fill His Church with scandals and will one day rise up against, and condemn before His judgment seat both the religious who suffers himself to be led into such a disorderly way, and the superiors who guide them in such fatal paths.

Secondly, every religious who engages himself in the service of Jesus Christ, under the rule of Saint Benedict, promises the conversion of his manners by the words of his profession, and to labor to be perfect according to the rule.[326] That is to say, he promises to form his life, to regulate and conduct himself according to the maxims, instructions, and practices laid down by that rule, and to labor for his sanctification, which is the end of all religious institutes, and that by the means which his rule prescribes. This truth is so evident that nothing would be more unreasonable than to call it into question nor less necessary than to spend time in proving it. This being so, can there be a more positive violation, a more distinct transgression, than to forsake those very rules, abandon all those means and practices, by which he promised God to labor in the conversion of his life? Can such conduct, when fixed and determined, be considered less than a transgression against the monastic state, and that those who follow it are professed prevaricators?

Thirdly, every person who is consecrated to God by religious vows is

---

[325] *De praecepto.* PL 182:863 (1854). / *Treatises I*, 109.

[326] RB 58.

obliged to tend to that which is most holy in a Christian life, and, as we have already said, to aspire to all that the gospel of Christ contains and proposes as most pure, excellent and perfect. This is what we are taught, not only by the saints of the primitive ages, such as Saint Basil, Cassian, Saint Climacus, and those who lived a long time after them, such as Saints Bernard and Thomas, but also by those of our own times who have written on the duties of religious perfection with the most enlightened piety, as Saint Teresa, Rodriguez, Father Saint-Jure; nor is there one who does not agree that every religious who is not in this disposition is not in the way of salvation.

Now this perfection is an end to which we can only arrive by the ways and means prescribed by the saints. All those whom Providence raised up to form monastic orders and congregations in His Church were careful to make laws, and to lay down rules leading to that end. In the rule of Saint Benedict, which we have selected as an example, the means and exercises prescribed by that great saint to all those of whom he was to be the father, are those of which we have spoken above, and of which scarcely the least mark or remnant any longer remains in the relaxed monasteries and mitigated communities. It seems to me that there is nothing more contrary to reason and good sense than to imagine that persons propose to themselves an end, and labor to attain it, when they not only reject the ways and means laid down by those who have been appointed by God to be their guides, lights and directors in the affair, but also, when they adopt others which are quite opposite and adverse to this end.

If I saw a man walking towards the west, and were to ask whither he intended to go, what could I think if he answered that he proposed to make China or Japan the route of his journey? Nothing less than that he had either lost his reason, or was gone astray without knowing it, or that his words were not conformable to his thoughts.

It is to such persons that Saint Augustine addresses himself when he says, "You pretend to arrive in the harbor by the road you are in, but you deceive yourself, for you are going full sail against the rocks."[327]

What could be said of a man, who being appointed to guard an important place in the midst of an enemy's country, would pull down all its fortifications and defense? Nothing, without doubt, but that he wanted to facilitate its capture, and to reduce it to a state of non-resistance when it

---

[327] S. Augustinus, *In Psalmum* XXXI. PL 36:256 (1845).

would be attacked. Do we not, then, have reason to think that those who imagine they do enough by proposing and saying that they mean to keep poverty, chastity and obedience as things essential to the religious state while they destroy, without fear or shame, the regularities, practices, and observances established by the saints to preserve those essentials? Have we not reason, I say, to think that they have a mind to give up the place, and that in truth they neither care for poverty, chastity, or obedience?

This is what happens precisely in the present affair. Saint Benedict enjoins fastings, watchings, abstinence, corporal labor and mortification to curb the concupiscence of the flesh, to acquire and preserve that purity which is so rarely found, and which is so opposite to all the thoughts and inclinations of nature. Is it not, therefore, deceiving oneself and others to pretend to the attaining of what that great saint proposes by leading a relaxed, effeminate life, and spending one's days in good cheer, sloth, unprofitableness, and in seeking after the satisfactions and pleasures of sense?

In order that we may acquire and preserve the calm of the passions, tranquility of soul, application to God, purity of heart and mind—in a word, that perfect disengagement in which every religious is bound to live—Saint Benedict establishes solitude, separation from worldly people, alienation from secular concerns, perpetual silence amongst the brethren, and that entire and sincere forgetfulness of ourselves, which the saints so carefully practiced. However, on the contrary, those persons to whom I allude pretend to acquire all the virtues of the saints by communicating with persons of the world, receiving and paying visits, entertaining themselves indifferently with everything that passes in the world—the remembrance of which ought to be forever effaced from their minds—continually filling their hearts with things that ought to find no place in them, and taking as much liberty, having as many familiar and frequent communications with one another as if no rule or law obliged them to silence. In this manner they flatter themselves with the hope of obtaining from the divine goodness that sacred repose, that remembrance of the last things, continual meditation of eternal truths, and all those other interior dispositions which sanctify men in the cloister, and make them worthy of and acceptable to the God to whom they are inseparably consecrated.

The same holy legislator—in order to form the religious to evangelical poverty and perfect obedience—deprives them of all superfluous things, leaving them only the use of such as are absolutely necessary, and moreover, depending on the permission of the superior. To all of this he enjoins that spirit of simplicity, which may hold up continually before their eyes the obligation that binds them to imitate the poverty of Jesus Christ. He regulates all their steps, words, actions, and every moment of their lives so that not one remains at his own disposal.

Notwithstanding all this, they seem to imagine that there can be no difficulty in acquiring the virtues and merit of poverty and obedience, by living in search of the ease, goods, abundance, ornaments, luxury, and vanity of the world, in libertinism, exemption from all subjection and regularity, reducing religion to and making it consist in the name, habit, a little order, and a few exterior ceremonies.

In the fourth place, to understand the religious state in the proper sense, it is a covenant made between the creature and God. The creature offers to the Lord all its time, goods, liberty, life, person and being, reserving to itself only the hope of the goods promised by Jesus Christ to those who renounce and forsake all things to follow Him. The religious promises to serve God according to the precepts, instructions, and practices contained in the rule he professes; and God, in exchange, promises him to accept his services, to make him happy, and to be Himself his happiness, His glory and reward. This obligation is reciprocal, for God engages, on His part, but on condition that the creature will be faithful to his promises, and constant in the observance of his vows.

This is what Saint Benedict teaches when, in the enumeration he makes of the means by which religious persons are to labor for their sanctification, he declares that God has attached the recompense to their fidelity, and that they ought not to promise themselves the enjoyment of it until they shall have constantly fulfilled, day and night, all the duties and practices laid down in the rule.[328] He says in another place that a religious who is not faithful in the accomplishment of all he has promised, insults Almighty God, who, on His part, will not fail to condemn him for his infidelity.[329]

By this it is evident that the religious who have dispensed themselves in the observance of those practices enumerated above, as in fasting, watching, manual labor, mortification, poverty, simplicity, separation from the world and its affairs, and who live in a manner entirely opposite to those

---

[328] RB 4.75.

[329] RB 58.

holy practices, it is evident, I say, that such persons have no right to hope that God will crown them on the last day with those rewards which He has promised only to those who shall have lived in the practice of the virtues to which they were bound, so that not having fulfilled the conditions of their engagement, they cannot produce either title or right to recommend them on the day of just retribution.

This sufficiently proves, that the mitigations of which we treat are nothing less than a violation of the law of God, a contempt of His orders, a decided, fixed, and public resistance to His will; in short, a ministry of iniquity and consequently a state of death.

Q. 3.—Can the truths, of which you have just spoken, be opposed by any solid and convincing reasons?

A.—To evade them, three reasons are employed. In the first place, it is said that the duty and principal obligation of a religious is to obey; that mitigations having been established, both by the authority and dispensation of superiors, and are, of course, lawful; and therefore, inferiors can embrace them with security of conscience.

In the second place, it is said that ancient customs, which are authorized by a great number of persons and over a long period of time, prevail over the authority of the law, according to the rules of prescription.

Finally, it is alleged that no one is obliged to more than he has promised, and that as the modern practices were those only which were then observed, the duties are fully accomplished by keeping them.

However, all these reasons are futile. To begin with the first, it is true, and we must agree, that the principal obligation of a religious is to obey and to be subject; but he ought to do so only in the manner he vowed. Now, as a religious does not bind himself to every sort of obedience without limits, but only to that according to the rule he professes, so he ought not to comply with the injunctions of his superior when they are contrary to the rule and tend to destroy it; nor has the superior any right to require his obedience in such cases.

Saint Bernard has already told us that the superior is not to follow the impulses of his imagination, in commanding those who are under him; but that he ought to remember that the rules have prescribed limits and measures which are not lawful for him to transgress; and that it is not enough for him to enjoin nothing but what seems proper and just, but it must be the very exact line of rectitude laid down by the holy rule; or at

least, pertaining to its spirit, and conformable to what has been instituted by Saint Benedict.

The same saint adds that the religious promises an obedience only according to the rule of Saint Benedict; and therefore, that he is not subject to every will of the superior, but only to such as is conformable to that rule; consequently, he is not obliged to obey him when he commands him to do something evidently contrary to it.[330] And it is certain that Saint Benedict never intended that a superior should dispose of the rule as he pleased, since he gives him power and authority only to make it observed.

Secondly, Saint Basil gave more extent to religious obedience than any other person, for he says that monks ought to imitate the obedience of Jesus Christ, and become obedient even to death. Nevertheless, he requires that in some circumstances, when the orders of the superior are manifestly evil, his subjects should examine them by the words of our Lord and compare them with the instructions and examples of the saints, and then decide, for they are not obliged to obey when his commands are evidently contrary to both these rules.[331]

Thirdly, Saint Paul says that the obedience of inferiors ought to be reasonable (Rom 12:1). Yet nothing can be less so than to obey men when we cannot do it without violating the law of God, and overturning the statutes of the saints, contrary to the engagements and solemn protestation we have made to observe them inviolably.

Superiors are to be respected and obeyed as Jesus Christ Himself, whose ministers and vicars they are, even though we should discover impropriety and disorder in their lives and conduct. But if it should happen that instead of assisting you in the exact observance of what you have promised and of raising you as they are bound to the perfection of a holy life, they lead you to the violation of your vows and the infraction of your rules; if they plunge you into the mire of a soft, licentious, relaxed *conversatio*,[332] unworthy the purity of your state, you should then consider them as those mercenary pastors of whom the prophet Jeremiah speaks, who destroyed the Lord's vineyard, trampled His inheritance under foot, and changed the delicious land He had reserved to Himself into a dry and barren desert (Jer 12:10).

---

[330] *De praecepto,* PL 182:866 (1854). / *Treatises I,* 112.

[331] S. Basilius, *Brevius,* PG 31:1162 (1857).

[332] In monastic parlance, an habitual way of living the monastic life

Then doubt not that you are in a situation in which you ought to say with the holy apostle: "It behooves us to obey God, rather than man" (Acts 5:29).

As to the second reason, which is deduced from prevailing customs, there is no more safety in adhering to it than to the former. A holy law cannot be annulled by an unholy custom. It subsists notwithstanding the abuses which militate against it. Moreover, if the strength it maintains does not effect the sanctification of men, it will undoubtedly procure their condemnation. If the law is of no great consequence, and no inconvenience can happen by its inobservance, the custom which has taken place may be followed. If it is important, but only annulled by another laudable custom that produces a good equivalent to that which the observance of the law itself would produce, the custom may still be adopted with safety.

However, if from the extinction of the law there accrue evils, public disorders, or serious disadvantages, in this case it is certain that custom can be considered only as an abuse and a corruption. Though it may be authorized by time, by the number and quality of the persons who have adopted and supported it, nothing can be deduced from that against the law. Otherwise, it would follow that evils themselves would become lawful when they could be found in the common practice of men. For the greater part of evils are only so because the law prohibits them, so that the law itself would be destroyed by every sort of custom, which would be, perhaps, of all confusions the greatest and most enormous.

The saints and all who have been guided by their spirit, adopted maxims entirely opposite to such false principles. Truth alone was their rule, and they followed in their conduct its dictates with an inviolable fidelity.

This was Saint Cyprian's opinion when he said: "Established customs ought never to take place of truth, nor hinder it to prevail. Custom without truth is no better than an inveterate error. Therefore," says he, "let us forsake error and follow truth, knowing that truth is most powerful, and always victorious, and that it will preserve its vigor and strength for all eternity."[333] And in another place: "If we are to hear Jesus Christ alone, we ought not to be much concerned about what some of those who have preceded us

---

[333] S. Cyprianus. *Contra Epistolam Stefani*....PL 3:1134 (1844)

thought best to be done; but we ought to consult Him who is before all men, and not them; for we are to follow the truth of God, preferably to the customs of men."[334] And although that great saint employed this maxim on an occasion, and in a cause that was not according to truth, yet it is not less holy nor less constant.

One of the greatest men of the same age, Tertullian, taught before him that nothing could ever prescribe against truth, neither the succession of ages, nor the authority of persons, nor the privilege of nations; and that almost every custom springs either from ignorance or foolish simplicity, and being strengthened by length of time, finds persons who support it against truth. [335]

Saint Basil was animated with the same sentiments. He tells us that we are frequently deceived by evil customs, that erroneous and corrupt traditions cause much evil, and generally spring from our sins and spiritual blindness.

Jesus Christ Himself teaches us the same thing, when He reproaches the Jews in His gospel for making no difficulty in forsaking the commandments of God that they might follow their traditions and customs (Mark 7:8). That which appears most strange is that there are Christians found who attack a truth so evident, and in an affair so important as is that of eternal salvation. For even pagans who propose to themselves nothing but temporal advantage and earthly emolument, acknowledge and complain that all our evils spring from men who suffer themselves to be guided by example and custom, and not by reason; that although we are not much induced to follow the example of the lesser, yet we think it not proper to make the least difficulty in going along with the crowd, as if the multitude who practice a thing could give it a rectitude which it has not. Thus where an error becomes public amongst us, it is considered as a real verity.[336]

The third reason employed in defense of mitigations, deserves no more attention than the two preceding. For how can any person consider himself at liberty to form the obligation of, and bind himself by a holy engagement to lead a life which, as we have repeated so frequently, is nothing less than a

---

[334] S. Cyprianus. *Ad Caecilium De sacramento Dominici Calicis*. PL 4 :385 (1844).

[335] Tertullianus. *De velandis virginibus*, PL 2:937 (1844).

[336] Seneca, Epistula CXXIII, *Epistulae, Pars Prima Sive Opera Philosophica*, Vol. 4 (Paris: Dondey-Dupre, 1829), 350.

violation of the law of God, a transgression of His orders, and an open and an avowed contempt of the statutes of the saints? Can a prevarication so manifest be considered as a religious consecration, or can we imagine that God can accept an offering so impure as a sweet scented sacrifice, or rather the persons themselves who are in a state so contrary to His designs, and so far from being qualified with the dispositions He requires in all those who are consecrated to His service?

Have they not reason to fear that He addresses Himself to them, in the words of the prophet, when He says:

> Your sacrifices are like murder, your criminal dispositions make them like so many acts of irreligion, rather than demonstrations of that sincere worship with which you pretend to honor me. He that sacrifices an ox, as if he slew a man; he that kills a sheep in sacrifice, as if he should brain a dog; he that offers an oblation, as if he should offer swine's blood; he that burns incense, as if he should bless an idol: all these things have they chosen in their ways, and their soul is delighted in their abominations (Is 66:3).

This is what made a celebrated doctor of the last century say that the religious who make profession in relaxed observances, and who propose to themselves no more than to live conformably to what they find established and practiced by others—that is to say, to violate the rule as they see it violated—and illude the Almighty even by the vows by which they give themselves to Him, are yet, notwithstanding, not less bound to observe the rule exactly, than if they had contracted the obligation in a regular and holy community.

A man must have closed his eyes to all light, if he cannot see that it is impossible to serve or please God in a profession which is nothing better than the corruption of a holy state. Nor if he cannot perceive that when anyone is so unfortunate as to find himself in a condition so deplorable, there is only one thing to be done, which is to employ every effort in endeavoring to rectify what has been improperly done, to place himself in the way appointed by God, to enter into the true spirit of this rule, to adopt its maxims and practices. Unless, that is, he intends to imitate the foolish man, of whom the scripture speaks, who lived content in his indigence, poverty and extreme misery, while the Lord pronounced the following terrible sentence against him: "Because thou sayest I am rich, I live in abundance and want nothing; and thou knowest not that thou art miserable, and wretched, and poor, and blind, and naked" (Apoc. 3:17).

Therefore, those who are in this unhappy state may say what they please, they may deceive themselves and lull their conscience into a false repose, but they can never give it a moral assurance. If they desire to enter the paths of true peace, they must renounce their mitigations, and commence the affair, by acknowledging that they are unlawful, that they dishonor both the majesty of God, and the dignity of their holy state.

It is to no purpose to say that the rules have their latitude, that it is not necessary to observe them in every point, and that nothing more can be required of people but what they have promised to perform. It is true that Saint Bernard allows, and every person agrees with him, that rules do not oblige to a positively literal observance, or that no article can be omitted without doing an injury to conscience. On the contrary, every institute, except the Cistercian order, may change or retrench something from its rules, according to the different observances. Yet that holy doctor says and insists that holy practices and customs are to be adopted and that temperance, justice and piety are to be observed.[337]

Now you may judge, my brethren, how very little those holy and rational dispositions agree with the mitigations of which we are speaking; and how very far Saint Bernard was from approving a manner of life so entirely filled with the spirit of the world, with licentiousness, liberty, sloth, irregularity, pleasures, vanities and independence. Here I stop my pen that I may not proceed to an enumeration of greater excesses. This suffices for your instruction, for the disorders which at present everywhere reign in the cloister are already but too well known.

I have frequently told you, my brethren, and I now repeat it again—as some of the most important advice I can give you—never give ear to those who do not speak the language of the saints, whatever may be their number, rank and authority. Through the organ and channel of the saints, God has made known His will. He has shown you the way by which you are to walk to eternal life by His servants, your founders and fathers, who were men replenished with His spirit, and according to His heart. You ought consequently to consider the instructions they have left you as the language of God Himself, for "What matters it," says Saint Bernard,

---

[337] *De Praecepto,* PL 182:887 (1854). / *Treatises I,* 141.

"whether the Lord speaks immediately Himself, or does it by the ministry of men or angels."[338]

Therefore, remember my brethren, to avoid those who address you in the language of deceit and seduction, however they may conceal their poison under the specious appearance of piety. "Place no confidence in lying words," says the prophet, "saying, The temple of the Lord, the temple of the Lord, the temple of the Lord"(Jer 7:4). If ever you shall find yourselves in such a case, forget not to employ the means the same prophet enjoins, who complained that those who were appointed to be the lights and guides of the people were filled with deceit and diffused error. He says, "Take heed, examine the paths, and enquire which is the ancient and good way, and walk in it, and you shall find refreshment for your souls" (Jer 6:16). That conduct is full of presumption, says Saint Basil, which forsakes the good paths of the holy fathers, and prefers the dictates of our own imaginations to their sentiments.

Q. 4.— Can it be safe to follow the example and conform to the practice of so many religious, who live according to maxims so contrary to the primitive rules ?

A.—It was prohibited in the Old Testament by Almighty God, my brethren, to follow the multitude in the ways of error (Exod 23:2), and in the New He declares by the mouth of His adorable Son that the way that leads to life is narrow, and found only by a few; but that the way leading to death is large and agreeable, and is chosen by the greater number (Matt 7:13).

Saint Basil, guided by this great truth, exhorts all monks to imitate the example of those whose lives are holy and exact, to imprint their actions deep in their heart, and beseech our Lord to grant them the grace to be of the small number. For, says he, All that is excellent is rare; and hence it is that so few will enter the kingdom of Jesus Christ.[339]

The holy abbot Paphnutius teaches the same thing in Cassian's conferences, where he says, speaking to solitaries:

> I fear much, my children, that there may be found at present as great a multitude of Christians as there was formerly of Jews who violated the law of

---

[338] *De praecepto.* PL 182:873 (1854). / *Treatises I*, 121.

[339] S. Basilius, *Exhortatione de Renunciatione.* PG 31:646c (1857).

God in the time of Moses; for of the six hundred thousand armed men who went out of Egypt, only two had the happiness to enter into the promised land. We must therefore quickly form ourselves according to the example of the small number who are walking in the narrow path; for that figure of the Old Testament is moreover confirmed by this oracle of the New, Many are called, but few are chosen (Matt 20:16).[340]

We learn something like this in the *Imitation of Christ*, when having considered the unlimited detachment and the eminent perfection of the primitive solitaries, we read that they were given as models to all monks, and that their example ought to excite and animate us more effectually in the pursuit of virtue than that of the great number of relaxed mitigated religious in leading us to adopt their dangerous systems.[341]

Hence, my brethren, we must be induced to follow those who walk in the ways of truth, however small their number may be, and to avoid the society of those who are in the paths of error, though they were as numerous as the sand on the seashore. The great depravity of the wicked receives a false authority from the great multitude who enroll themselves under the banners of sensuality. Thus it imposes on the ignorant and weak, who become its dupes, but it justifies neither the one or the other. The nature of error is not changed by its becoming universal. Those who indulge themselves in vices and excesses, which are common to them and the greater number of men, shall receive with them chastisements and pains, which shall be their common recompense.

Q. 5.—*Is it then possible to be saved in these mitigations?*

A.—The elect of God are disseminated through the whole world. There is no place or state in which He does not find some who belong to Him, and who are objects of His tender mercies. Thus, in the most relaxed and irregular congregations there are always some chosen souls, who, assisted by the light they have received from Heaven, and knowing the truth, withdraw themselves from the common disorders. By their efforts, prayers and continual aspirations; by the care and exactitude with which they regulate their lives, they find within their state sufficient means of salvation. They perform before God in the silence of their hearts what the

---

[340] *Collationes*, PL 49:568c-569a (1846) / *Conferences* 1.3.7 (NPNF2/11:323).

[341] Thomas a Kempis, *The Imitation of Christ*, Book I, Chapt 18.

disordered state of their monasteries and the violence of the persons to whom they are subject would not allow them to practice more publicly. They are like those olives of which the scripture speaks, which remains on the trees after the crop is gathered, or as those bunches of grapes that escapes the eye and hand of the vintager, or like Lot who preserved the fear of God in the midst of Sodom, or like Noah, who kept his innocence amidst the general corruption of the world.

Q. 6.— *What are the mitigations you call lawful?*

A.—The mitigations which we believe lawful are those which are established by the authority of the Sovereign Pastor and by the constitutions of the Church. Every one will indisputably allow that these are lawful, that they are to be considered in a manner entirely different from those relaxations of which we have been speaking, and that they can be embraced with a safe conscience. This is provided that they are adopted precisely as they have been approved of by the Church, without adding anything to the modifications it has pleased her to prescribe, or changing the rectitude of an alleviation that she has made lawful by adopting another which is unlawful. For otherwise the case would be just the same with regard to the lawful mitigations as the unlawful ones, in respect to the essence of the rule.

Now, in this three things are to be considered. The first is that the Church never mitigated rules except when she was compelled to it by the greatness or long continuance of relaxations, the magnitude of the evil being such as made it impossible to replace things on the basis of the primitive rules and constitutions. The Church in these unhappy circumstances, like a tender mother touched with the misfortune of her children, afflicted at their fall, stoops to raise them up, to support them in their weakness, and to prevent them from falling still lower. Moved with compassion for their weakness, she chooses rather to discharge them from the more difficult observances, the more austere practices, and the more laborious exercises, and to place them in an easier and less austere way, that they might be able to advance, however slowly, rather than to leave them in a public scandalous contravention, with so many obligations with which they were no longer acquainted, and for the fulfilling of which they entertained not a thought.

Secondly, every time the Church has been obliged to authorize those mitigations, she has done it with tears or evident demonstrations of sorrow, beholding the beauty of those great orders tarnished. These were formed by the hand of God as the master-pieces of His power and grace, orders which the saints consecrated with tears, labors and penance. They were the glory, ornament and strong support of the Christian world while they preserved their primitive sanctity. On all occasions she evinced the greatest desire to behold them renewed in their original perfection, exhorting the faithful to embrace their rules in their purity, and enjoining as she lately did in the Council of Trent: *"That all religious orders should be reformed according to the spirit of the saints and their first institutions."*

Therefore, it would be deceiving ourselves to conclude that these mitigations are the effect of her particular desires, for they have been extorted from her by compassion for imperfect persons. She granted them only to preserve these religious from sinking under their pressing wants and necessities. It might be said to those who instead of humbling themselves for being in a state which is nothing less than a condescendence, and ought consequently to be a constant admonition of their weakness, that they are endeavoring on the contrary to draw consequences injurious to the true spirit of the rule, the regularity and discipline of which they cannot endure. These words may be addressed to all such persons: *"Look to the rock from whence you have been hewn"* (Isa 51:1). Consider how much you have degenerated from the dignity of your birth, or those which our Lord formerly spoke to the pharisees. The hardness of your hearts alone prevailed in obtaining such permissions, for things were not so from the beginning (Matt. 19:8).

Thirdly, we must consider that when the Church authorized mitigations, she did no more than temper the austerity of the rules. She dispensed in the observance of some practices, some external exercises, in order to proportion the state to the infirmities of the members who could not be raised to a more perfect conversion. However, she never touched that which is essential to the monastic state. She never discharged the religious from the obligation imposed on them by Jesus Christ, of tending uninterruptedly to evangelical purity and to the perfection of a Christian life.

She is too zealous for His glory to be even inclined to diminish anything of the interior worship of the heart, which mankind are bound to give Him. This is a duty which Saint Bernard calls immutable, which can never admit of any change or modification on the part of men; so much so, that it can be truly said that a religious in the mitigated, as well as in the strict observance of the rule, are indispensably obliged to labor in the attainment of eminent virtue; that ordinary piety is not sufficient for them, but that they ought to serve our Lord in an exact accomplishment of all his counsels.[342]

Now as this obligation always subsists, it must be granted that mitigation destroy a great part of the means by which it may be accomplished. For we learn by reason and experience, as well as by the doctrine of the saints, that fasting, abstinence, watching, manual labor, silence, and other ascetic observances are those powerful and effectual auxiliaries that our holy fathers have left us to attain that end. Consequently, mitigations though holy and charitable in the intentions of the Church, are nevertheless states of relaxation, and frequently prove insufficient for the attainment of that religious perfection to which we are bound to aspire. They place to our account equitable and obligatory debts, and diminish the resources given us by the rule for liquidating them.

And now, my brethren, if you desire to form a true and just notion of a religious living in a mitigated order, take the following comparison, a figure of yourselves. Here is a man to whom a hard and painful task is enjoined, and who at the same time receives a prescription which points out the proper means for accomplishing it, such as watching, laboring in the heat of the sun, the use of several instruments heavy and difficult in their application, but proved above all others to be the most certain for advancing his work.

In the course of some time considering his weakness–rather of his will than that of his body–this man obtains permission of his master to use lighter instruments, to work at more commodious hours and times, but still without diminishing anything of the task which is to be completed at the appointed time. Now as the obligation of the work is always the same, so is that of the religious always immutable. As the same work is required of both, though one imagines that he is eased as to the manner of operating, so is the same perfection required of the other, though to make some allowance for his infirmity more apparently easy means are tolerated in his regard.

From all I have said, my brethren, you may infer that mitigations are full of inconveniences and dangers; that the Church only consented to their introduction when compelled to by necessity, and when she could find no other remedies to heal the evils, stem the disorders, and provide for the salvation of her infirm children.

---

[342] *De praecepto*, PL 182:865 (1854). / *Treatises I*, 110.

If after this you are anxious to know what a religious, in a mitigated observance should do to secure his salvation, I will tell you. He must enter into the intentions of the Church. Let him keep his heart properly disposed to receive all the graces which God annexes to everything that she approves. Let him embrace and remain inviolably attached to all she has enjoined, when she authorized the mitigated form. Let his exactitude be so punctual in all these points, that he may never omit anything prescribed, or diminish the least tittle of the yoke he has taken up. Let the sense of his weakness humble him continually. Let him be confounded and sigh at beholding himself so remote from the perfection, austerity and mortification practiced by the holy fathers. Let the remembrance of these relaxations make him enter into himself, and excite him to labor constantly in the dispositions of his heart by way of reparation for the backwardness that is found in the exterior state of his life. Let him exert himself by a continual application of his heart to preserve the spirit of his rule, as he has now almost lost it as to the letter.

Finally, let him endeavor to make himself worthy by a sincere conversion, by all the practices of piety, self-abnegation, humiliation, prayer, and obedience from which the Church has not dispensed him, nor will ever dispense any religious person. Let him, I say, employ all these means to obtain of God that interior disengagement, that purity of heart, that evangelical perfection which Jesus Christ will ever require—to the end of the world—of all those who have received of Him the grace of being consecrated to His service by the vows of religion.

Behold, my brethren, what I have been able to sum up in a few words concerning a subject that appears to me of an almost infinite extent. I feel impeded in saying any more concerning it, from my own very limited capacity, as well as my want of time.

Q. 7.— What can be said of a certain manner which is found in some observances that make profession of being reformed, and which may be considered as a spiritual mitigation?

A.—That kind of mitigation, my brethren, of which I have sometimes spoken to you, is not much less dangerous than those that are more gross and scandalous. The wounds they inflict are not less profound, though they are less sensible. It is a concealed evil, a malady of the soul quite interior. He who is a prey to it carries it with him, without perceiving it. Moreover, that which makes it incurable is that the world does not know it, and on that account it frequently extols those over whom it ought to lament.

This evil lies concealed in certain communities, which, having been reformed, and having re-established the observance of fastings, watchings, and other exterior regular exercises, but omit to purify the interior, neglect piety and the reformation of the heart. They forsake the simplicity of the saints, content themselves with the giving a certain edification to the public, and with exhibiting a distinction between their life and that of those religious who live in disorder and licentiousness.

Nevertheless, it should be remembered that religion is a state whose essence is contained in interior piety and unfeigned sanctity. Therefore, unless the whole system of its exercises be animated with the true spirit—which is that of the saints—so far from being what it ought to be, it is nothing less than an illusion, a mask, a human policy. The religious who are thus reformed have no more advantage over those who are not than the pharisee of the gospel–who boasted that he faithfully kept the law—had over the publican, who before his conversion made public profession of not knowing it all.

Saint Augustine gives a description of this sort of monk, when speaking in the person of Christians who are so only in name and profession, but not in truth. He says:

> "I rise early each day, I go to church, where I sing a morning hymn, and another in the afternoon, and I say three or four more in my house; I do not fail to offer up to God a sacrifice of praise; I even say or hear mass every day." You do well, but see whether all that is sufficient to place you in security; and whether God is not dishonored by your works, while you pretend to honor him with your praises: in a word, take heed lest you sing better than you live. [343]

This interior spirit with which those religious are not animated, the privation of which renders their life so fruitless and miserable, is that of Jesus Christ Himself. By the impression of His grace, He gives to all those in whom it is diffused, such qualities, maxims and holy dispositions, as are sufficient to sanctify them in the different states to which He calls them. Those which He communicates to all monks, and which are essential to their state, are the love of retirement and interior recollection, the love of humiliations, of mortifications, of penance, of compunction, of the

---

[343] S. Augustinus, *Enarratio in Psalmos,* In Psalmum XLIX. PL 36:580 (1841).

remembrance of God's judgments, of the meditation of death; in fine, the love of that poverty of spirit, and holy simplicity, of which our Divine Master gives us so many lessons in the gospel.

Although these sentiments are, as it were, so many indispensable duties for us, and although they always flourish when the religious state is observed in its purity, yet we pretend to be more wise and enlightened than the saints. We imagine that the rules have a latitude with which they were unacquainted. We consider their exterior practices as excessive, and believe it necessary to moderate such severity and rigor.

It has been asserted that the retirement and sacred repose in which monks found all their consolation and delight plunged souls into stupor and discouragement; that silence destroyed the vigor of the mind, and deprived the brethren of the innocent means they might have of giving each other demonstrations of mutual charity; that the remembrance of the divine judgments and the frequent meditation on death produced the phantoms and anxiety of a melancholy gloom; that humiliations disheartened well disposed souls; that such things were proper only for novices, but not for persons advanced in virtue.

The entire separation from the world was considered as an effect of gross rusticity of which men were no longer capable. Evangelical poverty and simplicity—which at all times were the ingredients of true sanctity and shone most bright in the character of the saints—were esteemed no better than folly and stupidity which dishonored the monastic state, and made the religious contemptible.

All these considerations were pretexts why monks thought it proper to forsake the ways of the saints, and to find out new ways according to their own taste. Solitude was made less exact, and consequently their life became less interior. There was more frequent commerce with men, and less with God. On pretext of recreation and necessary unbending the mind, permission was given to the brethren to converse together, to dispute on questions of doctrine, to speak of worldly affairs, to relate histories, pleasant anecdotes, and worldly news, and to indulge even in railleries, though nothing is more strictly forbidden by monastic rules, since they prohibit all unreserved conversation or words which might draw the religious from that recollection and interior disposition in which the rule requires they should pass their whole lives; and since it restricts the religious of consummate virtue in speaking even of such things as might edify and animate them to virtue and sanctity.[344]

They are allowed to make and receive visits, to engage in curious studies and researches. The more ancient members exempt themselves from humiliating practices and employments. Superiors who are bound to give good example, and to instruct as much by action as by word, make no difficulty to leave their monasteries, and to appear indifferently in all ranks of society, on pretext of attending to their temporal affairs. To preserve the least temporal interest of their houses, they undertake lawsuits and appear before every sort of tribunal. They pass their time in cities, and entangle themselves in worldly difficulties, the sequel of which frequently scandalizes the public, dishonors their state, disturbs the peace of their houses, and causes losses, which are not to be repaid.

In sum, from all those specious maxims they have composed a new code of rules, and organized a new body of religious who—having only a few traces or features of that which was formed by the saints—will never have before God the same merit, nor obtain the same recompense, whatever idea men may entertain concerning it. They are fallen into the unhappy state of which the prophet speaks, when he says: "They have forsaken me, the source of living waters, and have dug for themselves broken cisterns, that can hold no water" (Jer 2:13).

The greater part of men are often deceived in their judgments as to certain sins, because they attend only to the grosser sort of crimes. They have eyes only to behold great disorders, and they make no account of such as are exempt from scandalous deformities, though they offend the majesty of God, and are incompatible with the purity He requires in persons who are consecrated to Him. They regulate their duties and actions according to the existing customs and common practices, as we have already said. Or they decide in their own favor by comparing their observances with the excesses of those which are unlimitedly relaxed. Yet if they would consult the oracles of truth and examine things by the proper rules, they would have very different sentiments—they would undoubtedly condemn, as insupportable abuses what they usually tolerate as lawful or indifferent practices.

The saints, who had the Spirit of God and considered things with a view all pure and holy, were far from approving or authorizing dispositions

---

[344] *RB* 6.

and actions so adverse to the sanctity which ought to reign in the cloister. They required that monks should live in the practice of a pure and animated piety. Moreover, they considered as enormous crimes the designs of those who sought to introduce relaxation into those places of benediction, or to disturb the good order of those sacred dwellings, which God from all eternity has reserved to Himself, and in which He seeks to be adored in the spirit of eminent piety and perfection.

Saint Bernard, whose authority alone ought to weigh more with us than that of a thousand others, when speaking to his brethren, and complaining of some who conducted themselves improperly and exposed their salvation to imminent danger, has no difficulty in telling them that whoever shall presume to introduce vice into the house of God, and make His temple the retreat of devils, ought to consider himself as a traitor. [345]

Perhaps you imagine that he employs such a harsh term to denote only conspiracies, revolts, open rebellions, impurities, apostasies, and such like disorders; but so far from that, this saint so just and mild in sentiment, applies this expression to such disorders only as have at present become so common amongst monks that some commit them without remorse, and others behold them without being moved. Therefore, those religious whom he qualifies with the epithet of traitors are such as enervate discipline, diminish fervor, and disturb the peace and charity which ought to reign inviolably amongst the brethren.[346]

That man of God says that such religious have made a compact with death. They contradict the sanctity of their profession before the face of Heaven. They demonstrate by their actions that they indulge their former sensuality, and still remain faithfully attached to the dissoluteness and vanity of the world. He exclaims: "Undoubtedly you will deliver up an important fortress into the hands of the enemies of Jesus Christ, if you succeed in betraying Clairvaux to them." [347]

This infidelity seemed to him of a nature so horrible and atrocious, that he can scarcely find a punishment sufficiently great to avenge it. To what kind of torments can he be condemned, who shall be guilty of such a perfidy?

---

[345] *In Dedicatio Ecclesiae*, Sermo III, PL 183:525a (1854).

[346] *Dedicatio*, PL 183:525b (1854).

[347] *Dedicatio*, PL 183:525b (1854).

"A common death is too little; extraordinary pains and particular torments must be employed for that end."[348]

That no doubt might obscure his real sentiments he continues: *"What matter is it whether you forsake the place like an infamous deserter, if being obliged to guard and answer for it, you remain there in idleness, sloth, and negligence."*[349]

Surely everyone who has a true idea of the religious state, will think exactly in the same manner as did Saint Bernard. Entering into the designs of God, they will consider a religious community as an assembly of persons enrolled in a holy militia, and engaged in the service of Jesus Christ, in order to wage spiritual war for the glory of His holy name. These—being surrounded with enemies— are obliged to carry their arms continually, and to stand day and night with sword in hand, that they may not be surprised, knowing that since there can be neither truce nor peace found between them and their unrelenting foes, everything is to be feared; and that there is no aperture or breach, however small, through which they may not be suddenly attacked (Luke 18:8).

It seemed to me, my brethren, a duty to give you this last elucidation, so that as God has preserved you by His grace from those scandalous disorders, you may not be so inconsiderate or unfaithful as to fall into such an unhappy state, which, though spiritual, is not less to be feared. Also so that if you should ever feel tempted to adopt sentiments contrary to those you have embraced, or if any person should presume to propose them, you may remember that you are obliged to nothing less than to live as the saints lived. For it serves to little purpose to wear their habit and to have some of their exterior practices, if you have not their spirit and piety, because they were the faithful interpreters of the will of God, the sacred depositories of His divine ordinances, and consequently, it is by their instructions and examples we are to learn both.

Indeed, the necessity of regulating our lives and conduct by those of the saints was never more apparent than it is at present. For truth was never less found, either in the words or actions of men, than in these our unhappy times. Even those who ought to be the guides of others, and whose virtue is considered as the most enlightened, are so bewildered from what they

---

[348] *Dedicatio*, PL 183:525c (1854)

[349] *Dedicatio.* PL 183:454 (1854).

have continually before their eyes, that they cannot imagine how that can be reprehensible which is authorized by almost universal practice.

Therefore, we may say, according to the scripture expression, that their whole care consists in placing cushions under the elbows of sinners, instead of covering their heads with sack-cloth and ashes. But all this ought not to shake either your faith or piety, for you know, my brethren, that such things have been long foretold. Our Divine Savior Himself tells us in His gospel that there shall be days of sorrow and desolation, and that when He shall come on earth the second time, He shall scarcely find any faith among men.

Saint Nilus the great anchorite, inspired by God, opened a book in the presence of an Archbishop, and a great number of persons who came to visit him in his desert, and read a passage in which the following words were found:

> We have arrived to a time wherein of ten thousand persons scarcely one is saved, and some having cried out that it was a mistake, the saint replied, it is a truth which I can prove, both from the testimony of the sacred writings and that of the holy fathers.

Hence, my brethren, separate yourselves in everything relative to your state from those opinions which are called common, and from those maxims which appear under the title of popular. Let your thoughts and actions be conformable to the small number. Let us have courage and fervor to follow the example of the few who practice pure and solid virtue, for they are the number of the elect of Jesus Christ.

Imitate the actions of the saints, and imprint them deeply in your hearts. Do not imagine, as St. Basil says, that all those who find the way into the cloister will—merely on that account—obtain admission into the abodes of bliss. There are many who embrace this holy life, but very few who bear its yoke. For the kingdom of Heaven, according to the words of the scripture, suffers violence, and the violent only bear it away.

Therefore, bow down your heads, and take upon you the yoke of the Lord. Bind yourselves with those happy bonds, place this burden on your shoulders. Make it become light by the constant exercise of every virtue, by fasting, watching, obedience, holy retirement, singing the divine praises of your heavenly spouse; by prayer, tears, manual labor, patiently sufferin every tribulation, whether coming from the malice of the devil, or from that of men.

Never suffer the vanity of your thoughts, or the pride of your hearts, to induce you to relax any of your accustomed labors and austerities, lest arriving at the end of your course, destitute of virtue and works, Jesus Christ should close the entrance of His kingdom against you. Frequently say to God, for your comfort, what the prophet formerly said to Him: "Save me, O Lord, for there is now no saint; truths are decayed from among the children of men; they have spoken vain things every one to his neighbor; with deceitful lips, and with a double heart have they spoken." (Ps 11:2). Their words are fit only to seduce those who hear them.

Finally, my brethren, praise the Lord, because He has opened your hearts to His sacred truths, and bless Him, for He has at the same time given you the desire to practice them. Beseech Him, by continual prayers, to give you the grace never to be allured by opposite maxims (Tobit 12:6). Let your fidelity be your thanksgiving, and let your gratitude be demonstrated by your actions. Let your lives be as pure as your state obliges, that the influence of the Divine Mercy may shine even to remote parts, so that you may become the edification of men, the joy of angels, the confusion of devils, and in fine, that you may be eternally a subject of glory and triumph to our Lord and Savior Jesus Christ.

FINIS.

INDEX OF IMAGES

Page VI. The Flight into Egypt; the Holy Family walking with the young John the Baptist. Engraved by Claude Augustin Duflos le Jeun

Page XXIII. Holy Family with the Virgin reading, Giulio Carpioni

Page XXIV. Portrait of Abbé Armand Jean de Rancé by I. Lamsvelt in Joseph François Bourgoin de Villefore, 1652-1737, *Les vies des ss. pères des déserts, et des saintes solitaires d'Orient et d'Occident.* Tome IV (Amsterdam: P. Brunel, 1714), 356.

Page 2. "S. Crosne" in Villefore, *Les vies,* Tome I, 228.

Page 19. "Sainte Sylvie Vierge." Villefore, *Les vies,* Tome I, 328.

Page 27. "Aonez ou Eugéne " by M. Ceroni in Michel-Ange Marin, *Les vies des pères des déserts d'orient : leur doctrine spirituelle et leur discipline monastique,* Tome VI(Paris, L. Vivès, 1869), 446.

Page 37. "S. Hupace," by M. Ceroni, *Les vies,* Tome VI, 286

Page 47. "Paul de Telmise" by M. Ceroni, *Les vies,* Tome V, p. 86.

Page 60. "S. Cyriaque" by M. Ceroni, *Les vies,* Tome IV, frontispiece.

Page 68. "Two Monks in Contemplation in a Forest" by Carl Baron von Vittinghoff, 1809.

Page 75. "S. Elye" by Jean Mariette. In *Plates from Villefore's Les vies des ss. pères des déserts*[a title devised by the cataloger at Hathitrust, who notes it must have been published in Paris by J. Mariette, between 1708 and 1757], 173.

Page 83. "St. Theresa Kneeling in Prayer," Claude Mellan.

Page 90 "S. Theon" by Mathieu Elias, *Plates,* 45.

Page 93. "S. Agathon" by M. Ceroni, *Les vies,* Tome II, 84.

Page 97. "S. Basil le Grand" in Villefore, *Les vies,* Tome I, 294.

Page 103. "S. Possidonne" in Villefore, *Les vies,* Tome I, 218.

Page 112. "S. Jean Climaque" by Ceroni. Marin, *Les vies,* Tome V, 388.

Page 118. "The Crucifixion; a Square Small Plate. " Rembrandt van Rijn, 1634.

Page 120. "The Temptation of Christ." Leonaert Bramer, 1645-1655.

Page 127. "The Temptation of Christ." Lucas van Leyden. .

Page 133. "S. Antoine" by Mathieu Elias in Villefore, *Les vies,* Tome I (Paris, Desaint et Saillant, 1757), 26.

Page 141. "Saint Anthony the Abbot in the Wilderness," ca. 1435 by Osservanza Master.

Page 149. St. Anthony of Egypt Driving Away Devils, 17th century. Grégoire Huret.

Page 159. Satan offering Jesus Bread (Rembrandt).

Page 165: "S. Aphton" Villefore, Les vies, Tome I, 214.

Page 169. "S. Moyse." Villefore, *Les vies,* Tome I, 180.

Page 175. "S. Sylvain" by L. Mariette. Villefore, *Les vies,* Tome I, 200.

Page 184 "Solitaires de Therine" by M. Ceroni. Marin, *Les vies,* Tome II, 4.

Page 194. "S. Ammon Abbé" Villefore, *Les vies,* Tome I, 216.

INDEX OF IMAGES

Page 201. "St. Etienne Ancorete." Villefore, *Les vies*, Tome I, 206.

Page 211. "L' Abbé André" by Ceroni. Marin, *Les vies,* Tome V, p. 466.

Page 220. "S. Serapion le Sindonite," Villefore, *Les vies,* Tome I, 222.

Page 223. Monks Chanting, 1795, Jean Jacques de Boissieu.

Page 232. "The Virgin of Sorrows: The Crucifixion," engraved by Giorgio Ghisi 1575.

Page 243. "S. Eugenie," Villefore, *Les Vies,* Tome I, 322.

Page 267. "The Healing of the Blind Man and the Raising of Lazarus," Anonymous

Page 270. "S. Euloge" Mariette, *Plates,* 127.

Page 308. "S. Baradat," by M. Ceroni, *Les vies*, Tome V, frontispiece.

Page 326. "La Tentacion de Jesus Christ au desert" by Luca Giordano, (1634-1705) engraved by F. Holl (1815-1884). In John Kitto (1804-1854). *The gallery of Scripture engravings, historical and landscape, with descriptions, historical, geographical and pictorial* (London: Peter Jackson, 1900), 49.

Page 337. "The Holy Virgins Greeted by Christ as They Enter the Gates of Paradise," ca. 1467–70. Simon Marmion.

Page 344. Monk at his devotions, artist unknown, from Dresden, Germany.

Page 345. The Assumption and Coronation of the Virgin, from The Life of the Virgin, 1510. Albrecht Dürer.

Index of Scriptural Citations

Gen 3:19	168, 185
Gen 32:23	116
Exod 23:2	324
Deut 32:	41, 201
Deut 33:9	80
Joshua 7	200
1 Kings 4	200
Ps 5:12	73
Ps 12:4.	20
Ps 17:38	216
Ps 25:8	214
Ps 36:16	34
Ps 38:1	109
Ps 38:2	106
Ps 40:5	307
Ps 43:23	299
Ps 49:21	265
Ps. 74:9	304
Ps 76:3	20
Ps 84:11	80, 97
Ps 87:16	168
Ps. 93:19	17.
Ps 107:13	307
Ps 111:9	160
Ps 115:13	272
Ps 118:116	100
Ps 119:5	151
Ps Ps 119:7	42
Ps 141:8	151
Prov 15:19	187
Wis 4:13	287
Eccl 28:21	108
Eccl 28:28	108
Eccl 30:24	17
Eccl 34:30	99
Isa 5:8	249
Isa 30:15	108
Isa 33:9	11
Isa 48:18	20
Isa 49:10	88
Isa 51:1	328
Isa 51:3	88
Isa 58:7	56, 71
Jer 2:13	333
Jer 6:16	324
Jer 7:4	324
Jer 9:1	116
Jer 35:18	208
Lam 3:27	116
Lam 3:28	116, 108
Lam 3:30	116
Lam 4:1	250
Lam 5:16	20
Dan 5:27	303
Zech 13:5	168.
Mal 3:6	11, 289
Matt 5:39	30
Matt 5:48	30
Matt 6:24	62
Matt 6:33	28
Matt 7:13	324
Matt 8:20	50
Matt 8:22	65
Matt 10:34	62, 65, 152
Matt 10:36	63, 108
Matt 10:37	53, 60, 63
Matt 11:25	243
Matt 12:48-50	65
Matt 12:50	50
Matt 13:55	168

INDEX OF SCRIPTURAL CITATIONS

Matt 15:3	71	Eph 3:15	75
Matt 15:4	63, 79	Col 1:12	305
Matt 18:20	115	Col 3:3	35
Matt 19:5	45	Col 3:5	240
Matt 19:8	328	1 Thess 2:9	170, 189
Matt 19:29	65	2 Thess 3:10	177
Matt 20:16	325	1 Tim 5:8	71
Matt 21:19	187	Heb 12:2	283
Matt 25:6	214	1 Pet 4:11	160
Mark 6:3	168	2 Pet 2:19	60
Luke 1:15,17	117	James 1:17	289
Luke 2:49	51	James 3:6	108
Luke 6:12	213	Jude 1:23	287
Luke 6:30	29, 30, 31, 35	Apoc 3:17	322
Luke 9:62	61, 66		
Luke 10:41	154		
Luke 12:51	152		
Luke 14:19	284		
Luke 14:25	66		
Luke 18:13	298		
Luke 24:5	84		
John 5:14	276		
John 11:12	149		
John 14:27	21		
Acts 5:29	320		
Acts 10:13	1, 147		
Acts 20:34	189		
Acts 20:35	186		
Rom 2:24.	246		
Rom 6:11	246		
Rom 8:21	16		
Rom 12:3	195		
1 Cor 1:27	190		
1 Cor 4:12	189		
I Co. 6:7	30, 33, 34, 35		
1 Cor 15:28	73		
2 Cor 4:10	304		
2 Cor 6:5	171		
2 Cor 12:9	278		
Gal 6:17	84, 283		

Image Credits

All of the images in this volume are in the public domain:

Those on pages XXIV, 2, 18, 96, 102, 132, 164, 166, 168, 194, 201, 220, and 244 are from Joseph François Bourgoin de Villefore, *Les vies des ss. Peres de déserts, et des saintes solitaires d'orient et d'occident*, Tomes 1-4 (Amsterdam, P. Brunel, 1714). The images on pages 89 and 271 are from *Plates from Villefore's Vies des SS. Pères des déserts* a title devised by an Hathitrust cataloger for a volume without title or publishing information. Per Hathitrust all this material is in the public domain and Google-digitized.

Images on pages 26, 36, 46, 59, 92, 111, 210, 212 and 309 are found in the public domain and Google-digitized at https://catalog.hathitrust.org/Record/008976292 from Michel-Ange Marin, *Les vies des pères des déserts d'orient:leur doctrine spirituelle et leur discipline monastique*, Tomes 1-6 (Paris, L. Vivès, 1869).

Images on pages VII, XXIII, 67, 82, 118, 120, 140, 148, 224, 232, 269 and 337 are found on the open access page on the Metropolitan Museum of Art site, https://www.metmuseum.org. On February 7, 2017, the museum made all images of public-domain works in its collection available under Creative Commons Zero (CC0).

The image on page 126 has a CC0 public domain designation per The Art Institute of Chicago

The image on page 325 is from a book published more than 70 years ago and therefore is in the public domain.

*In religious life
a man lives more purely,
falls more rarely,
rises more quickly,
walks more cautiously,
receives more graces ,
rests more securely,
dies more confidently,
is purified more quickly
and in Heaven receives a
greater reward.*

Saint Bernard of Clairvaux

www.ingramcontent.com/pod-product-compliance
Lightning Source LLC
Chambersburg PA
CBHW071203240426
43668CB00032B/1871